Architecture *today*

HARRY N. ABRAMS, INC., PUBLISHERS, NEW YORK

Architecture *today*

CHARLES JENCKS

WITH A CONTRIBUTION BY

WILLIAM CHAITKIN

Photographs

p. 2:
RICHARD ROGERS AND
PARTNERS, ENGINEERS
OVE ARUP AND PARTNERS
Lloyds' Redevelopment, City
of London, England, 1978–,
model by Tetra Design Serv-
ices, Ltd.

p. 3:
MOORE, PEREZ ASSOCI-
ATES, INC., U.I.G., AND
RON FILSON, *Piazza
d'Italia*, New Orleans, Loui-
siana, 1975–80, modern
Serliana

p. 4 and on the dust jacket:
RICARDO BOFILL AND
TALLER DE
ARQUITECTURA, *Le Via-
duct Housing*, Saint-
Quentin-en-Yvelines,
France, 1981, exterior

p. 8:
JEREMY DIXON
St. Mark's Road Housing,
London, England, 1975–80,
facade

Executive Editor: Dr. Andreas Papadakis
Senior Editor: Frank Russell
Assistant Editor: Vicky Wilson
Research Assistant: Maggie Gilks
Designer: Kenneth R. Windsor

**Library of Congress
Cataloging in Publication Data**

Jencks, Charles.
    Architecture today.

    Bibliography: p. 336
    Includes index.
    I. Architecture, Modern—20th century.
I. Chaitkin, William, joint author. II. Title.
NA680. J448   1981   724.9'1   80-27124
ISBN 0-8109-0669-4

Copyright © 1982
Academy Editions, London

Published in 1982 by
Harry N. Abrams, Incorporated,
New York
All rights reserved.
No part of the contents of
this book may be reproduced
without the written permission
of the publishers

Published in Great Britain
under the title
Current Architecture

Printed and bound in Japan

CONTENTS

FOREWORD

FROM THE INITIAL CONCEPTION OF THIS BOOK, ONE principle has remained paramount: that it should bring together, within the confines of a single cover, important recent work which reflects the dramatic changes of direction within contemporary architecture. Now that the exclusivist and monostylistic Modern Movement has had its day, its purist theory has been superseded by an inclusivist and pluralistic view of architecture in which the criterion of truth has given way to one of comparative validity. In order to reflect this pluralism, we have commissioned two authors whose interests and experience transcend the usual doctrinaire or sectarian approaches. In addition, much of the information and illustrations have been supplied for publication by the architects themselves, and in this sense the book can be said to be a collaborative effort. Even in a work of this scope, however, we have been unable to include everything we would have liked, and our apologies go to those architects who have contributed material which for practical purposes could not be included.

Precisely those qualities which have made this undertaking both challenging and rewarding—the variety and complexity within the field of contemporary architecture—have also rendered it difficult. We make no claim to this being an encyclopedic record of recent built work, nor is it concerned with the technology of building. Works have been chosen for presentation on the basis of their relevance to the current architectural discourse, and although we are dealing essentially with built works, a number of projects are included for which ground has not as yet been broken, or which may never be built although intended for completion. Nor is this a *post facto* history, but rather an international survey which seeks to define and interpret contemporary *architecture in the making*, a "freeze frame" of the Great Train of History as it rushes past the camera. This contemporaneity obviates some of the historiographic problems which normally face the historian; however, it also raises other interesting questions which time alone, perhaps, will resolve.

The book is divided into three major sections, corresponding to the three identifiable developments of architecture today, each prefaced by an evolutionary chart which we hope will give meaning and coherence to the proliferation of different approaches and help the reader through this ultimately rewarding if at times seemingly confusing or contradictory discipline.

Andreas C. Papadakis
& Frank Russell

1 MICHAEL GRAVES, *Portland Public Service Building*, Portland, Oregon, 1980–, perspective from Fifth Avenue

Introduction

THE EVOLUTION AND MUTATION OF MODERN ARCHITECTURE

SINCE ABOUT 1960, MODERN ARCHITECTURE, OR THE International Style and its related models, has changed dramatically. It has evolved into a new style, a "Late" version of its former self, and, at the same time, has undergone a mutation to become a new species—"Post"-Modern. Such changes in architectural history have occurred before—Late-Minoan, Late-Gothic, and Late-Baroque are all examples of historical periods when a previous style was exaggerated—and Late-Modern architecture also exaggerates the period it comes after, the Early- and High-Modern architecture produced from 1920 to 1960. By contrast, Post-Modern architecture is a more definite split from the preexisting tradition, just as the Renaissance broke away from the Late-Gothic: but it is a selective, not total, rejection of the previous era. Post-Modern architects were trained, after all, by Modern architects, and they have to adopt contemporary constructional methods; so there are several important ways in which they too are an evolutionary species.

The differences between Late- and Post-Modernism are simple to define as long as we focus on broad categories. Late-Modern architecture takes the ideas and forms of the Modern Movement to an extreme, exaggerating the nature and technological image of a building in an attempt to provide amusement or aesthetic pleasure. It tries to breathe new life into the Modern language of architecture, a language which many people find monotonous and alienating. Post-Modernists also react against the visual dullness of Modernism, but their solution involves combining the Modern language with another one. Thus a Post-Modern building is doubly coded, one-half Modern and one-half something else (often traditional building), in an attempt to communicate with both the public and a concerned minority, usually architects. If we are looking for historical parallels for the movements, we can find them in the Mannerist period (1518–80), when both Raphael and Michelangelo were reacting against the dullness of straightforward, repeated solutions and wanted to enliven the classical language by inventing new tropes, or rhetorical figures. In a more recent reaction, the Modernist Ludwig Mies van der Rohe's slogan "Less is more" was countered in 1965 by Robert Venturi's answer, "Less is a bore." It was not only the Post-Modernist Venturi who was bored, however, but also the Late-Modernists, and both groups reacted as the Mannerists did to produce highly elaborate, witty, complex, and difficult inventions.

If we look briefly at a Late-Modern masterpiece by Richard Meier, analyzed more fully in a later chapter, we can see some defining characteristics of the late style (2). The Atheneum uses a Modern language of pure, white forms, ribbon windows, flat roofs, ship railings, and many of the structural and functional elements found in Le Corbusier's Villa Savoye, Poissy (1929–31)—for example, the ramps and freestanding columns. However, where Le Corbusier sought a harmonious integration of flat planes, curves, and grids, Meier intends a dissonance of elements. Grids are skewed at a five-degree angle; volumes are violently juxtaposed; solid, void, and their opposition are exaggerated to give the opposite of Le Corbusier's harmonious integration. If in the twenties the grid represented rationality, order, and perfection, then now the skewed grid represents an imperfect perfection—the idea of reason cast in doubt, but still asserting its presence.

By contrast, the Post-Modern Classical work of Michael Graves, for example his Portland Public Service Building, uses only a few Modern elements—for instance, the large plate-glass windows representing the public space—and combines them with quasi-traditional ones: the colonnade, square window, sconce, swag, sculptural group, and keystone (1). A traditional urban form is adopted to hold the street line and create positive urban space (wherein the outdoor space between buildings is given definite form and character), as opposed to the Modern and Late-Modern notion of the "skyscraper in the park" (or parking lot as it often becomes). Yet as in Late-Modernism, the language is complex and mannered. Classical motifs are used both conventionally to communicate with the public and in a distorted way (the *three-story* keystone). If to the Modernists of the twenties eclecticism represented compromise, indecision, and a pandering to jaded tastes, then for Post-Modernists it represents pluralism and communication with the many cultures which make up a large city.

Since roughly 1975, the period which occupies the greater part of this book, Western Classicism has become, more and more, one-half of the style toward which Post-Modernists turn. In 1980 Post-Modern Classicism came into its own as the reign-

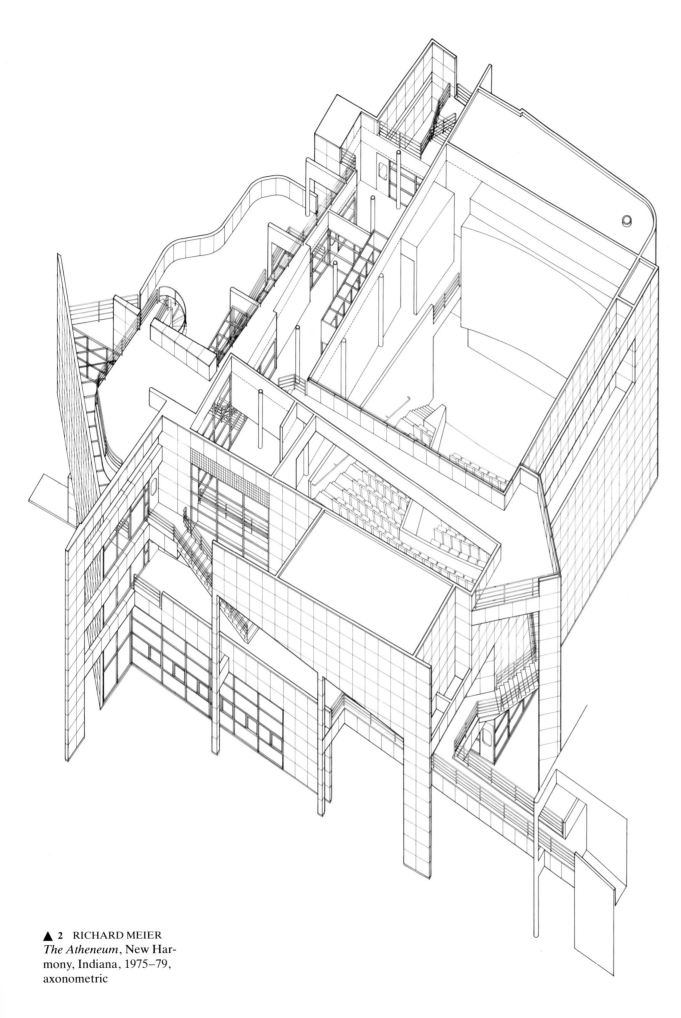

ing, elitist style, summarized at best in the work of Michael Graves, and at length in the 1980 Venice Biennale (3). Back were all the recognizable motifs—columns, capitals, arches, moldings, and polychromy. Even the deeper humanist ideals had returned in part—the classical balance between nature and culture, anthropomorphism, the notions of harmony, proportion, and (almost) beauty. However, this revival is not neoclassical as is commonly supposed, but Post-*Modern* Classical, because of its evolution from Modernism and its non-canonic nature.[1] It does not try to achieve the integration, consistency, and propriety of a Vitruvian or Palladian language, but rather attempts to reach out to a variety of languages—including the industrial style—in an effort to be more broadly based.

Designs which indicate that Post-Modern Classicism has become a consensus among international architects include James Stirling's museum in Stuttgart (282–283), Michael Graves's Fargo-Moorhead project (217–219) and Portland Public Service Building (1), Ricardo Bofill's Les Arcades du Lac (265–266), Philip Johnson's AT&T Building (194), Charles Moore's Piazza d'Italia (181–185), Arata Isozaki's Fujimi Country Club (307–309), and most of the recent work of Robert Stern, Robert Venturi, Hans Hollein, Aldo Rossi, and Leon Krier. In short, major creative architects from many countries have settled upon a style as recognizable and yet as varied as the International Style was in 1927. Yet unlike the architects of the twenties, these architects may also practice other styles, including Late-Modern ones, and so the consensus exists within a larger frame of pluralism. Nevertheless, a new, shared tradition is growing, and the virtue of this for architecture, the public art, is that it allows conventions to develop and an important link to be made between the architect and society. The broad intention of this tradition, voiced by all the above architects at one time or another, is to engender an architecture that communicates with the public. To criticize these architects for failing to live up to their intention is possible, but one should remember that Post-Modernism is at most fifteen years old, and the classical consensus has only just been achieved. Confusion still reigns, not least among those who should give architects the lead—the critics.

CONFUSION AMONG CRITICS

ONE REASON THAT THE LABEL POST-MODERN HAS BECOME accepted is the vagueness and ambiguity of the term. Like "modern," which has been used variably as a key term since the fifteenth century, it refers to a variety of movements grouped loosely under a single

▲ 2   RICHARD MEIER
The Atheneum, New Harmony, Indiana, 1975–79, axonometric

umbrella, and can be supported by many people for different, even opposite, reasons. Historians Arnold Toynbee in 1938, and Geoffrey Barraclough after him, used the term Post-Modern to describe the pluralistic age of our civilization, in which coexistence and cultural relativism have been inevitable outgrowths of "modernism" (i.e., the triumph of Western civilization) since the fifteenth century.[2] This usage relates to the one adopted here, and it should be distinguished from the way in which the sociologist Daniel Bell used the term, in 1976, to refer to those artists, writers, and philosophers who emphasize the breaks in tradition, the new and unique in art, the uncommunicable and uncommunicative in creation. This is an extreme position, as defined by Bell: "A post-modern line developed which carried the logic of modernism to its furthest reaches. In the theoretical writings of Norman O. Brown and Michel Foucault, in the novels of William Burroughs, Jean Genet, and, up to a point, Norman Mailer, and in the porno-pop culture that is now all about us, one sees a logical culmination of modernist intentions."[3] A similar definition of the term can also be found in the writings of the literary critic Ihab Hassan, who stresses its disruptive and anti-conventional nature: "Post-Modernism . . . is essentially *subversive* in form and *anarchic* in its cultural spirit. It dramatizes its lack of faith in art even as it produces new works of art intended to hasten *both* cultural and artistic dissolution."[4]

I find these intentions *opposed* to those of Post-Modernism and, unlike the architect Robert Stern, who partially follows them, I would consider them a defining aspect of *Late*-Modernism. Indeed, the debate on Post-Modernism has been confused because of the absence of a concept of Late-Modernism and because most critics do not see the dialectical relations between these two traditions and Modernism itself. Before looking at these links we should note the confusing way the term Post-Modern is applied by architectural critics, partly as a result of the literary usage cited above.

For example, Arthur Drexler, Director of the Department of Architecture and Design at The Museum of Modern Art, New York, refers to Post-Modernism in a contradictory and reductive way, equating it first with just *one* of its elements—historical reference—and then with another which he imputes to this tradition—"trivialization."[5] This reductive interpretation reveals an apparent distaste for the movement, and is partly derived from the literary usage of Irving Howe, who again stresses the Ultra-Modernist sense of the term, so that it seems to retain the progressivist flavor of its parent—Modernism.[6] The way the term Post-Modern can be used both confusingly and with progressivist

overtones is also shown by the writer William Hubbard and his reviewer, architecture critic for *The New York Times*, Paul Goldberger. Goldberger, who previously applied the term to such Late-Modernists as Hardy Holzman Pfeiffer, entitled his review of Hubbard's book—*Complicity and Convention: Steps Towards an Architecture of Convention*—"Architecture: After Post-Modernism."[7] Here we have the *Zeitgeist* out front: "after . . . beyond . . . post-Post-Modern." Many lecture titles and not a few books adopt this progressivist tone quite consciously and as a joke on the supposedly soon-to-die Post-Modernism. But what happens if we read Hubbard or Goldberger on this?[8] We find the typical confusion of Late and Post-Modernists—Richard Meier, the early Michael Graves, Hardy Holzman Pfeiffer, and Peter Eisenman are all called Post-Modernists[9]—and Post-Modernism is attacked for being anti-conventional, although convention is one of its oldest motives. Yet it is curious that Hubbard and Goldberger hold up for praise, as the summation of their arguments,

◀ 3 HANS HOLLEIN AND MASSIMO SCOLARI, *Venice Biennale*, 1980, facades

▼ 4 CHARLES JENCKS *"Garagia Rotunda,"* Truro, Massachusetts, 1976–77

precisely the building on which I focused the ending of my *The Language of Post-Modern Architecture*—Kresge College (1965–74) by Charles Moore and William Turnbull (**179, 351–353**).

What we have here is a typical confusion—Late-Modernism being mistaken for Post-Modernism—with the argument over convention obscured as a result. To lessen this confusion *somewhat* (a little vagueness, an overlap, is consonant with the facts), I have constructed a chart (see p. 16) which contrasts Modern, Late-Modern, and Post-Modern architecture and shows, through thirty variables, that these three schools are distinct, although there is some overlap in design ideas and stylistic motifs. One basic distinction is that Modern architects of the twenties practiced the International Style, or else believed that there was no style to be followed except that which resulted as a by-product of rational investigation. Late-Modernists follow a similar notion of "unconscious style": one does not have stylistic discussions with Norman Foster and I. M. Pei, or at least they are not known to favor them. Post-Modernists, however, have been discussing style—its suitability for a particular task, its comprehensibility and aesthetic qualities—regularly since about 1960. Indeed, the characteristic Post-Modern double coding, or mixture of styles, can be traced to this sixties historicism.[10]

▲ 5 CHARLES JENCKS *"Garagia Rotunda,"* Truro, Massachusetts, 1976–77, rotunda

▶ 6 CHARLES JENCKS *"Garagia Rotunda,"* Truro, Massachusetts, 1976–77, interior

By going through the chart point by point, we can see many strong ideological and stylistic differences between the three schools, and also how damaging it is to the architects' intentions to confuse them.[11] Carried to an extreme, this confusion would make understanding impossible because it would break down the categories of classification and undermine the genre within which buildings are experienced. To experience Cesar Pelli, Hardy Holzman Pfeiffer, and Kevin Roche as Post-Modernists, as has been done by reputable critics, is to do an injustice to their work, as well as to misunderstand the concept.

Perhaps it is unnecessary to make as many distinctions as thirty, but the fundamental ideological oppositions should be borne in mind if the dialectic between the movements is to make any sense. Late-Modernists still believe in the technological imperative, or in the beauty of an extreme technological image. They use this technology, particularly the curtain wall, with far greater facility than Post-Modernists. Their articulation of structure is greater, their handling of open space is more repetitive; in nearly every one of the thirty variables there are differences. It *does* matter that critics achieve a relative consensus on these points, and that the public understand the issues at stake.

APOLOGIA

TO WRITE A BOOK ON CURRENT ARCHITECTURE IS TO invite several obvious objections. Some of the architecture discussed here will not be current, even in terms of last year's magazines, because (among other reasons) the recent past must be called upon to explain the present. Secondly, the breadth of vision, knowledge, and sympathy required to enter into the wealth of architectures from different cultures is beyond the capacity of one or two individuals, even those who espouse pluralism. If opposite approaches, different styles, and ideologies had been explained by different voices, this would have resulted in a book with different stories to tell, perhaps some incompatible with others. Here, we have struck a compromise—William Chaitkin explains several strands of alternative architecture, while I cover Late- and Post-Modernism. My sympathy for parts of these traditions is very unequal, and a brief personal digression may help to explain why certain architects are present and valued while others are excluded or faulted.

In 1966 I wrote an article, "History as Myth," which argued that the major architectural historians of this century—Sigfried Giedion, Nikolaus Pevsner, Bruno Zevi, Henry-Russell Hitchcock, Vincent Scully, Reyner Banham, etc.—wrote a type of history

MODERN (1920-60)	LATE-MODERN (1960-)	POST-MODERN (1960-)
IDEOLOGICAL		
1 one international style, or "no style"	unconscious style	double-coding of style
2 utopian and idealist	pragmatic	"popular" and pluralist
3 deterministic form, functional	loose fit	semiotic form
4 *Zeitgeist*	late-capitalist	traditions and choice
5 artist as prophet/healer	suppressed artist	artist/client
6 elitist/for "everyman"	elitist professional	elitist and participative
7 wholistic, comprehensive redevelopment	wholistic	piecemeal
8 architect as savior/doctor	architect provides service	architect as representative and activist
STYLISTIC		
9 "straightforwardness"	supersensualism/slick-tech/high-tech	hybrid expression
10 simplicity	complex simplicity—oxymoron, ambiguous reference	complexity
11 isotropic space (Chicago frame, Domino)	extreme isotropic space (open office planning, "shed space"), redundancy, and flatness	variable space with surprises
12 abstract form	sculptural form, hyperbole, enigmatic form	conventional and abstract form
13 purist	extreme repetition and purist	eclectic
14 inarticulate "dumb box"	extreme articulation	semiotic articulation
15 machine aesthetic, straightforward logic, circulation, mechanical, technology, and structure	2nd machine aesthetic, extreme logic, circulation, mechanical, technology, and structure	variable mixed aesthetic depending on context; expression of content and semantic appropriateness toward function
16 anti-ornament	structure and construction as ornament	pro-organic and applied ornament
17 anti-representational	represent logic, circulation, mechanical, technology, and structure, frozen movement	pro-representation
18 anti-metaphor	anti-metaphor	pro-metaphor
19 anti-historical memory	anti-historical	pro-historical reference
20 anti-humor	unintended humor, malapropism	pro-humor
21 anti-symbolic	unintended symbolic	pro-symbolic
DESIGN IDEAS		
22 city in park	"monuments" in park	contextual urbanism and rehabilitation
23 functional separation	functions within a "shed"	functional mixing
24 "skin and bones"	slick skin with Op effects, wet-look distortion, sfumato	"Mannerist and Baroque"
25 *Gesamtkunstwerk*	reductive, elliptical gridism, "irrational grid"	all rhetorical means
26 "volume not mass"	enclosed skin volumes, mass denied; "all-over form"—synecdoche	skew space and extensions
27 slab, point block	extruded building, linearity	street building
28 transparency	literal transparency	ambiguity
29 asymmetry and "regularity"	tends to symmetry and formal rotaion, mirroring, and series	tends to asymmetrical symmetry (Queen Anne Revival)
30 harmonious integration	packaged harmony, forced harmonization	collage/collision

CLASSIFYING MOVEMENTS ACCORDING TO THIRTY VARIABLES
Architects usually classify movements according to a few stylistic categories, but here a more extended list of variables is used to bring out the complexity of the situation: the overlap, contradictions, and differences among movements

that was necessarily biased toward the values they were promoting, either explicitly, as in the case of Giedion, or implicitly, as in the case of Hitchcock.[12] The conclusion was that a succession of viewpoints does much to correct the deficiencies of any single one, and that a historian might try to overcome this limitation by presenting a plurality of traditions, and a characteristic list of those architects he was excluding. This I tried to do in *Modern Movements in Architecture* (1973), a book which first of all put the plural in the word movement and, secondly, showed how many discontinuous strands were submerged under this portmanteau word. The *Zeitgeist* then, as now, simplified things too much.

Concurrent with these writings was an attempt to reestablish the notion, underrated by Modernism, that architecture conveyed meaning through a language. *Meaning in Architecture* (1969), "Rhetoric and Architecture" (1972), and finally *The Language of Post-Modern Architecture* (1977) all emphasized that architectural symbolism was based on convention, the importance to the architect of consciously understanding how meaning is conveyed, and the idea that he might even learn various aspects of rhetoric in order to facilitate intended meaning. My preoccupation with rhetoric has extended to the present, and the reader will find that rhetorical concepts such as oxymoron recur in several chapters. Rhetorical figures—for example, volumetric elision—may unite architects into a school, as in the case of the so-called Whites. Rhetoric is the underlying theme of my two sections, and it is placed polemically in contradistinction to the Modernist position "Without Rhetoric," as enunciated by the English architects Peter and Alison Smithson.[13]

Furthermore, because of my polemical attitude toward Modernism, being at first a defender of the faith and then later an apostate, the reader will detect an occasional irony and suasive tone. I have argued, half-jokingly, that Modernism is dead because its ideology is so moribund. Nonetheless, and presumably out of habit, Modern buildings are still built. One will not find them defended here, or perhaps anywhere today, because the ideology has lost its credibility, and its great defenders. In spite of the fact that several of its ideas have remained current, Modernism lacks its Le Corbusier, and out of respect for the intensity of his and others' beliefs we should distinguish sharply between Modernist ideals and the Late-Modernism with which they are often confused. Having myself studied with members of the European congress of Modern architects, C.I.A.M. (Congrès Internationaux d'Architecture Moderne)— Walter Gropius, José Lluis Sert, Sigfried Giedion, and others at Harvard—and having written a book

partly defending Le Corbusier, I am acutely aware of the difference between the social, ethical, and aesthetic ideas of the pioneers of Modernism and those of, for instance, the designers of the Pompidou Center (**64–69**). Since Late-Modernists are not as critical of their patrimony as Post-Modernists, I am less sympathetic to them and hence the reader will find the occasional dissenting remark in the sections discussing their work.

My own work as an architect, confined to a few small buildings, is intended as another polemic in support of Post-Modernism. A studio I built on Cape Cod in 1977 (**4–6**) was intended polemically to show a continuity with Modernism—being in part a cheap, prefabricated garage—combined eclectically with other languages: the Cape Cod vernacular, the San Francisco painted building, and the geometrical Palladian villa. Hence the ironic name "Garagia Rotunda," hence the garage door lifting over the entrance to form a baldacchino, hence the one-inch rotunda and its steps, echoing Palladio's Villa Rotonda near Vicenza (1566–67). On the interior, shades of blue emphasize the basic structure—the four-by-four-inch studs which are stressed by horizontals, furniture, and *trompe-l'oeil* painting of the same dimension. The two rhetorical devices of simplicity and redundancy are used to make the interior a comment on structure, axis, and order—that is, on classical ideas. This classicism is echoed in the pediments, quoins, and aedicule with its permanently billowing curtain (an echo of the winds of revolution blowing through the tennis court at Versailles).

On the other hand, the widow's walk, spindle, and shingle are more a part of the builder's vernacular, although they might have evolved from the classical tradition. My intention in combining vernacular and classical, prefabricated and handmade, was to create links which had been severed by Modernism, and to communicate specific emotions and concepts. The major idea—that of a study located in the woods— finds particular expression in the Chinese tradition of the *chai*, the simple garden pavilion, built in quiet natural surroundings, where a scholar can work, drink wine, and look at hand scrolls or paintings.[14] Everything in a *chai* should aim to express quiet isolation and allow contemplation of framed vistas of nature. A related idea in my own study, meant to be conveyed literally through color, was the feeling of the Cape. Typically the Cape sky changes through infinite varieties of blue, causing the structure of the studio to disappear as parts of it are absorbed into the dark or light tones above.

These were the main metaphysical ideas meant to be conveyed by the "Garagia Rotunda," while in a more purely polemical context the ornament was

meant to be read semantically, and understood by everyone. The symbolism and ornament of this studio were, I hoped, comprehensible because they were partly conventional—a mixture of cliché and new usage. Or such was my intention, one which has been dwelt on because so much of the current discussion on Post-Modernism is concerned with historical reference rather than communication.

IF COMMUNICATION, RHETORIC, AND LANGUAGE HAVE been the filters through which I have seen architecture, then they are clearly limited filters. Buildings *work*, in addition to being experienced, and many of the ways in which they work effectively (the recent history of environmental controls, of new energy devices, etc.) are not illustrated in this book. Exotic new environments constructed over the sea are not discussed; nor are the pressing issues of building economics, land control, and patronage. William Chaitkin and I have discussed such issues only insofar as they have led to buildings or projects which we consider relevant *architecturally*, and clearly that category is a lot wider for the whole architectural world than even our expansive net. We have both tried to aim at a more coherent pluralism than is achieved in most recent histories of architecture, a coherence which is helped by the aid of charts and evolutionary trees. We hope the reader will enjoy threading his way through the labyrinth which is present-day architecture, creative and multiform, but will understand if from time to time the variety becomes overwhelming. As a Chinese adage put it, "May you be cursed to live in interesting times." The charts, we hope, will lessen the curse.

RICHARD MEIER, *The Atheneum*, New Harmony, Indiana, 1975–79, west facade

Late-Modernism

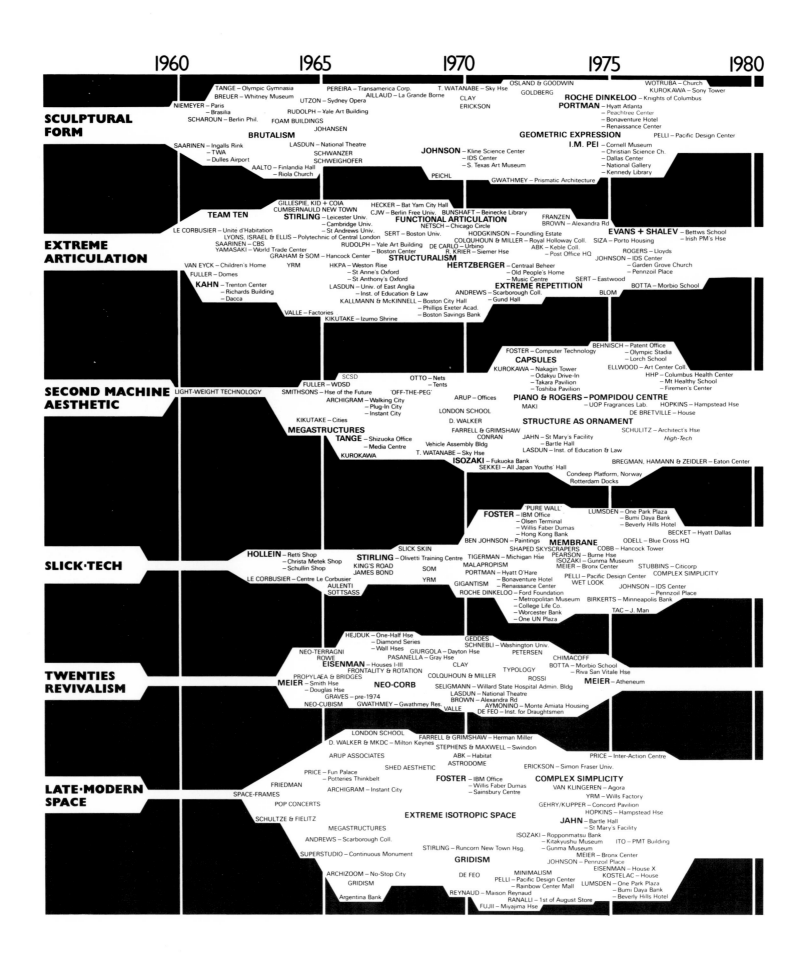

■

LATE-MODERN
DEPARTURES

THERE ARE MANY WAYS TO CHARACTERIZE LATE-Modern architecture and most of them can be reduced to the simple notion of exaggeration. Late-Modernism takes Modern architecture to an extreme in order to overcome its monotony and the public's boredom with it: in this it is like other Late styles coping with "aesthetic fatigue."[1] Familiarity with white, cubic boxes has bred if not contempt, then exaggeration, and architects such as Aldo Rossi, who has revived this Early-Modernist style, have reduced it to *extreme* blankness: white wall and shadow.[2] But there are as many types of exaggeration as there are modes of expression, so that one finds, for instance, structure and construction turned into ornament, the blank-walled box undulated into organic shapes and eroded violently with holes, and room shapes expressed externally where there was once a single, impersonal envelope. The categories of exaggeration sometimes overlap, and because Late-Modernism is a recent notion without a long history of analysis, none of the labels feels quite permanent. Thus Arthur Drexler, in his book *Transformations in Modern Architecture*, distinguishes several approaches, based partly on morphological categories ("Blank Boxes"), partly on historical ones ("Brutalism"), and partly on constructional ones ("Cages"). These categories are neither logically comparable nor exclusive: a single building might fit into several of the classes.[3] The same is true of the categories proffered here: they are logically mixed, overlapping, and of variable cogency.

This chapter treats three rhetorical exaggerations—sculptural form, extreme articulation, and the second machine aesthetic—whereas later chapters are devoted to more cohesive traditions, such as the slick-tech style based on developments in the curtain wall. The three exaggerations treated here are often related to each other within one building—an internal relationship which has often been called Brutalist.

▶ 7 PAUL RUDOLPH
*Art and Architecture
Building*, Yale University,
New Haven, Connecticut,
1958–64

SCULPTURAL FORM AND HYPERBOLE

AFTER LE CORBUSIER'S NOTRE-DAME-DU-HAUT, RON-champ (1950–55), Post-Modernists started to develop a metaphorical architecture while Late-Modernists took off in a more purely sculptural direction. During the sixties the latter began to use reinforced concrete in an ultra-expressive way, a trend which continued to develop into the seventies. Sometimes the results are overwrought and confusing, and often they make use of the rhetorical device of hyperbole to create extravagant forms meant to impress by their grand, overpowering sweep. One finds this sort of architecture in World's Fairs, airports, stadia, city halls, and architectural schools—where the hyperbole is either appropriate or acceptable.

For instance, Paul Rudolph uses a violent contrast between horizontal and vertical "beams," which are themselves exaggerated in size, and "corduroy" texture (7). Here one could say that Frank Lloyd Wright's Larkin Building, Buffalo (1903), and the spatial interpenetrations of the Dutch De Stijl movement are being taken to an extreme and combined with the later work of Le Corbusier. In fact, "Late-Corb" is responsible for much Late-Modernism just as Michelangelo is responsible for much Late-Renaissance (i.e., Mannerism and Baroque), and both protean figures have straddled stylistic periods. Rudolph carried out his exaggerations of Early-Modernism with a gusto that at the time (1964) looked bombastic, but which now, because of subsequent developments in the genre, looks more normal, and simply muscular.

Other buildings of this period which helped to extend the vigorous use of sculptural form were

▼ **8** GOTTFRIED BÖHM
Pilgrimage Church, Neviges,
West Germany, 1972,
interior

▶ **9** GOTTFRIED BÖHM
Pilgrimage Church, Neviges,
West Germany, 1972

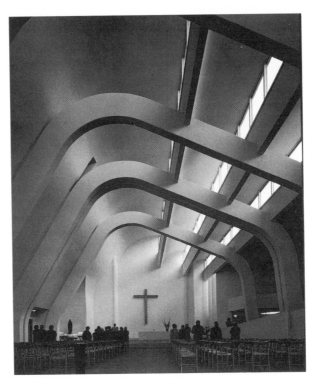

◀ **10** ALVAR AALTO
Riola Church, Bologna,
Italy, 1966–78

▲ **11** ALVAR AALTO
Riola Church, Bologna,
Italy, 1966–78, interior

▶ **12** GUSTAV PEICHL
ORF Studio, Salzburg, Austria, 1970–72, central hall
with radiating corridors

Jørn Utzon's Sydney Opera House (1956–73); Eero
Saarinen's TWA Terminal, New York, of 1958–62
(designed after Saarinen had judged Utzon's project)
and his Dulles Airport, Washington, D.C. (1962–64);
Kenzo Tange's Olympic Stadia, Tokyo (1961–64);
Marcel Breuer's New York University Lecture Hall
(1957–61); Denys Lasdun's National Theatre, London (1967–76); Hans Scharoun's Berlin Philharmonic
Hall (1956–63); and Gottfried Böhm's Neviges
Pilgrimage Church (1972). This heterogeneous but
representative list of sculptural formalism and hyperbole shows a variety of motivation. Some of the work
was motivated by metaphorical concerns: the idea of
introducing explicit similes such as wings, sails,
birds, arms, and snails into the architectural language. Late-Modernism, however, was more concerned with sculptural form as an end in itself, or else
as a consequence of structural developments (the thin
shell, the catenary curve, etc.). Böhm's church has a
mixed motivation and metaphor. In profile it resembles the glass mountains of the Expressionist architect
Bruno Taut (**9**), while on the inside it recalls a moody
fundamentalism prevalent in the Expressionism of
Rudolf Steiner (**8**). But the Brutalist formwork, the
folded plates, the rigid columns, and the ubiquitous
reinforced concrete—with the idea that one material
can do everything—mark it as a work of the early
seventies and a definite part of a Late phase. Indeed,
one of Alvar Aalto's last works, the Riola Church in

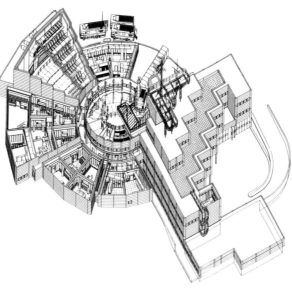

Bologna, can be seen as a late working out of an Expressionist syntax (**10–11**). Here structural hybrids, column/beams, bend and twist down in a way that recalls the ambiguous lighting effects of his church in Imatra (1957–59)—but without extending the basic idea. Rather, it is distorted, mannered, made bonier and simplified—perhaps showing the diminishment of the creative powers of a designer who was by then in his late seventies.

The problem of any Late style—a drift into mannered repetition—can be seen in a whole class of foam buildings which sprouted, or squirted, onto the scene in the sixties and seventies. Basically they remain undeveloped variations on Frederick Kiesler's Endless House (first project 1923, mature project 1960) and Hermann Finsterlin's viscous amoeboids of the twenties.[4] Slightly anthropomorphic in shape, with a plethora of orifices and folds of skin, they become as monolithic and humorless as the square world they are meant to replace. Sprayed foam, while potentially cheaper than other production methods, has yet to find its Antoni Gaudí, or even its Buckminster Fuller. It has the potential to lead the sculptural movement, given its essential comparability to clay, but its great masterpiece dates from the very start of the movement—Le Corbusier's Ronchamp—the building that used free-form curves (and sprayed concrete) with other shapes and materials.

Indeed, the sculptural potential of architecture seems most impressive when it is partly resisted and partly contrasted with non-sculptural shapes, whether utilitarian, orthogonal, or planar. Thus a particularly effective example, or examples because it was reproduced five times, is the ORF (Austrian Radio and Television) Studio designed by Gustav Peichl and built in Linz, Salzburg, Innsbruck, Dornbirn, and Eisenstadt (12–14). Here, pie-shaped studios contrast with rectilinear office forms and a highly sculptural set of discs whirls around a central hall to be offset by a staggered, box-like form. The two opposed morphologies overlap, or bite into each other, producing an effective juxtaposition of circle and square, complete form and eroded form. Indeed, the contrast between regular and irregular is carried through as the underlying idea: a perfect Platonic form is implied by the circle and is modified by the different wedges, just as a square is implied by the orthogonal forms and modified by the erosions. From the ground, the long, low horizontals line up to form a silver-gray battleship, with outstretched antennae, plying its way through the Austrian fields beneath the white-capped mountains and the fortress of Salzburg. Here is the contemporary equivalent of the bastion, the power center, the nerve center, flashing out its centralized culture to the region, plugging in the populace the way organs of government did in the past, except now with invisible media. Peichl has captured the fantasy involved in this meritocratic enterprise with an image comparable to that projected by Hans Hollein in his "Aircraft Carrier in the Austrian Wheatfields" (1964). The Expressionist sketches Peichl made for the studios show that the image is intentional.[5]

An equally compelling image of advanced technology under corporate control is found in Kisho Kurokawa's Sony Tower in Osaka, a ten-story block that looks much bigger than it is because of its sculpted head (15–17). The curved and angled "hat" hides the mechanical plant, lifts up to allow the elevator core to continue, and reaches down to become part of the stair system. This anthropomorphic quality, the ability of form to become animated

with active properties so that it "rises, falls and embraces," is then contrasted with the inanimate repetition of rectilinear forms—the offices in the back and the plug-in, stainless-steel capsules in front (factory-assembled packages of toilets, etc.). One form dovetails another; materials contrast; horizontal, vertical, and diagonal lines play in juxtaposition. The whole is a highly sculptural play with architectural form. No doubt it stems from a twenties functional Expressionism, but the sleek handling of gleaming forms and hybrid expression marks it as part of the Late phase of Modernism. Kurokawa's later work has kept the contrast of various materials, and a few underplayed capsules, but has incorporated this variety within a neutral grid and "ambivalent gray"[6]—which he has turned into a new philosophy known as "Rikyu Gray" (18).

Stemming from Le Corbusier's plastic handling of form, and from Brutalism and Expressionism, is a major tradition which might be called Geometric Expressionism. In the hands of American and Japanese architects this became, surprisingly, a leading style for public buildings of the seventies. Thus older architects such as Kunio Maekawa, Marcel Breuer, and Philip Johnson used it on grand civic buildings, while relative newcomers (Gwathmey, Isozaki, Takeyama, Roche, Lumsden, Portman, and Pei) developed its Mannerist qualities, its slick-tech surface. On reflection, however, it is perhaps not altogether astonishing that large corporations and governmental bodies should adopt Geometric Expressionism as a major mode of presenting themselves to the world, since it combines a relatively new aesthetic with a crisp formality. Underneath the smooth exteriors, however, is a violence and distortion odd for the public realm.

Philip Johnson (perhaps influenced by Charles Gwathmey) used an ultra-white Expressionism on his Texas museum (19) and then an angular silver composition for his drive-in California church (20–21). Both buildings reduce architectural form to a single, monolithic material which expresses a geometric shape: cylinder, rectangle, wedge, steps—and void for a door. This is all that is left in the reductive style. Its precisionism is quite surreal. The machine-like finish, bereft of all fabrication marks, without age, locale, or scaling devices (such as base, molding, or top), takes on an hallucinatory quality which calls attention to the form as form. Precisionism obviously appeals to the insecurity of the business community, its desire for rectitude and precise answers, as critic Vincent Scully has pointed out, and I.M. Pei has turned this *aperçu* into a distinctive style. With Johnson precisionism is a constant, and thus his work has a concomitant primness about it.[7]

The Garden Grove Community Church, however, mixes Geometric Expressionism with a delicate filigree of silver pipes—a space-frame which can sometimes obscure vision, depending on the light and angle of view. This ambiguity between precise solid and diaphanous void is heightened by the angled surfaces and scaleless walls. The whole building is like the mysterious cathedral of crystal which Expressionist poets prophesied for the future world brotherhood, and the fact that it has been realized as a drive-in church (with the majority of the congregation at home in front of a television) can be counted an irony which the Expressionists themselves would not have enjoyed. If one subtracted the commercial and kitsch elements from the program, the building would have that euphoric airiness and crystalloid form which the Expressionists sought.

That commercial interests adopted Geometric Expressionism for their own purposes is apparent also in the work of John Portman, Roche and Dinkeloo, Anthony Lumsden (22), and many other large American practices. Portman's Detroit Renaissance Center, estimated at six hundred million dollars but completed at a cost of over a billion, is the ultimate Late-Modern exaggeration of program, geometry, interior space, slick-tech, and cost (23–24). Dark glass towers house a massive concentration of power, the bastion of Henry Ford's financial monopoly—a pure expression of the over-concentration of wealth within late-capitalist society. What was once dispersed in the fabric of the city has now been hoarded into one point, and, to use a metaphor inspired by the shape, stacked like black coins at the gaming table. Portman at least provides a diverting interior with trees cantilevered thirty feet above the ground, the "plastic rain" which Bruce Goff handles with wit (249, 251), and a suitable degeneracy (like the Rome Piranesi sketched with plants growing out of the ruins). However, the architecture itself adds little to the tradition from which it derives—the hyperbole of Paul Rudolph and Archigram.

Without doubt the master of Geometric Expressionism and the late-capitalist agglomeration is Ieoh Ming Pei, a China-born American architect who has a very large practice and the temerity to handle gargantuan commissions which swallow up large chunks of the city.[8] A case in point is the glass-faceted New York Convention Center, which will hover over four city blocks, encasing them, like a wrapped Christo building, in a dumb, primitive silence.

Pei is nothing if not an opportunist, in the better sense of that word, grasping the basic drives of late-capitalist accumulation and turning them, where possible, into precise geometric slabs of expression— usually in reinforced concrete. His Dallas City Hall turns a triangle upside down, and then increases the drama by contrasting black glass with smooth concrete and horizontal cornice with vertical slab (25). The hyperbole of the building verges on bombast: a marching figure of stepped shapes culminates in a giant concrete exclamation point; an amplified dentil frieze one thousand times too big is placed between sloping glass walls; entrances, balconies, and columns are all scaled to the size of the city and to the size of the conglomerate and thus, because capital is here collected as hardly before, beyond a customary scale. The sublime effect depends on this exaggeration in scale and finish, on the precisionism that has turned rough concrete into a steel-like material, and on the hovering massiveness that gives one the same feelings of pleasant terror as are obtained by standing under a mountain of cantilevered stone in the Grand Canyon. Pei, like the eighteenth-century French architects of the sublime, Etienne-Louis Boullée and Claude-Nicolas Ledoux, turns his geometric forms into acts of nature, wonders of the world, grand public events meant, like all monuments, to memorialize a shared institution or a communal memory. He has gained two of the most important civic commissions in America, a new building for the National Gallery of Art in Washington (26–27), and The John Fitzgerald Kennedy Library, south Boston (28–29). Both buildings might have been supreme monuments of Geometric Expressionism, as well as great American celebrations, but both, in their way, are disappointing.

The National Gallery starts to create a dynamic tension with its upturned table legs, precisionist

▲ 15   KISHO KUROKAWA
Sony Tower, Osaka, Japan,
1976

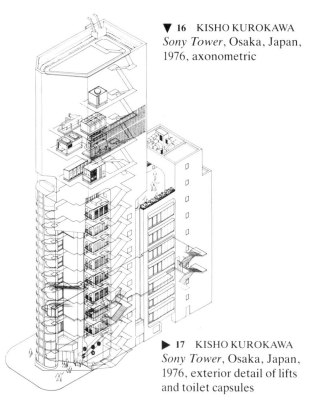

▼ 16   KISHO KUROKAWA
Sony Tower, Osaka, Japan,
1976, axonometric

▶ 17   KISHO KUROKAWA
Sony Tower, Osaka, Japan,
1976, exterior detail of lifts
and toilet capsules

finish, and sharp angles, but this is dissipated by the overbearing flatness, even dumbness, of the blank surface. A long horizontal lintel is stretched taut over the gigantic entrance, but this effect is then weakened by its flaccid repetition in the background. A grand interior space is given over to an Alexander Calder mobile which, like the Henry Moore sculpture at the entrance, is meant to summarize everything in a single statement. But can sculpture and Minimalist architecture sustain interest at such a scale? When one understands that the building itself is the major sculpture and that much other art has thereby been relegated to minor rooms and insignificant placement, when one compares the emptiness of these diagonal juxtapositions with the tension created by Richard Meier in his Atheneum (139–143) there is regret at the lost opportunity.

The same may be said of The John Fitzgerald Kennedy Library, in which sculptural form is skewed fashionably at various angles to achieve rather heavy-handed juxtapositions. Circle, square, triangle, black space-frame, and white cubic figures are set into rotation at the end of a dramatic peninsula. Again, however, the drama is dissipated by the expanse of empty surface and the dumpiness of the horizontal volumes. That Pei can do much better is evident, but that he has a weakness for corporate reticence is also clear. Good taste and expression fight it out in the large corporate practices—and usually boredom wins.

EXTREME ARTICULATION

A REACTION AGAINST THE BOREDOM INHERENT IN blank surfaces, however sculptural, may be seen in another rhetorical convention which became exaggerated in the sixties and seventies: the articulation of the surface into "skin and bones," "structuralism," obsessively repeated joints, and emphatic details. Louis I. Kahn, in his last buildings, took this convention to a beautiful extreme.[9] Eschewing any decoration that did not come from the material or construction, he made a very high-minded ornament from the pour joints in concrete and the juxtaposition of beige-colored elements. At the Kimbell Art Museum, travertine, metal, wood, carpet, and concrete dovetail, while the clear diffused light and highlights bring harmony to the composition (30–31). Tender harmony is the figure conveyed by these interiors. The blend and dissonance of warm hues provide a perfect museum setting for the art, unlike Pei's more assertive new National Gallery building. Simple barrel vaults of light are set off by troughs whose shape is an inverted vault cut in half. Downlighter, travertine slabs, and concrete piers are accentuated as incidents, but always remain restfully subservient to the geometric order. Although Kahn's geometry is sometimes as

gargantuan as Pei's, it is handled with a greater delicacy and gravity. The Roman vaults repeat themselves across the field, slicing space into steady rhythms of high and low ceilings of greater or lesser length, and this essentially simple idea achieves a certain complexity and richness.

On the outside, the pedestrian entrance is at right angles to the front door and so one has to make several surprising and delightful turns, under vaults and through a grove, before arriving inside. Since the scheme has a Beaux-Arts axial layout, this asymmetrical sequence provides a subtle counterpoint. Indeed, Kahn's work may be considered as an interplay between a Beaux-Arts emphasis on constructional logic and selected Modern principles of composition. But in all of his work there is an articulation of construction (or THE BUILD, as it often appears) so that this becomes the subject matter, second only to the geometrical order (or ORDER). The relation of this construction and order to place and particular meaning is often tenuous, no matter how spiritually convincing, and one can ask embarrassing questions: Where is the major car entrance? (Suppressed in back.) How is the building related to the art displayed, to Texan culture, or to the city of Fort Worth? (No more than an almost purely Beaux-Arts museum by the American architect Cass Gilbert

of seventy years previously would have been.) Late-Modernists do not engage these questions the way Post-Modernists do, as they hope to override them with convincing aesthetic answers. Louis Kahn, like James Stirling who also articulates constructional elements in an extreme way (**32**), makes us suspend such questions of symbolism or propriety, at least for a while, as we concentrate on THE BUILD.

Extreme Articulation became almost a style in itself during the sixties and seventies and was widely practiced around the world. Most of the convincing work was in reinforced concrete. Kallmann and McKinnell finished their muscular Boston City Hall in 1968 (with Edward Knowles) and their smaller but delightfully articulated Boston bank in 1972 (**33**). This bank has the push-pull of elements, fashionable at the time, and a slightly brutal handling of the beam ends, which were probably intended to be tough and unfinished. Brutalism, the architectural movement led by Alison and Peter Smithson and supported in the writings of Reyner Banham, obviously had an influence on much Late-Modernism, particularly its chunky, massive articulations, as here.[10] But Kallmann and McKinnell, like Kahn who influenced them, have tempered the harsh, literal aspects of this approach with warm colors and a fan of structure and light which provides order and

rhythm. A "noble bank hall" was asked for and, given the curve of the site, it has been achieved with an exterior colonnade and unobstructed interior space. The building also manages to be an understated part of the urban fabric, linking two streets and orienting toward the triangular plaza in front.

Fumihiko Maki created many highly articulated structures in Japan which relate to Kahn and to Brutalist work, while in England such practices as Colquhoun and Miller carried on this approach in a more straightforward way. Denys Lasdun, in his Institute of Education and Advanced Legal Studies Building, gave extreme articulation to the theaters, circulation elements, and window-wall (**34**); Neave Brown expanded this kind of linear syncopation to an even greater extreme in his Alexandra Road housing (**35**). In America, Craig Ellwood articulated the structure so strongly that it swallowed the building (the truss-bridge wraps the functions; **36**), while Bruce Graham combined the articulation of the truss with that of the columns and mullions to set up an opposition of visual forces which gives scale and delight to the dumb box (**37**). In Harvard's Gund Hall, John Andrews combined the articulation developed in both styles—concrete and steel—to produce a hybrid that has many references: both "skin and bones"; on the interior a latticework of white space-frame glisten-

▲ 20 JOHNSON/BURGEE
ARCHITECTS, *Garden Grove
Community Church*, Cali-
fornia, 1976–80, model

ing overhead like a trellis; on the outside, a series of
rocket launchers aimed at an angle; and on the front,
an entablature reaching over the street on thin columns (**38–39**). Such elaborately articulated buildings, where structure, circulation, and construction
form the pretext for expression, are all Late-Modern
in their use of a functional premise for a supra-
functional exuberance.

The tensions inherent in this opposition are obvious,
and they can lead to sustained high drama in the
hands of a convinced Modernist such as José Lluis
Sert, who will keep within the bounds of a functionalist style but strain against its restrictions. His
housing schemes in New York, "Eastwood" and
"Riverview," develop ideas for low-cost housing
which stem, roughly, from Le Corbusier and Dutch
traditions, but pushed in a more picturesque direction (**40–41**). The emphasis is on mixture and
hybrids.[11] High buildings on the major street step
down to low buildings on the river, tower turns into
slab, roof terraces (presently unused) are mixed with
courtyards, white concrete contrasts with brown tile,
and vertical elevator cores with horizontal "streets
in the air." (The elevator stops only on every third
floor to lessen the cost and increase pedestrian use of
the "streets in the air.") Such economies and mixed
types (there are a variety of apartment sizes) are
given a degree of articulation which takes some of the
pathos from mass housing, and undoubtedly a
major motivation of extreme articulation is to in-
dividualize the monolithic image which Modernism
has bequeathed its successor. There are many
European examples of this direction, stemming from
Team Ten, and particularly apparent in the work of
Giancarlo de Carlo and Mario Botta. But perhaps
the most powerful example is the work of a school of
Dutch architects, led by Aldo van Eyck, who carry
on the intricate close packing of De Stijl and have
tried to find ways of making the big small.[12]

Piet Blom takes 188 dwellings, raises them on
columns or tree trunks, rotates them diagonally to the
column, and breaks up the surface into a patchwork

▲ 21 JOHNSON/BURGEE
ARCHITECTS, *Garden Grove
Community Church*, Cali-
fornia, 1976–80, exterior
under construction

▶ 22 ANTHONY LUMSDEN
AND DMJM, *East Los
Angeles Medical Center*,
California, 1979–80

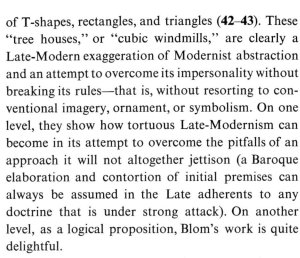

◀ 23 JOHN PORTMAN AND ASSOCIATES, *Renaissance Center*, Detroit, Michigan, 1977

▶ 24 JOHN PORTMAN AND ASSOCIATES, *Renaissance Center*, Detroit, Michigan, 1977, interior of the Plaza Hotel

▲ 25 I.M. PEI AND PARTNERS, *Dallas City Hall*, Dallas, Texas, 1977

of T-shapes, rectangles, and triangles (**42–43**). These "tree houses," or "cubic windmills," are clearly a Late-Modern exaggeration of Modernist abstraction and an attempt to overcome its impersonality without breaking its rules—that is, without resorting to conventional imagery, ornament, or symbolism. On one level, they show how tortuous Late-Modernism can become in its attempt to overcome the pitfalls of an approach it will not altogether jettison (a Baroque elaboration and contortion of initial premises can always be assumed in the Late adherents to any doctrine that is under strong attack). On another level, as a logical proposition, Blom's work is quite delightful.

The amusing extremes to which Late-Modernism may go in its attempt to humanize abstract form can best be seen in the work of Van Eyck himself (**44–45**). His Housing for Single-Parent Families is, like his Amsterdam Children's Home (1957–60), a sensitive essay in the small-scale and poetic use of industrial materials. Here mirror strips on columns, and painted steel set against concrete, take on a decorative quality

in themselves. Rigorously excluding conventional Dutch imagery, which he used in housing at *Zwolle* (1975–77), Van Eyck nevertheless fits the scheme into the Amsterdam fabric in size and texture. The basic Amsterdam morphology of a thin, vertical building is acknowledged by the columnar uprights, while the basic mass is eroded by the entrance and given a counter theme with a cascade of steps. This emphasis on transition, on the threshold as an in-between space mediating between inside and outside, occurs in his earlier work, as does the basic modular organization.

His new concern, however, is with color and glass. The large glazed areas are meant to relate the inhabitants to the street life, while the Serlian motif in steel which enframes the glass is supposed to relate to people of different height rather than to this Italian motif.[13] Van Eyck says of the color: "The facade on the building line is blue, three different blues in sequence of the window, then two greens and, as the street is scooped out, it goes from green to yellow, climbs up to orange and orangey-red, then vermilion,

26 I.M. PEI AND PARTNERS, *National Gallery of Art—East Building*, Washington, D.C., 1978

▶ 27 I.M. PEI AND PARTNERS, *National Gallery of Art—East Building*, Washington, D.C., 1978, interior

▲ 28 I.M. PEI AND PARTNERS, *The John Fitzgerald Kennedy Library Complex*, south Boston, Massachusetts, 1979

▲ 29 I.M. PEI AND PARTNERS, *The John Fitzgerald Kennedy Library Complex*, south Boston, Massachusetts, 1979, interior

crimson and back via violet to blue, following the hollowing out . . . As the rainbow is completed, it becomes more like a posy . . . Instead of choosing a colour combination, I chose the spectrum."[14] The emphasis on "gay colour" is meant to contrast with the harshness of advertisements and the omnipresence of dirty brown. With this rainbow, and the contrasting of many industrial materials with wood and tinsel mirrors, Van Eyck is trying in effect to bypass the more conventional Post-Modern ornament by inventing an urbane equivalent of Simon Rodia's ad-hoc decoration, based on castoffs and broken glass. Characteristically, Late-Modernists have a distaste for anything historicist, and yet they still wish to overcome the blank surfaces and *tabula rasa* of Modernism. This pushes them toward the sophisticated primitiveness of Van Eyck's decoration, and even more toward the frenetic articulation of structure.

Structuralism is the name often given to the expression of structure and space together, that integration which Louis Kahn defined as "Structure is the space."[15] This is beautifully realized in Van Eyck's project for a Protestant church in Driebergen (1965), where cylinders and skylights are located asymmetrically to each other to create the ambiguous figure—center/non-center—and, with more complexity, in Herman Hertzberger's Centraal Beheer Office Building, where space cells and structure are conceived on a diagonal grid (46–49). Here, extreme articulation really has reached an extreme, with every parapet, corner, glass brick, and concrete block receiving separate emphasis.

The intention is obviously to break down the monolithic office typical of Modernism yet still keep some of its organizational principles (*Bürolandschaft* or open office planning) and abstraction (repetition of industrial materials) in a modified form. The building, for an insurance company, houses eleven hundred people in four hundred spaces each about nine feet square.[16] Various work islands focus on a cruciform space that often unites three levels to allow views across space while keeping the identity of a small location. Like the casbah planning of Van Eyck and Blom, where a complex of low-level, cellular places are connected on their streets, this scheme gives a sense of place through small scale. In certain respects the complexity is overwhelming and the "filing cabinet" of Modernism has been overcome by creating a veritable rabbit warren. The impersonality of repeated concrete block is an equivalent of the repeated window in Mies van der Rohe's Seagram Building, New York City. There is no acceptance of different taste cultures, for instance that of traditionalists, in spite of the fact that Hertzberger claims to be designing democratically, "Architecture for People."[17] Nevertheless, as an alternative to the usual monolith, this intricate Chinese puzzle, with its daylit "streets," coffee bars, and interior gardens, is a small step in a welcome direction.

A typological problem within the work of the Dutch Structuralists is the relation of their small cells to the fabric and typology of the existing city. Van Eyck's Children's Home, Hertzberger's Centraal Beheer Office Building and his Old People's Home (1974), and Blom's various tree houses do not relate to

◄ 33 KALLMANN AND MCKINNELL, *Boston Five Cents Savings Bank*, Boston, Massachusetts, 1972

▼ 34 DENYS LASDUN AND PARTNERS, *Institute of Education and Advanced Legal Studies Building*, University of London, England, 1965, 1973–78

▲ 35 NEAVE BROWN *Alexandra Road Development*, London, England, 1973–78

▼ 36 CRAIG ELLWOOD *Art Center College of Design*, Pasadena, California, 1970–75, central bridge and south wing

existing city streets or blocks, but rather set up their own small world. A partial attempt to break this impasse is evident in Hertzberger's Vredenburg Music Center in Utrecht (**50–52**). Here the usual structuralist elements articulate a pleasant labyrinth of small space cells (Van Eyck's "labyrinthine clarity" defines the duality of ordered modules set into a complex order); here are the concrete block, the nooks and crannies, the views across levels, and the primitive columns and capitals. But the important departures are the way the central auditorium breaks out and above the cellular mass, the creation of a major interior street which connects the existing urban passages, and the way the building mass creates exterior street conditions. By contrast, the previous buildings had a tyranny of small-scaled cells, as if the Dutch architects, like anarchists, considered any group larger than four people a corrupting influence. Here a fifteen-hundred-seat main hall (used mainly by the Utrecht Symphony Orchestra) has an octagonal plan set against a stepped cellular module; a large centralized space mediated by tiers of seating.

The latent contradictions of extreme articulation may be seen as virtues or vices depending on the context and the views of the critic. Absolute Platonic form, a consequence of Kahn's structuralism, is mediated either by picturesque multiplications, by erosions, or by both. Thus the typically Late-Modern figure of oxymoron is established and focused on the contradiction—perfect/imperfect.[18] We will see many Post-Modernists using this figure as well. Secondly,

where a democratic, open form is intended by Van Eyck and Hertzberger, or where they speak about architecture as aiding "homecoming," as "provocation," or as a plurivalent structure with many possible functions, one can laud their intentions and see in them a critique of Modernism. No doubt their work does provoke more personalization than Eero Saarinen's CBS Building in New York City (1960–64), an ultimate exercise in corporate control. But their displacement of pluralism to the level of formal complexity has, for some, engendered a new kind of subtle coercion. Van Eyck and Hertzberger are, in a sense, pushing Modernism as far as it can go in an attempt to humanize its language, and this leads to an exaggerated emphasis on structural articulation, in fact to structure as ornament.

THE SECOND MACHINE AESTHETIC

THE BRITISH ARCHITECT AND WRITER ROBERT KERR, IN 1869, distinguished four types of relation between structure and ornament: "structure ornamentalized (or rendered in itself ornamental), ornament structuralized (or rendered in itself structural), structure ornamented, and ornament constructed." [19]These distinctions may not matter in certain cases where the ornament, structural shape, and constructional detail have an identity. Indeed, in Late-Modernism one can find all four types, and a mixed motivation in creating any single one. Basically, however, it is the first type which Late-Modernists emphasize—structure ornamentalized, particularly in an extreme, or gigan-

▲ **37** BRUCE GRAHAM AND SOM. *John Hancock Center*, Chicago, Illinois, 1965–70

▲ **38** JOHN ANDREWS *Gund Hall*, Graduate School of Design, Harvard University, Cambridge, Massachusetts, 1968–70

▶ **39** JOHN ANDREWS *Gund Hall*, Graduate School of Design, Harvard University, Cambridge, Massachusetts, 1968–70, interior

▶ 40 SERT, JACKSON AND ASSOCIATES, *"Eastwood" Housing*, Roosevelt Island, New York, 1971–75

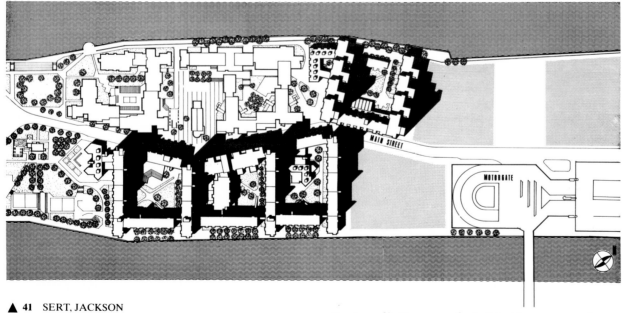

▲ 41 SERT, JACKSON AND ASSOCIATES, *"Eastwood" Housing*, Roosevelt Island, New York, 1971–75, site plan

tic form.[20] One can find this idea expressed most clearly in the sixties in megastructures, where heavyweight constructional systems are, for the most part, monumentalized.[21] But there is another, lightweight tradition, stemming from Buckminster Fuller ("Madam, do you know how much your house weighs?"), from the work of Archigram and their designs for responsive architecture, and from Frei Otto and the lightweight tents which he has inspired.

The most extraordinary of these lightweight structures, which was turned into ornament at a geological scale as well as at the tiny scale of the joint, were the tents at the Munich Olympics of 1972 (**53–55**). Here we see acrylic panels flying in the air, glistening like the oily skin of a fish, or from below, as light and airy as a cobweb flinging its regular mesh in an irregular way to reach between supports. The tents were seen as "umbrellas," "sails with masts," and were related to a host of structural models from which they were derived. All of these images were conceived, ideologically, in opposition to the heavy Fascist architecture of the thirties, a point which was brought out when Günter Behnisch bitterly attacked the Post-Modern Stuttgart museum of James Stirling for being crypto-Fascist.[22] Indeed, the Olympic tents *were* an alternative to the heavy public monument, or to its consumerist equivalent, Disneyland. Here the rather carefree and joyful shapes are without past associations—except those I have mentioned—and they *do* have a connection with the undulating landforms. Their non-centric, non-hierarchic, non-historicist shape was conceived as the apotheosis of the free,

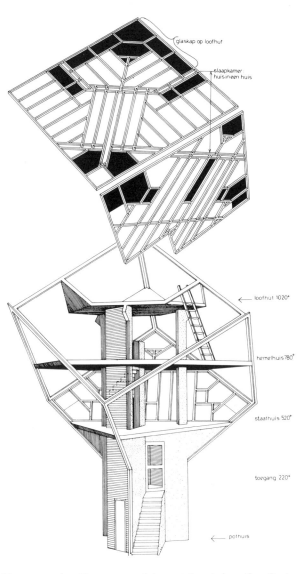

◀ 42   PIET BLOM
Speelhuis Leisure Center,
Helmond, The Netherlands,
1975–78, cutaway
perspective

▼ 43   PIET BLOM
Speelhuis Leisure Center,
Helmond, The Netherlands,
1975–78

Democratic German spirit, at least by the Late-Modernists. This connects certain engineer-architects such as Frei Otto with the Dutch Structuralist school, and differentiates them from Americans such as Hardy Holzman Pfeiffer, who use structure as ornament to express technology (**56**), or from the Japanese, such as Kisho Kurokawa, who use structure as ornament to express growth and change (**58**).

The second machine aesthetic was different from the first, the work of the pioneers of Modernism, in several important respects. As in Archigram's work, for example the "Walking Cities," its emphasis was on flexibility, change, and movement, whereas previously even Futurism had turned movement into static monuments. The second machine aesthetic also claimed variety instead of standardized production (because computerized assembly lines could vary components with ease) and responsiveness: architecture was meant to become like clothing, or like a responsive robot fulfilling every individual wish. Although these images, and the ideas of Archigram, Buckminster Fuller, Yona Friedman, and others, remained for the most part on paper (except at Expo '70), they had an enormous effect on practice around the world. Many moderate firms, such as Farrell and

▲ 44   ALDO VAN EYCK
Housing for Single-Parent Families, Amsterdam, The Netherlands, 1976–80, facade

▶ 45   ALDO VAN EYCK
Housing for Single-Parent Families, Amsterdam, The Netherlands, 1976–80, facade detail.

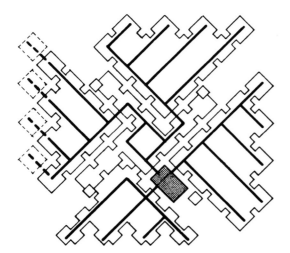

▼ 46 HERMAN HERTZBERGER (with LUCAS & NIEMEYER) *Centraal Beheer Office Building*, Apeldoorn, The Netherlands, 1972, diagram of service ducts emerging from technical tower

◄ 47 HERMAN HERTZBERGER (with LUCAS & NIEMEYER) *Centraal Beheer Office Building*, Apeldoorn, The Netherlands, 1972, interior

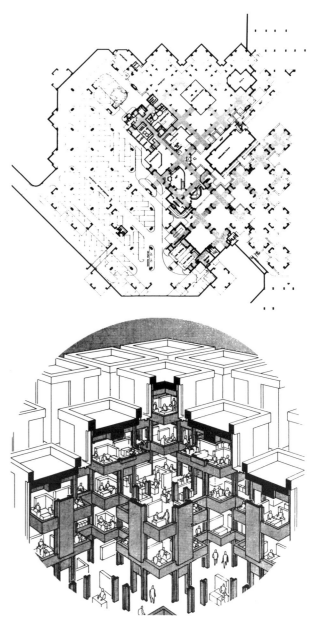

▲ 48 HERMAN HERTZBERGER (with LUCAS & NIEMEYER) *Centraal Beheer Office Building*, Apeldoorn, The Netherlands, 1972, aerial view

▲ 49 HERMAN HERTZBERGER (with LUCAS & NIEMEYER) *Centraal Beheer Office Building*, Apeldoorn, The Netherlands, 1972, plan and cutaway perspective

◄ **50** HERMAN HERTZBERGER, *Vredenburg Music Center*, Utrecht, The Netherlands, 1979

◄ **51** HERMAN HERTZBERGER, *Vredenburg Music Center*, Utrecht, The Netherlands, 1979, interior

▶ **52** HERMAN HERTZBERGER, *Vredenburg Music Center*, Utrecht, The Netherlands, 1979, plan

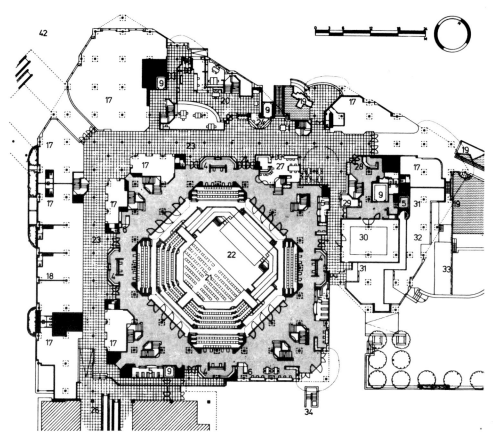

◀ 53 BEHNISCH & PARTNER (with GÜNTHER GRZIMEK), *Olympic Stadia*, Munich, West Germany, 1972, seen from above

▶ 54 BEHNISCH & PARTNER (with GÜNTHER GRZIMEK), *Olympic Stadia*, Munich, West Germany, 1972, aerial view

▼ 55 BEHNISCH & PARTNER (with GÜNTHER GRZIMEK), *Olympic Stadia*, Munich, West Germany, 1972, seen from within

Grimshaw, adopted a flexible building approach which treated building systems in their totality as a "kit of parts" to be selected from. In certain cases, the owner of a factory could even pick up the ready-made panels himself and clip them into place. Norman Foster developed the same assembly techniques on a larger scale, and therefore less responsive to the individual (**57**).

Two houses that architects built for themselves—one in London, the other in Los Angeles—show the expressive virtues of the "kit of parts" approach. Helmut Schulitz's house in Los Angeles is a lightweight steel building cantilevered from the side of a hill: the trusses, corrugated metal, I-beams (painted yellow), balcony rails (in red), vents, and chimney (in silver) are all "off-the-peg" and have, therefore, an abstract, impersonal quality (**59**). Painted in bright primaries, which contrast with each other and with the site, they become a form of construction as ornament. Schulitz justified his approach by its economic potential: such industrial ad hocism could be generalized for mass housing, and the home builder could select his particular gamut from the

totality. The idea is a Late-Modern version of Fuller's and Le Corbusier's ideas of industrializing the building process, with the emphasis changed from the producer to the consumer. Michael Hopkins achieves a subdued London version of the same idea (**60–61**). Here the "kit of parts" is even lighter, the plan more regular and open. Hopkins has given the glass pavilions of Mies van der Rohe and Philip Johnson diagonal braces, thinner articulations, and Venetian blinds which form a kind of trellis-wall. It is all very delicate and elegant, not the kind of thing an average consumer would knock together, but rather a highly abstract and airy filigree of components. In fact, the idea of an industrial Meccano set providing infinite flexibility, great economy, consumer choice, and abstract, machine-age aesthetics was limited to two taste cultures: elite, academic architects with fastidious taste or alternative architects who worked in dropout communities. Only in rare instances did the second machine aesthetic become accepted by the middle class or on a large scale.

One case is the interior of the house, at the level of details, appliances, and industrial hardware. The book *High-Tech*, aimed at the mass market, helped further the taste which was already developing.[23] Up-market firms such as Design Research, Habitat, and Conran purveyed the products with a careful admixture of traditional and vernacular accents, and usually the accompanying potted palm. The French architect François Deslaugiers persuaded the Department of Income Tax in Nemours to accept a clip-together industrial system (**62**), and Renzo Piano managed to build lightweight, industrial housing in Perugia. More typical of large urban commissions is Eaton Center in Toronto, where the multistoried arcade is articulated with lightweight technologies and movement systems—glass elevators and hot and cold air ducts (**63**). A linear space and a repetitive structure are made picturesque and full of incident by using mechanical systems as a form of decoration.

▲ **56** HARDY HOLZMAN PFEIFFER ASSOCIATES *Occupational Health Center*, Columbus, Indiana, 1973, interior

▶ **57** FOSTER ASSOCIATES *Sainsbury Centre for the Visual Arts*, University of East Anglia, Norwich, Norfolk, England, 1975–78, exterior detail showing ready-made panels

▶ **58** KISHO KUROKAWA *Takara Group Pavilion*, Expo '70, Osaka, Japan, 1970

▲ 59 HELMUT SCHULITZ
Architect's Home, Los Angeles, California, 1976–77

▶ 60 MICHAEL HOPKINS
House in Hampstead,
London, England, 1978,
exterior detail

This whole trend of Late-Modernism came to a glorious climax in the Pompidou Center, a building whose imagery and ideas were projected as early as 1963 (by Archigram) but which was not finished until 1977 (**64–69**). Here there is no doubt that all the elements of Modernism are taken to an extreme: logic, technique, circulation, repetition, mechanical services, structure, construction, and, as we shall see in a later chapter, isotropic space.

This megastructure consists of thirteen bays made from trusses constructed by Krupp in Germany (and smuggled through the streets of Paris at 6 A.M., partly because they were so long). The clear span of the truss is 156 feet, they are 42 feet apart, and a perimeter space of 19 1/2 feet stabilizes the whole structure in every direction (hence the cross-bracing and cantilevered arms, the famous *gerberettes*). Con-

ceptually the structure is placed on the outside and interrelated through a series of cantilevers so that it acts like an exoskeleton: the perimeter space is like a gigantic truss and allows circulation on one side and mechanical equipment on the other. The main circulation up to each floor is by a tube of cantilevered escalators, painted red underneath, which gives a significant diagonal to the rectilinear exoskeleton. This forms a figure in two important ways: firstly, it can be related to the other tubes—horizontal caterpillars—which run along this side, and secondly, it becomes the main focus of the exterior piazza and *the* major architectural content of the building. People often ride the escalators just to see Paris at different levels, or a major Gothic landmark framed sympathetically by the *gerberettes* and braces. On the ground, the sloping piazza space always has a collec-

▼ 61 MICHAEL HOPKINS
House in Hampstead, London,
England, 1978, ground- and
first-floor plans

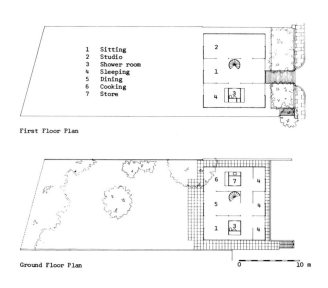

1 Sitting
2 Studio
3 Shower room
4 Sleeping
5 Dining
6 Cooking
7 Store

First Floor Plan

Ground Floor Plan   0   10 m

▲ 62 FRANÇOIS
DESLAUGIERS, *Centre
Régional d'Informatique*,
Nemours, France, 1975–79

tion of performers—fire-eaters, jugglers, acrobats, as well as curious wanderers. Because of these celebrations of Parisian public life, the building really does become a fitting twentieth-century monument, and transcends its technocratic content.

Of course, some Parisians do see the Pompidou Center as a supermarket of culture. Because the building centralizes many artistic activities—museum, exhibition space, ICRAM (Institute for Research and Coordination in Acoustics and Music), industrial design center, *cinémathèque*—and monopolizes arts finance and book collection as a public library, it has had a negative effect on other cultural institutions, just as a huge shopping center drives out small competitors. The supermarket atmosphere of bemused consumption is not appropriate to cultural activity in any case. Given this drawback, the building has to be seen as the typical Late-Modern failure (as well as its crowning success)—a failure of content, a failure where the means of architecture, its technology, have predictably taken over its ends. Even with this negative assessment, however, one has to admit to countervailing advantages: for many of the thirty thousand who come on a successful day the center provides

▲ 63 BREGMAN AND
HAMANN, ZEIDLER
PARTNERSHIP, *Eaton
Center*, Toronto, Canada,
1973–77

▶ 64 RENZO PIANO AND
RICHARD ROGERS
Pompidou Center, Paris,
France, 1971–77, general
view

▲ 65　RENZO PIANO AND
RICHARD ROGERS
Pompidou Center, Paris,
France, 1971–77, exterior
from the piazza

◀ 66　RENZO PIANO AND
RICHARD ROGERS
Pompidou Center, Paris,
France, 1971–77, exterior
from the piazza at night

◀ 67 RENZO PIANO AND RICHARD ROGERS
Pompidou Center, Paris, France, 1971–77, street side "wall of services"

▶ 68 RENZO PIANO AND RICHARD ROGERS
Pompidou Center, Paris, France, 1971–77, escalator

contact with the arts and with information on culture which they might not otherwise have had.

On the street side, the technology has become even more obsessive (**67**). Here a "wall of services" proclaims its responsive technique in several different colors: the layer of circulation is a black cage, above are red elevator engines, to either side green pipes, and in back are silver cross-braces, heavy blue ducts, orange metallic cabinets, and finally a gray wall. Color clearly accentuates the notion of structure and construction as decoration: in fact the canonic elements of Modernism have been turned into ornament.

An interesting aspect of this elevation is its marked similarity to the morphology of the Parisian hôtel, and, more generally, to the Baroque palazzo.[24] No doubt the Pompidou Center is trying to huddle down into its Parisian context, but it also has the paired columns of the Louvre, and a division into base, *piano nobile*, and attic. Such contextual references, consciously sought by Post-Modernists, are here mostly fortuitous, although the architects are aware of them.[25]

In conclusion then, the Pompidou Center manages to summarize most of the positive trends outlined in this chapter, and not a few of the negative ones. It has the extreme articulation and responsiveness which we have emphasized as aspects of the second machine aesthetic, although the responsiveness is more in the imagery of technical change than in its reality. It seeks democratically to address large numbers yet fails to articulate minority interests. It becomes a piece of sculptural form, particularly at its base, where the air-conditioning ventilators are featured as three white exclamation points. And it turns the means of architecture, above all the circulation system and exoskeleton, into the ends, the ultimate content. The paradox is that the utilitarian means can transcend their ostensible purpose and be perceived as a spiritual expression. Indeed, the *gerberettes* are almost arm-like bones which reach out to catch the passerby and raise with him a discussion about the human body which also transcends its utilitarian base.

▲ 69 RENZO PIANO AND RICHARD ROGERS
Pompidou Center, Paris, France, 1971–77, escalator view of the piazza and Paris

SLICK-TECH
THE RHETORIC OF CORPORATE PROFICIENCY

AFTER MODERN ARCHITECTURE WAS ACCEPTED BY THE large corporations in the fifties as a fitting style for the business world and, on occasion, for corporate identity, it underwent a modification that all successful styles soon follow as they become commercial: it became more elaborate, distorted, and extreme. Structural logic became structural exaggeration—structure as ornament. The restrained curtain wall of Mies van der Rohe was by now too familiar; it had to be replaced by a mutation. In short, the slick-tech aesthetic replaced the straightforward expression of the pioneers of Modern architecture.

Slick-tech, as the appellation implies, is an exaggeration of a technological image toward the glossy and ultra-smooth.[1] Sheet steel, polished aluminum, glistening plastic, bright enamel, and mirror-plate glass are the distinctive materials, and they often achieve an oily wet-look and sleek sfumato, a smoky mixture in which highlights and darkness blend into each other without distinct transition. The materials existed in the twenties when their rhetorical effects were exploited by Art Deco designers, but it was only in the mid-sixties that they started to be dramatized by architects. A seminal example, one of Le Corbusier's last works (**70**), used sheet steel, multicolored

enamel panels, and a superabundance of bolts and screws in a decorative and functional way (the pavilion was designed to be changed internally, and perhaps even moved around). The Centre Le Corbusier consists of a grid of paneled space placed under a double butterfly roof which rises on one side and falls, symmetrically, on the other. This airy structure exaggerates the opposition of form as well as slick technology: heavy pier is opposed to thin column, a pediment opposes an inverted pediment, steel roof opposes enamel boxes. Opposition, contrast, inversion, antithesis—these are the rhetorical figures which heighten the drama and make this modest pavilion an extraordinary building. Its function, an exhibition center, is perhaps too minor, given the vigorous expression. Like other slick-tech work, the form is more important than the building task.

This imbalance can be seen more clearly in the early work of the Viennese architect Hans Hollein, who also exploited the slick-tech look in the mid-sixties. His tiny Retti Candle Shop (1965) creates a violent contrast between sheet aluminum plane and cutout void (**71–73**). Here, the metal is cut out and bent back as if it were paper, a rather surprising metaphor and an intriguing paradox. The contrast between metal and paper is heightened by the paradox of the sfumato effect; where the metal moves from flat to curve, the color and tone change from gray to silver to bright white without a clear transition. The paradoxical qualities of slick-tech are all evident in this early example. One material changes to another, chameleon-like, yet we know it is still the same material. The rhetorical figure of oxymoron (a condensed paradox) is used to focus our attention on a rather banal content: selling candles, lumps of wax. The curved aluminum has multiple oxymoronic qualities: a soft/hardness, a masculine/femininity. This last paradox is underscored by the doorway itself, two R's

◀ **70** LE CORBUSIER
Centre Le Corbusier,
Zürich, Switzerland,
1964–66

▶ **71** HANS HOLLEIN
Retti Candle Shop, Vienna,
Austria, 1965

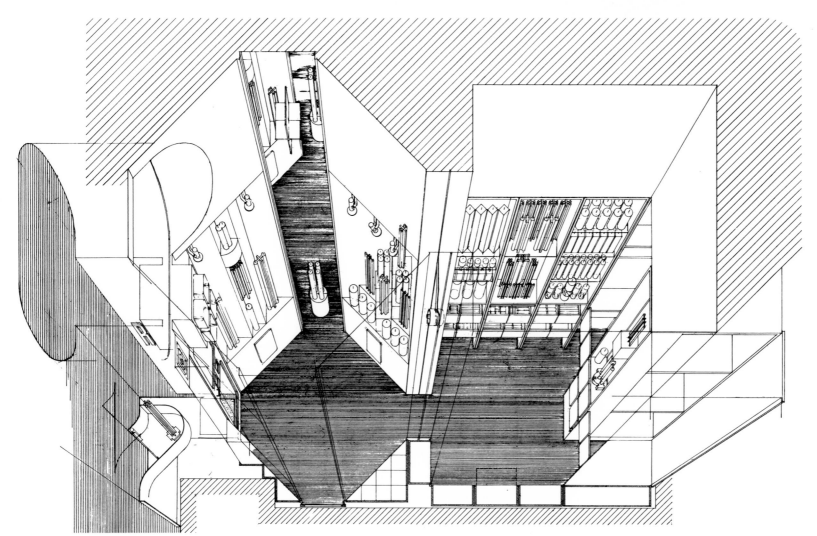

set back to back, signs of the Retti Shop which also form a gigantic phallic symbol (Hollein often exploits anthropomorphism or body metaphors—a major concern, as we shall see, of Post-Modernism). On the very small interior, further oxymoronic devices are used to increase the feeling of space. As in Adolf Loos's tiny Viennese shops of sixty years earlier, from which this one is surely derived, opposed mirrors are used to set up an infinitude of reflections— here of giant white bulbs. This familiar *trompe-l'oeil* device is made more paradoxical by the mirroring of the light source itself—four globes separated by dark plexiglass that *looks like* a mirror. Thus we have an illusion of an illusion which sets up a multiplication of illusions. The further handling of interior space is both hieratic and ritualistic. Axes, cross-axes, and diagonal axes focus on candle clusters and slick-tech mechanical equipment. We are in a temple of consumer society where products are displayed as sacred icons, highlighted, spotlighted, and backlighted like a Baroque tableau by Bernini.

The rhetorical figures of Hollein's work were immediately taken up by other small commercial enter-prises, particularly those on fashionable streets in Rome, Los Angeles, and Paris. On Carnaby Street and King's Road in London the slick-tech shop, boutique, and disco are given a flat, polished aluminum front which is again cut out into a giant logo, as if it were paper. The names—GIRL, I SPY, JUST LOOKING—reflect the narcissism inherent in shopping for clothes, just as the materials used literally reflect the narcissist (**74–75**). In this there is a correspondence between the form and the content, which is very suitable for the slick-tech aesthetic. On the inside, the warped shapes and glistening mirrors disorient the customer as much as the multitrack stereo—usually turned too high— confuses his senses. The body is enveloped in a soothing symphony of sounds and colors which at once break down consumer resistance and heighten the feeling of youthful sensuality.

These temples of the youth cult, with its religion of the body, were further developed in Milan. The annual furniture trade fair, the magazine *Domus* which celebrated its products, shops such as O-Luce or clubs such as Alto Mondo, and above all the gifted designers Gae Aulenti and Ettore Sottsass made Milan the world center of Supersensualism. This found international recognition in the exhibition, "Italy: The New Domestic Landscape," which was held at The Museum of Modern Art, New York, in 1972.[2] Here the organizer Emilio Ambasz distin-guished several aspects of a movement of which Supersensualism (not so named by him) was just one. He identified the ritualized fetishism inherent in collecting domestic equipment and displaying it in the house as an altarpiece for a domestic liturgy (**76**). Now plastic furniture and chromium lighting fixtures glistened and sparkled with the sacred light usually reserved for stained glass or the reliquary. The "House for an Art Lover," a favorite Art Nouveau commission, had become the "Temple for the Ob-ject Collector." Furniture, jewelry, and art were the icons of the new consumer religion.

Perhaps the greatest temple to this cult was Hans Hollein's Schullin Jewelry Shop, located in the main shopping street in the center of Vienna (**77–80**). As in most of Hollein's work, there is a complexity of meaning which goes beyond the immediate and undeniable impact of the primary image. Here, the

▲▼ **74,75** *Boutiques on King's Road*, London, England, 1968–70

◀ **76** GAE AULENTI
Art Collector's House, Milan, Italy, 1970

▲ **77** HANS HOLLEIN
Schullin Jewelry Shop, Vienna, Austria, 1974

basic image is a contrast between polished black granite, laid in squares, and two voids—one a fissure of skin-like bronze in different hues and the other a rectangle. The fissure is again clearly a sexually provocative sign, a warped uterus violated by the polished air-conditioning pipes which lead into an enclosed, dimly lit, womb-like interior. But there are other metaphors—and in this it is a Post-Modern work—of landscape and sea. The folds of skin slide around the door to become contour lines, ridges in an estuary where the tide has gone out, leaving waves of sand. The way one metaphor penetrates another (antithesis) is similar to the way one syntactical element violates another (elision and metathesis). Why all these rhetorical devices? To sell jewelry, to answer the rhetorical question. Jewelry and the building become interchangeable; jewelry and mechanical equipment, lighting, doorway, logo, display case are all in the same semantic key. Yet there is a certain

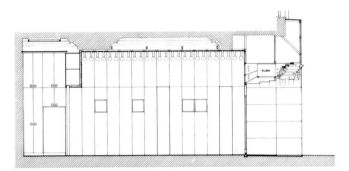

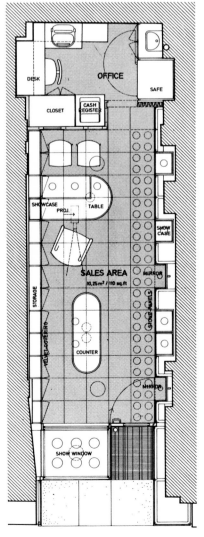

◄ 78 HANS HOLLEIN
Schullin Jewelry Shop,
Vienna, Austria, 1974,
exterior detail

▲ 79 HANS HOLLEIN
Schullin Jewelry Shop,
Vienna, Austria, 1974,
interior

► 80 HANS HOLLEIN
Schullin Jewelry Shop,
Vienna, Austria, 1974,
plan and section

irony, a sophisticated irony of acceptance, introduced by the fissure, by the crumble of perfect masonry. We can see in the "ruined stone" a single admonishment to narcissism, even a conventional one: "Time ruins beauty." Nevertheless, the ease with which this note of doubt is introduced does not challenge the consumer ethos. There is no tension or *Angst* in the fissure, just a sweetly flowing crack which dissolves into golden folds of hedonistic pleasure and reverie. The slick-tech aesthetic is being used to celebrate and sell the products of late-capitalist society. In spite of the latent metaphor and symbolism, the Schullin Jewelry Shop thus remains a Late-Modern building, a partial step toward Hollein's more recent Post-Modernism.

The American architect Stanley Tigerman also used the slick-tech aesthetic in one of his Late-Modern buildings—a house overlooking Lake Michigan (81–83). Here, aluminum panels fracture their

way around a curving plan, giving a steady staccato beat.[3] The tense pulsation is emphasized by the alternation of black gasket and panel, an alternation Tigerman afterward wished he had smoothed over with an even slicker continuous surface (an ideal of slick-tech reached by Norman Foster in the "pure wall"). Instead, the curves are broken into segments of flat panels—aluminum or glass. Positively, this gives scale and incident to the surface, and a surreal, "perfect" look to the corner block housing the observatory. The fantasy latent within slick-tech of the perfectly functioning machine has come to the surface. It corresponds to the created fantasy of the owner, the founder of Gimix, Inc., who can here do just about anything at the press of a button (on a pocket-relay computer he can turn on lights, heat and ventilate the house, open and close doors, and defrost the driveway, among other things).

This house approaches the James Bond elysium

▶ 81 STANLEY
TIGERMAN, *Private Residence*, Lake Michigan,
1972–76, lakeside view

▼ 82 STANLEY
TIGERMAN, *Private Residence*, Lake Michigan,
1972–76, observatory
facade

where everything, including the female human body,
is manipulated, cleansed, perfected, and pampered
by advanced technical equipment. In the late sixties
and early seventies the Bond films did as much as
King's Road to further the slick-tech aesthetic (**84**).
Boardrooms in these films would always have a few
high-gloss chrome torture machines, while the
dénouement usually occurred in a giant womb of sheet
steel (and usually ended as an explosion of silver
metal and silicon chips). The ideal, however, was not
the disastrous end of technology, but the exploration of its manipulative power and superhuman
proficiency. It is this theme which underlies the

◀ **83** STANLEY TIGERMAN, *Private Residence*, Lake Michigan, 1972–76, interior

▼ **84** Slick-tech interior from the James Bond film *You Only Live Twice*

greatest use of slick-tech: by the large corporations. The most obvious emergence of this new aesthetic is not in the home but in downtown areas and in the public, pseudo-mythologies of *2001*, *Star Wars*, and *Star Trek*. In these films we can find the dreams of corporate proficiency made explicit.

An early essay in this genre is James Stirling's Training School in Haslemere, England, for Olivetti's young corporate executives (**85–88**).[4] Located in a sprawling Edwardian estate and surrounded by lush, exotic horticulture, the center provides an ultimate contrast to its setting. Two-toned GRP (glass-reinforced plastic) slithers and undulates its way around corners and over the top of the building, eliding all distinctions between base, wall, and roof: the distinctions made in normal syntax. Two rhetorical devices increase the drama and perplexity of the structure: synecdoche (the substitution of a part for the whole—here the allover panel), and illusion (the *trompe-l'oeil* perspective of the glass wing). To this is added the slick-tech sfumato and distortion caused by reflections and highlights. Inside the auditorium, panels are placed between a battery of Hollywood-like lighting fixtures which can be raised or lowered to create four possible room conditions. A master control panel, the James Bond archetype, surveys the

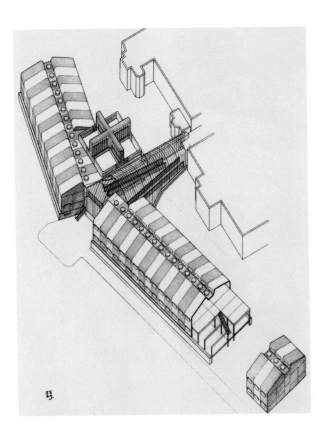

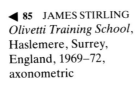

◀ 85 JAMES STIRLING
Olivetti Training School,
Haslemere, Surrey,
England, 1969–72,
axonometric

▶ 86 JAMES STIRLING
Olivetti Training School,
Haslemere, Surrey,
England, 1969–72, exterior
detail of auditorium and
wing

▲ 87 JAMES STIRLING
Olivetti Training School,
Haslemere, Surrey,
England, 1969–72, interior
controls

▶ 88 JAMES STIRLING
Olivetti Training School,
Haslemere, Surrey,
England, 1969–72,
auditorium

auditorium through rounded, gun-slit ribbon windows.

This building implies an effortless mechanical control—the ideal of corporate power, as well as the specific goal of Olivetti. A comparison to their rounded calculators and electric typewriters is often made. Basically, the building is a blown-up piece of domestic equipment or a giant executive toy. This metaphor underlies much subsequent slick-tech work: buildings are meant to be implicit icons, felt, if not completely seen, as amplified versions of the product they represent. A change in scale, from small to large, makes the forms rather hallucinatory, and the hieratic way in which they are treated gives them a slightly religious overtone.

The Hyperrealist painter Ben Johnson brings out these meanings in his precisionist *Domed Roof Lights* (1974), a painting of the circular glass domes in the middle of each wing of Stirling's building (89). Here we can see an artist exaggerating the precision, the controlled symmetry and above all the highlights, reflections, and ambiguities inherent in slick-tech. The scale is reduced from large to small, the context is subtracted, and we might well be looking at the metaphor behind the building—its existence as a yellow submarine (the ambience, incidentally, of the control room) or as a space capsule with portholes (Stirling visited Cape Kennedy in 1965). It is a testimony to Stirling's complexity, however, that there are quite other meanings which resist and counter

the above—a picturesque, dissonant massing, a classical base and symmetry of parts, and a rhythmical contrast of color meant to recall marquees and other impermanent structures. (Stirling was prevented from using a strong contrast of green and purple on the exterior.) As with Hollein's work, there is always a lot more than the slick-tech definition of the overall mood.

With the corporate design groups who work for large organizations the situation is somewhat different. Here, we find the reduction of architecture to a few simple ideas, a strong, indeed overwhelming, expression of these ideas, and a gigantism fitting in its way to late-capitalist commissions (which can now be over one billion dollars—as was Detroit's Renaissance Center). One of the problems of Modernism, which led to both Late- and Post-Modernism, was its gigantic scale: its expansion of a single idea, and the diagram of that idea, into the whole building. Late-Modernists have, by and large, kept this diagrammatic quality (and they have certainly tried to keep the gigantic commissions) but they have enhanced its simplicity by Minimalist expression. Using the rhetorical devices of Minimalist Art— ellipsis, brevity, distortion, amplification, and geometrical simplicity—they achieve, at best, a surreal fantasy and primitivism. At worst, they achieve a childish bathos. The work of Gunnar Birkerts, I.M. Pei, Kevin Roche, John Portman, and sometimes Philip Johnson falls into, or between, these categories.

They call on Piranesi, Boullée, and Ledoux—the grand tradition of megalomaniac architecture—and sometimes it responds.

Gunnar Birkerts's Federal Reserve Bank for the city of Minneapolis (90) is a blown-up M and an eleven-story bridge with a catenary curve supporting 275 feet of column-free space. Two towers hold a giant steel truss (the "lintel") from which are suspended cables and two glass walls, one behind the other, which form a pleasing counterpoint. The image is that of a giant, primitive gateway: a Minimalist triumphal arch turned upside down and filled in the middle. This inversion of syntax and weight has odd and disturbing effects because it presses down on the opening below at the very point where one expects and wants openness. The image of the "blocked gate" is an example of the rhetorical device of architectural malapropism (unintentional, inappropriate meaning) which we find throughout Late-Modernism as it becomes more self-important. An excessive amount of money and a large commission serve to liberate the architect's imagination from the restraints of good sense. The results, in many American cities, provide enjoyable landmarks and a considerable amount of mirth, particularly for visiting Europeans.

Yet many of the most interesting malapropisms have been committed by European emigrés in the "land of opportunity," and these "slips of the metaphor" have certain redeeming virtues when placed in a dull environment.

Birkerts's monumental M, in a downtown Minneapolis of parking lots and street lights, works like a giant Chinese gateway located in the middle of a traditional city. Its bulk, size, and stability constitute a sign of civic permanence which architecture must provide. John Portman's slick-tech monuments in Atlanta, Chicago, San Francisco, Los Angeles, and Detroit also clearly provide this civic permanence (91–94).[5] They are isolated landmarks which pull many functions together into an intense "culture of congestion" (as Rem Koolhaas has termed New York skyscrapers). They usually consist of a simplified geometrical figure, a square, surrounded by glistening towers of colored mirror plate, with an interior lobby ("or atrium") filled with potted plants, "sidewalk" cafés, kinetic sculptures, lightly tinkling fountains, and a set of glass elevators clothed in bronze and gilt as if they were Baroque pulpits about to ascend heavenward. This last is an *intentional* malapropism, if that is possible. The hotels, reminiscent of Kenzo Tange's

▲ 89 BEN JOHNSON
Domed Roof Lights. 1974,
Acrylic on canvas,
48 x 72"

◄ 90 GUNNAR BIRKERTS
AND ASSOCIATES, *Federal Reserve Bank of Minneapolis*, Minnesota, 1967–74

91 JOHN PORTMAN AND ASSOCIATES, *Hyatt Regency O'Hare Hotel*, Chicago, Illinois, 1967–71

92 JOHN PORTMAN AND ASSOCIATES, *Hyatt Regency Hotel*, Atlanta, Georgia, 1964–67

megastructures, provide the public spectacle and almost the *res publica* of European cities—the piazza space without, alas, either its civic functions or historical depth. Absent are the town hall, the church, the palazzo, and the mixture of building types; present is a vertiginous covered space that zooms and angles, in the case of the San Francisco hotel, one hundred and seventy feet high. Spectacle and whimsy have replaced ritual and public life.

Considered as serious contributions to the Western tradition of grand public space, these hotels must be seen as impoverished, no matter how commercially successful they might be. And it is interesting to compare the imagery with that of the European tradition from which it stems. Boullée wrote that "the poetry of architecture is acquired by giving monuments their proper character," and Ledoux that "the character of a building must reflect its function"—in short that poetry and *proper* character are related. Here again, Portman's hotels are only somewhat successful. The play of glass cylinder against concrete honeycomb does indicate certain functional distinctions; it is an *architecture parlante* of a sort. But the overwhelming massiveness of the cylinders, the squatness of proportions, the awkward juxtapositions and inelegant volumes (an inelegance one supposes to be caused by giving a preeminence to sculptural hyperbole) are not particularly proper for

hotel rooms or urban space. Perhaps if these monoliths were surrounded in the future by a sensitive urban infill, rather than parking lots or wide highways, their monumentality might become more acceptable.

Kevin Roche and the firm Kevin Roche, John Dinkeloo and Associates also produce grand atrium spaces and urban monuments sheathed in slick-tech skins. Their Ford Foundation Headquarters in New York City encloses a tree-filled garden with much more conviction and surety than Portman's hotels, but the *res publica* is even further reduced. A strange Egyptian tendency can be seen in two of their monuments: the triple glass pyramids for the College Life Insurance Company (**95**) and the single glass pyramid for The Metropolitan Museum of Art in New York City. The truncation and asymmetry of the pyramids mark them obviously as Late-*Modern* rather than revivalist. The way they meet the sky and ground—they slam into it without transition—underscores the oddness of the imagery and the malapropism of the overall conceit. Why these slick, truncated pyramids for an insurance company? Why three of them? Why the diagrammatic handling of detail? Roche perfects his large sculptures in a "model chamber" specifically devoted to the shaping and testing of external volumes. They thus all have a well-thought-out formal consistency, but remain nevertheless diagrammatic. Even his successfully modeled United Nations development (**99**) opens a "stiff upper lip" to swallow visitors at the entrance.

◀ **94** JOHN PORTMAN AND ASSOCIATES, *Bonaventure Hotel*, Los Angeles, California, 1974–77

▼ **95** KEVIN ROCHE, JOHN DINKELOO AND ASSOCIATES, *College Life Insurance Company of America Headquarters*, Indianapolis, Indiana, 1967

◀ **93** JOHN PORTMAN AND ASSOCIATES, *Hyatt Regency Hotel*, San Francisco, California, 1972–74, interior

The rigidity of this entry probably resulted from the intention to use a single formal system everywhere, even when this system could not accommodate the required shape and mood. A Post-Modernist, by contrast, would have changed material and form for this most important symbolic focus. Positively, this large building breaks down the mass by tripling the usual division between floors; and cutting back, or projecting out, at various heights. It is one of the most distorted of shaped skyscrapers: that recent genre of Late-Modernism which seeks to provide interest to the dumb box. Aside from the scale changes and distortions already mentioned, the building achieves this interest by synecdoche and the overall use of one form. The green glass and silver rectangle march in and out, over and under the entire building. Conceptually, it becomes one homogeneous sculpture which is, paradoxically, many buildings at the same time (the separate planes act as if they were several skyscrapers or a cityscape of towers). This is a typical Late-Modern curtain wall: the slick skin as *membrane* rather than trabeated mullions, as a volumetric, light skin rather than wall.

An even more successful essay in this genre is Henry Cobb and I.M. Pei's John Hancock Tower in Boston (**96–98**).[6] This building also breaks down the weight and scale of its large size, sixty stories, by facets and irregularities—the plan is a rhomboid distorted to hold street lines and inflect toward the important Copley Square. Henry Cobb describes the rise of reflective glass as aiding in the breakdown of mass and as destroying the volume as an inert shape.

▲ **96** HENRY COBB OF I.M. PEI AND PARTNERS *John Hancock Tower*, Boston, Massachusetts, 1968, 1973–77

▶ **97** HENRY COBB OF I.M. PEI AND PARTNERS *John Hancock Tower*, Boston, Massachusetts, 1968, 1973–77, detail of reflective glass

The reflections of the buildings opposite, as well as passing clouds, cut up the volume into discrete areas. Reflections also make one read each facade as a separate plane rather than as part of the overall mass.

But it is as an ultimate metaphor of skyscraping and a sympathetic foil to the adjacent structures that the building works particularly well, with its slick-tech mirror plate which takes up and changes toward its surroundings like a chameleon. Same/different, light/heavy: these are the obvious oxymoronic figures. This ice-blue skyberg really does tear the passing clouds to shreds—with its angled corners it slices them up into large chunks, with its serrated edges it cuts them finer, and with its precise, mirror-finish flat edge it positively scrapes their bottoms flat. Its forerunners, the Flatiron Building in New York City (1902) and the Pirelli Building in Milan, Italy (1961), both skywedges, did not scrape so convincingly.

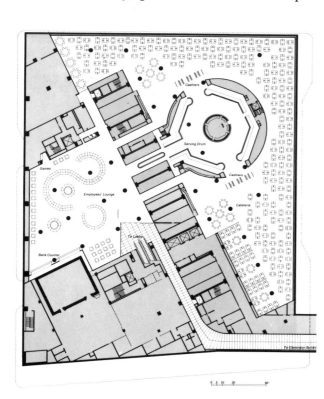

◀ **98** HENRY COBB OF I.M. PEI AND PARTNERS *John Hancock Tower*, Boston, Massachusetts, 1968, 1973–77, ground and typical floor plans

▶ **99** KEVIN ROCHE, JOHN DINKELOO AND ASSOCIATES, *One U.N. Plaza*, New York City, 1969, 1974–76

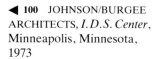
100 JOHNSON/BURGEE ARCHITECTS, *I.D.S. Center*, Minneapolis, Minnesota, 1973

▶ 101 JOHNSON/BURGEE ARCHITECTS, *Pennzoil Place*, Houston, Texas, 1976

▼ 102 JOHNSON/BURGEE ARCHITECTS, *Pennzoil Place*, Houston, Texas, 1976, plan

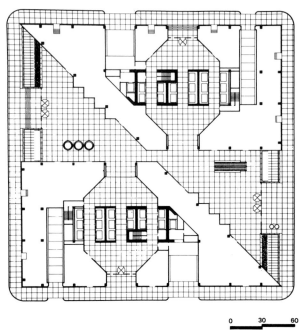

A property of the slick skin membrane is that because it allows a greater volumetric articulation than the previous curtain wall, it breaks down the mass.[7] One way of doing this is to destroy the four-square morphology (the building as a rectangular volume) by adding or subtracting facades; or, as Philip Johnson has done in the I.D.S. Center in Minneapolis, by making a facade—here a broken one—of the corner (100). Here, once again, the shaped skyscraper is conceptually a sculpture constructed from a single form—the rectangular module —yet paradoxically it is at the same time many buildings, not one. The rhetorical figure of one into many is from another angle the oxymoronic figure of complex simplicity, and this can best be seen in Johnson/Burgee's Pennzoil Place in Houston (101–103), where visual paradox adds interest to the twin towers.

The towers appear at first like the dark, simple boxes of Mies van der Rohe, with their regular I-beams and spandrels. But their simplicity is complicated—a double whole, or one building split in two, implying a third trapezoid in the space between. The same surface appears different from any viewpoint because of the light angle (opaque transparency). The two black wedges, set very close on edge, cut a tall sliver of light straight up for three hundred feet and, at the top, inflect toward each other to create an energy charge, like two powerful electrodes. From within the atrium space, the walls seem to lean in and fall over the space-frame roof— a disorienting experience, especially when increased by the optical buzz of the repeated structural members. Reflections of one building in the other, or the reflection of passing clouds, dissolve the surface and give another oxymoronic contradiction—soft hardness. The way the slanted roof forms complement

◀ **103** JOHNSON/BURGEE ARCHITECTS, *Pennzoil Place*, Houston, Texas, 1976, interior

▼ **104** LARRY BELL *Iceberg Palace*. 1975, height 8′. Installed in Philip Johnson's Art Museum of South Texas

each other suggests still another reading: that of a single trapezoid halved diagonally with the two resultant pieces placed at an angle. Finally, the chamfered roof planes, set against the orthogonal geometry of the floor lines, create the last paradox, a diagonal rectangle. Thus, like the Minimalist sculpture of Larry Bell from which they are perhaps derived (**104**), the buildings capture our interest by their distortion of very simple and well-known motifs. They take the skyscraper clichés, visual codes which bore every urbanite, and literally bend and warp new meanings into them.

Anthony Lumsden's buildings and projects achieve a more serene and facile distortion of similar codes. His project for the Bumi Daya Bank is the ultimate in slick-tech membrane building, with its silver skin bending on two sides, faceting on two sides, and flaring out at the base (**108**). Here is an implicit metaphor suitable to the banking function (the silver standard), as well as to the means of wealth which may undermine it (the oil-slick surface). Appropriate metaphor is not a strong point of Late-Modernism, but when it comes to expressing meanings of corporate power, efficiency, and precision, there is a natural affinity between the slick-tech aesthetic and the goals of big business. Is the undeniably phallic shape of the building intentional, or is it a kind of inspired malapropism? To raise this question is to probe into a Late-Modern taboo, the suppressed symbols and motivations of the large practice and large corporation. It is obvious from Lumsden's other buildings, and from his statements, that he is concerned with the free manipulation of the membrane, the clear separation of its modulating surface from structural requirements. This separation allows him a freer plan and morphology than in the usual Miesian skyscraper. Instead of a classical box with predetermined facades and axes, Lumsden

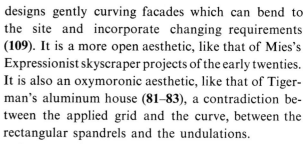

designs gently curving facades which can bend to the site and incorporate changing requirements (**109**). It is a more open aesthetic, like that of Mies's Expressionist skyscraper projects of the early twenties. It is also an oxymoronic aesthetic, like that of Tigerman's aluminum house (**81–83**), a contradiction between the applied grid and the curve, between the rectangular spandrels and the undulations.

A masterpiece of the silver slick-tech aesthetic was created by Welton Becket and Associates in their

◀ **105** WELTON BECKET AND ASSOCIATES, *Hyatt Regency Hotel*, Dallas, Texas, 1976–78

◀ **106** WELTON BECKET AND ASSOCIATES, *Hyatt Regency Hotel*, Dallas, Texas, 1976–78, rear view

▲ **107** WELTON BECKET AND ASSOCIATES, *Hyatt Regency Hotel*, Dallas, Texas, 1976–78, interior

◀ **108** ANTHONY
LUMSDEN AND DMJM
Bumi Daya Bank Project,
Jakarta, Indonesia, 1972–
76, model

▼ **109** ANTHONY
LUMSDEN AND DMJM
Manufacturers Bank, Los
Angeles, California, 1974

Hyatt Regency Hotel, Dallas (**105–107**).[8] The reflective rectangular module is used once again all over the building in curves and in seven stepped volumes. The segments of a curve made from flat surfaces again set up a familiar staccato beat. But now the sfumato effects are even more pronounced, due to the scale and high reflectivity of the surface, and a smoky black merges·and bubbles its way into a glowing silver. Black whiteness, soft hardness, rectangular curves: these are the oxymoronic figures we might expect in 1976, a point at which the slick-tech aesthetic had become conventionalized. The building as a blown-up piece of domestic equipment is another familiar conceit. There are two probably unconsciously created figures, however, which also give excitement to the scheme: its appearance from the back as an Art Deco table, and from the side as a twisting animal with head and tail (the five hundred and sixty foot tower with its restaurant). And finally a conscious simile: at night when its krypton bulbs are lit, the tower becomes a sparkling star or moon.

There are two architects who have concentrated on the slick-tech aesthetic and developed its possibilities more than other designers: Cesar Pelli, an Argentinian who worked for Eero Saarinen and headed the Yale School of Architecture in the late seventies and early eighties; and Norman Foster, a Manchester-born designer who was trained at Yale and works mostly in Britain. Cesar Pelli has concentrated on the ambiguity and layering inherent in the slick-tech look. In his Pacific Design Center, he detaches the taut membrane of the building from the structure, modulates and fractures its surface, and then sets up ambiguous relationships between different surfaces (**110–112**). Transparent, semi-transparent, and opaque glass meet at several points, such as the escalator cylinder, to double the image, fracture reflected views of the environment, and allow partial glimpses of the interior. Images are thus superimposed to give three different and sometimes contradictory meanings. This ambiguity is also taken up in the plan and

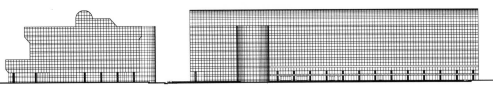

◀ **110** CESAR PELLI
Pacific Design Center, Los
Angeles, California, 1975

▼ **112** CESAR PELLI
Pacific Design Center, Los
Angeles, California, 1975,
escalator tower

▶ **113** BEN JOHNSON
Dock Reflections (detail).
1973, Acrylic on canvas,
60 x 80″. Painting of
Foster Associates' Fred
Olsen Passenger Terminal
in London, England (1971)

▶ **111** CESAR PELLI
Pacific Design Center,
Los Angeles, California,
1975, ground-floor plan
and front and side
elevations

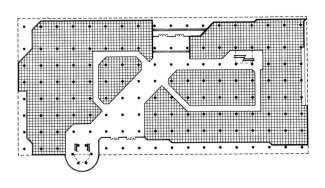

section. For instance, the linear, extruded shape projected on the end elevation would seem to indicate that circulation takes place along an axis and at right angles to this axis, whereas in fact it often occurs on the diagonal. The semi-cylinder seems to suggest a vertical circulation ramp, whereas movement is by escalator at right angles to this circle. In other words, we have a Mannerist contradiction between expectation and result, a Mannerism not confined, as many critics argue, to Post-Modernism.[9] Pelli's articulation of the surface, with its rippling wet-look, furthers this Mannerism, since a "flat" panel is actually undulating slightly (such panels do bend) to produce that wobbly and slithery look typical of slick-tech. When thousands of panels ripple together, the "Blue Whale" (as it is known) seems to shimmer its hide and move through the landscape. The skin membrane has become an explicit simile to be enjoyed as an end in itself.

Norman Foster also makes an expressive virtue of the wobbly flat, an effect which has been focused on by the painter Ben Johnson (**113**).[10] In his *Dock Reflections*, we find the reflected world broken up into rectangular patches by a very thin mullion line while the reflections themselves wobble as they cross the panels and bend. The painting brings out another rhetorical property of the mirror-wall: as a *trompe l'oeil* it distorts reality slightly and enhances its

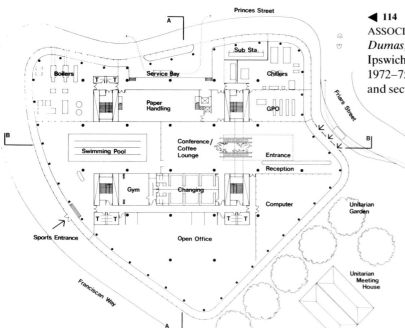

◀ 114 FOSTER ASSOCIATES, *Willis Faber Dumas, Ltd., Head Office*, Ipswich, Suffolk, England, 1972–75, ground-floor plan and section

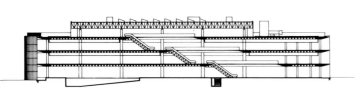

▲ 115 FOSTER ASSOCIATES, *Willis Faber Dumas, Ltd., Head Office*, Ipswich, Suffolk, England, 1972–75, exterior by day

◀ 116 FOSTER ASSOCIATES, *Willis Faber Dumas, Ltd., Head Office*, Ipswich, Suffolk, England, 1972–75, exterior by night

▶ 117 FOSTER ASSOCIATES, *Willis Faber Dumas, Ltd., Head Office*, Ipswich, Suffolk, England, 1972–75, facade detail

cleanliness and precision. Johnson's painting, a two-dimensional illusion of this *trompe l'oeil*, is thus a type of double paradox, or lie, which depends on our perception of the difference between reality and distorted reality for its drama. As Foster further developed the slick membrane, reducing the mullion more and more until it finally disappeared, the illusions became stranger and stranger. The climax of this story is his Willis Faber Dumas building, the last word in the slick-tech look and one of its most delightful and paradoxical realizations (**114–117**). Here nine hundred and thirty panels of specially toughened, half-inch-thick, bronze-tinted "antisun solar control glass" are suspended from a continuous rail running around the roof perimeter. The panels are connected at the corners with metal plates and the gaps between sealed with translucent silicon, while stiffening is supplied by vertical glass fins.

The aesthetic result of this is an undulating, staccato beat of black glass and bumpy-wobbly distortions of the environment. The building holds the site and street lines, taking on a shape which has led to its being called the "Big Black Piano"—an inadvertent metaphor, not quite a malapropism. But the real fascination is not in these fortuitous images but in what the glass does to different views: from any one point the building is part transparent, part opaque,

and part reflective, while one part slithers into the next, eliding these images with a sfumato as it wobbles them. Perhaps the oxymoronic figure bumpy-wobbly is not the absolute termination of the development of the slick-tech membrane because one can imagine a pure, curved wall with no joints and segmental planes (which may be built as glass technology becomes even more developed, although it seems unlikely at present).

We have reached then, with Foster's "Big Black Piano," a *ne plus ultra* of the slick-tech look, a perfect expression of the corporation's dreams of proficiency. Precision, technical mastery, the mystery of black box technology, impersonality, the building as blown-up instrument, sfumato, oxymoron, ambiguity—these figures and ideas are summarized, unlikely as it may seem, in the town of Ipswich, England. The building is inevitably a Late-Modern dream of a twenties fantasy: the ideal of corporate efficiency and egalitarianism leading to a Brave New World commandeered by Captains of Industry. It is hard to sustain a belief in such a world given the realities of late-capitalism—its gigantism and inequality to name only two—but Foster comes close to persuading us of the potential beauties behind that reality.

3

TWENTIES REVIVALISM
THE WHITE, IDEAL PAVILIONS OF PRIVATE LIFE

IF THE SLICK-TECH LOOK ARTICULATED A PUBLIC fantasy of corporate perfection in the seventies, then the white, neo-Corbusian aesthetic was one representation of the ideal private domain in the same period. The neo-Corbusian villa replaced the neo-Palladian villa, at least in some sectors of American society, as *the* sign of arrival and social probity. For the American architects who designed these villas (at times as unusable as Palladio's Villa Rotonda) the abstract, white lyrical style symbolized an ideal world of pure architectural integrity. For European architects, the style symbolized rich clients (indeed *nouveaux riches*) who should either not exist, or better still, should move back across the Atlantic and commission the original inventors of the style. For many practicing architects, the style represented both an exercise in nostalgia and a form of intellectual gymnastics. For certain students it meant the one true faith of Modernism, reborn with a new fervor and dogma.

These, the major attitudes toward twenties revivalism and its protagonists, The Five,[1] gave strength, notoriety, and international significance to the style. They convey an ambivalence which it is hard to avoid, for the movement is at once reactionary and progressive, populist and elitist, pretentious yet not without integrity: In this chapter, the Late-Modern aspects of twenties revivalism, lasting roughly from 1963 to 1974, will be treated; whereas certain spatial complexities and symbolic concerns, notably those of Michael Graves, will be discussed in the Post-Modern sections where they more appropriately belong. As in other cases, such as the work of Arata Isozaki, there has been a recent trend of Late-Modernists toward Post-Modernism.

The Smith House of Richard Meier (**118–120**) is, as the architect has said, a combination of Le Corbusier's Citrohan and Domino houses; a reworking of propositions which all of The Five modify in different ways.[2] Its entrance "back" is a planar, wall architecture, while its garden "front" is opened up, on a free plan, to the view. This Mannerist inversion of front and back is just one of several inversions of customary usage and Corbusian syntax. The effect is dramatized by exaggerating the difference between a front that looks like a back (with small holes puncturing wooden siding) and a back that looks like a front (very large glazed areas that Le Corbusier could not achieve with twenties technology). Furthermore, there is a Mannerist distortion of materials: what looks like a reinforced concrete villa is in fact a combination steel, brick, and load-bearing wood structure—painted white and presented for publication in black-and-white photographs, as were the twenties International Style buildings, to give maximum contrast and abstraction to the image. It is this lyrical, white, abstract quality which is most apparent in the photographs, especially those taken without people or much furniture (aside from a few abstract, twenties revival pieces). They correspond to the beautiful, cryptic plans and sections which Meier draws—pristine, elegant, unlabeled, and often ambiguous in their distinction between inside and outside space. This cool ambiguity and over-refined intellectualization, again common to The Five, can be compared to similar qualities in the virtuoso Renaissance work of Michelangelo and Giulio Romano, as well as to the grand tradition of the Western villa. For as Colin Rowe has shown in "The Mathematics of the Ideal Villa" (1947), an essay that has influenced all this work, there is a traditional connection between the pure, geometric block placed in an untouched Virgilian landscape and the notion of the ideal villa.[3] This Platonic villa may be Roman, Albertian, Palladian, Corbusian, or now even Meierian. And yet there are certain semantic problems unacknowledged by Meier, or not dealt with by him adequately—such as his application of a twenties egalitarian aesthetic to private houses for, if not the jet set, then, according to Meier, the readers of *House Beautiful* (where many of his houses are published).

Of course there is nothing inherently wrong in building beautiful houses and purveying them through the pages of consumer magazines, nor indeed in appealing to an elite, *nouveau-riche* class: the most creative architecture of the last two hundred years has often found its support in this way. Nor is it morally suspect to resemanticize previous languages of architecture—all creative movements do this. What is disturbing is the way this is achieved, the naiveté and lack of irony with which it is done. As Peter Papademetriou has shown, in his article "Le Corbusier à la mode, Revolution for the Sell of It," Meier's Smith House (**118–120**) can be appropriately used in advertisements selling the youth cult, Magnavox equipment, helicopters, and jet-set living precisely because it is so successful in resemanticizing an egalitarian form language.[4] There is no doubt, irony, or social tension in Meier's forms, and furthermore, in his reply to his critics ("My Statement," 1976), he naively assumes that his architecture still carries an egalitarian message because it goes against other elitist taste cultures (those supporting a neo-Vernacular) and because it is formally integral and challenging.[5] The irony that he has become, or, one supposes, intended to become, the ultimate American villa architect, proffering answers to the private dreams of the rich, finds no expression in his buildings or statements. As a result, we have to treat his work as reduced in meaning to a commentary on previous architecture. It is architecture about architecture—particularly that of the preceding generation.

Thus the Smith House uses the round, columnar grid of Le Corbusier's Domino houses as a rotational element opposed to the frontal layering of his Citrohan houses. This opposition between frontality and rotation is, as Kenneth Frampton has pointed out, a major subject of The Five's architecture, even if its meaning is rather empty.[6] Private space is tight and layered while public space is open, with diagonal vistas and a slight feeling of rotation caused by the round columns set close up to a glass wall. The horizontal and vertical oppositions of the seaward side (**120**) are particularly successful at

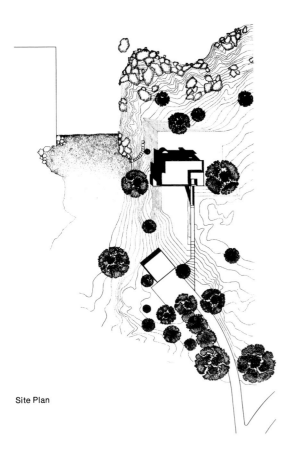

Site Plan

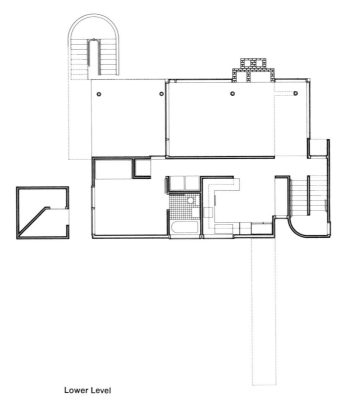

Lower Level

▲ **118** RICHARD MEIER
Smith House, Darien,
Connecticut, 1965–67,
southeast facade

◀ **119** RICHARD MEIER
Smith House, Darien, Connecticut, 1965–67, site and
lower-level plans

▼ **120** RICHARD MEIER
Smith House, Darien, Connecticut, 1965–67, entrance
facade

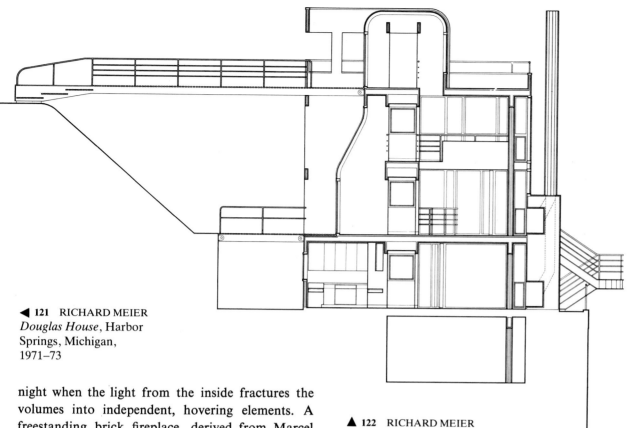

◀ **121** RICHARD MEIER
Douglas House, Harbor
Springs, Michigan,
1971–73

▲ **122** RICHARD MEIER
Douglas House, Harbor
Springs, Michigan,
1971–73, section

night when the light from the inside fractures the volumes into independent, hovering elements. A freestanding brick fireplace, derived from Marcel Breuer but here placed on the outside away from the wall, contrasts with a precisionist interlocking of horizontal planes, derived from Richard Neutra's Lovell House, Los Angeles (1927–29), and a thin treatment of stretched mullions derived from the Stick Style. Le Corbusier, Breuer, Neutra, Stick Style—all these quotations are finished with a craftsmanship and elegance which the readers of *House Beautiful* and *The Journal of the Society of Architectural Historians* can enjoy. Meier is the craftsman of architects' architecture, just as Frank Stella, with whom he worked, is the craftsman of painters' painting.

Another of Meier's important modifications of twenties syntax is the Douglas House, which is an even more dramatic evocation of the Virgilian dream—a pure, white, geometrical frame, with two glistening, silver flues, set on a steep hillside in a green forest beside Lake Michigan (**121–122**). Here, as in the Smith House, we cross a bridge entrance to a private front/back, which then gives way to a public back/front opening out onto an extraordinary view. It is nature untouched, and architecture as an expression of man's intellect. The opposition nature/culture could not be more heightened by color, form, and material: the apotheosis of the Corbusian villa set off from the organic world. The Greek temple and certain Renaissance churches also play on this extreme dichotomy, and it is of course the opposite of organic architecture and all that work of Frank Lloyd Wright and Bruce Goff which seeks to make a continuum between nature and culture. It creates feelings

which are usually associated with shrines: a sense of awe, solemnity, dignity, and quiet. Again, the absence of people (apparently the house is used only as a retreat by the Douglas family) and the presence of twenties furniture in a hieratic way (Le Corbusier and Mies reproductions) add to the religious solemnity. This is *the* temple to private life, and like Palladio's Villa Rotonda it is too difficult and expensive to inhabit for long: one cannot live up to the ritual and cleanliness it entails.

Again, the quotations come rolling off the tip of the critical tongue: Le Corbusier's ship-rail pipes set against Neutra's Von Sternberg House; Breuer's fireplace on the entrance axis set against Le Corbusier's triple-height space (now carried through four levels to outdo the master); gridded, Corbusian Domino block with stretched mullions indicating Corbusian columns and floor lines. Meier's work, like that of Charles Gwathmey, was labeled Post-Johnson-Corb by admirers and critics in the early seventies. It applies the precisionist fastidiousness which Philip Johnson has made a hallmark of his style to the more rough and ironic work of Le Corbusier, sleeking over the bumps, grain, age, and dissonance which were an inseparable part of his later buildings. In fact, there is a bit of Late-Corb in Meier's bridges and distended stairways—it is not all *twenties* revivalism. Just as Graves and Hejduk make use of Le Corbusier's

▲ **123** CHARLES
GWATHMEY, *Gwathmey
Residence and Studio*,
Amagansett, New York,
1966–67

Carpenter Center for the Visual Arts at Harvard (1961–64) for its detachment and fragmentation of parts, and above all its ramps and erosions of volumes, so too does Meier. The stair and parapet of the Douglas House cantilever out over a precipitous drop; the cubic volume is eroded at the corner to

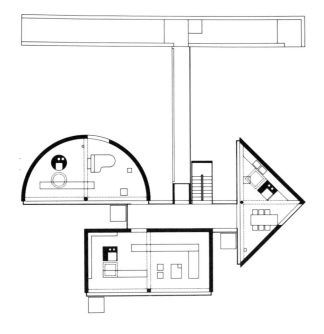

▶ 125 JOHN HEJDUK
*Diamond Series Project:
House 8*, 1962–66, entry-
level plan and projection

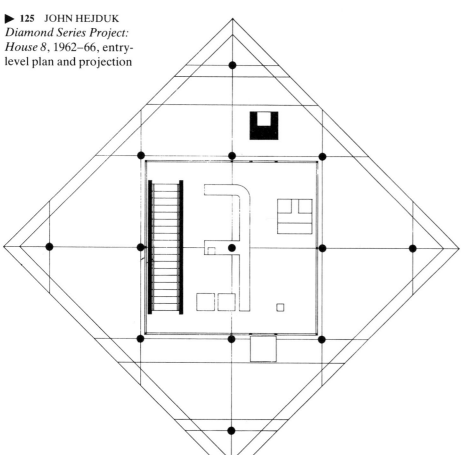

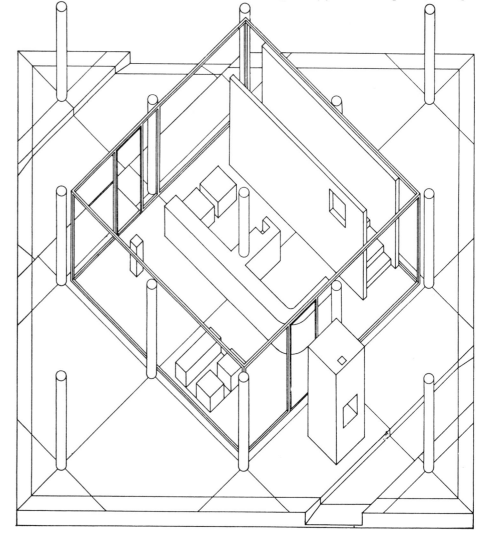

allow a negative volume of space to penetrate through four stories. The mullion rhythm (A, A, B, A, C, A, B reading from left to right on the lakeside) is syncopated and non-symmetrical, as in Le Corbusier's later work, to introduce an open, unfinished note into this image of perfection—and thereby generate a tension in Meier's work. As we will see, Meier has more recently pushed this fragmentation and tension onto a larger scale, making it take over entire facades of a building. What are minor curves, discontinuities, and collisions within the Douglas House have become major themes on the outside of his Atheneum (**139–143**).

Turning Corbusian syntax inside out, upside down, or on its side is as much a theme of Charles Gwathmey as it is of Richard Meier and John Hejduk. Gwathmey's residence and studio for his parents (**123**) takes Le Corbusier's concrete forms, renders them in cedar siding (appropriate to Long Island), fragments them into demi-forms (one-half square, one-half circle and triangle), and then elides all these fragments together. The result is a very disturbing and enjoyable bloating of scale. Stair curves become heavy, inert semi-cylinders; blank walls become giant pieces of cardboard; triangular skylights become massive wedges. These are children's building blocks, awkwardly thrown together but finished with a miraculous polish. The oxymoronic figures—awkward perfection, concrete wood, and childlike sophistication—are given a Surrealist emphasis in the photographs of this scheme, again without people or the usual signs of identity and place. These and later Gwathmey buildings look as if René Magritte had played intellectual billiards with Corbusian toys, a conjunction which is even more apparent in the work of John Hejduk, an architect who admires Magritte.

Hejduk's One-Half House Project is, like all his work, an extraordinary proposition about the ordinary based on a variable metaphysical idea (**124**). In this case, three primary solids (cylinder, cube, and prism) are cut in half and placed pinwheel fashion at the end of a circulation spine. The circulation is at right angles to a solid entry wall, so again, as in Meier's work, we have a rotational scheme set against a frontal entrance. Now, however, the rotation is conceptual as well as perceptual: the mind circulates from one primary demiform to the next trying to put them together, trying to understand their relationship, trying to fathom their *raison d'être*. Certain semantic clues are given (cylinder for piano, triangle for kitchen, rectangle for study) which prove helpful in understanding different areas, but are ultimately enigmatic in their significance. As with Magritte's *Collective Invention* (1934), a painting showing the inverse of a mermaid with a female tail and fish's head, the enjoyment consists in perceiving a reverse logic. Conventionally functional shapes—the cylinders, rectangles, and prisms popular in the twenties—are given a precise but arbitrary function, and the whole building is paradoxically exploded into three separate parts and an entry. We try to put it together in our mind as rectangular base, semi-circular door, and pitched roof—forms which have fallen on their sides. This is like a chiastic figure (for example, Oscar Wilde: "Work is the curse of the drinking classes") where usual meanings are transposed, although here the semantic transposition is not precise. The syntactical order is, however, worked through with exactitude. Each demi-form is itself halved, in each left half is an emblematic chimney, and each half has its midpoint placed on a relevant axis about which it appears to have been rotated, thus adding a conceptual rotation to the perceptual one.

In Hejduk's Diamond Series Project, developed since 1962, the rotational elements were pushed even further (**125**). Here, the inspiration was Piet Mondrian's *Foxtrot* (1927), Theo van Doesburg's canvases which also set up two grids rotated at forty-five degrees to each other, and Frank Lloyd Wright's plans of the twenties. One should also add to this twenties revivalism and the sixties Carpenter Center of Le Corbusier, about which Hejduk wrote: "The shape of the structural columns is round, indicating a centrifugal force and multi-directional whirl."[7] In the Diamond Series, round columns set in a tight space close to walls also create a centrifugal force. To this is added the whirl of L-shaped space created by partitions which always partly enclose and partly leave open a room. They spin about an implied center like a whirligig or exploding, twirling firecracker. A walk through this maze would force one to go into a spin, or at least a constantly turning route. In nearly every room two right angles are contrasted with the rotational diagonal.

It would appear that Hejduk is merging ideas from several different sources: the open planning and sliding planes which Mies van der Rohe used mostly outdoors; the labyrinth, which is also an outdoor form; and the concepts from painting and architecture mentioned above. There is no obvious *raison d'être* to this merger beyond formal exploration and creation. It does extend the spatial research of Le Corbusier and others, and it is somewhat paradoxical (the inside-outside labyrinth). But it is as a ruthless metaphysical proposition worked through to

one conclusion that this and other Hejduk projects gain their conviction. The Metaphysical School of architecture is largely Post-Modern, as we will see (pages 178–199), and Hejduk might be considered one of its members except that his concerns are more purely formal than metaphysical. He has created a primitive semantic architecture (the Babar House, the Bye House, etc.) and that Post-Modern concern makes him more difficult to classify as a Late-Modernist. But his semantic coding remains more private than public, more hermetic than shared. Likewise, as Kenneth Frampton has pointed out,[8] his architecture implies an isolated, rural landscape rather than an urban one; it stands apart from any context as the supreme, detached monument, rather than forming part of an order. For this reason it is interesting to compare it to urban schemes of the Rationalists which are also based on a twenties revivalism and rotational order.

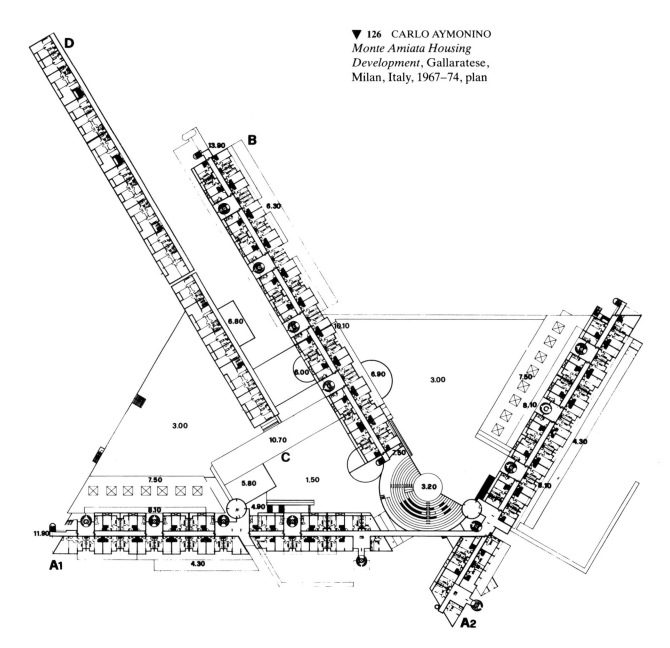

▼ **126** CARLO AYMONINO
Monte Amiata Housing Development, Gallaratese, Milan, Italy, 1967–74, plan

Carlo Aymonino's Gallaratese neighborhood in Milan, planned for two thousand four hundred inhabitants, consists of four linear slab blocks rotating around a three-quarter circular, outdoor theater (**126**).[9] The slabs, mixtures of a traditional street architecture and Modern double-loaded corridor plan, are set in the arms of equilateral triangles, while the bases of these triangles are left open and implied, so that the entire urban fabric seems to spin, rather like certain Constructivist plans of the twenties. The ends of some slabs are canted at sixty degrees to reinforce the triangular geometry, while a double frontality is set up by parallel slabs and the implied base of each triangle. The result is a curious mixture of an open, Modernist landscape and a closed piazza, although finally the fragmentation and openness prevail. The collective center, the *res publica* of the theater, does not hold the spin. In like manner, the Constructivist-inspired facades become restless and

▲ 127 VITTORIO DE FEO
(with FABRIZIO AGGARBATI
and CARLA SAGGIORO) *Esso
Service Station Prototype*,
1971, perspective

▲ 128 VITTORIO DE FEO
(with ERRICO ASCIONE)
Institute for Draftsmen,
Terni, Italy, 1968

▶ 129 PETER EISENMAN
House II: Falk House, Hardwick, Vermont, 1969–70

animated in their fragmentation and extreme articulation. Figure predominates over ground, object over
texture, as in Hejduk's work, and as opposed to the
urbanism of Aldo Rossi, who designed one block
of the Gallaratese group.

Vittorio de Feo, another Italian architect who has
been influenced by twenties Constructivism, and has
written a book, *U.R.S.S. Architettura 1917–1936*
(Rome, 1963), on it, has designed several schemes
which violently oppose rectilinear and angled geometries, notably his Regional Administration Center
at Trieste and his prototypical Esso Service Station.
The latter mixes Roy Lichtenstein supergraphics with
Constructivist graphics derived from El Lissitzky to
produce a highly communicative, appropriate architecture that is really Post-Modern in intent (**127**).
Vectors of speed, wedges, and gasoline pumps placed
at an angle; the distortion from the frontal ESSO sign
to the bended tube of automobile movement—these
forms have a direct communicative impact and suitability for aiding movement at high speed. Frontality,
rotation, and the dialectic between them have a
purpose.

This purposeful use of a Constructivist language is
not so apparent in De Feo's Institute for Draftsmen
(**128**). Here, primary forms are combined and rotated
in ways which recall Hejduk's inventions. One wall of
a slab is rotated back to produce a monopitched
wall-roof and a right-angled triangular figure. This
paradoxical surface can be sat on and thus used, as
Constructivist buildings were sometimes used, as an
outdoor linear grandstand (is foot-racing part of the
draftsmen's training?). Lecture theaters are on the
smaller underside of these leaning wall-roof-stands,
while Palladian cutout motifs light the interior corridor. Thus there is some functional justification for
these highly arbitrary formal moves, but it is as a
formal, paradoxical game that the scheme really
achieves its interest. Besides the paradoxes already
mentioned, there is the grand trope, a distortion of the
simplified house so that it lies down at an angle:
rusticated base, Palladian window, and roof cover
are all implied by the surface.

Formal games played to heighten the perception of
pure syntax are the special concern of Peter Eisenman. He rigorously tries to exclude the semantic
dimension of architecture, but this being impossible,
his work necessarily sets off a chain of associations:
the white architecture of Mykonos, the Cistercians,
Le Corbusier, and above all the Italian Rationalist
Giuseppe Terragni. The signs of twenties revivalism
are as apparent in his constructions as they are in
the work of any of The Five, where twenties syntax
is distorted and extended. Thus the reticulated grid
of Le Corbusier's Domino houses is present in

Eisenman's House II (**129–131**), but the round column is changed to a frontalized square pier and moved to the surface. It is then elided with the white planar wall and, at some corners, with the volume of the building. Elision is one of the most pronounced rhetorical figures used by Late-Modernists, as, for example, the slick-tech architects who omit junctures and run a homogeneous skin over all parts of their building. Eisenman does the same, producing what he calls a conceptual, "cardboard architecture": the actual building looks like a cardboard model and this forces one to read it conceptually from above, turning it over in the mind as one would with a model.[10]

There is another oxymoronic figure Eisenman adds to the building/model and reinforced concrete/cardboard: the column/wall/volume, in which one element transforms itself into another as it runs around or through the building, a figure we can term volumetric elision. Like the chimera, or perhaps Magritte's inverted mermaid, one thing becomes another before our eyes: no transitions, moldings, decoration, or parts that are customarily distinguished. This forces a new kind of reading of architecture on us. Perceptually, we read the grid and its rhythms in combination with the voids. Figure and ground are equated. This produces very complicated rhythms which nonetheless evoke classical buildings. Thus the south elevation of House II (**130**) can be read simply as a two-story palazzo with a major triadic rhythm of three bays (A, A, A). When we look more closely, however, we see internal rhythms: that

A includes a further subdivision c, d, c—vertical rectangle, horizontal rectangle, vertical rectangle (on the ground floor, left). If we now add to this complication the perceptual fact that the figure is also the ground, a pier is a wall or void, and give this pier the letter b; and if we add the cues in depth which we perceive, we get a very complicated rhythm overlaid on the simple triad (b, c, b, c, d, c, b, c, d, c, b, c, e, c, b, c, b and A = c, d, c). It is almost a gentle syncopation.

In fact, according to the way Eisenman has designed the house, marking internal transformations on the outside, these rhythms sometimes refer to a change in internal wall, volume, pier, or circulation area. We do not know which changes are being marked,

▼ **130** PETER EISENMAN
House II: Falk House,
Hardwick, Vermont,
1969–70, south elevation

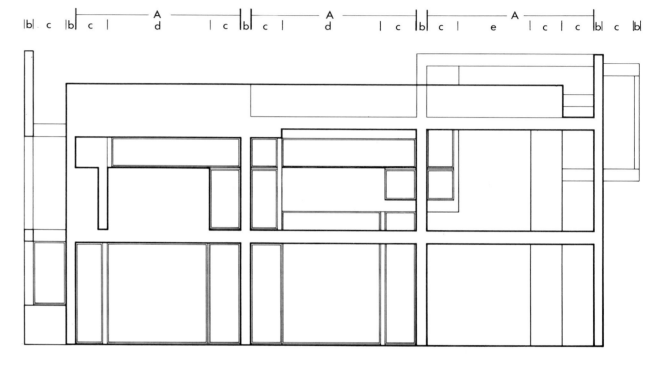

▼ **131** PETER EISENMAN
House II: Falk House, Hardwick, Vermont, 1969–70,
six steps of transformation

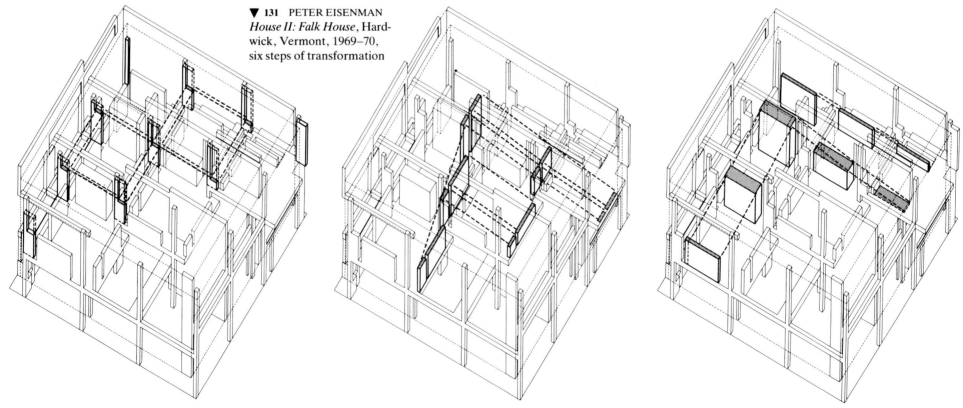

and even if we stand in front of the south elevation with his diagrams in hand, it is hard, if not impossible, to tell. Perversely, Eisenman admits that he does not care about this because the actual building is really important only as a sign of the process by which it was designed: the transformational drawings are more important than the building, they *are* what the building ultimately signifies.

This is at once a cynical and interesting idea. It is rather as if one said that the dome of St. Peter's in Rome signifies the transformational drawings by which Michelangelo, and others, designed it. To many architectural historians, this signification may be the prime concern; to the worshipers, of course, it is of minor importance. If one is exclusively interested in architects' architecture, and architecture about the process of design, as Eisenman is, then this inversion of priorities is understandable. It is cynical because it makes the client, his desires, and architectural languages totally subservient to, and manipulated by, the concerns of the architect. A set of transformational drawings cannot be inhabited, as some of Eisenman's clients have found.

The elitism of this stance, combined with the hermetic and ultimately incomprehensible markings on the surface, is typical of Late-Modernist attitudes in general—although Eisenman holds his position with greater tenacity and extremity than any other architect. In treating architecture as reified process, as extreme technical virtuosity, as exaggerated and

esoteric sculpture, as a paradoxical game of nonsense, Eisenman does what the other Late-Modern elitists do, but with a refreshing, self-conscious defense of elitism.[11] It is an open question whether anyone can perceive the "dual deep structures" inherent in House II, the two grids which are shifted in relation to each other on the diagonal, one made up of a pier grid, the other of planes set on the diagonal. The "tight, layered space" between these two grids (c) is, however, quite apparent.

In a later work, House III (132–133), the presence of the dual deep structure becomes more apparent because the two grids are rotated at forty-five degrees to each other and thus set up angular collisions throughout the house which are dramatic and even violent. The reticulated grid and rotated planar grid are much more explicitly coded, while the volumetric elision and the erosion of this volume, in large chunks of empty, framed space, are stronger. The perceptual and conceptual enjoyment this creates consists, once again, in rotating the building in our minds through several transformations. Because of volumetric elision, we can turn the building on its side, or upside down, or any-which-way, and it remains equally plausible. Architectural enjoyment consists, among many other things, in this game of mentally manipulating relationships, inverting and rotating them. The clients of this house particularly enjoyed these syntactic transformations, even when they played havoc with domestic functions.[12]

In summary, this building, whose complicated relationships can best be experienced with the quiet and time that domesticity affords, is yet another white temple to private life. In the hermetic privacy of its language games, its disregard for context and semantics, it is typical of Late-Modernism, while in its complex, layered spatial surprises, it is, as we shall see, typical of Post-Modern space.

The same could be said of Michael Graves's early buildings—the Hanselmann House, Benacerraf House, and Snyderman House—although these *do* have semantic concerns. The problem with their meanings, such as the "celestial soffit," is that they are coded with a seemingly willful obscurity.[13] They challenge the reader to discover their significance if he can, and judging by the response of most architectural commentators, he cannot. These buildings are perceived by many as being merely essays in twenties revivalism, a language they no doubt use, but an architecture whose meaning they do not share.

The Hanselmann House, for instance, is coded as a public building, a freestanding monument that might also be a grandiose doctor's office, with its overtones of crisp sterility, or an idiosyncratic temple, with its ceremonial stairway, propylaeum, bridge, and near-symmetrical entry (134–135). If we pass over this questionable semantic inflation and concentrate on the hermeneutic codes, a more rewarding reading of the building can be made. Once again, it is a Man-

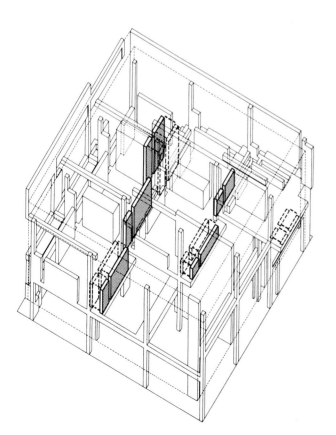
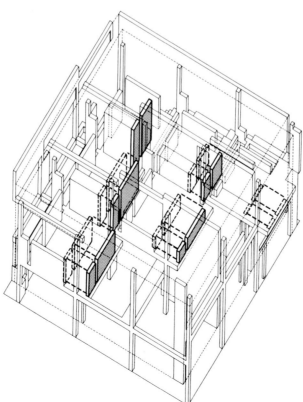
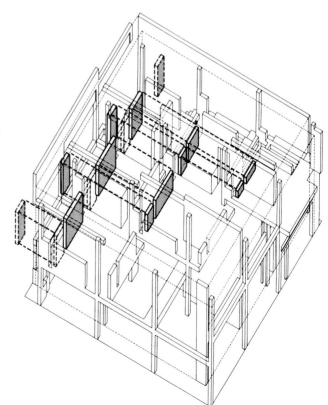

▲ **132** PETER EISENMAN
House III: Miller House,
Lakeville, Connecticut,
1969–70, view from the
southeast

nerist distortion of twenties syntax. The frontality demanded by the approach propylaeum (not built) and bridge set at right angles to the front plane is offset by an erosion of both elements to their left side. The white diagonal on the front, indicating the stairway, and the one-sided open ribbon window above both increase the rotational movement. But this is counteracted by a renewed frontality once one is inside the entry: the slots of tight rectangular space set up between the column grid, walls, partitions, and views up and down. Here we have that vertical and horizontal layering of space which Colin Rowe and Robert Slutzky analyzed in an article that influenced The Five.[14] There is also a contrast of planar "cardboard" surfaces with a reticulated structural grid which we find in Eisenman's work, although the

two are now more separated, and volumetric elision does not result. The image has more stability than in the other work of The Five, partly because of the closure of the square volume and partly because the square is repeated and doubled many times. A square, or cube of space, is implied between outside propylaeum and front; the plans and elevations are fragmented squares; entry is dead center of the square. Thus the Hanselmann House is basically a square, frontal building with rotational fragments introduced, which signify a kind of doubt concerning the rationality of the right angle.

A later Graves building, the Snyderman House, takes these doubts and fragmentations further, indeed so far that they explode the square (**136–138**). The reticulated structure can still be seen, especially on the east facade, where it is a useless cage supporting nothing but itself. Here, in a sense, is the ultimate inversion of twenties semantics: for the functional arguments underlying the Domino block, the reinforced concrete frame, and the Chicago steel frame, Graves has substituted an argument for the "useless frame." The notions behind this are twofold. Firstly, by expressing its own uselessness and by exaggerating its scale and identity, the frame accentuates its existence as a principle of order, not function: it becomes, like a decorated Doric column, the *sign* of architectural order and of the trabeated structure within. Secondly, it frames the richly colored, moving planes within and the views of trees and sky without. A rather simple rhythm (A, A, B, A, A)

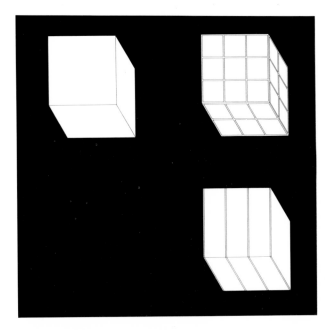

allows the diagonal stairs and cantilevered study to be pronounced as variations on this theme.

This gridded order, which runs through the whole building, turning from square frame to round column, is much more complex on the south facade, which looks, semantically, like a pink Juan Gris painting trying to get out of a gray-and-white Mondrian. The pink guitar-shaped terrace is the most notable form and its curves recall the kidney-shapes of Hejduk's schemes, as well as other less-mentionable biomorphic parts of the body. Graves has com-

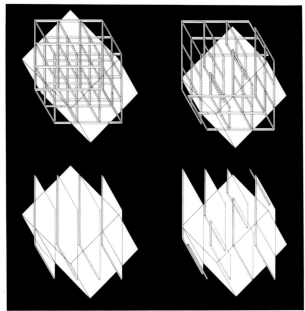

▲ **133** PETER EISENMAN *House III: Miller House*, Lakeville, Connecticut, 1969–70, transformational drawings

▼ **134** MICHAEL GRAVES *Hanselmann House*, Fort Wayne, Indiana, 1967, entrance facade

mented on the basic duality here: "The 'natural' is taken to mean that which shows the attributes of nature—irregularity, lyricism, movement. Similarly, 'man-made' becomes synonymous with idealised form, geometry, stasis. . . . Polychromy is used to refer to both natural and man-made elements.

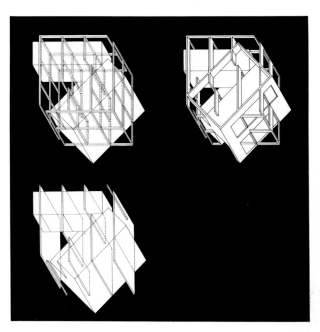

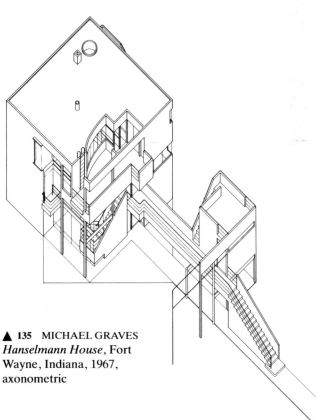

▲ **135** MICHAEL GRAVES *Hanselmann House*, Fort Wayne, Indiana, 1967, axonometric

The colours modify the perfection assumed in the white frame and make allusions to the adjacent landscape."[15] The allusions are more elusive than elucidating. The color coding (pinks, light blue, gray, green-black) is not *conventionally* related, here in Fort Wayne, Indiana, to any of the surrounding greenery or landscape. The white frame would probably be perceived as referring to perfection and to the white, ideal pavilions of private life, partly because Richard Meier, The Five, and Le Corbusier, among others, have established this convention. But basically, the Snyderman House remains the last, most complicated work in an inaccessible language which Graves was to modify in his switch to Post-Modernism. It did, however, have an enormous effect on other Late-Modernists, and on no one more than Richard Meier.

Meier's Atheneum in New Harmony, Indiana (**139–143**), sets up a dialectic between "ordered utopia" and "disordered reality" (as Meier characterizes the duality underlying the utopian community founded there by Robert Owen in the early nineteenth century). Meier expresses this dualism, as one would guess, as a dialectic between frontality and rotation and a semantic confrontation between ideal grid and irregular guitar shapes. Many Gravesian motifs from the Snyderman House can be found here: the curved guitar cut by a ribbon window, symbolizing nature; the stairway rotated at an angle to the grid; and the perspective enlargements and diminishments caused by skewing space within the confines of

◀ **136** MICHAEL GRAVES *Snyderman House*, Fort Wayne, Indiana, 1972, east facade

▼ **137** MICHAEL GRAVES *Snyderman House*, Fort Wayne, Indiana, 1972, south facade

▶ **138** MICHAEL GRAVES *Snyderman House*, Fort Wayne, Indiana, 1972, first-floor plan

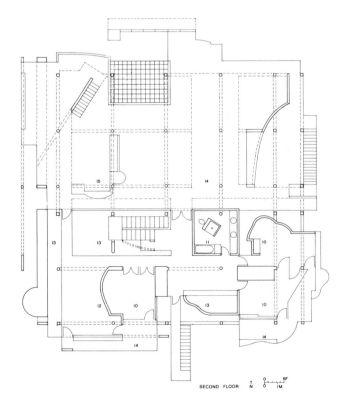

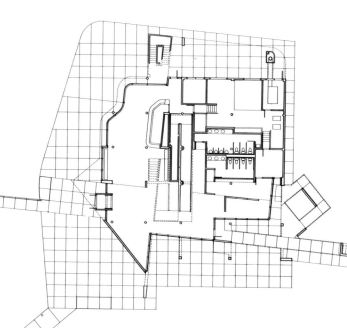

the grid (a later Gravesian motif). Again, the complexity and ambiguity of spatial layering are Post-Modern while the esoteric coding of the elements, in an abstract, white, machine aesthetic, is Late-Modern. This code does not relate to the function (exhibition and reception center for New Harmony), to the taste cultures of the users (basically Middle American), or to the locale. As an elitist, self-referential monument, however, the Atheneum is superior to other monuments in this Late-Modern genre because its syntactical collisions are so carefully and elegantly worked through.

One approaches the white exploded box up a ramp from the east. This is in fact the back entrance, but because of size and disposition it looks like the front. Straight ahead is a blank wall (the auditorium) and an exterior staircase cantilevered out into space and set at forty-five degrees to the frontal surface. This gigantic staircase, more sculptural than useful, acts as a kind of propylaeum or gateway, except that one does not move through it; the articulation of size and geometry makes it a symbolic entryway. There are slight Mannerist distortions even here, as the entry ramp is slightly angled to the front and the "gate" is shifted away from the path. One then moves to the bridge, which is sheltered by a plane of wall cut at an angle which continues that of the ramp, except now positive and negative volumes are reversed. This inversion, or anastrophe, is a very pleasing figure in itself. Next one proceeds into the building with its interior ramped space which goes through four stories, or one goes to a room with a dramatic view of the river. The natural landscape is here represented by gentle undulations and the guitar shape.

◄ **139** RICHARD MEIER
The Atheneum, New Harmony, Indiana, 1975–79, east facade

▲ **140** RICHARD MEIER
The Atheneum, New Harmony, Indiana, 1975–79, ground-level plan

▼ **141** RICHARD MEIER
The Atheneum, New Harmony, Indiana, 1975–79, south facade

absence of the painting, sculpture, and traditional ornament which were so much a part of the Zimmermanns' populist language. In the Atheneum we have, by contrast, the white light of the Enlightenment: a cerebral and Protestant light rather than the Catholic South German light. We have, to push the analogy further, the white, silver light of the twenties and seventies, implying the egalitarianism and crystalline straightforwardness of the one and the slick proficiency of the other. Here, the logic and clarity implied in Le Corbusier's Domino houses is broken apart by freestanding, detached elements. Platonic perfection is evoked only to be questioned.

Twenties Modernism has been stood on its head: unclear clarity, ambiguous straightforwardness, rotated frontality, silver whiteness, imperfect perfection, and back front are the oxymoronic figures built into the form. Finally, then, an aesthetic which was conceived for the ideal pavilions of private life has gone public and introduced a note of questioning celebration into the *res publica*. The ambiguity of this celebration makes the Atheneum one of the great monuments of Late-Modernism.

◀ 142 RICHARD MEIER
The Atheneum, New Harmony, Indiana, 1975–79, west facade

▼ 143 RICHARD MEIER
The Atheneum, New Harmony, Indiana, 1975–79, interior

The explosion of white light, almost shadowless because it enters from so many angles and is reflected, echoes the explosion of forms and creates further ambiguity about the distinction between inside, outside, and intermediate space. As in the drawings, a perceptual ambiguity is set up by equating things which are different—solid and void, wall and structure, figure and ground—and thus there is a greater volumetric elision, and hence rotation, than in other schemes. Everything seems to spin, gyrate, whirl, and finally explode in the ultra-bright light. One is reminded of Dominikus and Johann Zimmermann's rococo churches, where white light also suffuses and dematerializes all parts of the structure. But as soon as this comparison comes to mind, one notices the lack of conventional iconography, the

LATE-MODERN
SPACE
A SIGN OF AGNOSTICISM

A PROMINENT ARCHITECTURAL CONCEPT OF THE SIXTIES was that of the giant industrial shed which could be used to shelter a variety of functions. This idea was already manifest in two existing building types, one extremely practical, the other just extreme: the supermarket and the megastructure. Inherent in these building types, and in the proposals put forward to justify them, was the concept of great size, and, by extension, of a great marketplace. Outdoor pop concerts attended by a quarter of a million people were held; minimal shelter was provided for a weekend. Supermarkets, shopping centers, and new, large, covered entertainment facilities such as Houston's Astrodome were seminal building types of this period, and even if they were not altogether new, their scale and back-up services were greater in extent than before. A partially new type of social organization had developed, dependent on mass culture and advanced technology, and ideologically committed to a type of egalitarianism: the democracy of large numbers. Such an ideology obviously related to late-capitalism, with its emphasis on world markets, multinational companies, mass consumption, and cultural growth. Not surprisingly, Late-Modernist architects sought out late-capitalist commissions, the megabuildings. These designers developed a new formal typology, based on the Chicago frame, the warehouse, and the supermarket: extreme, isotropic space, the space sandwiched between floors of structure and service which is equipotential and everywhere the same. The Modernist Domino block of Le Corbusier was exaggerated in length and breadth to give a new, Late-Modern space—sublime in its purity and flat extension, and sometimes very boring.

One of the first architects to develop a philosophy and formal solution for this large, multipurpose space was Cedric Price. As Price was working within the English tradition, it is not altogether surprising that his commitment was to the social, welfare side of large mixed-use buildings, or megastructures, as they came to be known. He looked to the state rather than to late-capitalist monopolies to provide architecture as a public, free service. His Thinkbelt and its architecture, the anonymous, well-serviced shed housing an educational aid program for depressed areas, should, he said in a striking phrase, make education as readily available as the National Health Service makes free teeth.[1] In the event, Price did not find state backing, but he nevertheless produced several designs which influenced the way students and bureaucrats thought about large buildings—namely, the Fun Palace (1964), the Potteries Thinkbelt (1966), and the Inter-Action Centre, which was actually built. These designs and buildings all develop an impersonal, industrial style known as the shed aesthetic, a kind of down-market version of high-tech. Industrial systems and products are used for their functional and economic potential; the emphasis is on utility and flexibility, not economic power. Thus Price developed an informal ad-hoc aesthetic, barely distinguishable from an engineer's approach, and hard for most people to see as architecture at all. Yet his style has its nuances which relate it to the Brutalist tradition of architecture and the poetic use of industrial objects in their "as found" state.

The Fun Palace expands the shed to enormous size and equips it with a romantic technology of movable gantry cranes and other instruments which can change the isotropic space from a pop-concert setting to a scientific observatory with supposed ease. The Inter-Action Centre also uses ready-made industrial products in a new way (144–145). External walls are clad in plastic-coated decking, fixed to roof trusses which are here used vertically. Portakabins, one of the cheap prefabricated room systems manufactured in England, are used for the center's wet services (lavatories, darkrooms, changing rooms, etc.) while Finnish kit-built log cabins are provided, appropriately, for children's activities. The informal, haphazard appearance of these elements slung under the open space-frame, together with the attached stairway and mechanical equipment, should indicate and encourage change. According to local authority plans, the center has to be demolished after the year 2000, and Price wants to represent this transience.

Of a more monumental and expressive nature is Farrell and Grimshaw's treatment of the shed aesthetic. Their warehouse for Herman Miller, Inc. remains within the British tradition of architecture as an anonymous service, which is characterized by painting the pipes, duct work, and structures different colors and threading them through each other in a complicated manner (156). Thus, as in other extreme isotropic spaces, the ceiling plane becomes the sole point of architectural expression. The floor of the shed has to be flat and unarticulated and the walls,

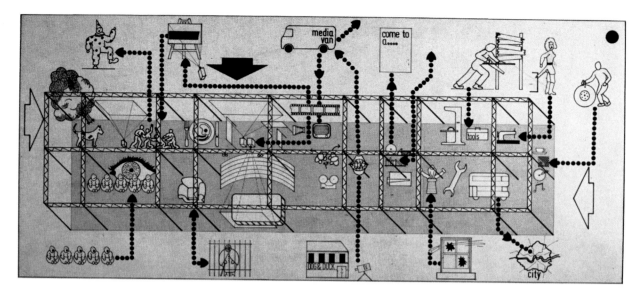

◄ 144 CEDRIC PRICE
*Community Centre for
Inter-Action Trust*, London,
England, 1972–77, axono-
metric

▼ 145 CEDRIC PRICE
*Community Centre for
Inter-Action Trust*, London,
England, 1972–77, aerial
view

usually, movable; only the ceiling is left free for architecture.[2]

During the late sixties two Italian groups, Superstudio and Archizoom, started to examine late-capitalist building types such as the supermarket for their spatial implications. Superstudio developed their ironic Continuous Monument (1969) from this and other types (such as the World Trade Centers which were springing up vertically in major capitals). The Continuous Monument was a sublime, isotropic grid of endless identical units which was to be continued around the world. The totalitarian, democratic sameness which unified all supermarkets would now be applied to all functions, but in such a beautiful way that no one would notice.[3] Or if they did, they would enjoy the "sweet tyranny." Archizoom, a Marxist group of designers, was equally ironic about extending capitalist and socialist trends of gigantic growth to extremes. Their No-Stop City was, as the name implies, an endless isotropic grid of open space sandwiched between an endless (or at least large) vertical grid of floors.[4] Imagine ten Macy's Department Stores stacked, or Chicago's Merchandise Mart extended indefinitely; imagine this space evenly lit and well-serviced with necessary elements such as partitions, lavatories, and stairs spread evenly, like randomized patterns on wallpaper, and you have the late-capitalist ideal of pragmatic organization: maximum efficiency and control combined with infinite flatness. Archizoom foresaw the subversive egalitarianism developing within consumer society and took it to a sublime, nightmarish extreme.

Inevitably, the image had a compelling force and logic, and it was applied by others in a less extreme manner. Derek Walker and a team of architects, the Milton Keynes Development Corporation (MKDC), applied it to the central shopping building at Milton Keynes, one of the largest such facilities in Europe (149). A series of glass, gridded rectangles hold eight large stores, three supermarkets, a variety of specialist shops, and, not surprisingly, a consumer advice center (which might aid navigation through this "No-Stop" consumer grid). The Miesian aesthetic was exaggerated to a new thinness and more extreme repetition. But the Platonic roof trusses and

cosmic orientation, which gave a certain intensity to the boxes, were not perceptible to the consumer. He could only appreciate by way of architecture the isotropic space and randomized repetition of mullions, service units, and planting. The Platonic wallpaper of Archizoom had become a reality.

An articulated version of the shed aesthetic which provides more drama is the Eindhoven agora, designed by Frank van Klingeren and other Dutch architects (146). Here, the isotropic tendency of the roof truss is countered by triangular skylights, and the grid is varied in plan. The structures can thus characterize the separate uses—social, cultural, and educational, as well as commercial—with different lighting, colors, and spatial size. Nevertheless, the industrial aesthetic classifies the overall ambience as one of utility, exchange, and efficiency.

The pathos of these agoras, several of which have now been built, shows how far Late-Modern architects are from understanding the historical and semantic properties of the building type they recall by name. Like the American "atrium" spaces of the Hyatt Hotels, the agoras are commercialized versions of the *res publica*—an agora without its politics,

power, or social vision. As Late-Modern spaces,
however, and considered in the abstract, they show a
counterpoint between the isotropic grid and the
multicentered foci.

Late-Modern space becomes more impressive when
it seeks to do away with all articulation and, instead,
to enlarge its horizontal extension. Its inherent
qualities, brought out by Archizoom, can lead to a
mild agoraphobia, or fear of large open spaces, which
is not displeasing when under control and tempered
by other meanings. Just as the skyscraper makes expressive use of vertigo, so Late-Modernism makes
positive use of negative visceral reactions. In Helmut
Jahn's Bartle Exhibition Hall in Kansas City, the
extreme horizontality is reinforced by the extreme
repetition of triangular trusses above and seats below
(**148**, **152**).[5] The building contains two hundred
thousand square feet of column-free exhibition space
and, on the perimeter, vertical circulation, mechanical equipment, and service rooms. This organizational scheme has become the archetype for Late-
Modern space (perimeter supports and services;
column-free isotropic center; mechanical distribution
housed in floor and ceiling sandwiches). The trian-

gular trusses are expressed on the outside in a way which recalls a Miesian design, but the dazzling, optical buzz of the trusses is more exaggerated than Mies van der Rohe would have allowed—another example of the way Late-Modernism takes a Modernist idea to a Mannerist extreme.

Helmut Jahn's Athletic Facility for St. Mary's College, South Bend, Indiana, is a lighter version of this kind of structure and space (**151**). Here, red trusses, blue pipes, and yellow ducts play above one's head in a very delicate filigree of layered ceiling

space, while the sides glow with light. The light quality here is generalized and well distributed, since direct light comes through the curved acrylic clerestory windows, glowing light comes through the translucent fiber-glass panels, and reflected light bounces off gray floor and ceiling. The ceiling plane is thus kept light and airy at the edges, the point where it usually becomes heavy, and the space has that bright, clean cheeriness which one associates with collegiate basketball. It is a fitting semantic use of the long spanning truss.

The Pompidou Center of Piano and Rogers has perhaps the most dramatic example of extreme isotropic space stacked vertically (**147**).[6] Again, services and structure are on the perimeter and the ceiling plane becomes the focus of architectural expression with a zigzag of polished, silver pipes held by white elbows. The spatial quality is more varied than we might at first think, given the repetition from floor to floor. This is caused by the depth of the truss, set off against the blue, and the shallowness of the mechanical ducts. One finds a

◀ **151** HELMUT JAHN OF C.F. MURPHY ASSOCIATES *St. Mary's College Athletic Facility*, South Bend, Indiana, 1977, interior

▼ **152** HELMUT JAHN OF C.F. MURPHY ASSOCIATES *Bartle Exhibition Hall*, Kansas City Convention Center, Missouri, 1976, plan

▶ **153** FOSTER ASSOCIATES, *Sainsbury Centre for the Visual Arts*, University of East Anglia, Norwich, Norfolk, England, 1975–78, exterior

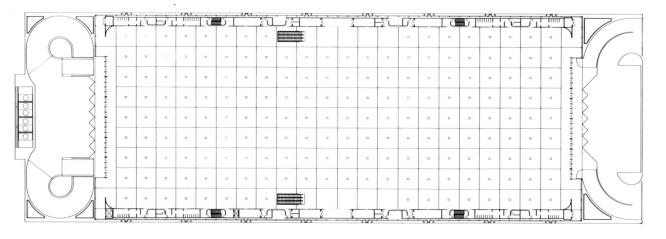

regular bay rhythm, an even tempo set at right angles to circulation, which is counterposed by the longitudinal bank of lights. Thus the usual isotropic space is mostly articulated by contrary rhythms. One can, of course, criticize the suitability of such space for a cultural center, the way the shopping center is equated with the museum, but the iconic way structure is treated as decoration raises the Pompidou Center above its utilitarian origins.

Once again, however, it is Norman Foster, who worked previously with Richard Rogers, who takes a Late-Modern idea to a beautiful conclusion.[7] The edge of his Willis Faber Dumas building has an open perimeter of glass where the heat and light intensity are different from those at the center. This perimeter is for circulation, while the more controlled and isotropic center is the work area. Ethereal open space flows in all directions, toward the blue-tinged wall and beyond, out into the view of the townscape (150). A feeling of freedom and openness is conveyed, particularly in the photograph which shows the space uncluttered by furniture or people. This might be a *parterre* at Louis XIV's Versailles, or a green carpet (with concealed electrical outlets) and a repetition of columns, mechanical ducts, and long, very long, lines of acoustic baffles. These last accentuate the perspective diminishment and the rush of space toward a vanishing point. The two flat, uninterrupted planes provide ample opportunity for surveillance and flexibility, requirements of the centralized monopoly now just as they were in the newly centralized France of Louis XIV. And the transformation of these pragmatic considerations into signs of the sublime is

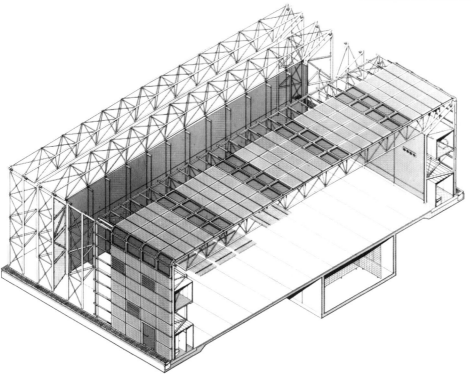

▲ 154   FOSTER ASSOCIATES, *Sainsbury Centre for the Visual Arts*, University of East Anglia, Norwich, Norfolk, England, 1975–78, interior

◄ 155   FOSTER ASSOCIATES, *Sainsbury Centre for the Visual Arts*, University of East Anglia, Norwich, Norfolk, England, 1975–78, axonometric

▶ 156   FARRELL AND GRIMSHAW, *Herman Miller Warehouse*, Bath, Somerset, England, 1977–78, ceiling and walkway

achieved by Foster, as it was by Le Nôtre in the gardens of Versailles, by taking repetitive devices of order beyond their usual extent and rendering them with a pristine absoluteness.

Foster's Sainsbury Centre for the Visual Arts (153–155) also contains a collage of activities between two absolute planes, but now the isotropic space is oriented along a spine to the view of the surrounding countryside.[8] A grand entrance canopy, reminiscent both of an airplane hangar and of Le Corbusier's High Court at Chandigarh (1952–56), transforms the trussed space into a gigantic portico, an expanded temple front. Amplification and simplicity, two rhetorical devices, are then combined with anamnesis (the recollection of things past) to produce a very dignified and haunting image, made more strange by the slick-tech aesthetic. On the inside, unusual distortions of familiar forms intensify these feelings of strangeness. Are we in a super-

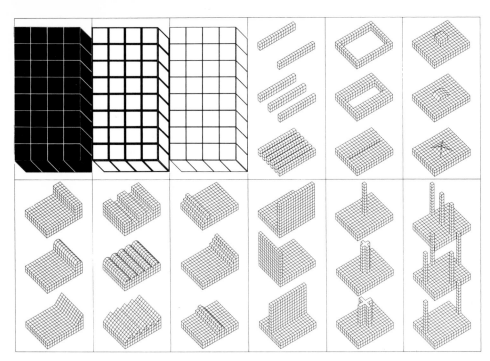

"universal" space we have discussed. Its inherent geometric properties of reversibility and rotational equality are tied to theoretical properties of simplicity, representation, and synecdoche. If isotropic space is everywhere the same, then gridism, the surface equivalent of this space, implies that all surfaces are the same. Of course, the consistent ideal of gridism is rarely achieved in a real building.[9]

The French artist and sculptor Jean-Pierre Reynaud has approached this ideal in a house he built for himself, and his art, in Paris (158). Nearly all the interior surfaces are covered in white tile squares (approximately six inches square) which are outlined by black cement. The floors are covered in black or white rubber. There is no furniture as such, just geometric shapes constructed from the white-and-black grid. The only exceptions to the grid are the floor, doors, and lighting fixtures. The connection

◀ **157** SUPERSTUDIO
*Istogrammi d'Architettura
Project*, 1969

▼ **158** JEAN-PIERRE
REYNAUD, *Maison Reynaud*, Paris, France, 1970–72, interior

market, an airplane hangar, a factory, a greenhouse, or an office building? The museum space and study areas seem at first dwarfed and overwhelmed by these alien associations. The equation of art with mass production and consumption, a metaphor of the Pompidou Center, again seems too inappropriate and pragmatic. Yet these opposed meanings are allowed to merge because of the subtle handling of the light and the beautiful detailing of the structure. Motorized louvers buzz overhead to set up optical as well as acoustic vibrations. A delicate, dappled, even light spills over the space, equating all parts. Wall, ceiling, and floor planes are equated by a similar silver finish, and so extreme isotropic space, the sign of equality and the sublime, is supported by isotropic surface, the sign of mass production. All activities are banished to the perimeter or dwarfed behind partitions as the universal space of Mies van der Rohe reigns triumphant over time, function, and locale.

Architects have always sought the supremacy of pattern over activity and signs of time. Greek and Roman trabeated architecture suppressed transient functions and equated different ones. This tendency of architecture toward the repetitive and permanent was summarized in Superstudio's Continuous Monument, and architecture's dependence on the trabeated grid was epitomized in their Istogrammi d'Architettura (**157**). Here, we have a representation of an ideal Cartesian cage of space and its transformation and deformation into Platonic solids to incorporate different functions (e.g., the sawtooth profile of factories).

The applied grid of mullions is thus equated with the "ideal" white grid of structure, which The Five and the Rationalists used, and with the isotropic,

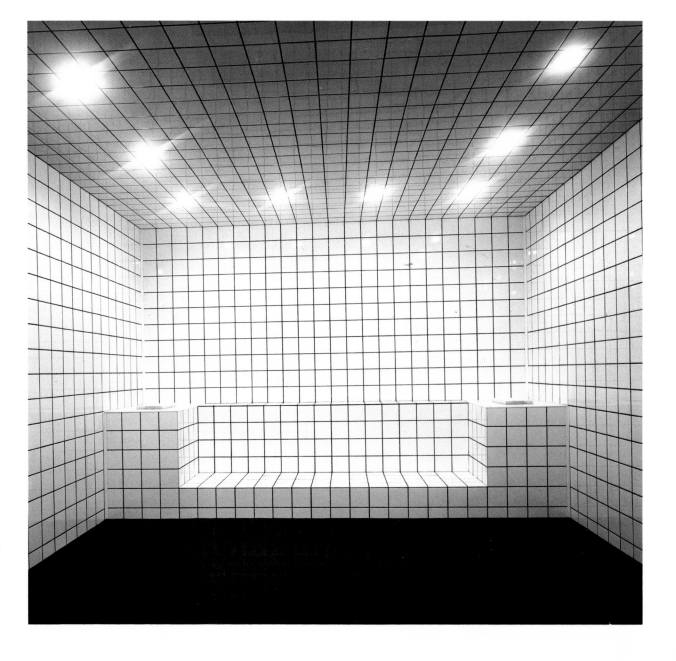

between this brilliantly white environment and a hospital, abattoir, or morgue is not fortuitous, and Reynaud speaks of his art as being an "homage to both nature and man in the persons of the marble-workers and the constructors of gravestones." The white grid has washed away all memory and time; objects seem caught and bracketed off in its matrix, like pure geometric or algebraic propositions. Walls and ceilings can be mentally rotated or mirror reversed. Since the scale is small and all exterior cues and light are cut off, an ambiguity of size results. Is it a very big or small space?

This abstractive function of the grid underlies much Late-Modern work—slick-tech and twenties revivalism as well as the neo-Rationalism of the Europeans. Several Japanese architects such as Kisho Kurokawa, Toyo Ito, Monta Mozuna, and Hiromi Fujii have developed the grid's potential for produc-

▶ **159** HIROMI FUJII
Miyajima House, Tokyo, Japan, 1973, interior

▼ **160** TOYO ITO
PMT Building, Nagoya, Japan, 1978

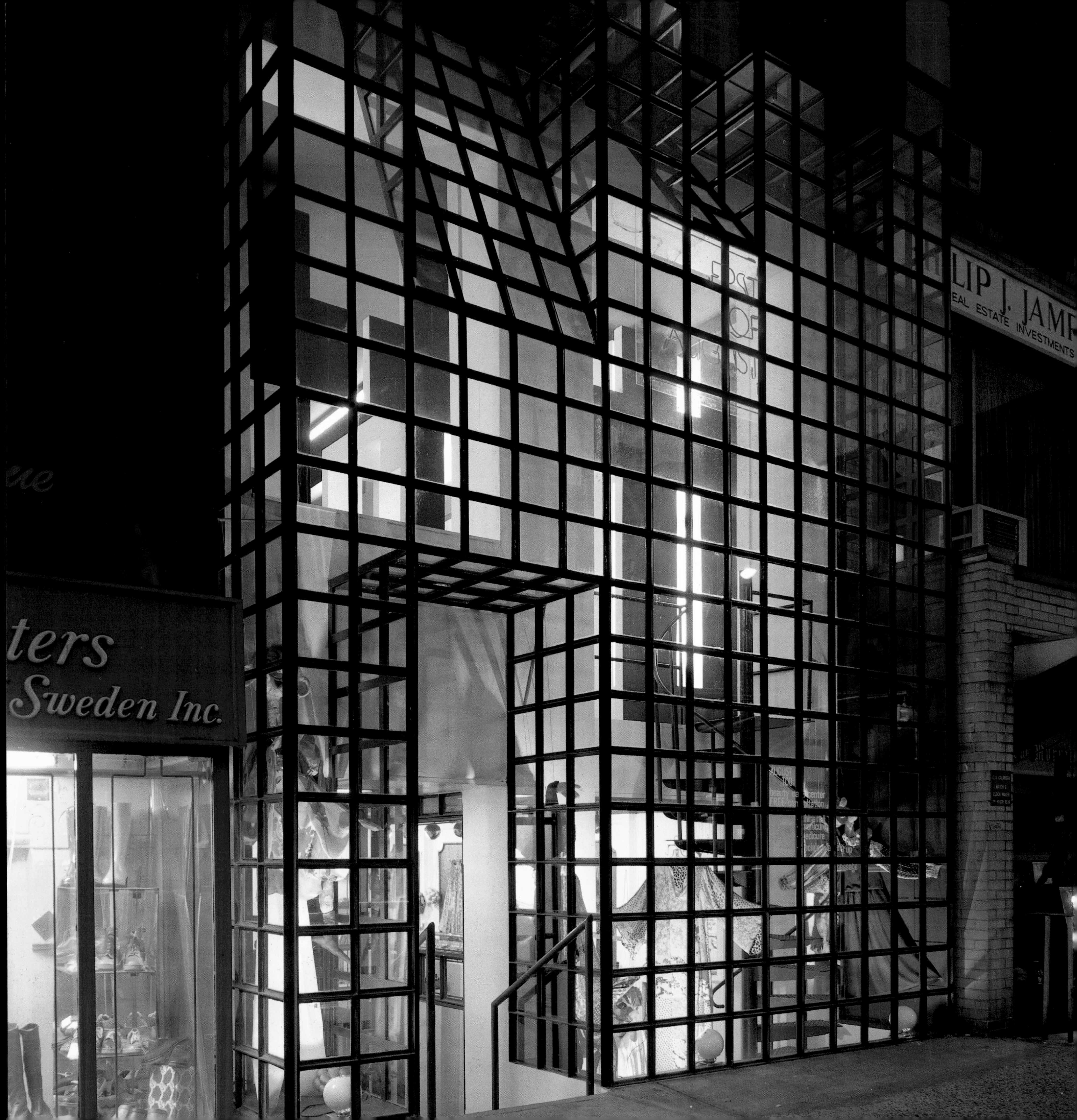
ters
Sweden Inc.
LIP J. JAM
EAL ESTATE INVESTMENTS

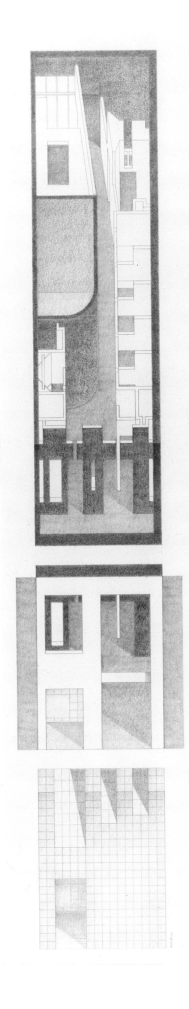

ing paradoxes of size and orientation. For instance, Hiromi Fujii telescopes grids inside each other in his Todoroki House ("Box within a Box") so that plan, elevation, and section become ambiguously merged.[10]

As in his Miyajima House, window details and wall are equated with furniture and the floor in a neutral gray. The result again destroys orientation and any familiar cues of time and place (**159**). What was a Modernist principle of rationality and order, the applied grids of Viennese architects Otto Wagner and Adolf Loos, has now become both a comment on that principle and a subversion of it. Anonymity, neutrality, and background order are here the content of the architecture, not a utilitarian device. Toyo Ito's PMT Building also shows this irrational rationality, the bent grid which is no longer structural or inherent but applied as a scenographic facade (**160**). Taking a Modernist cue and upholding its formal brilliance, while at the same time tying to it an advertising logo ("Heidelberg") and warping it, produces a strange extension of Modernist ideology. Ito wishes to show the superficiality behind consumer culture, while still proving that this can produce challenging results. Perhaps only Modernists who have been brought up with the code "grid = rationalism" can fully appreciate the irony of his inversions. More accessible to everyone is the gentle sfumato produced as the glistening grids warp and the light quality blends indistinctly from darkness to brilliance across the building.

A more clearly decorative use of the grid is found in George Ranalli's store in New York City which merges the grid with other forms (**161–162**).[11] Ranalli changes material and color so that the rotational aspects inherent in gridism are lost. Instead of using it throughout as a homogeneous surface, he applies it to a window-wall. At several points breaks occur in the rectangular figure to create ambiguities of depth as transparent grids are superimposed on each other. The most pleasing ambiguities occur at dusk when the light is on inside the store and the fractured grid glows out from its background. This reverses the intended meaning of the neutral form, which was supposed to fit into the close scale and grain of a New York street. The dull ordinariness of the grid suddenly jumps out of its lowly station in architectural life.

Anthony Lumsden achieves an even more extraordinary displacement of banal associations with the undulating grids he uses in his buildings and in his project for the Beverly Hills Hotel (**163**). This unbuilt design was conceived in the "silver aesthetic" as a blown-up machine, perhaps an electric typewriter.[12] The "roller" is here repeated seven times,

each one flowing into the next as they stagger upward and to the side. Elision, amplification, and a stepped figure which ends in a climax: these syntactic figures are tied to the metaphor of a great, domestic machine. The rolling ends are given a neoclassical mullion pattern, like a doubled fanlight. With its allover warped grid of reflective silver, the hotel would have been a summation of Beverly Hills cultural life, although perhaps the rolled shapes were too reminiscent of packaged coins for the clients' comfort.

Richard Meier has used the allover silver grid in a school for physically disabled and mentally retarded children. The Bronx Developmental Center (**164–165**) is a gleaming institutional jewel made from anodized, natural-colored aluminum panels which wrap everything except the roof.[13] This obsession with a single material is matched by the grid fetish, and as if to compensate for these two endlessly repeated motifs, Meier has articulated them with countless variations. The floor plan is flat on the more public side, and staggers in individual L-shaped units on the residential side. Bedrooms are articulated by smaller windows, ventilation louvers by tablet-like horizontal slits, and living rooms by larger windows placed in quarter-circle cantilevered rec-

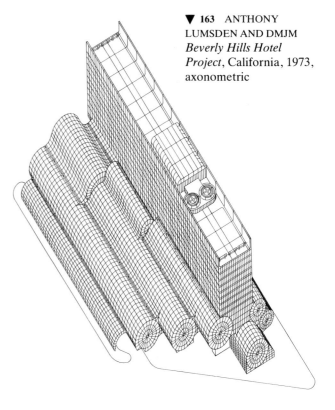

▼ **163** ANTHONY LUMSDEN AND DMJM *Beverly Hills Hotel Project*, California, 1973, axonometric

◀ **161** GEORGE RANALLI *First of August Store*, New York City, 1976–77, facade at night

◀ **162** GEORGE RANALLI *First of August Store*, New York City, 1976–77, combined elevation, section, and axonometric

▲ 164 RICHARD MEIER
*Bronx Developmental
Center*, New York City,
1970–76, exterior of residential buildings

▶ 165 RICHARD MEIER
*Bronx Developmental
Center*, New York City,
1970–76, axonometric

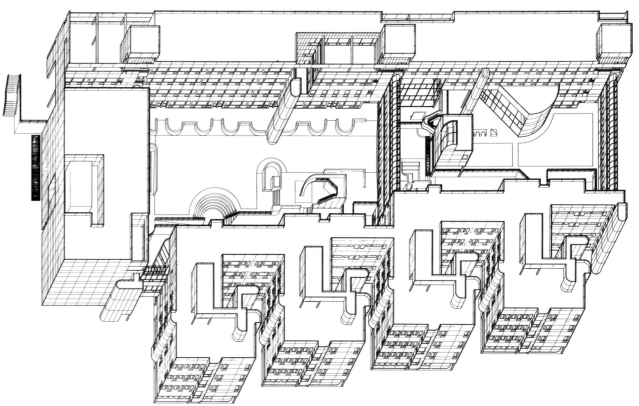

tangles. Further articulation is achieved by dividing the basic 11 1/2-by-12-foot panel into three horizontal sections and, when needed, stamping out holes. Refinements in the gridded aluminum indicate the 7 1/2-inch dimension of the panel (at certain end joints), the 1 1/4-foot aluminum-sheeted column (sometimes held flush with the surface), panels on reentrant planes, and vertical circulation (2 feet by 10 1/2 inches). Thus for an architectural aficionado keyed up to read subtle cues of aluminum articulation, this building speaks a sensible language; for the mentally retarded, not to mention the average New Yorker, its meaning must surely be quite different. They would probably be struck more by the incessant repetition of form and material than by the subtle distinctions of plane. The associations of aluminum with hygienic institutions and cars, buses, or trains are the most apparent within the popular code, and thus the overall meaning of a mechanistic, controlling institution must predominate. The residences are less of a home than the architect would wish, and more like the elegant head office of a multinational corporation. This malapropism is, however, tempered by the extreme beauty and care with which each part is detailed and built at the factory. The overall image then fluctuates back and forth as the oxymoronic sign it is: impersonal personality, indifferent caring, institutional home, or, in terms of the chapter, non-gridded gridism.

Meier is not particularly interested in the way non-architects might read his buildings. He hopes, in any case, to reach this constituency with the craftsmanship of his details and the logic of abstract form rather than with the semantic appropriateness of his imagery. The same might be said of Arata Isozaki, an admirer and friend of Meier, except that this Japanese architect is particularly concerned with communicating philosophical ideas.[14] This fact distinguishes his gridism and isotropic space from Late-Modernists' and places him somewhere on the road to Post-Modernism.

Isozaki's Nagazumi Branch of the Fukuoka Mutual Bank (166) is, on the inside, a very simple, poetic statement of the applied grid. White and gray surfaces, subtly related and almost neutral, set up a very quiet atmosphere. This background architecture, again a Modernist idea related to the abstract grid, is then given slight nuances which jump out at those who are attentive to them. The variance of a line from the grid, the placement of a door or railing off the system: these minor distortions are experienced, as in a Zen work, as major emphases. Isozaki in fact uses Minimalism very dramatically to communicate both variations from the pattern and a metaphysical neutrality and nullity.

His Gunma Museum (167–169) uses the square throughout at different scales and in different materials, although the color is kept to the gray tonality of aluminum and concrete. Isozaki calls this method of repeating the square at different scales "amplification" (after one rhetorical term), as it is the expansion and transformation of a single idea. The square aluminum panel can be seen reversed in the square window and then transformed in the tiled floor and gridded ceiling. The "deep structure" of squares sets up a basic rectilinear framework from which the most important part of the museum, a private collection, is rotated. The most enigmatic part of the building is the entrance lobby, where the square marches off in three or four directions and then, in the distance, in marble, gets larger as it recedes. This anti-perspective device, related to artist M.C. Escher's drawings of impossible buildings, is another oxymoronic sign of irrational rationalism, the crazy grid.

The junctures between different planes of the museum pick up this figure in details. One wall is run into another without transition, moldings, or a change of detail; the aluminum squares can change direction and function, as the overall volume can, without any change in articulation. This elision and synecdoche are typical Late-Modern devices, as we have seen in examples of the slick-tech aesthetic, and they serve to speed up perception of the building. One's eyes run over the surface of the whole building very quickly; parts are ambiguously merged and the same square detail works, miraculously, for everything. If there are any great doubts about this *tour de force*, they concern, once again, the semantic dimension. The slick-tech surface is not appropriate to all kinds of art; the pervasive machine metaphor is not very suitable for a museum; the omnipresence of the aluminum surface at such a scale is rather trying. As in Meier's Bronx Developmental Center, one formal idea is made into a fetish so that other, more traditional forms cannot be accepted. At Gunma, for instance, the requisite Japanese tea-ceremony room is built, as it must be, in a traditional wood style, but is suppressed, as an embarrassment to the slick-tech seventies, in the basement.

Admitting, then, that this building has Late-Modern shortcomings—it does not relate to function or traditional patterns—there are nevertheless qualities which it is eminently suited to convey. As mentioned, Isozaki sees an ultimate significance behind his gridded cages and the particular silver-gray color. He interprets these qualities metaphysically in terms of twilight and illusion. "Shadows give things differentiation and a sense of actuality. Shadowless twilight is a metaphor for the suppression of visual differen-

▼ 166 ARATA ISOZAKI
Nagazumi Branch of the Fukuoka Mutual Bank, Fukuoka, Japan, 1971, interior

tiation. Minimizing differences reduces disturbances caused by information from the outside to the lowest level and makes possible the creation in architecture of something like artificial twilight. Covering the exterior of buildings with endless series of uniform units (a process I call amplification) minimizes differences and produces a twilight effect of non-differentiation . . . Pale colours in limited distribution cause shadow and shade to unite with the base tone and thus obscure the distinction between actuality and illusion."[15] We can see these ambiguous properties in the gray-gridded Gunma Museum best when it is twilight and its form has merged imperceptibly into the broken silhouette of the industrial landscape.

As another, more metaphysical reason for resorting to the neutral cage, Isozaki cites our present lack of

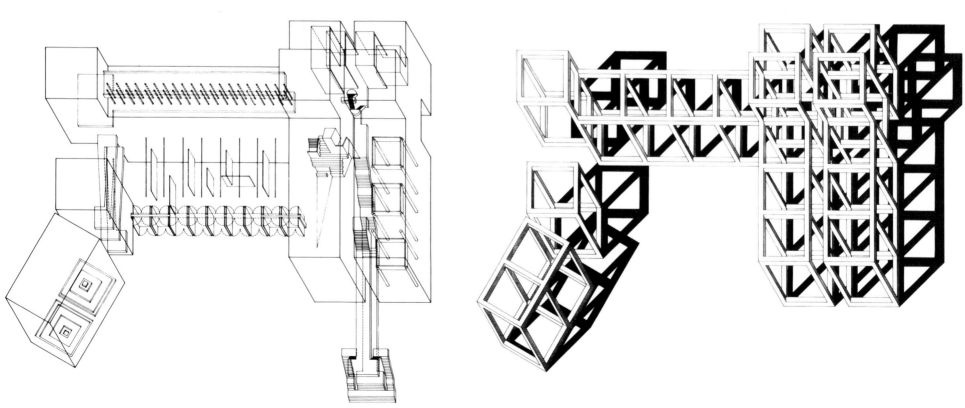

◀ 167   ARATA ISOZAKI
*Gunma Prefectural Museum
of Fine Arts*, Takasaki,
Japan, 1971–74

◀ 168   ARATA ISOZAKI
*Gunma Prefectural Museum
of Fine Arts*, Takasaki,
Japan, 1971–74, deep
structure and supplemental
structure

an accepted ideology or religion. "We have no means of becoming clearly cognizant of the universe; we have lost our context; and everything seems isolated, unique, and unrepeatable. Not only has God disappeared, but we have become incapable of aiming at an interpretation of the universe that all of us can share . . . illusive images surround us with a mosaic that lacks classical balance, consistent clarity of arrangement, harmony and order. We have no way of recognizing relative, wildly dispersed world images. It may be that there is no longer any one theme deserving expression. I represent this set of circumstances by means of a metaphor of degree zero, or a void at the centre."[16] This particularly clear statement of metaphysical agnosticism, or nullity, explains not only so much of Isozaki's silent grids, but also some

of the Post-Modern architecture of the Metaphysical School (discussed below). It suggests another, semantic meaning of the isotropic space and gridism we have looked at, albeit a meaning accessible only to the happy few. Late-Modern space expresses a dignified quietism for several architects, an honest neutrality and agnosticism toward a society which cannot make up its mind what to value. Clearly this agnosticism is not adequate as a general position, as Isozaki himself has acknowledged in later works, but it has a limited honesty and integrity.

▲ 169   ARATA ISOZAKI
*Gunma Prefectural Museum
of Fine Arts*, Takasaki,
Japan, 1971–74, interior
entrance space

HANS HOLLEIN, *Austrian Travel Bureau*, Vienna, Austria, 1978, interior

Post-Modernism

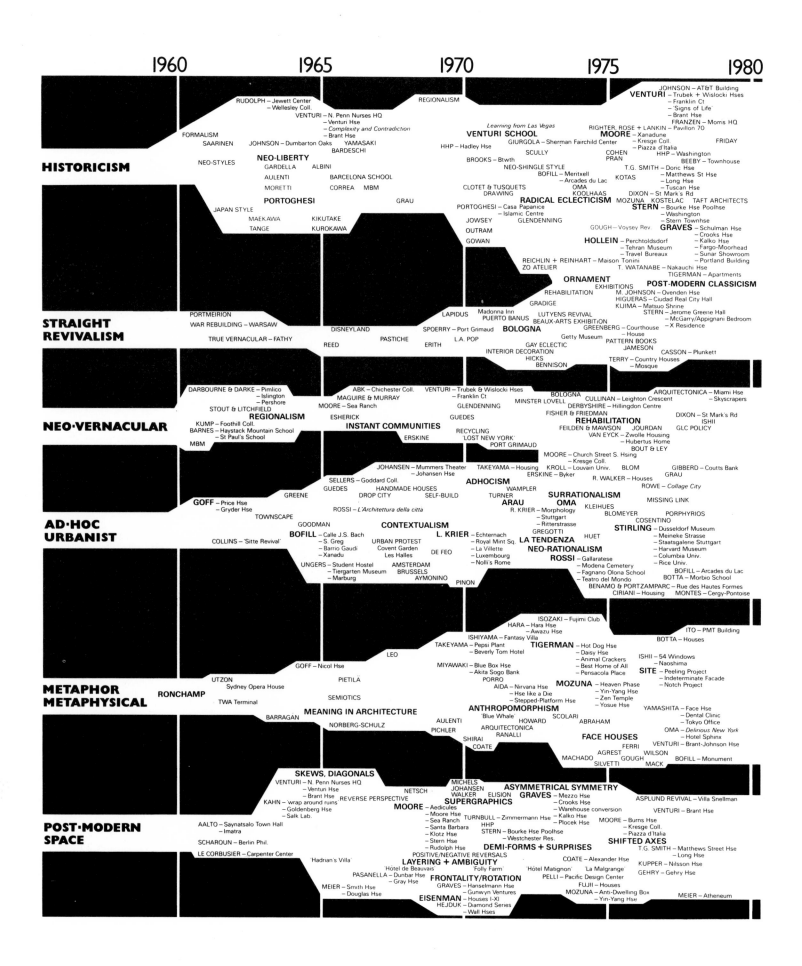

INTRODUCTION

POST-MODERN IS A PORTMANTEAU CONCEPT COVERING several approaches to architecture which have evolved from Modernism. As this hybrid term suggests, its architects are still influenced by Modernism—in part because of their training and in part because of the impossibility of ignoring Modern methods of construction—and yet they have added other languages to it. A Post-Modern building is doubly coded—part Modern and part something else: vernacular, revivalist, local, commercial, metaphorical, or contextual. In several important instances it is also doubly coded in the sense that it seeks to speak on two levels at once: to a concerned minority of architects, an elite who recognize the subtle distinctions of a fast-changing language, and to the inhabitants, users, or passersby, who want only to understand and enjoy it. Thus one of the strong motivations of Post-Modernists is to break down the elitism inherent in Modern architecture and the architectural profession. Sometimes Post-Modernism is confused with Late-Modernism because, as we have seen, that movement is also a Mannerist play on a former language. Some architects practice both approaches, and there are also, inevitably, buildings which are transitional. But, as pointed out in the Introduction and chart (pages 12–17) there are many philosophical and stylistic points which separate the two movements. Once these have been grasped, the major distinctions between Late- and Post-Modernism can be clearly perceived.

The term Post-Modern has a complex genesis which I have tried to untangle in *The Language of Post-Modern Architecture* (1977, revised 1978 and 1981). It was used in a non-architectural context as early as 1938 by the English historian Arnold Toynbee, and applied to architecture by Joseph Hudnut in 1949, but its first use in the currently accepted sense was in my own articles of 1975. A year later, and quite independently, the architect Robert Stern (apparently influenced by Peter Eisenman) and the critic Paul Goldberger were using the term in the United States. By 1977 the usage had become popular (for example,

Douglas Davis was asked by his editor to put it in the title of his book *Artculture: Essays in the Post-Modern*, although, characteristically, the term is not defined, nor even used). The same may be said of C. Ray Smith's book *Supermannerism: New Attitudes in Post-Modern Architecture* (1977) in which the term appeared in the subtitle only because it had become fashionable. Because of this loose usage I attempted in 1978 a definition to distinguish Post-Modern from Late-Modern architecture and to focus on the positive notion of double coding instead of historicist imagery alone (which was the major American definition). The two usages, European and American, were somewhat different although both schools of thought focused on the important work and theories of Robert Venturi and Charles Moore. They differed, and still do, over the emphasis placed on urbanism, participation, ornament, and image: Americans stress the latter two aspects, Europeans the former two. But as the term is an umbrella covering a variety of schools, this division should not be overstressed. There was a wide enough general agreement for a large exhibition on the subject, the 1980 Venice Biennale organized by Paolo Portoghesi. There, seventy architects from around the world, who have sharp differences among themselves, were loosely grouped under the banner Post-Modern. Both the heterogeneity and commonality of current Post-Modern work should be kept in mind in the six chapters that follow.

▲ 170 KIYONORI KIKUTAKE, *Tokoen Hotel*, Yonago, Japan, 1964

FROM HISTORICISM TO RADICAL ECLECTICISM

DURING THE LATE FIFTIES, WHEN THE INTERNATIONAL Style was enjoying its commercial success, many designers and theorists became concerned about its urban implications and its lack of cultural signification. Modern offices and dwellings quite obviously failed to relate positively to their context, or to the codes of architecture that their users understood. The attacks on these failures are too well known to need recounting, but one should emphasize that they were made in many countries, especially America and Italy, and by many non-architects, including the writer Norman Mailer and the sociologist Herbert Gans.[1] Architects trained within the Modern Movement, sensitive to their failures, were somewhat at a loss: their anti-historical training and bias toward "The Tradition of the New" made it difficult for them to use historical allusion positively to fit their buildings into the context or relate them to the needs of the users.[2] Their attitude toward history was at once embarrassed and sardonic: historical quotations were borrowed rather arbitrarily from any period of architecture and applied to the new creation as fragments. Architects lacked a theory of eclecticism, and it showed.

The most explicit historicist *appliqué* came from America, which produced a volume of kitsch buildings about which it is best to be silent (unless one is celebrating the genre). Minoru Yamasaki, Ed Stone, Eero Saarinen, Philip Johnson, and Paul Rudolph all produced historicist essays with uncertain historical justification.[3] Perhaps the best of these works was Johnson's extension to the Museum for Pre-Columbian Art, Dumbarton Oaks, Washington, D.C. (1963), a series of domelets which could be justified because of their association with the museum collection. And certainly Johnson's amusing quips on his not being able to "not know history"—the double negative showing the tentative and defensive attitude of the time—helped free architects from their anti-historical bias.[4] The most convincing historicist work of this period was produced in Japan and Italy, where strong building traditions still existed. The

"New Japan Style," a phrase used by Robin Boyd,[5] can be seen in the sixties work of Kunio Maekawa, Kenzo Tange, Kisho Kurokawa, and Kiyonori Kikutake which incorporates rationalist and traditionalist elements within a basically Corbusian syntax. For instance, Kikutake's Tokoen Hotel (170) recalls the traditional post-and-beam construction and gentle roof curves of the Japanese temple—tatami mats within the hotel rooms and a Japanese garden outside. The old wooden forms are translated into a new material, reinforced concrete, and detailed with a precision and care which goes beyond the diagrammatic historicism present elsewhere.

In Italy the revival periods were more heterogeneous and covert. The 1900 Liberty Style was revived by Ignazio Gardella, Gae Aulenti, and others, while Luigi Moretti, Franco Albini, Carlo Scarpa, and GRAU (Roman Group of Urban Architects) produced a neo-Roman and neo-Vernacular revival. The deepest commitment to historical precedent, however, was that of Paolo Portoghesi, an architect and historian who wrote key analyses of Bernardo Vittone (1702–1770), Francesco Borromini (1599–1667), and Victor Horta (1861–1947) and during the fifties and sixties investigated Baroque and Art Nouveau architecture from the position of semiotics and rhetoric. In one major book after another, he showed how architectural language flourished as a communicative tool in some periods and waned in others. His most creative book, *The Rome of Borromini: Architecture as a Language* (1967), showed that Borromini used a highly rhetorical set of figures and complex language because he was strongly motivated to com-

▲ 171 PAOLO PORTOGHESI AND VITTORIO GIGLIOTTI *Casa Papanice*, Rome, Italy, 1969–70

er because of the thinner structure which allows space and light to break through the corner supports themselves, and to explode the column into a ring (abacus) and four separate colonnettes (capitals and shafts). Portoghesi proffers a metaphorical interpretation of the structure which aligns him with other Post-Modernists (the shafts are "like hands during the act of prayer"), but it is perhaps the sheer exuberance of these structural members, a Modernist conceit, which is most apparent.[11] They are like a Pier Luigi Nervi structure except more purely expressive. From the ring-abacus three ribs shoot out at each point to make that point part of three different geometrical systems (two orthogonal and one diagonal). This gives an ambiguity and complex struc-

◀ 172   PAOLO PORTOGHESI AND VITTORIO GIGLIOTTI *Mosque and Islamic Center*, Rome, Italy, 1976–77, interior perspective

▶ 173   FRANCESCO BORROMINI, *Re Magi*, Rome, Italy, 1662–64, ceiling detail

municate specific religious and structural ideas to a wide audience and to sustain interest in, and continual reinterpretation of, these ideas.[6] The multivalence of Borromini's work was thus explicitly elucidated by Portoghesi and it acted as a challenge to his own.[7]

Portoghesi's early work of the late fifties showed, not surprisingly, a mixture of Borromini's spatial ideas and the more open aesthetic of Modernism. By 1970, however, in the Casa Papanice (171) he had formalized these ideas to generate sets of overlapping spatial foci: "pools" of space marked by concentric circles over the traditional "hearts" of the house (the dining table and fireplace), and "directed space" marked by curved walls focusing on a tree or view.[8] The continual horizontal flow of space on the inside was reminiscent of Borromini's use of the heavy, unifying cornice, while the vertical stripes, discs, and semi-curves were reminiscent of twenties architecture. This double coding also included the incorporation of kitsch motifs, as did the work of other Post-Modernists such as Venturi and Moore, and for the same reasons: that other, non-architectural taste cultures had a legitimate right to be recognized in architecture.

Portoghesi's later work continues the "search for a lost language of architecture."[9] His Mosque and

Islamic Center in Rome (172) carries forward his structural and spatial ideas which are here clearly doubly coded, the most obvious historical references being the minaret, courtyard, and domes of the mosque. These last have the characteristic profile of Islamic domes: the gentle curve ending in a point, the four-centered arch with its slight ogee, or reverse curve. The doubling of the ribs and their intersections are also meant to recall the Re Magi of Borromini (173). As Portoghesi says, his own works can be seen as cinematic "lap dissolves" in which the old forms overlap and dissolve into the new.[10] Thus Islam and Rome are alluded to, but with modern technical means: thin, linear, structural members of reinforced concrete.

It is natural for one's eyes to fix on the structural invention of the mosque because this is so emphatically the keynote of the design. As in other Portoghesi buildings, concentric curves provide the focus. Here they overlap, as in the vaults of Guarino Guarini's SS. Sindone in Turin (1667–90), to allow a diffused and checkered light to shine through. But these curves are also combined with doubled ribs on the diagonal to create a more open, non-centric space. Indeed, although the spatial flow and airiness are reminiscent of Guarini's buildings, the effect is light-

tural pattern—two rhetorical figures that had been used as early as A.D. 785 in the Great Mosque at Córdoba and later by Guarini to create a similar sense of religious awe. It is a mark of the quality of Portoghesi's historicism that his work can be compared to such precedents without embarrassment.

No other practicing architect has such a complete and creative grasp of history, nor is such a good historian in his own right. Robert Venturi, whose *Complexity and Contradiction in Architecture* (1966) established historical precedent as a major source for Post-Modernism, is no doubt equally creative in his investigations, but is less of a scholar.[12] He *uses* historical lessons (ambiguity, contradiction, tension, etc.) rather than explores the past in a disinterested way.

While working on *Complexity and Contradiction in Architecture*, Venturi was also applying several historical conceits to the small buildings he was designing. They have, as a result, that double coding which shows his training: part Le Corbusier and part Edwin Lutyens, part Louis Kahn and part the Mannerists. Indeed, his house for his mother in Chestnut Hill is a Mannerist work of Modernism: it takes the flat plane and simple volumes of Modernism and decorates and distorts them (174). Technical elements

▼ 174   ROBERT VENTURI
Vanna Venturi House,
Chestnut Hill, Pennsyl-
vania, 1962, rear view

▶ 175   VENTURI AND
RAUCH, *Brant House*,
Greenwich, Connecticut,
1971–73, garden facade

◀ 176   VENTURI AND
RAUCH, *Trubek and Wis-
locki Houses*, Nantucket
Island, Massachusetts, 1970

▶ 177   VENTURI AND
RAUCH, *Brant House*,
Tuckers Town, Bermuda,
1975–78

are used in a pragmatic, straightforward way, but to these are added applied moldings which increase the scale and occur at odd points (they bisect windows). The shifted axis on the front, a device Venturi borrows from Lutyens, has since become a conventional motif of Post-Modern space (see pages 200–201). On the back, traditional elements are also used, but in a distorted way: a very large Roman lunette window increases the scale, as does the stringcourse, while the pitched roof and sides provide a traditional sign of homestead at a gargantuan scale. The combined pitch implies a building twice the size, and the ellipsis between them implies a fracture. To these rhetorical figures is added the asymmetrical symmetry common to the Queen Anne Revival and the Shingle Style, about which Vincent Scully had been writing in the fifties.[13] This modest house, along with Venturi's book, had an enormous effect on all subsequent Post-Modernism. Both incorporated historicist lessons in a carefully articulated way.

Subsequent buildings, writings, and exhibitions of Venturi and his team (his wife Denise Scott Brown and the designers Steven Izenour and John Rauch) confirmed a serious commitment to both the present and the past. This is not the place to evaluate their contribution, but certain points essential to the argument of Post-Modernism can be summarized. In the book *Learning from Las Vegas* (1972) and the

exhibition "Signs of Life: Symbols in the American City" (1976) the Venturi team analyzed the popular, commercial vernacular of architecture as a language or sign system. This work paralleled semiotic research in Italy and that carried out in England under George Baird, Geoffrey Broadbent, myself, and others.[14] One important lesson in all this investigation was the simple, but previously disregarded, idea that architecture is a language perceived through a code. The attendant notion that different people have different codes was followed up by the Venturis, more in their writings than in their buildings. They emphasized that other taste cultures, besides the professional and avant-garde elite, had the right to see their tastes and meanings of architecture confirmed. Unfortunately, the way their meanings were perceived was mostly ironic: as kitsch, schlock, gigantic billboards, "ducks" (buildings in the shape of a recognizable object), or cliché. Furthermore, the Venturi team was not able to build for the mass audience their polemic implied. Instead, and predictably, they built for those who shared their values and background—the educated elite.

The Brant House in Greenwich (**175**) was built for a family which has a collection of Art Deco objects—hence the green-glazed brick, shiny and stepped back in an Art Deco stagger, the flat streamlines, and chrome-like cornice. Other intended references, to a

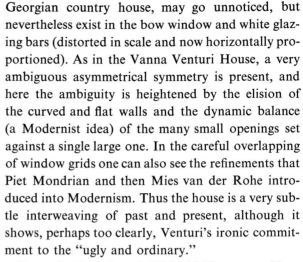

Georgian country house, may go unnoticed, but nevertheless exist in the bow window and white glazing bars (distorted in scale and now horizontally proportioned). As in the Vanna Venturi House, a very ambiguous asymmetrical symmetry is present, and here the ambiguity is heightened by the elision of the curved and flat walls and the dynamic balance (a Modernist idea) of the many small openings set against a single large one. In the careful overlapping of window grids one can also see the refinements that Piet Mondrian and then Mies van der Rohe introduced into Modernism. Thus the house is a very subtle interweaving of past and present, although it shows, perhaps too clearly, Venturi's ironic commitment to the "ugly and ordinary."

Venturi's Trubek and Wislocki Houses on Nantucket Island use the local Cape Cod vernacular in a more straightforward and convincing way (**176**). Here all the arguments for the neo-Vernacular, discussed in chapter 7, might be invoked to justify the choice of language. The historicism is much more clearly presented than in Venturi's previous houses; its roots are closer to the prototype, and indeed closer to the surrounding buildings. The two wood shingle houses sit on the seaside landscape in clear relationship to each other, calling up familiar echoes of the lonely summer house or the more ancient fisherman's cottage. Certain distortions are introduced—an eroded corner, a Palladian window with asymmetrical parts —which tie the two houses together and distinguish them from the vernacular, but these distinctions are not overwrought and polemically "ugly."

The later Brant House, in Tuckers Town, Bermuda, extends this mixture of straightforward vernacular and ironic distortion (**177**). Regular bay rhythms are set up, arches and columns which relate to the surrounding colonial architecture. These are then counterposed by a different rhythm of windows. Since the columns and arches themselves do not line up, one has a syncopation to be read twice, horizontally. Above this the roof pitches sometimes follow the expected order, and fall to the edge, and sometimes go against it, rising from the sheer edge. Chimneys also do what they normally do, *and* violate their accustomed position. Perhaps the greatest joke, which these other careful dislocations announce, is the lantern which falls, not rises, between two roofs. The meshing of curves, moldings, and traditional details is also masterful and relaxed. In plan, a collage of Baroque demi-forms gives an informality to the grandiose language; in detail the bisection of an *oeil-de-boeuf* window by a cornice gives a certain freshness. Venturi thus achieves a more convincing synthesis of taste cultures, and past and present, than in his previous work. The "ugly and ordinary" are

by color and decoration from a white, arcaded background (**179**). We will examine in chapter 10 the series of planned surprises which are designed into the scheme.

Charles Moore often works very closely with his clients, interpreting their desires and sometimes combining them with his own. He is more responsive to a *variety* of taste cultures than most other architects and, because he uses various methods of participatory design, he can get closer to the clients' actual tastes than architects who merely theorize about pluralism.[16] He has designed several schemes using modeling techniques which allow the participants to work through their images and ideas—the final result naturally being a combination of Moore's design skill and their notions. (Participation without this skilled interpretation would be fruitless in architectural terms, and it is a measure of Moore's open-

◀ **178** CHARLES W. MOORE ASSOCIATES *Xanadune*, St. Simon Island, Georgia, 1972, aerial view of model

▼ **179** MLTW/MOORE TURNBULL, *Kresge College*, University of California at Santa Cruz, California, 1965–74, laundromat and arcades

present but not insisted upon; cliché and kitsch are incorporated into the meanings of the building by way of detail, but do not dominate because of the syntactic inventions and syncopations.

The use of kitsch for non-kitsch ends has been a special feature of Charles Moore's work, although not its major motivation. Like Portoghesi, Moore has tried to make links with past languages of architecture, partly to establish a distinctive feeling of place (in a Modernist environment of abstract spaces) and partly to bring into play memory (*The Place of Houses,* 1974, and *Body, Memory and Architecture,* 1977, were two books Moore co-authored).[15] The establishment of a sense of place through historicist memories that are not too explicit could summarize his particular concern.

In the sixties, with his partners Donlyn Lyndon, William Turnbull, and Dick Whitaker, Moore developed a series of distinctive formal ideas which could absorb historicist recollections. For example, the notion of the aedicule, the little house, first enunciated by the English art historian Sir John Summerson in an essay "Heavenly Mansions" (1949) led Moore to the layering of small enclosures within larger ones, and to the idea of centeredness as significant. His interest in the vernacular and in ordinary technology, together with his Modernist background, allowed him to accept everyday techniques, stucco. walls, and ultimately the cutout cardboard aesthetic which we have seen even architects as apparently different from Moore as The Five exploit. His Sea Ranch Condominiums, for example, established a sense of place by combining cutouts with aedicules, all in a vernacular language (**235**), while a later project, Xanadune (**178**), played the same game at a

larger scale, and with a more formal language: that of Palladio and the nineteenth-century resort hotel. The exterior of the scheme is kept low to respect its dune setting, while the interior creates a much larger and more colorful public realm, with arches painted in strong yellows, reds, and oranges, and a variety of window shutters picked out in different hues. This opposition between a sober, contextual outside and a rich, rhetorical inside was realized at Kresge College, which consists of a series of mundane "monuments" (telephone booths, laundromat) distinguished

minded agility that he has even conducted two participatory exercises on a television phone-in basis.) A modest building resulting from a modest interaction of differing ideas is the David Rodes House, which has a double cube room derived from Inigo Jones and a bed placed next to a sliding door, an idea borrowed from Thomas Jefferson. Both these design ideas were from the client. The eighteenth-century, French image of the house was also the client's wish (**180**), but this image is tied to others—some of a local nature (the stucco box, the pronounced *portes-co-*

chères) and some personal to the three architects (notably the swelling curve and interior spatial ambiguities). The notion of teamwork, which Modern architects such as Walter Gropius held as an ideal, has here reached fruition because it is based on an inclusivist aesthetic.

Participatory design and teamwork have made Moore's architecture more pluralist than that of other Post-Modernists and have pushed it in a direction I have termed Radical Eclecticism. The adjective Radical, no doubt a fashionable one, is meant to distinguish a more thoughtful eclecticism than the easy shuffling of styles popular in the nineteenth century, which was then termed "indifferentism," or damned as "macaronic architecture." Radical Eclecticism has its basis in a philosophy of pluralism and the related theory of justifying different styles in different situations.[17] With the notion of pluralism, it insists that almost any city is made up from several different taste cultures, each with its relatively distinct code of architecture and view of the good life (which is, after all, what architecture is meant to celebrate). The justification for using a given style, or mixture of styles, is based on three main determinants: the context of the building (its urban or rural background); the variety of its functions; and the specific taste cultures of its users. When all three of these determinants have had an important effect on the design, the building can be termed Radically Eclectic. A good example is the Piazza d'Italia (**181–185**), designed by Moore in loose association with a Los Angeles group, U.I.G. (Urban Innovations Group), and a local New Orleans firm, Perez Associates, Inc. As usual, Moore played a catalytic and mediating role as well as that of designer, flying back and forth, literally, between the two design teams and shaping the project without determining all its details.[18]

As the site plan of the scheme reveals, the piazza is set in a mixed area of New Orleans. This contextual setting is the first justification for the highly rhetorical forms of the piazza: they are meant to contrast with the more regular outside, as figure against ground, void against solid, climax against repetition. Without these contrasts, and with the restaurant as yet uncompleted, the forms seem overly rhetorical, a condition which will change if the scheme is finished. Obviously, the piazza partially gains its formal motifs from its context: for example, from the nearby Modern skyscraper, whose black-and-white graphics have been taken up as a motif to generate the graduating series of rings. This circular form, at once a Modern bull's-eye and a Baroque urban form (like the Place des Victoires, Paris), radiates out into three streets to give a cue to the passerby that something unusual occurs behind the existing buildings. This

▼ **180** MOORE, RUBLE, AND YUDELL, *Rodes House*, Brentwood, California, 1979–80

setting up of an expectation, and the use of veiling devices that at once proclaim and hide—namely, the archway and pergola (**182**)—dramatize the approach. We are pulled toward the center of the bull's-eye, where we expect to find a symmetrical, circular culmination. What actually occurs both satisfies and contradicts this supposition. There is indeed a center and circular forms, but these do more than just confirm the Baroque centrality; rather, they set up new expectations because the circles are partial discs, screens of columns that spin asymmetrically on the diagonal of movement toward a new culmination point, the tallest point, an archway, in fact a modern Serliana (**183**).

The diagonal movement here is reinforced by the cascade of broken forms which shape the boot of Italy, focusing on the highest plateau, the "Italian Alps." Thus we have a clear organization of form and content. As Italy rises toward the northern Alps, so too do the five orders of Italian columns, culminating in a new sixth order which enframes the future restaurant. Moore calls this invention of an architectural order for a German restaurant the Deli Order, partly because of its neon necklaces and partly be-

cause it will vie with the sausages hanging in the restaurant's windows. One may take exception to the bad taste of this pun, but as an example of Radical Eclecticism one cannot doubt that Moore's invention does characterize the function: bad taste and good food are conventionally associated in our century.

The plurality of meanings within this scheme could not have been successfully incorporated by one designer: participation with a team and clients gives a density and conviction of meaning which cannot ordinarily be achieved by someone working alone. In this case, two designers from Perez Associates, Inc., Allen Eskew and Malcolm Heard, Jr., supplied much of the local cultural knowledge: they were the ones to stress the importance of the annual St. Joseph's Day festival, the pretext for the fountain, piazza, and its strong symbolism. Once a year, on the day of its patron saint, the Italian community comes to the fore to celebrate its presence in New Orleans with a carnival. Since the ostensible reason for the piazza was to give identity to this community in a city where other ethnic groups dominate (the French, Spanish, blacks, and Anglos), there was a sufficient pretext for historicist rhetoric and explicit content. Without this

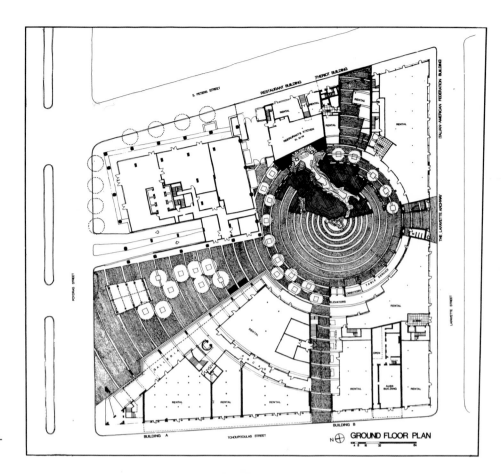

▶ 181 MOORE, PEREZ ASSOCIATES, INC., U.I.G., AND RON FILSON, *Piazza d'Italia*, New Orleans, Louisiana, 1975–80, site plan

current technologies (the neon and concrete); for the lover of pure architectural form there are the cutaway imposts finished in speckled marble and a most sensuous use of polished stainless steel. Column capitals glisten with this material as water shoots out of the acanthus leaves, while the stern, squat Tuscan columns are cut from it to evoke razor-sharp paramilitary images like the silhouettes of Greek helmets. Thus, the overall impression is a sensuous and rhetorical one.

Conceptually, the scheme is a convincing example of Radical Eclecticism in that it fits into and extends the urban context, it characterizes the Italianness and public nature of the various functions, and it takes its cues for content and symbolic form from the local taste culture, the Italian community. Moreover, it provides that community with a center, a "heart," to use that Post-Modern concept which Moore and others have done so much to publicize. In comparison with a later Moore collaborative effort, the Bunker Hill project for Los Angeles, it has a much stronger focus and sense of place.

The Bunker Hill scheme (186) had an extraordinary array of talented participants, including Cesar Pelli, Lawrence Halprin, Ricardo Legorreta, Hardy Holzman Pfeiffer, Frank Gehry, Barton Myers (who

content, the rhetoric would have been empty and the eclecticism weak.

What is the content? Italianness, clearly, as symbolized by echoes of Rome's Trevi Fountain, the five rather than three orders, the strong earth coloring, the Latin inscription ("This Fountain was given by the citizens of New Orleans as a gift to all the people"), and most obviously the plan of Italy (with the Adriatic and Tyrrhenian seas represented by moving water). Since the community is made up mostly of Sicilians, this island occupies the center of the bull's-eye, an emphasis which is increased by another focus, the black-and-white podium, which can function as a speaker's platform on St. Joseph's Day, when the piazza works as a *res publica* and the mayor addresses a large audience. This particular function is the kind of detailed social content that emerges only after patient exploration into a culture, and it is the way this function is *characterized* which makes the scheme an example of Radical Eclecticism.

Another Radically Eclectic aspect of the piazza is the plurality of taste cultures to which it is addressed. For historians there are references to the Marine Theater of Hadrian and the triumphal gateways of Karl Friedrich Schinkel (two images Moore had in mind); for the Italians there are references to archetypal piazzas and fountains; for the Modernists there is an acknowledgment of skyscrapers and the use of

▲ 182 MOORE, PEREZ ASSOCIATES, INC., U.I.G., AND RON FILSON, *Piazza d'Italia*, New Orleans, Louisiana, 1975–80, pergola

▶ 183 MOORE, PEREZ ASSOCIATES, INC., U.I.G., AND RON FILSON, *Piazza d'Italia*, New Orleans, Louisiana, 1975–80, modern Serliana

stitched the schemes together), and Harvey Perloff (who coordinated the designers). This was one of the first large-scale collaborative efforts by noted architects for a long time (the Berlin Interbau, 1957, comes to mind). The result, while creative and certainly more interesting than run-of-the-mill city development, lacks just that sense of precise social detail and participation which makes the Piazza d'Italia a success. Its metaphors and symbolism (for example, the "banana peel" tall building of Pelli, the "dominoes" of Hardy Holzman Pfeiffer, the "frozen waves" of Halprin, the "telescoped arches" of Moore) are certainly striking, but without a sense of urgency, or profound justification.

Clearly the lack of content in the building tasks given the architect by a consumer society poses a problem. Without significant and shared social values, the architect has little to represent except the ingenious metaphors he may derive from technique (the "banana peel" above consists in one stretched skin peeling away to reveal another skin, where the sun strikes the building from a different angle). Even in a consumer society, however, there are a few building tasks which *do* have a modest significance. The ski lodge Pavillon Soixante-Dix by Righter, Rose, and Lankin celebrates the public nature of skiing (**187–188**). Historicist forms borrowed from Palladio, such as the open arms of the exedra toward which the skiers aim, are mixed with local forms and those of traditional resort hotels. There are also elements of Moore's cutaway aesthetic, not surprisingly since the architects were taught at Yale University when Moore was chairman of the Department of Architecture there. In describing this building, the designers have emphasized the way in which its symbolism relates to other public buildings of the past and to the taste culture of skiers, but absent from their thoughtful list of references (which make this another Radically Eclectic work) is perhaps the most obvious one: the main facade, with its twin towers, high center, and lower sides, looks vaguely like the front of a cathedral. We can almost imagine it a classical *Westwerk* of the tenth century, showing a nave and two aisles, except that the neon decoration and the entrance remind us of other things, the commercial present.

This present was engaged quite directly in form and content in the designs for a Best Products storefront exhibited at The Museum of Modern Art, New York, in late 1979. Here, in designing a false front for an anonymous behind, the invited architects had to confront, head-on as it were, the problem of content in a commercial society. Two of the historicist solutions, those of Michael Graves and Robert Stern, show interesting attitudes to commerce.[19]

▲ 184 MOORE, PEREZ ASSOCIATES, INC., U.I.G., AND RON FILSON, *Piazza d'Italia*, New Orleans, Louisiana, 1975–80, Tuscan columns

▶ 185 MOORE, PEREZ ASSOCIATES, INC., U.I.G., AND RON FILSON, *Piazza d'Italia*, New Orleans, Louisiana, 1975–80, Lafayette Arch

▶ **186** U.I.G. TEAM ORGANIZED BY HARVEY PERLOFF, *Bunker Hill Project*, Los Angeles, California, 1980, model

curved screen-walls in an overall Shingle Style (**191–192**). A quite complicated and well-worked-out relation between structure, space, and roof reminds one of Eisenman's transformational drawings, which influenced the scheme. Walls inflect from an orthogonal grid to announce an entryway, or push the view toward the fireplace. Volumes are eroded at these junctures to reinforce the content (the traditional emphasis on door and hearth) and to allow in light. It is the brilliant quality of this light, reflected off the pool and walls, sometimes bouncing several times on back-lighted elements, that makes the poolhouse such a celebration of the sun, and thus quite appropriate to its summertime function. Details of the scheme, such as the erosion of the shingle line to accentuate column capitals, prefigure Stern's later interest in a highly mannered classicism. An example of this can be seen in the McGarry/Appignani bedroom, which uses the Tuscan order and voussoirs at giant size and in the wrong place (**193**). Columns to either side of the bed taper both ways and have mirror-image capitals at the base; the keystone and voussoirs sink under the bed and the false windows. The overall figure could almost be turned upside down, an example of anastrophe and amplification which Lutyens would have enjoyed. Indeed, Stern's later work seems to have swerved toward a Lutyensesque straight revivalism, as we will see in the next chapter.

Graves takes a generalizing approach, and gives a monumental, "Roman" colonnade of giant red cylinders surrounded by a "sky" blue cornice of glazed elements and a "pediment" sign, absolutely symmetrical, which steps up rather than down like a typical pediment (**189**). This heroic facade transcends its commercial content, just as a Roman aqueduct or stadium elevates its relatively banal social function. By contrast, Robert Stern's design adopts a socially realistic solution; it is quite the most hideous, ill-proportioned, and blatant facade produced for a long time (**190**). One has to go back to those lovably monstrous turn-of-the-century works of Hector Guimard, Henri Sauvage, or Lucien Weissenburger, to the absolute standards of Herculean ugliness. Stern's "fat women," made from bloated Doric columns, have wonderfully blank, flat faces that advertise the Best products within. The red and yellow/orange color dissonance is also suitable to the type of products sold. Here classical pastiche, the recurrent sign of consumer kitsch, finds its ironic representation—half a good advertisement and half so consistently awful that one knows it could not be an accident.

Very little Stern does is accidental. Like his mentor Philip Johnson, he is ultraconscious of every move in the evolution of Post-Modernism and of every possible influence on his own design. Basically, as he has outlined in two articles ("Bow-fronted Houses" and "Influences"), these influences are late-nineteenth-century (both Shingle Style and Lutyens), the Philadelphia School, the entire work of Venturi, and the "spaces within spaces" of Louis Kahn.[20] Vincent Scully, a friend and teacher of Stern, is another influence who has written, in *The Shingle Style Today* (1974), about Harold Bloom's theory concern-

ing the "anxiety of influence."[21] With Stern, ready to tell all before being asked, there seems to be no anxiety at all—he has given up the Modernist pretense of total originality and the concomitant hiding of traces. Yet he does, of course, "swerve" from these influences, as Bloom's theory has it, and like any creative architect he builds on his sources.

The poolhouse Stern built with partner John Hagmann for the Bourke House combines skylights with

▼ **187** RIGHTER, ROSE, AND LANKIN, *Pavillon Soixante-Dix*, St. Sauveur, Canada, 1976–78, axonometric

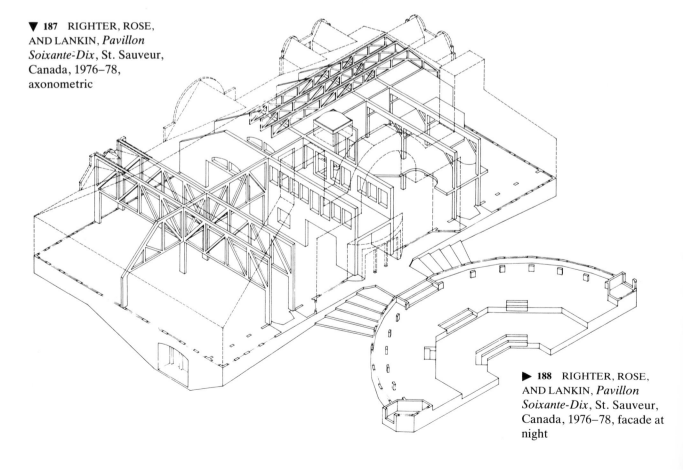

▶ **188** RIGHTER, ROSE, AND LANKIN, *Pavillon Soixante-Dix*, St. Sauveur, Canada, 1976–78, facade at night

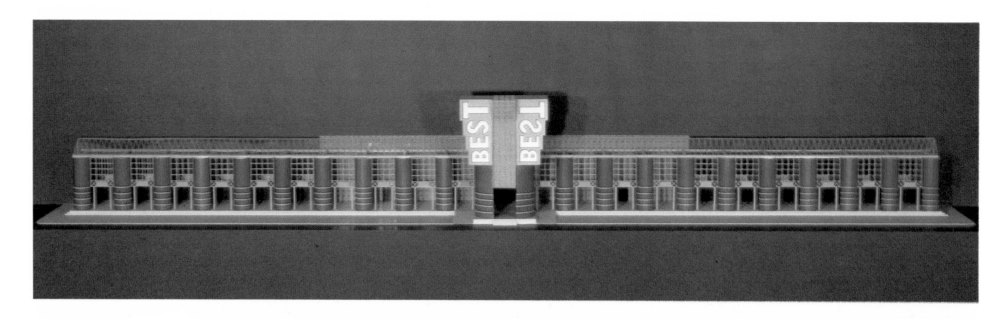

▲ **189** MICHAEL GRAVES *Best Products Showroom*, The Museum of Modern Art, New York City exhibition project, 1979

▶ **190** ROBERT A.M. STERN, *Best Products Showroom*, The Museum of Modern Art, New York City exhibition project, 1979

This trend toward a more explicit historicism has occurred for many reasons: writings such as Conrad Jameson's which stress the importance of traditional patterns (and pattern books) for domestic situations; the presence of straight revivalists such as Quinlan Terry and Allan Greenberg; the logical point that if tradition is to be revived it might as well be engaged directly; and the influence 'of younger designers such as Thomas Gordon Smith, who have themselves looked to Pre-Modernists, including the Californian architect Bernard Maybeck, for their original use of the classical tradition. Many Post-Modernists now consider that the most fruitful period to study is Pre-Modernism, when the Western tradition was accommodating itself to the new technology and space without altogether succumbing. The figures of Otto Wagner, Edwin Lutyens, Charles Rennie Mac-kintosh, Hendrik Berlage, Bernard Maybeck, Antoni

Gaudí, Henri Sauvage, John Belcher, J. J. Joass, Josef Hoffmann, and all those who could loosely be called "free style" architects loom large for these designers.

Philip Johnson, as usual, was relatively quick to grasp this new direction, quick at least for those who design large corporate buildings. His AT&T Building is in the tradition of the 1910 New York sky-scraper with its classical ordering of base, shaft, and capital (**194**). This traditional tripartite morphology is further subdivisible into historicist images: the base is a fairly straightforward reproduction of Brunelleschi's Pazzi Chapel in Florence (1442–61); the shaft is like a turn-of-the-century Louis Sullivan structure in its distinction between colored piers and anonymous infill; and the top is related to three sources—the iconic architecture of Ledoux, the up-turned crown of a Chippendale highboy, and the

radiator of a Rolls Royce. This design caused an
international sensation after it was unveiled at a
press conference because it was the first instance of
a large corporation commissioning a Post-Modern
building for the center of a major city. It was featured
on the front pages of *The New York Times, The
New York Times Sunday Magazine,* and *Time* magazine and in London in *The Times* (where no project
had ever been previewed). Its time had come (to use
a pun about a building produced on the run). The
imagery was interesting but certainly not deep
enough to warrant its being the most publicized design since, perhaps, the Eiffel Tower.

Younger designers in America have taken Pre-
Modernist sources in a very colorful and vigorously
modeled direction. Thomas Gordon Smith and other
San Francisco architects have used the informal
classicism of Bernard Maybeck and John Hudson

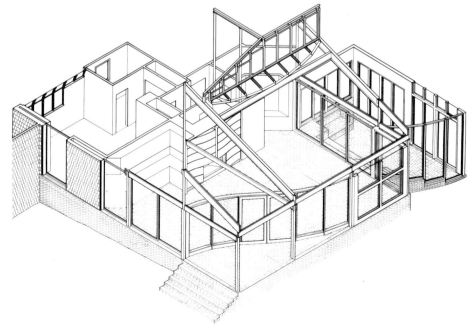

▲ **191** ROBERT A.M
STERN AND JOHN S.
HAGMANN, *Poolhouse for
the Bourke House*, Green-
wich, Connecticut, 1974

◄ **192** ROBERT A.M.
STERN AND JOHN S.
HAGMANN, *Poolhouse for
the Bourke House*, Green-
wich, Connecticut, 1974,
isometric

◀ **193** ROBERT A.M. STERN, *McGarry/Appignani Bedroom*, East Hampton, Long Island, New York, 1979

▼ **194** JOHNSON/BURGEE ARCHITECTS, *AT&T Building*, New York City, 1978–, perspective

Thomas which permeates the architecture of the Bay Area and which helped develop the California bungalow. Smith combines both high and low architectural sources with European ones. Thus his Matthews Street House Project is, in back, an informal stucco bungalow while, up front, it is an asymmetrical temple with a Michelangelesque broken pediment (**195**). A single column, vigorously modeled and colored like the rest of the design, sits in the garden: it at once recalls classical ruins placed in a garden and the fact that one column is missing from the portico. This architectural conceit and the explicitness of the historicism would seem overdone if it were not for the Bay Area tradition which encompasses the painted fantasies of the Newsom brothers, the carpenter-built extravaganzas of the Gold Rush era (of which fifteen thousand remain), bungalows with gnomes or worse in the garden, and Bernard Maybeck.[22] Critics of Thomas Gordon Smith tend to forget this context.

Smith's Tuscan and Laurentian Houses in Livermore, California, again use classical fragments in a poetic and witty way (**196–197**). Pastel-shaded walls in blue, rose, buff, and yellow provide a richly patterned background for the architectural and sculptural elements, which are rendered in more saturated colors. The columns, varying from the Doric to Tuscan and Ionic, and from the useless to the useful, serve to combine into one virtual space the outdoor areas of the two houses. The roof forms and courtyards acknowledge each other to form the oxymoronic figure-fragmented whole, as do the architectural orders. The paradox of unified dualities is further heightened by the Tuscan arcade which combines, in one doublet of paired columns, two orders. As in Smith's other houses, the wall itself changes rhythm as it moves from public front to private back. An elision of wall with colonnade and triumphal arch, combined with ellipsis (parts of the colonnade and arch are missing), make these modest bungalows highly rhetorical works.

Young American architects have used historicist motifs in an eclectic manner to revive the earlier tradition of the false front—the planar facade attached like a billboard to a modest back in order to give public presence and dignity to a building. In Philadelphia, Friday Architects have designed a community center which uses traditional motifs in an informal way (**198**). A grand public stairway marks the double entry which is, however, ironically mediated by large brick piers on the corner. The Art Deco (and classical) pediment above clearly breaks over the roof line to show its representational nature. Gothic windows, picked out in white trim according to nineteenth-century practice, remind one of previous communal buildings, as do the stagger and checkerboards within. It might be a twenties municipal building in the Art Deco manner except that the exaggerations in scale and informality show the influence of Robert Venturi. A twenties influence is also apparent in Taft Architects' addition to Quail Valley Municipal Control Building (**199**). Here, very subtle games are played with the Art Deco classicism. The false front is carefully accentuated as a thin plane detached from the modest lunchroom and office behind. Red tile unites one set of disparate elements which are all located on the same plane: the sides, parapet top, and implied central pilasters (with their white globe capitals). Then, again on the same plane, a stepped motif in white stucco turns into an arch and broken pediment. As if to confuse things

▲ **195** THOMAS GORDON SMITH, *Matthews Street House Project*, San Francisco, California, 1978, perspective

▲ **196** THOMAS GORDON SMITH, *Tuscan and Laurentian Houses*, Livermore, California, 1979–80, perspective

▶ **197** THOMAS GORDON SMITH, *Tuscan and Laurentian Houses*, Livermore, California, 1979–80

even further, the windows, still on the same plane, go in and out of both systems. This rhetorical equation of things which are different and separation of things which are the same provides a pleasing ambiguity in a sober facade, just as the colored flowerburst in the tympanum adds a decorative irony. Both buildings are appropriate, if modest, eclectic mixtures of the ordinary and symbolic.

In Europe historicism has also become more explicit and classical, although not to the degree that it has in America. The Barcelona Taller de Arquitectura, led by Ricardo Bofill, has constructed several monuments which mix historicist motifs in a Surrealist way. Their "pyramid" on the French/Spanish border is a monument to Catalan autonomy built from the earth and rock left during the construction of a motorway (**200**). The pyramid form creates a natural perspective diminishment which is heightened here by the cypress trees, planting, and sculpture, all of which seem to be falling down because the slope is treated as a flat plane. At the top, highly figurative architectural elements rotate and combine conventionally separate forms such as column, pier, wall, and pyramid. The way these forms merge and are transformed in masonry materials recalls similar transformations within the work of that previous exemplar of Catalan nationalism, Antoni Gaudí. In a sense, then, the monument is an appropriate symbol of continuing Separatist hopes.

Ricardo Bofill's religious center at Meritxell also makes appropriate use of existing forms, in this case the ruins of a Romanesque chapel (**201**). Here, the original shrine was to be expanded into a bridge, like the Roman Pont du Gard, which would span a mile and a half between two peaks (**202**). The Romanesque arches are thus expanded, both literally and metaphorically, to make a new shrine, and cultural center, dedicated to Andorra's autonomist aspirations. As Geoffrey Broadbent has written, "The *function* of the Meritxell project is 'to symbolize,'" and he goes on to analyze how: "The Taller envisage a symbolic progression, of which the main features are to be a mountain path, a terraced amphitheatre open to the landscape, and a giant staircase. Andorra's cultural

aspirations will be symbolized by a path across the bridge, the crossing, and the arching of the viaduct over an artificial lake. A vertical monolith and the arching of the viaduct over grass will symbolize her political aspirations while, in addition to the Virgin in her new shrine, the ruins of the shrine will be retained for their symbolic value . . ."[23]

Other European architects, also loosely associated with the Rationalist movement, achieve a restrained and dignified type of historicist symbolism. Bruno Reichlin and Fabio Reinhart have built several neo-Palladian villas with stripped-down details in a hard-edge reinforced concrete. Their Maison Tonini (**203–204**) takes Renaissance themes—the symbolic arch framing a view, the rhythmical bay system, the

"house within a house"—distorts them slightly, and builds them with present-day technology. Because this crossing of traditions is done in a straightforward and direct way it seems quite natural, not the extraordinary mix it really is, and only on close inspection does one notice the Mannerist emphasis on eroded edges, the grid *appliqué,* the neo-primitivist farmhouse image, and the rotated symmetry. One reflects on how surreal Palladio's Villa Rotonda (1566–67) must have seemed when it was built; a centralized church turned into a suburban villa. The same kind of latent symbols are present here.

The European master of the latent symbol is, as we have seen in the chapter on slick-tech, the Viennese Hans Hollein. Vienna must always be seen as the

background to Hollein's work, even when he designs for other cities, because his buildings have the sophisticated irony and cosmopolitan wit associated with his native city. Gustav Klimt, Sigmund Freud, Adolf Loos, Ludwig Wittgenstein, Otto Wagner, Johann Fischer von Erlach, *Sachertorte,* logical positivism, the end of an Empire: Hollein knows it all, as well as much of the rest of the world from his wide travels and readings. Consequently, his architecture is bound to contain a complexity of meaning which is often hidden, as we have seen, by surface brilliance.

His Perchtoldsdorf Town Hall renovation, like many of his other works, thrives on exploiting a small, difficult site, and the result, quite logically, is architecture conceived of as large furniture (205–206). Decorative wavy lines in blue and chrome mediate between the existing ceiling and the new table and floor ornament. Thirties revival chairs for the councillors are packed tightly together to give, like the portraits of previous Mayors, a feeling of intense concentration and political discussion. Subtle ironies are built into this image of the *res publica:* the door to the Conservatives' chamber is slightly articulated by an upside-down wave; the Mayor seated at the head of the oval table sees the front of every councillor's place as equal because of visual differ-

ences made to produce this illusion; stylized grapes and vines in the center of the oval provide a visual distraction during an interminable debate; the grapes have a golden hue to indicate that wine is the source of the town's wealth; air-conditioning ducts and lighting elements are introduced as punctuation marks in the rococo ceiling. Everywhere the contrast of new and old is mediated by the harmony of these two systems. The chrome wave, for instance, has a light rococo feel to it; the thick entablature of the new table gives it a weight consistent with the old doorway. This produces the effect of accommodation with irony in the old Viennese tradition of sophisticated diplomacy.

Hollein's Museum of Glass and Ceramics in Tehran is even more sophisticated in its interweaving of opposite meanings. Here, Hollein has restored an old Quajar mansion to a better-than-original condition, upgrading the lighting and finish, and then collaging on and threading through his own architecture. The result is a set of rooms which are characterized theatrically in various ways, with the kind of eclectic opposition of meanings that an eighteenth-century architect such as Filippo Juvarra might have achieved. Where the rococo stucco was worth preserving, giant display cases have been introduced, "brass hats" or "black columns," each with a quite different mood, which leave the stucco walls free to become an exhibition in their own right (**207–208**).

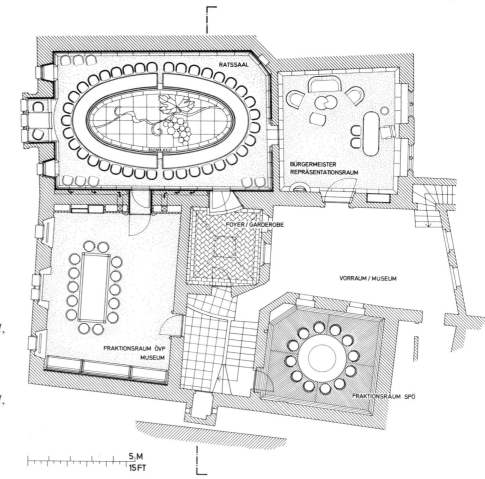

◀ **205** HANS HOLLEIN
Perchtoldsdorf Town Hall, Austria, 1976, council chamber

▶ **206** HANS HOLLEIN
Perchtoldsdorf Town Hall, Austria, 1976, plan

▼ **207** HANS HOLLEIN
Museum of Glass and Ceramics, Tehran, Iran, 1977, first-floor showroom

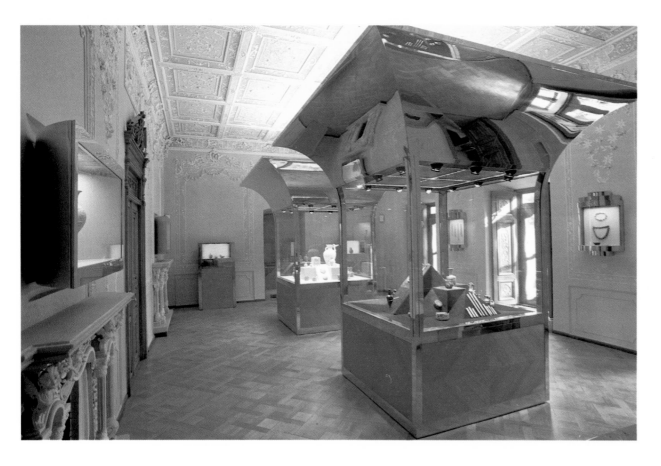

These cases then provide an indirect light, which bounces off the coffered ceiling, and a kind of miraculous, glowing light (which is Hollein's secret) that seems to illuminate the objects from within.

On the second floor, where the rooms are not so significant, Hollein has collaged a space away from the wall to create yet other moods: a semi-circular fan of cases in a distended, floating space of orange, and a brass-gridded room which seems to be another Rationalist mortuary of abstract squares (**209–210**; see chapter 4). Indeed, death and the gravestone have been preoccupations of Hollein since the late sixties, and one can conceive of many of these cases as caskets pulled from the wall and turned upright.[24] The "brass-gridded room," for instance, has rectangular cases which seem to fit the voids left at viewing height. We mentally slot them back into this wall, just as we mentally complete the volume of every eroded case. This theme of beautiful erosion is most apparent in the "black-column room," where a cube has one edge missing, a rhomboid is incomplete, and the columns are cut in two—all these incisions made as if by our gaze, which they instantly focus. Through such elegant means Hollein makes his showcases as

interesting as the objects they display. The paradoxical graves he has designed, with their missing parts and magical light, are perhaps suitable metaphors for this collection with its archaeological past and uncertain future. An eclecticism which can accept the past in parts and transform it elsewhere, as appropriate, is again more radical than a simple mixing of styles.

Another example of characterizing functions, and thus Radical Eclecticism, is Hollein's Austrian Travel Bureau (211–213), in which we can read the meanings and their distortions quite clearly because they are in a popular code. Hollein plays upon the slight fantasy of tourism through the use of stereotypes. Thus travel to Egypt is signified by part of a pyramid lying up against (and going through?) the wall. Desert travel is communicated by bronze versions of the palm columns of John Nash's Brighton Pavilion (1815–21)—or is it travel to an exotic land, or to England, or to the nineteenth century? The references are both vague and specific. A woodcut of Sebastiano Serlio's perspective, representing the theater, is blown up in scale and draped with an inert, metal theater curtain (the place to buy theater tickets). Ship flags fly frozen in glass, birds sail in mid-air: both abstract signs of travel which take on a Surrealist dimension. One can ruminate on all these enigmatic symbols under a bronze solar topee, a sign of India or colonization, which is decorated like a Hollywood dressing

▲ 208 HANS HOLLEIN
Museum of Glass and Ceramics, Tehran, Iran, 1977, first-floor showroom

▼ 209 HANS HOLLEIN
Museum of Glass and Ceramics, Tehran, Iran, 1977, second-floor showroom

▶ 210 HANS HOLLEIN
Museum of Glass and Ceramics, Tehran, Iran, 1977, second-floor showroom

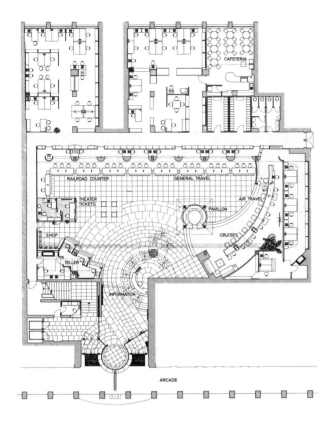

table. A ruined column, signifying Italy or Greece, is impaled from above by a slick-tech shaft. One pays for all these fantasies, and travel, through a chrome Rolls Royce grill. Surrounding everything is a Pre-Modernist, abstract grid, and geometrical figures in the floor, reminders of Vienna, Otto Wagner, and the fact that one can tour without leaving home. The agency is collaged into a preexisting block, and respects the surrounding color and geometry while discreetly announcing itself. Thus Hollein searches for hints in the program—the context, the functions, and the taste culture of the users—for his symbolism. He speaks directly to a mass culture by using its stereotypes, but avoids the kitsch usually attendant on such situations by a careful craftsmanship and use of symbols.

Michael Graves, in his more recent work, also looks to the program of the building for its symbolic potential. Since about 1975 he has moved away from a Late-Modern abstract style toward a more accessible language with historicist references.[25] A key scheme is his Crooks House (1976), which translates the concerns of his painting onto the facade and into

the garden, but this will be discussed later for its Post-Modern spatial implications (347). The Claghorn House additions (1974) start to use an historicist vocabulary, but the references, such as the half-split pediment, are so implicit as to be unrecognizable, and the fragmentation is so extreme as to defeat a coherent reading.

The first realized building of Graves in which one can see a shift toward a more explicit coding is his Schulman House additions (214). Here the fragments are brought into mutual interaction to produce a multivalent work that allows many readings. The street facade uses the existing clapboard motif at different scales to enforce half an illusionist space, diminishing toward the entrance, which is celebrated and articulated in a traditional way, but with a distorted keystone and pediment and thin, layered steps of Art Deco inspiration. This "ziggurat" not only marks the door but also reiterates another key center, the fireplace. Thus a favorite dualistic theme of Graves is set up to be repeated in other places, such as the garden. On the street itself there is a further duality, created by the repetition of columnar

◀ 211 HANS HOLLEIN
Austrian Travel Bureau,
Vienna, Austria, 1978,
interior

▲ 212 HANS HOLLEIN
Austrian Travel Bureau,
Vienna, Austria, 1978, plan

▶ 213 HANS HOLLEIN
Austrian Travel Bureau,
Vienna, Austria, 1978,
interior

shapes, which sets up two readings. If we look at the fireplace column we can see that its "capital" has jumped off and landed in the middle of the facade; if we look at this point we can see that the missing center has jumped to the right. Either reading gives us multivalent linkages which tie the meanings together. Dualities are repeated in the pairs of windows, the column that divides the facade in half, and its overall asymmetrical symmetry, a major rhetorical figure of the Queen Anne Revival. Indeed, the explicit coloring (the green earth and blue sky), and explicit use of strongly colored moldings to end a theme, remind one of this accessible language of architecture.

The antecedents that Graves likes to draw upon include Roman, Renaissance, and Baroque architecture and the work of Claude-Nicolas Ledoux (1736–1806), Edwin Lutyens (1869–1944), Gunnar Asplund (1885–1940), and Le Corbusier as well as elements of Art Deco. To this heterogeneous list should be added Synthetic Cubism, Purism, and landscape gardening,

particularly the art of topiary. In his mature work these sources are generalized and unified under his own unmistakable aesthetic. Indeed, the importance of Graves can be gauged by the fact that he is one of the few architects of the last twenty years to have generated a new, personal style (Robert Venturi, Hans Hollein, and James Stirling, perhaps Aldo Rossi and Leon Krier, are others). This style is developed through his paintings, drawings, and sketches and clearly it is based on a graphic facility. None of the architects mentioned above gives so much time to painting and sketching. Indeed, one has to return to Le Corbusier (whom Graves can mimic with ease) to find an equally wide visual commitment. Not surprisingly, Graves's murals have something of Le Corbusier's Purist canvases about them: recognizable architectural details set in a shallow, proportioned space (**215**). With Graves, however, spatial systems are superimposed in fragments. Thus he uses elevation, plus oblique projection, conventional perspective, and rotated, Cubist perspective. As in his architecture, the fragments of these different systems are elided as well as divided by edges. Thus, in the "Easel Mural," a perspectival space to the left blends into the shallow, layered space of the center, but is divided from it by two white "cuts." The feelings evoked by the coloring and subject matter (*parts* of couches, easel, chair, plan, ribbons, moldings) place it within the post-Cubist, Mediterranean tradition of Picasso.[26] Blue sky, pink stucco, and ideal, white structure call up memories of the heroic twenties, but these are mediated by memories of the Ecole des Beaux-Arts or the nineteenth-century artist's studio. These paintings seem to fluctuate, like the fragments of which they are composed, somewhere between Mediterranean primitivism and hothouse academicism.

Such double coding is also evident in the New York Sunar Furniture Showroom for which the mural was painted. Because the rooms are cut off from the outside, and since the fabrics displayed have an origin in nature, Graves decided to introduce the metaphor of nature into his scheme to provide relief from the artificially enclosed and serviced space (**216**). A "metaphorical garden" was created through which the customer walks, with the fabrics draped somewhat

▲ **215** MICHAEL GRAVES
Sunar Furniture Showroom,
New York City, 1979,
"Easel Mural"

◀ **216** MICHAEL GRAVES
Sunar Furniture Showroom,
New York City, 1979, textile room

like vines on a trellis. Views through false windows are implied at various points to decrease the claustrophobia, as if one were looking into the house from the garden. Other, more familiar images are also encoded with these windows: the anthropomorphic visage, always a suggestion of a window with its "eyes"; the Serliana motif suggested by a cutout pediment and flanking, red columns. Elsewhere in the showroom heavy red columns rest on heavier gray blocks and support smaller golden capitals—a reminiscence of a Cretan column, although here upside down. This anastrophe can be seen in other elements such as the thick moldings—below the windows rather than above.

Everywhere in this mature work meanings are suggested without being named, as if Graves were following the advice of a nineteenth-century Symbolist poet, or at least that of Oscar Wilde. This device of suggesting a plethora of possible meanings can also be found in Le Corbusier's Ronchamp chapel, a building I have analyzed elsewhere as a supreme example of suggested metaphor.[27] The virtue of this rhetorical device, as opposed to the explicit reference, is its ability to imply more than it says, and thereby to induce a penumbra of meanings. The mind races over and over the associative links but is never allowed to come up with a final interpretation. Clearly, this device can be used for obfuscation as well as amplification. As many critics have shown in their analyses of Shakespeare's *Hamlet,* the enigmatic protagonist of this play uses suggested metaphor to both ends, and so too does Graves.

The Fargo-Moorhead Cultural Center (**217–219**) is both explicit and implicit in its use of references, and it is this combination which makes it a most powerful example of Radical Eclecticism. The subject matter is fairly straightforward: the Center is a bridge/building which is meant to unite two cities divided by a river and a state line—Fargo in North Dakota and Moorhead in Minnesota. Many signs of a unified duality are used, perhaps the most obvious of which is the broken arch in the center of the bridge which seems to reach toward an unattainable unity with its outstretched curves. The duality is restated by adjacent, massive columns and the separate buildings on each shore; the unity is restated by the "keystone window" and the frozen water which rushes, Ledoux-like, from a semi-cylinder.

Other formal repetitions underline the oxymoronic figure of two in one: the red masonry and blue glazing which interweave throughout the whole scheme. The anthropomorphism implicitly coded in the central bridge reiterates this same message: two legs, one head, two eyes, one chin. The image of some crawling animal is suggested just enough to work on our subconscious. Indeed, the historicist references are kept at a level of abstraction to give them a kind of halo effect—the penumbra we have mentioned. The tripartite division of the bridge is implicit, but becomes explicit in the two side buildings (as Graves explained it, the river is the rusticated basement, the bridge and vehicular access is the *piano nobile,* and the light canons, the half-arches of the art museum, are the attic). References to the Ponte Vecchio in Florence, the pyramid at Sir John Vanbrugh's Castle Howard (1699–1712), Ledoux's cylindrical buildings, a Serliana pergola, and Borrominian lantern are more obscure; their point is not so much to be perceived and understood as to be suggested and to suggest. Besides heightening the drama, an effect already mentioned, the varied stock of half-remembered visual codes from which they are drawn provides richness and depth. Horizontal bands are vaguely reminiscent of rustication, diagonal checkers recall trelliswork (a favorite motif of Graves), and glass grids refer back to the twenties. The giant, heroic entrance to the Concert Hall and Communication Center recalls the entrance to primitive basilicas at

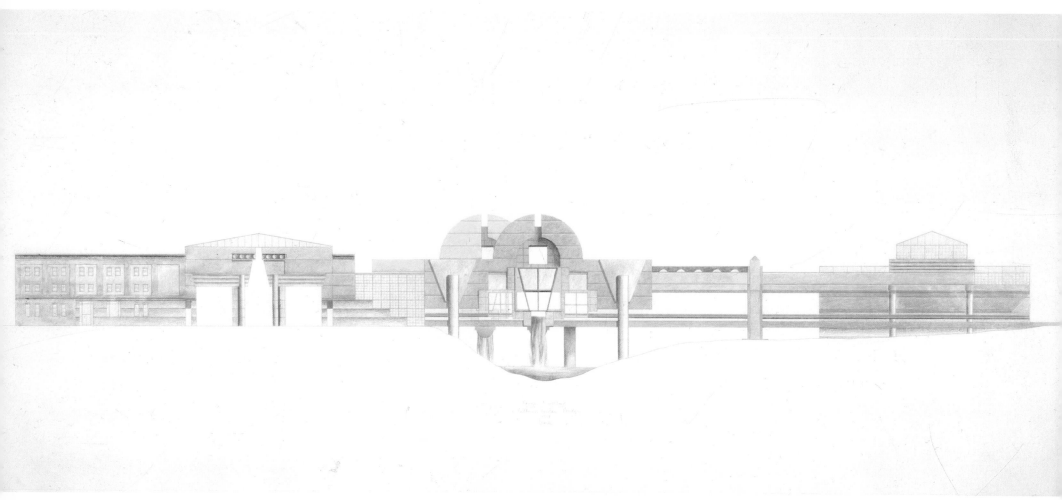

Ravenna. We then get a wide spectrum of memories ranging from the classical tradition to the garden, from the factory to the church, and it is this extensive semantic field which is probably most clearly perceptible. Like Hollein's eclecticism, it acts to characterize functions with a variety of moods, some of which are appropriate to concert-going, others to river life, or to the history museum (reading from left to right across the south elevation).

The plan shows how this variety of space and function is stitched together. A basic pinwheel motion of axes rotates around the center of the bridge. The Communications Center to the south incorporates an existing three-story building into its grid and bends toward the curve of the river. The History Museum to the north keeps to the same grid, but erodes it toward the parking lot and skews fragments of other grids toward the center. The Cultural Center itself resolves these two orders and the river bend with a shifted axis, a favorite motif of Graves and other Post-Modernists.[28] This connects indoors and above with outdoors and below, focusing on the "voided keystone" through which water is pumped. "The voided keystone is also seen as a scupper which collects the sky and replenishes the river below through a waterfall which issues from its base. The water is pumped from the river by a windmill which is part of the history museum and reflects the agrarian base of the communities. In this way, the individual elements

of the composition are seen as parts of a larger narrative."[29]

We have then, in 1978, a much deeper historicism than that of twenty years earlier, one which finds reasons in the site, the culture, and the functions for its eclectic form. These reasons give contemporary historicism greater meaning.

◀ 217 MICHAEL GRAVES
Fargo-Moorhead Cultural Center, Fargo, North Dakota, and Moorhead, Minnesota, 1977–78, south elevation

▲ 218 MICHAEL GRAVES
Fargo-Moorhead Cultural Center, Fargo, North Dakota, and Moorhead, Minnesota, 1977–78, south elevation bridge detail

◀ 219 MICHAEL GRAVES
Fargo-Moorhead Cultural Center, Fargo, North Dakota, and Moorhead, Minnesota, 1977–78, site plan

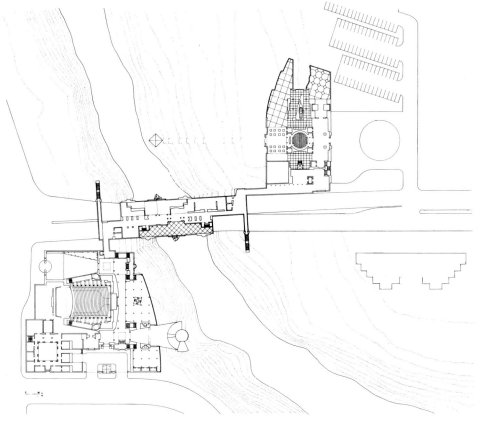

FROM STRAIGHT REVIVALISM TO DISTORTED ORNAMENT

MANY ARCHITECTS AND HISTORIANS HAVE ARGUED that traditional architectures, and above all the classical tradition, died a slow but inevitable death in the twentieth century. Henry-Russell Hitchcock, the dean of historians, put the organic metaphor this way: "The causes of death are still disputable, but the fact of dissolution is by now [1958] generally accepted."[1] In spite of several mini-revivals—Stalinist Baroque or the stripped classical architecture of the thirties— (or, critics would say, *because* of them) there is no live tradition, if by live we mean unbroken building activity carried on by both elite designers and the construction industry. By this definition, historical styles are indeed dead; there are no first-class, creative talents pushing the extension of a traditional language, nor is there a significant craft-based organization capable of carrying out such work. Yet period revivals continue to be built by both individuals and teams, and on a large scale where "repro" details are mass-produced in modern materials. Indeed, in industrial societies there is a lot of straight revivalism —what are called the neo-styles to distinguish them from an unbroken tradition such as that of eighteenth-century Georgian, which grew gradually from a combination of the vernacular and classical traditions.

Neo-styles may vary from scholarly reconstructions to pastiche, but most of the architects who work in these areas are not Post-Modernists because they were not trained in Modernism in the first place. However, their influence on Post-Modernism has been important: they have pushed Post-Modernists toward a more literal use of historical forms, and provided a valuable standard by which to measure some of the latter's more excessive creations.

Conrad Jameson, who has emerged in England as the major polemicist for a traditional approach, argues for its superiority in the area of mass housing.[2] Using traditional pattern books—any tradition as long as it is Pre-Modern and unbroken—he shows that traditional approaches can produce housing which is cheaper, more suitable, and more enjoyable than any modern housing estate. The arguments are elaborate, the evidence complex—based on measuring real social costs, looking at delays caused by unnecessary innovation, and interviewing those people who live in modern estates. Whether or not we believe that these arguments logically lead to a traditional approach for all housing, we can accept them insofar as they offer a further alternative, a matter for choice in a pluralist society. Jameson argues that a traditional pattern of building should be followed and only modified *piecemeal* to accommodate new uses such as the automobile and refrigerator. He contends that housing is a social craft and not a place for expression—or for individual creation.

There have been several examples that carry through this approach in part: the rebuilding of European cities, such as the center of Warsaw, Poland, that suffered damage in World War II; the building of vernacular housing and arcaded streets in cities such as Bologna, Italy, where a communist Mayor oversaw a communal program which is really quite unique in its success; or Hassan Fathy's Gourna

▶ **220** HASSAN FATHY
Gourna New Town, Egypt, 1945–48

New Town, Egypt, built with traditional five-thousand-year-old Egyptian techniques (**220**). Fathy recreates mud-brick villages with tight streets, flat domes, and whitewash finish.[3] He revives the craft tradition of drying mud bricks and teaches peasants to construct spheres and barrel vaults with them. Such constructions are cheaper, better insulated, and more varied than their mass-produced counterparts, at least for these Egyptian villages. It may well be, as Fathy and Jameson contend, that traditional building should be augmented in many parts of the world.

What is usually produced, however, and will continue to be produced in a consumer society, is not traditional but traditionalesque building. A pastiche of the past is what society often seeks, and what its commercial designers are trained to produce. Since Williamsburg, Virginia, was restored by the Rockefeller Foundation in the twenties, there has

been a strong Williamsburg revival all over the United States. Since Portmeirion, Wales, was finished by Clough Williams-Ellis in 1956 and Port Grimaud, France, by François Spoerry in 1969 there has been a strong Mediterranean port revival all over Europe. Port Grimaud (**221**) is a mass-produced, reinforced concrete marina with controlled parking areas, modern services, and occasionally front lawns, although from a distance it looks like a traditional Provençal fishing village. Its superiority to comparable modern villages by the sea led Modernists, such as the English architect Peter Smithson, to reappraise their form of urbanism. It caused the same challenge to Modernism in Europe that Disneyland and the Madonna Inn caused in America: pastiche had turned out to be

more functional and appropriate than Modern building. The ultimate irony of this reappraisal occurred when Maurice Culot, a Belgian Marxist, proposed Port Grimaud, the ultimate consumer luxury resort, as a model for mass housing and urban renewal.[4] His protest group ARAU (Atelier de Recherche et d'Action Urbaine) used this populist prototype in an attack on the very bourgeoisie who had produced it, an irony Marx, Lenin, and Stalin would have applauded with their love of bourgeois art. The people who were shocked at this turn of events were the old-time Modernists and socialists, trained in other codes of perception, and the bourgeoisie who were tearing down old Brussels and rebuilding it in the Modern, corporate style. To explore this collision and inversion of taste cultures might be interesting, but it would take us beyond the confines of the subject at hand.

221 FRANÇOIS SPOERRY, *Port Grimaud*, France, 1965–69, aerial view

222 QUINLAN TERRY *Waverton House*, Moreton-in-Marsh, Gloucestershire, England, 1979–80, southeast facade

223 QUINLAN TERRY *Newfield*, Mickley, Ripon, Yorkshire, England, 1980–81, forecourt elevation of first design

Straight revivalism, practiced as a discipline, sometimes demands a rare combination of arrogance and modesty. Quinlan Terry, a designer trained by Peter Smithson in the tenets of Modernism (the education didn't take), combines these opposite attributes in his work.[5] He builds large country houses for the English upper class, in an era when such houses are thought not to be created anew, and has the temerity to produce them without irony, without acknowledging either that the Modern Movement existed or that the British Empire has ceased. For a Bahai Temple in the Middle East (1973–76) he mixes classical Roman grammar with colonial Indian architecture. For two country houses in England (**222–223**) he uses a Palladian grammar without the slightest trace of expression, or deviation from the canon (although finials may be in glass-reinforced polyester). The results are more incongruous than if they had been

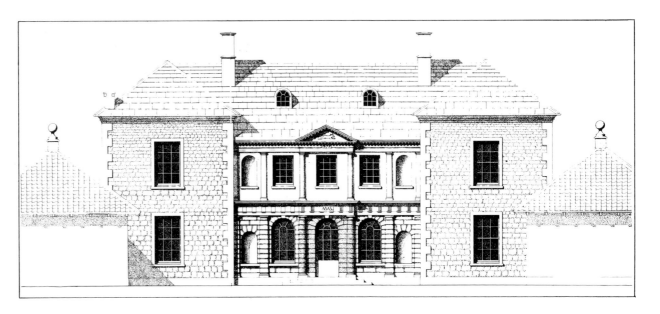

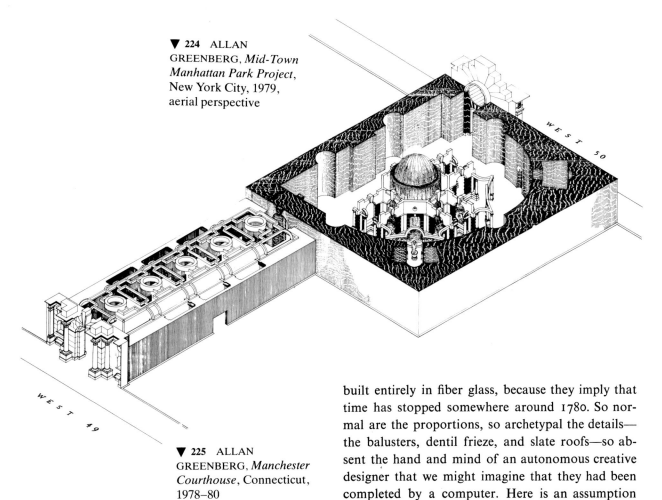

Terry forces us to reconsider, as Andy Warhol does in his replications and Conrad Jameson with his theorizing: does architecture have to be a creative art, or can it successfully be an applied craft? Cannot the architect, like the musician who performs a classical symphony, be intent on modestly rendering a previous score with maximum fidelity (even supposing that, for the architect, this score exists in a tradition rather than a single manuscript)? Herein lies the modesty which is tied to the arrogance that overlooks time and cultural space.

Terry's virtues (and those of the buildings published in *Classical America*)[6] are those of the craftsman, and he spends an impressive amount of time and energy getting skilled laborers to fabricate just the right capital detail. The pediments, quoins, pedestals, stucco pilasters, and stonework are all of a quality usually achieved only in restoration work. Perhaps his buildings should be seen as preemptive restorations of would-be ruins? Perhaps they will act, as aging cathedrals did in the eighteenth century, as anachronistic relics which keep alive a tradition about to be revived? One asks these tangential questions because the cultural relevance of the work is not immediately apparent.

Easier to comprehend is the relevance of Allan Greenberg's classical revivalism, based loosely on the

built entirely in fiber glass, because they imply that time has stopped somewhere around 1780. So normal are the proportions, so archetypal the details—the balusters, dentil frieze, and slate roofs—so absent the hand and mind of an autonomous creative designer that we might imagine that they had been completed by a computer. Here is an assumption

free style of Edwin Lutyens, which he has studied. Many Post-Modern architects have been influenced by this Pre-Modernist, and one can speak of a mini Lutyens revival. Robert Venturi, Robert Stern, Michael Graves, Philip Johnson, as well as Allan Greenberg, who organized a Lutyens show at The Museum of Modern Art, New York, have been influenced by his plans and ironic use of the "high game" of classicism. In England, Roderick Gradidge, and several writers including Nikolaus Taylor, Colin Amery, David Watkin, and Gavin Stamp, have brought Lutyens back into the mainstream of discussion.[7]

Allan Greenberg designed a Lutyensesque park, at the request of The Museum of Modern Art, New York, which connects two streets (**224**). At either end are exaggerated and distorted keystones (a motif Graves used somewhat earlier) which proclaim the machine-tooled and highly muscular classicism within. As one would expect from these grandiloquent fronts, and as in the work of Lutyens, there are all sorts of rhetorical inversions of the traditional language. Topiary and architecture exchange roles conceptually; a fountain turns into the implied dome of a church; round cylinders (reminiscent of Lutyens's tennis racket metaphors at New Delhi?) remind one of pergolas and restaurant kitsch; the plan

of the "cathedral" is yet another ode to Hadrian's Villa, as well as a ruin (or inside-out building). Thus we find double meanings, puns, oxymoron, and ad-hoc combinations: the kind of high-minded wit we would expect of Lutyens, and here quite appropriate to a dense, urban site.

Another Greenberg project, the conversion of a supermarket into a courthouse, also shows an appropriate use of the classical language for a civic function, but here the Mannerism is more low-keyed (**225**). Quoins step up the side and diminish like an Art Deco marching figure, occasionally turning into a broken stringcourse or entablature (that elides with a pediment and keystone). The horizontal emphasis and flat sides may allude to Modernist conventions, but the meanings most apparent to the public are those of municipal classicism. Because Greenberg's treatment of the language is so close to stereotype, some may miss his creativity altogether, a result many straight revivalists would applaud.

Robert Stern's revivalism is, by contrast, based more on representation and recollection than on replication of stereotype. Where he uses a direct quotation from a Pre-Modernist, it is to communicate a general idea and harmonize with a preexisting environment rather than to seek to recall a prototype

in full. The Jerome Greene Hall renovation for law students at Columbia University uses signs of a gentleman's club—the heavy furniture and clean, cheery classicism—which Stern presumes the students find welcoming and appropriate to their future condition (**226**). Robert Venturi, Stern's mentor, might have added a few ironic touches to such an accommodating message, to indicate perhaps a begrudging acceptance of the elite, but Stern prefers to play it straight. The square niches which in a nineteenth-century club might have held a member's portrait or uplifting statement are blank, but not ironically so. Rather, they form a Lutyensesque layering of tight space and part of the symmetrical, aetiolated ornament system which plays tricks with the scale of the room (it makes the large, vertical dimension smaller). Such conventional revivalism, like Greenberg's and Terry's, implies that all is well with the legal world, and that justice will be done.

Other Stern revivalism, which verges on the eclecticism discussed in the previous chapter, is more creative in its use of stereotype and thus shows less satisfaction with the world as it is. A solar-heated, luxury pool borrows motifs straight from the architecture of the Vienna Secession and from John Nash's Brighton Pavilion, but combines these quotations to send new messages (**227**). We recognize the bright, checkerboard sparkle of the tiles as a familiar Secession image but nevertheless delight in the way it erupts, on the corner, between the two female figures formed as ad-hoc combinations of window (head), keystone (torso), and column-quoin (legs). These playful figures provide suitable poolside amusement, just as the jewel-like tiles appropriately take up the splash and shimmer of the water.

The contrast between these two examples of Stern's work clarifies an important distinction between straight revivalism and Radical Eclecticism: the former may seem stultifying and smug in its presumptions about the status quo, whereas the latter may seem more liberating in its creativity. I use the word "seem" because this will appear differently to other taste cultures, and what is being read is a *representation* of the world, not the world itself.

The forces inherent in revivalism are probably contradictory. On the one hand, there are the demands of the existing language, its rules of combination and the limitations of its imagery; on the other, there is the pressure to use modern fabrication techniques, for traditional materials and methods of construction have become expensive. These opposite forces, combined with the creative will of the designer, push straight revivalism toward a distortion of the stereotype. There is a trend of design emerging which might be called distorted ornamentalism be-

◀ **226** ROBERT A.M. STERN, *Jerome Greene Hall*, Columbia University School of Law, New York City, 1975–77, interior

The strange, even sinister feeling, is increased by large dark windows set against tiny, gun-slit holes cut in the thick masonry. Individual volumes are accentuated by pitched roof caps, and individual parts of the house are characterized by different materials, details, or tiles—all recycled from former buildings. What makes this house rather frightening is the literalist and precisionist way the ornament has been handled. Details are borrowed directly from medieval architecture, the Vienna Secession, Victorian and classical modes, and rendered with a hard-edge blankness. This also gives the house a charm associated with the mystery of age: an old/new building whose provinciality is rescued by paradox.

Provinciality, anachronism, nostalgia—these are the three epithets that latch onto straight revivalism like leeches, draining it of significance for those brought up with progressivist ideals. To overcome these inherent prejudices, architects sometimes re-

◀ **227** ROBERT A.M. STERN, *Cohn Poolhouse*, Llewellyn Park, New Jersey, 1980–, interior

▼ **228** FERNANDO HIGUERAS, *City Hall*, Ciudad Real, Spain, 1970

▶ **229** MARTIN JOHNSON *Ovenden House*, Liskeard, Cornwall, England, 1975–, north and east elevations

cause it uses recognizable motifs with a strange, new feeling: a haunting precision.

The acceptance of applied ornament started in the sixties with the neo-Liberty movement and the work and writings of Robert Venturi, which placed emphasis on the symbolic role of decoration. Ornament had many functional and aesthetic roles in the past which were revived one by one in the sixties and seventies: for example, it broke down the mass of a large building and gave it scale at different distances; it modulated the light into various shades and qualities; it "hid faults in construction," a purpose for which it was faulted by Modernists; it mimicked the qualities of expensive materials with cheap ones; it provided an inert wall surface with visual rhythms, complexities, and hidden motifs; it "beautified," "adorned," and "lifted up" the thing or person to which it was applied. When the Modern Movement purged ornament from the repertoire of architecture, or reduced it to structure and construction, a host of important qualities were lost together with the superficial ones for which it was attacked. In the seventies several conferences, exhibitions, and magazines were devoted to outlining these roles of ornament.[8]

Together with the eclectics who use ornament and new versions of the architectural orders in their work, there are also some architects who concentrate specifically on ornament.[9] Martin Johnson, a young English architect trained at the Architectural Association in London, has built, in conjunction with the Ruralist painter Graham Ovenden, a house and studio for the artist (**229**). The building resembles a Victorian polychromatic church, with flying buttresses and finials: rather an odd image for a house.

North Elevation

East Elevation

A House in Cornwall for the Ruralist painter G.S. Ovenden ◆ Elevations ◆ Martin Johnson ARIBA AADip, Architect ◆ Beech Cottage, Holmbury St. Mary, Dorking, Surrey ◆ ¼"=1'0" ◆ January '74

▶ **230** YASUFUMI KIJIMA
Matsuo Shrine, Kumamoto,
Japan, 1975–76

sort to a knowing nostalgia, or to the self-conscious, ironic sign of the past in which the ambiguity may defuse the cliché of its cloying power. Such is Fernando Higueras's Ciudad Real City Hall in Spain, a "pre-cast Gothick" building which uses concrete rosettes and repeated rib mullions in an hallucinatory way to pick up local rhythms and signs of the piazza **(228)**.

The master of hallucinatory ornament, however, is Yasufumi Kijima, a Japanese architect who has worked with Le Corbusier's collaborator, Pierre Jeanneret, and with Kenzo Tange, and who has definitely rejected part of this Modernist training. Kijima distorts traditional ornament, which he fabricates by modern means, just enough so that its model is at once recalled and denied. We can recognize what the source is, yet there has been no attempt to copy it

with exactitude. Thus Kijima uses another form of the double meaning inherent in parody: he reduces and intensifies previous architecture, making the allusion dream-like. His Matsuo Shrine is a barrel-vaulted colonnade placed at right angles to an existing Japanese shrine. The traditional upturned roof, *chigi,* and brackets are set against Pantheon-like coffers and a temple colonnade **(230)**. Further details make the building still more unearthly. The concrete columns have thinner proportions than masonry ones, with zigzag capital decorations which recall Art Deco sources; the precisionist arch and machine-tooled cladding give a delirious quality to hand-crafted symbols.

This typical Post-Modern ornament—prefabricated decoration—is obviously the kind which Modernists found unacceptable both because it was not

carved by hand and because it does look brittle. Like much nineteenth-century decor, it looks machine-tooled, impersonal, and notional, not the result of craftsmen expressing their ideas and delight in fabrication. Hence the damnation of similar ornament by John Ruskin and the distaste with which it is regarded by many today. Yet if we stop judging such decoration by pre-industrial canons and start appreciating its positive qualities, we can see that it does share something with the Modernist aesthetic. It has the sharp, pristine, hard-edge quality attained by mechanical control. The exact dimensions of the curved arch and T-shaped capitals make them look as if Mies van der Rohe had designed their forms in steel.

This is one more hallucinatory image within the Matsuo Shrine, together with the unnerving mixture

▲ 231 YASUFUMI KIJIMA
Matsuo Shrine, Kumamoto,
Japan, conceptual drawing,
1976

▼ 232 YASUFUMI KIJIMA
White House, Minami
Azabu, Japan, conceptual
drawing, 1977

of Eastern and Western sources. One can, however, justify such an excessive emphasis on delirious and magical imagery for a building type which conventionally lifts our spirits by seeming to do the impossible. Kijima himself has pointed out an important function of ornament: "One of the major points in style is the ability of ornament within a style to communicate a definite mood."[10] Style and ornament therefore classify an ambience; they set the tone which allows one to read the other meanings in a particular way. To underscore the importance of ornament in creating mood, Kijima provides interpretive drawings, "Making an Image Sketch after the Building is Finished"—if the building continues to inspire him (231–232). These image sketches of buildings floating in a hazy cultural landscape use M.C. Escher's perspective tricks to establish the impossible/

possible. The barrel vault zooms toward us from the oculus of the Pantheon; the flutings of an upside-down Corinthian column turn into a colonnade; viscous sea creatures dissolve into the ornamental capitals. Chiasmus, transformation, hyperrealism are the typical rhetorical figures.

With Kijima's drawings and buildings we have come a long way from the understated revivalism advocated by Jameson and practiced by Fathy and Terry. Style and ornament are recognizably traditional, in fact their hyperrealism accentuates this aspect, but at the same time they are distorted for a particular function and to convey a particular mood. The mood is not nostalgic in a significant sense, but precious, intense, mysterious, and reverent. We pass through levels of parody to reach a feeling of sanctity which has always lain within the orbit of ornament.

It is perhaps characteristic of our time that we have to pass through the trials of kitsch and cliché to arrive at this state. Adornment is usually the monopoly of the cosmetic industry.

NEO-VERNACULAR
THE SIGN OF AN INSTANT COMMUNITY

ONE OF THE CLEAREST REACTIONS AGAINST MODERN architecture, and its planning ideology of comprehensive redevelopment, was the neo-Vernacular movement which arose at more or less the same time in several countries.[1] In the mid-fifties groups in Italy started to design housing developments which mixed vernacular and Modern technologies to recall traditional villages on a larger scale. In Britain, Darbourne & Darke introduced a neo-Vernacular brick style which recalled the picturesque housing of the nineteenth century, again at a greater scale and density (233). This popular alternative to Modernism had caught on in Britain by the seventies to become the accepted approach for most council housing built by the State.[2] One can see its obvious advantages over the slab blocks and building systems approach of Modernism. And we can see that it brought a sense of community which was being eroded by, among other things, the State itself.

The Lillington Street Housing of Darbourne & Darke broke down the scale of the large blocks by varying their profile and surface. Deep balconies with staccato indentations attempted to give a sense of individuality to each flat, while the overall picturesque massing took into account an important brick church on the site, and provided variety and drama—two qualities conspicuously lacking in more Rationalist architecture. But above all, it was the range of functions, the mixed use and mixed ages of the buildings that gave the scheme its significance, an approach which Jane Jacobs was proffering at the time (1961) in her anti-Modernist polemic.[3] Here were corner pubs, an old people's home, a library, and outdoor spaces filled with trees, all merged with mass housing and existing nineteenth-century brick buildings. The mixture of functions provided the continual activity, safety, and economy of village life which was lacking in so many Modern housing estates, while the mixed ages provided a cultural continuity. The scheme's success, relative to other social housing, led even outside England to many variants which developed toward the original vernacular model—whatever it might be.

In England, Maguire and Murray, perceived as the humanist architects of the moment, combined concrete block, pitched roofs, and traditional village scale for colleges as well as housing estates (234). They tried to achieve the qualities of rural stone architecture, which they had studied, with new "vernacular" materials such as the concrete block.[4] Anonymity of craftsmanship, but personalization of each house; wide picture windows, but pitched roof; rationalized layouts and plumbing, but variable massing as if the buildings had been constructed over several years—these were the contradictory signs of neo-Vernacular. The point, apparent to everyone, was that the vernacular was not straight, scholarly, shared by the community or unselfconscious. In pre-industrial societies it had existed, like regionalism,

► **233** DARBOURNE & DARKE, *Lillington Street Housing*, London, England, 1961–68, courtyard

as a consequence of many factors, most of which had disappeared. Now it was being reimposed by architects as the sign of a lost community. No doubt architects of this period shared with parts of society a real desire to recapture a former communal language—such a desire even underlay the Modern Movement—but because the conditions which developed this language had been eroded, architects had to admit that their choice of a communal language was as arbitrary as any other Post-Modern approach. As Oscar Wilde said in another context: "To be natural is such a difficult pose to keep up." In a consumer society, which yearned for roots, it was difficult but financially rewarding.

In America, countless middle-class communities, with their integrated neo-Vernacular and total package of services, were built as exclusive suburban enclaves. Westlake Village outside Los Angeles is an example, but there are so many such villages, built by large developers and medium-size contractors alike, and they are so well known that illustration seems unnecessary, and just a few architect-designed counterparts will be mentioned.

Edward Larrabee Barnes started the fashion in the United States for the monopitch shed aesthetic of the neo-Vernacular. His Haystack Mountain School of Arts and Crafts in Maine (1962), with its allover Shingle Style, or his buildings for St. Paul's School, New Hampshire (1969), and Emma Willard School, Troy, New York (1969), with their allover masonry, show how self-conscious the neo-Vernacular is as a style. The careful composition of picturesque groups, more rigorous exclusion of diverse materials than in actual vernacular, and stark opposition between flat wall and recessed, black-tinted window—these signs mark it as a sophisticated form of naturalness, just as Marie Antoinette's little farmyard at Versailles was distinct from the real thing. Charles Moore and MLTW in their Sea Ranch Condominiums acknowledged the artificial nature of their proposals, and their neo-Vernacular is probably more convincing for this self-consciousness (235). Again, monopitch and shingle, redwood siding and chimney provide the familiar images of home, just as the cluster of buildings provides the image of community (much more apparent than real with these vacation homes). But the sharp rise and fall of profiles, the ad-hoc additions of glazing, and, above all, the Post-Modern interior space show very clearly that this is Vernacular, not vernacular. The influence of Sea Ranch has been widespread, not just on the West Coast, and now there are assortments of monopitched, shingled "ranches" all over the United States.

One of Charles Moore's expressed desires was to create a "sense of place" and avoid the abstract

234 ROBERT MAGUIRE AND KEITH MURRAY *Student Housing Court 3*, University of Surrey, Guildford, England, 1968–70

▼ 235 MOORE LYNDON TURNBULL WHITAKER *Condominium 1*, Sea Ranch, California, 1964–65

space of Modernism, a goal he shared with (and perhaps derived from) European architects and theorists.[5] Christian Norberg-Schulz proposed the importance of a lost "genius loci"[6] and Aldo van Eyck, in attacking the Modernist C.I.A.M. group, proposed the return to a concept of place (1959). His early schemes achieved this sense of place through a Late-Modern extreme articulation, as in his Children's Home in Amsterdam (1957–60), where every functional block and building block was carefully separated. His more recent buildings, designed with Theo Bosch, achieve a greater sense of place by actually using a locally based vernacular, albeit in distorted form. The Zwolle Housing follows the existing, medieval street lines, uses a traditional row-house form, and adds to this balconies, outdoor sheds, and a communal walkway (**236**). The insertion of parking space and the Dutch gable, which is given a flat top, mark this as a recent, not a traditional, scheme. The double coding carries a touch of irony and a considerable amount of *Angst*, from an architect who dislikes explicit historicism. His infill housing and Housing for Single-Parent Families continue this mixture of vernacular and Modern, Dutch brick and De Stijl, Palladian motif and Brutalism (**44–45, 237**).

◄ **236** ALDO VAN EYCK AND THEO BOSCH *Zwolle Housing*, Amsterdam, The Netherlands, 1975–77, house units

▲ **237** ALDO VAN EYCK *Housing for Single-Parent Families*, Amsterdam, The Netherlands, 1976–80

◄ **238** FEILDEN AND MAWSON, *Friars Quay Housing*, Norwich, Norfolk, England, 1972–75, aerial view

► **239** ANDREW DERBYSHIRE OF ROBERT MATTHEW, JOHNSON-MARSHALL AND PARTNERS *Hillingdon Civic Centre*, London, England, 1974–77

In an attack on Post-Modernism which I was privileged to hear (New Orleans, 1979), Van Eyck evinced his contempt for nostalgia, historicism, and the conventional use of decorative elements, and he reaffirmed his commitment to Modernism (by which he meant a celebration of the everyday, egalitarianism, and the "Tradition of the New"). He justified the Palladian window of his Housing for Single-Parent Families on functionalist grounds (it accommodated different height children) and averred a distaste for brick used in a sentimental way.[7] The difference between his statements and his buildings is apparent and it should be emphasized since it is shared by so many architects of his generation. It points to an ideological crisis, far from over, in those who believe in the tenets of Modernism: they wish to establish place and identity in their buildings but have an abhorrence of a traditional and conventional language which might do this. Vernacular provides an acceptable model for design (as it did for Le Corbusier) as long as it is underplayed and unselfconscious. Here lies the poignancy and tension in their work, for, as we have argued, today's conditions only allow neo-Vernacular.

To understand this inherent contradiction is a key to understanding some of the European motivation. The style is offered as a kind of egalitarian necessity: the cheapest way to build acceptably for the masses and a compromise between many supposed determinants among which is the idea that brick is flexible, that it will blend more easily into an existing urban fabric, and that most people can identify with its scale. These sorts of arguments motivated Feilden and Mawson's housing in Norwich (238), which again follows traditional village and house patterns (the North European merchant's house, with an extra floor slipped under the roof). On an institutional level, such arguments also justify the Hillingdon Civic Centre, a veritable collision of pitched roofs and allover brick (239). Here, the architect set out "to design a building that spoke a language of form intelligible to its users (its occupants as well as the citizens of the borough) and used it to say something they wanted to hear . . . Pitched roofs [are] the protective, welcoming element."[8] A study by environmental

psychologists Linda Groat and David Canter called "Does Post-Modernism Communicate?"[9] showed that the Hillingdon Civic Centre communicates its intended meanings very well on the outside, and that non-architects do relate it to the vernacular and traditional building types they know and enjoy. No doubt the omnipresent brick, the picturesque massing, and low-pitched roofs were perceived as welcoming. All this attention to user reaction and the codes of the inhabitants is commendable and, by extension, even more relevant to housing, especially mass housing, where the social meaning of form is most crucial.

Again, a spectrum of attitudes and approaches to the neo-Vernacular can be illustrated to show the mixed attitudes of architects who have left Modernism with reluctance. Edward Cullinan's Westmoreland Road housing scheme mixes a Modernist slab morphology with a traditional walk-up (**241**). Cullinan, like Van Eyck, dislikes the neo-Vernacular label applied to his work and, as can be seen by the details of this housing, keeps one foot in Modernism. The result, characteristically, is the double coding of Post-Modernism: a white, symmetrical block, reminiscent of twenties architecture, is articulated by African

▲ **240** KAZUHIRO ISHII *"54 Roofs" Nursery School*, Okayama, Japan, 1979

▶ **242** ARQUITECTONICA *Spear House*, Miami, Florida (first design Rem Koolhaas, 1975), 1977, aerial view

▶ **243** JEREMY DIXON *St. Mark's Road Housing*, London, England, 1975–80, facade

▼ **241** EDWARD CULLINAN, BRENDAN WOODS, AND SUNAND PRASAD, *Westmoreland Road Flats and Maisonettes*, London, England, 1979

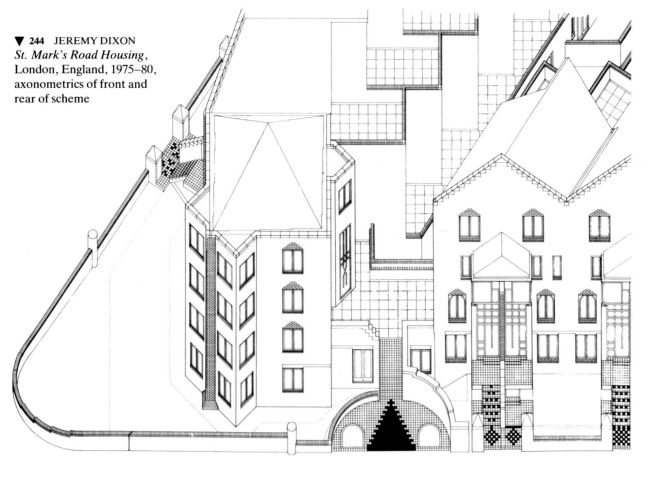

▼ **244** JEREMY DIXON
St. Mark's Road Housing,
London, England, 1975–80,
axonometrics of front and
rear of scheme

But when more complex examples of architecture are analyzed, the limits of the concept are stretched and it becomes less clear. There is a considerable amount of work at this edge of the definition: the rotated, pitched-roof boxes of Piet Blom (**42–43**); the multiplied aedicules of Kazuhiro Ishii (**240**), pitched roofs repeated in ghost form to act as a sign of house (which they are not); a building by the group Arquitectonica based on the local Miami vernacular, but also using the vernacular of twenties Modernism (**242**). If the vernacular one alludes to is itself recent (in the Spear House the stuccoed concrete block, Modern steps, and Miami pinks), the arbitrary nature of *neo*-Vernacular is suddenly clarified. Here the irony of the approach is manifest, for the vernacular is Moderne and Modern; to revive this style of Miami of the twenties is to be at once revivalist and contemporary. The members of the group Arquitectonica, like Rem Koolhaas who influenced their design, are aware of this irony and seek to establish an urban architecture in its image.

The way trends and concepts of Post-Modernism overlap at their edges can be seen in Jeremy Dixon's recent housing in London, which could be regarded as an example of Radical Eclecticism because of the way

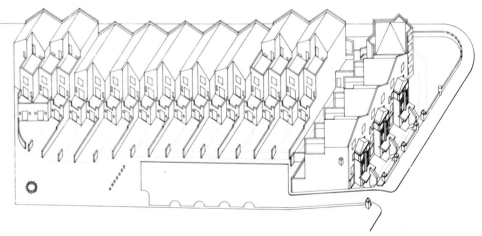

hardwood details, brown-stained window frames, blue-stained balconies with Rietveld lap joints, and protruding rafter ends which give a rural, Italianate profile. Curiously enough, these mixtures of meaning are like those found in nineteenth-century London terrace housing, and in that sense constitute a neo-Vernacular for the area.

Richard MacCormac, Eric Lyons, and Ralph Erskine are three more architects who produce Post-Modern hybrids with variable reluctance. They often like to think of themselves as carrying forward the social message of the Modern Movement, with its basis in rational design, egalitarianism, and straightforwardness, although in fact, like other architects, they have been influenced by fashion and public

opinion toward a style and approach which is quite different from that of their predecessors. Their work is socially conscious, but now in a particular, not general, way: it responds, unconsciously, to the codes of the users. Few of these architects would like to admit to designing in a style, or would admit to acknowledging the tastes of the users, because they believe in a combination of problem-solving and personal expression. Nonetheless, the aesthetic of the inhabitants is incorporated, surreptitiously, within their brand of neo-Vernacular.

Defining neo-Vernacular as a style and movement is easy as long as one confines the view to the most obvious examples of brick or shingle housing, the use of the pitched roof and traditional urban details.

it revives a common language (**243–246**). Like the examples of Dutch neo-Vernacular, this is a traditional type of brick housing, incorporating even Dutch gables and crow-step articulation. As in nineteenth-century Queen Anne Revival, an *English* style is allowed to be eclectically foreign while remaining still recognizably British. Other historicist quotations include Art Deco ziggurats and Rationalist grids, but it is the local contextualism which is most striking.[10]

The scheme accepts the existing street line and setback, the traditional layout (except for a striking diagonal plan generated by the site and quite contrary to traditional patterns), the bay windows of the adjoining Edwardian houses and their emphasis on

▼ 245 JEREMY DIXON
St. Mark's Road Housing,
London, England, 1975–80,
lower ground-floor plan and
section

▶ 246 JEREMY DIXON
St. Mark's Road Housing,
London, England, 1975–80,
oblique street view

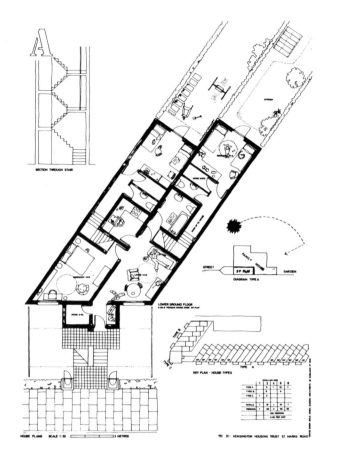

stairway, door, and front step (the stairs lead to two front doors or down to a small flat). Thus the inhabitants can recognize their traditional language and requirements through stereotypes used in a relatively straightforward way, as stock as the London brick of which the scheme is built. But then, on further inspection, there are meanings in a more esoteric code which are more accessible to the architect, or to the inhabitant who cares to search for them: the physiognomic visage with the stare of the face now divided between two houses; the repetition of the aedicules in each entry unit (the little house is an image of domesticity which goes back to ancient Greece and which has signified homestead ever since); the stained glass and color syncopations in blues and greens which identify each house; the aedicular entrance gates which hide garbage cans. Indeed, the aedicule becomes the main theme, which is given further variations in the roof and windows.

This scheme, then, shows a richer set of meanings than most neo-Vernacular, and a deflection of the style's pathos: rather than the instant community which is evoked so hopefully elsewhere, the scheme implies a continuity of communities, a reaching back to existing social groups and outward to new ones. It speaks of a London one hundred years old, and reaches back further to more primitive patterns without becoming nostalgic. The straight detailing and realistic treatment of every element has a sober elegance which is honest without being Brutalist.

8

AD HOC
AND URBANIST
TOWARD A CITY WITH MEMORY

A CHARACTERISTIC DEFICIENCY OF MODERN CITY planning which Modern architects themselves pointed out, *late* in their careers, was its inability to provide images of cultural continuity. The building of New Towns in Britain, or whole new cities like Chandigarh in India and Brasilia in Brazil had revealed a recurrent problem evident to architect, planner, and citizen alike: the new creation, however imaginative, was oversimplified and lacked the complexity of life and the continuity with the past which any old, bungled city, with all its faults, possessed. The failures were inevitable for a new city or town, but the problem of rootlessness was exacerbated by Modernist theory. C.I.A.M., the official organ of the Modern Movement, had in the twenties proffered a *tabula rasa* approach toward planning, which included the division of the city into major functional blocks, a dis-

regard for existing patterns and buildings, and a dislike of historicizing architecture. When the reaction to such city destruction set in and people started criticizing the *tabula rasa* of Modernists and developers, the architects were not equipped with a theoretical answer. All they could do, lamely, was to propose that the new city should have a "heart" or "core," a downtown center full of bustling citizens; but they went on largely as before, designing superblocks with parks threaded through them, cores with the "new space concept" fragmenting this core apart, hearts which had no clear, recognizable image.[1] Even Team Ten, the breakaway party of C.I.A.M., could not altogether fashion a new theory to provide the qualities of identity and place which they were themselves demanding. They kept the anti-historicist bias of the Modernists, substituting, it is true, a host of "webs," "grids," and small-scale "infrastructures" for the functional separation and large-scaled superblocks.[2] These modifications were not enough to change the theory and practice of urbanism. Only piecemeal, and through many diverse contributions, has that theory begun to change and, inevitably, at an urban scale, practice lags far behind to await culmination in the eighties. We will look at many of these contributions in turn, commencing at a modest scale with architects who fashion houses ad hoc from the fragments of past and present systems.

Bruce Goff, like the turn-of-the-century Catalan architect Antoni Gaudí before him, is an architect

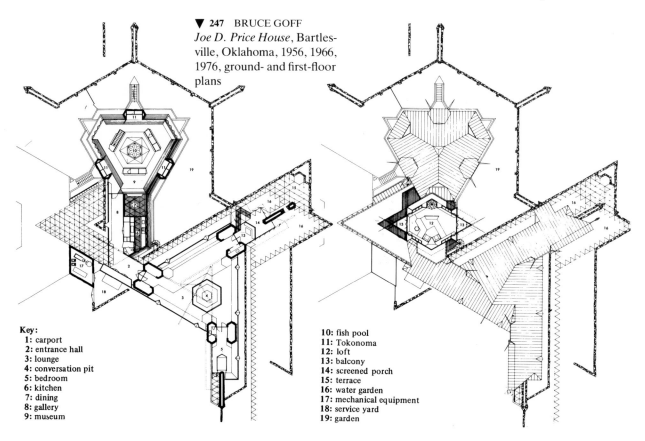

▼ 247 BRUCE GOFF
Joe D. Price House, Bartlesville, Oklahoma, 1956, 1966, 1976, ground- and first-floor plans

Key:
1: carport
2: entrance hall
3: lounge
4: conversation pit
5: bedroom
6: kitchen
7: dining
8: gallery
9: museum

10: fish pool
11: Tokonoma
12: loft
13: balcony
14: screened porch
15: terrace
16: water garden
17: mechanical equipment
18: service yard
19: garden

pletely absorbed reverberant sounds so that one's perception of space was altered and the experience was basically that of an enveloping womb. Contrasting with this was a masculine, rugged exterior of rubble masonry, and crystal, blue glass cutlet—all discarded materials.

This exotic environment inevitably changed when Price married a Japanese woman, Etsuko, and started to build up an important collection of Japanese screens and paintings. Extensions, studios, bathing areas, and museum space were added in a way which recalls the Emperor Hadrian's additions to his pleasure villa, built as a coll age of Greek, Egyptian, and Roman set pieces. Pure geometric shapes, variants of the triangle and hexagon, or prismatic volumes, were collaged into each other in a picturesque manner. This mixture of geometric perfection and incident is, as we will see, a mark of the new urbanism, and Hadrian's Villa has become one of its models.

who builds with traditional materials and with those outside the usual repertoire of architectural practice.[3] Many of his works, such as the Bavinger House in Norman, Oklahoma (1950–55), use both materials found in the area—rubble masonry, trees that have to be cut down—and those from non-architectural sources—biplane braces, a bomber-blister for a light globe, and oil-drilling pipes. The cost of such assemblies is often well below that of usual construction, partly because the material is cheap or trade surplus and partly because the owners in this case charged admission for people to watch the house under construction—and fifty thousand customers thereby helped pay for it.

Such ad-hoc assemblies are not only strange and quite beautiful, but they also have a density of meaning and reference which Modernist constructions, using only one or two building systems, lack. History, time, and place are literally built into them. The Joe D. Price House, built over several years in Bartlesville, Oklahoma, shows this richness of reference (**247–249, 251**). Originally in 1956 the scheme was designed as the ultimate bachelor's pad, a retreat in the countryside which was intended to be unconventional. As Price said, it was "an escape from business . . . Away from the stifling blanket of false morality."[4] To characterize these intentions, Goff designed a very thick-pile carpet (four inches deep) which covered many surfaces including some walls and the sunken conversation pit—placed beneath a skylight filled with "plastic rain" and white goose feathers (stuck into latex cement!). This mixture of the exotic and the ordinary actually created a tactile environment which was quite different from anything designed before: the carpet and goose feathers com-

◀ **250** DAVID SELLERS
AND JOHN MALLERY
Design Center, Goddard College, Plainfield,
Vermont, 1970

▶ **251** BRUCE GOFF
Joe D. Price House Addition, Bartlesville, Oklahoma, 1976, Japanese bath

individual spaces and individual functions and at the same time he seeks to bring the scale of his reduced volumes into a Modern spatial continuity through the use of colour, port-hole windows, and roof lights. Others are doing similar things. In all this mannered complexity Walker is essentially one half Modern and one half Post-Modern . . ."[9]

John Johansen achieves an even greater fragmentation and identification of parts in his Mummers Theater in Oklahoma City (**254–255**). This was designed, on the analogy of electronic circuitry, as a series of connections between "components and sub-components" which were neither composed nor related in a classical sense.[10] Rather, functional parts —two theaters, a silver-painted cooling tower, red steel circulation tubes, etc.—were attached so that each kept a maximum identity in color and form. Again, ad-hoc components and down-market materials were used: light steel framing, plain wood decking, raw concrete, corrugated steel. In part, this resulted in a Late-Modern image of plug-in technology, the Archigram image from which it is derived; but its improvisatory relationship of pure forms is again reminiscent of Hadrian's Villa and the theory of "Collage City" developed by Colin Rowe in the late seventies.

Johansen's pyramidal house for himself combines the ad-hocist approach with a symbolic one to produce a clearer opposition between the archetypal and changing (**256–257**). The flat-topped pyramid, an obvious sign of centeredness, covers what Johansen describes as a "neolithic cave"—comprising the fireplace, pool, and rock garden—signs of dwelling which deserve a special importance and permanence. Against this is a very light, ship-like aesthetic of rigs, tackle, steel frame, cables, and sixty-four attachment points which allow decks to hang out in different ways, or allow the surface to be tuned to the prevailing weather conditions. The contrasts of natural materials and rubble masonry remind one of Goff's interiors, while the elegant, lightweight technology recalls Charles Eames's ad-hocist house for himself in Santa Monica (1949). These images, combined with more archetypal ones explicitly derived from Carl Jung and the towers he built for himself, give the design a dimension in time which the technological image alone denies.

Ralph Erskine is another architect trained, like Johansen, in the Modern Movement, who has modi-

---

The Price House absorbs into its geometrical figures a corresponding diversity of references: decorative details reminiscent of Gustav Klimt's jewel-like paintings, American Indian finials, television aerials, and Japanese hot tubs. The perfection of the prismatic shapes is shattered as planes intersect and one material passes through another.[5] To keep the Japanese screens from cracking, humidity is provided by a pool in the center of the living space. Its transparent, plastic bottom allows a shimmering light through to the Japanese bath located directly below it, a bath whose tiles take up the abstract, crystalline forms overhead. Thus from triangular plan to prismatic decoration, from refined art to consumer kitsch, a series of brilliant interrelationships is established.

This ad-hoc approach has been extended to a large scale by architects such as David Sellers, Roger Walker, John Johansen, Ralph Erskine, and Lucien Kroll.[6] David Sellers and John Mallery directed students in building a design center and sculpture studio at Goddard College.[7] Here, used window and door elements were absorbed into the shed aesthetic to produce a very rich mixture of shapes that also had linkages across time—both with traditional clapboard houses and vernacular classicism (**250**). Like the "woodbutcher's art" which produced thousands of personalized shacks across the United States, or the idiosyncratic concoctions of Clarence Schmidt,

this self-built environment broke all sorts of syntactic rules, including, for example, the placement and consistency of windows. The fragmented results are rather like populist versions of Michael Graves's works, a *pot au feu* to which a lot of ingredients are gradually added rather than the premeditated *bouillabaisse* which is characteristic of Graves.

Roger Walker, a young New Zealand designer who had completed eighty private houses, a shopping precinct, and an airport building by his thirty-fifth birthday, uses the ad-hoc method of design to give maximum identity to different room spaces.[8] He fragments a house or larger building into many small, pitched-roof spaces, exaggerating the scale of structural members—the timber posts and diagonal struts —and then juxtaposing them with vigorous curves which have historical overtones (**252–253**). Like Bruce Goff and Osamu Ishiyama, Walker takes the sewer pipe out of its lowly station in life and uses it in a new way, for example, as a window. Also like them he uses standard junctions in some areas so that the builder can work without continual supervision. As Russell Walden has written: "Walker uses the High Victorian language of steeply pitched roofs, finials and criss-cross bracing juxtaposed against Modern Movement motifs such as port-hole windows, domed roof lights and drooping roof standards. Further, in planning terms Walker uses the High Victorian device of dividing the domestic scene into

fied a Rationalist and technical approach toward a more meaningful, expressive one based on ad hocism, or the combination of past and present systems.[11] His most well-known design, the "Byker Wall" in New-castle, shows his unmistakable, informal aesthetic, even though it was designed in consultation with the eventual inhabitants (**258–259**). Like Charles Moore's participatory work mentioned previously, there is a fruitful interaction between the skills and biases of the designer and the desires of the users. This inter-action gives the form a deeper conviction and mean-ing than it would have had as an abstract exercise, as can be seen from a comparison with Erskine's other housing.

At Byker, the site is shaped into a series of public spaces and outdoor gardens which are organized, like a typical English garden, to give variety and a sense of surprise. The spatial sequence winds through small piazzas, tight pedestrian streets, and parking areas to culminate in an informal garden under the grand wall. Here, a pergola wraps around to one side, while classical fragments left from previous buildings are used as seats. The "ruin in the garden" has its counterpart in the "factory and swimming baths in the wall"—nineteenth-century buildings which are restored and incorporated as part of this noise buf-fer. The outside of the wall is an ad-hoc assemblage of various colors and patterns of brick, small win-dows, brightly painted air-conditioning units, and

blue shed roofs. Erskine, even more than Johansen, feels that his informal aesthetic works best when he does not try to compose it according to an *a priori* idea. On the garden side of the wall, this picturesque approach works well in breaking down the massive scale and giving identity to individual apartments. Exterior walkways and rest areas, as well as balconies, use green-stained wooden members that have the rickety quality of a shanty town. This increases the sense of place, even as it somewhat undermines one's sense of security. The Byker community has been helped by this housing, probably the best public housing in Britain, and the Erskine team's partici-patory endeavor, despite its faults, remains the stand-ard for other schemes.

Lucien Kroll's participatory architecture is even more ad hoc than Moore's and Erskine's. In his Para-medical Faculty Buildings for the University of Louvain near Brussels (**260–261**), he and the students have designed an urban equivalent of Bruce Goff's work, or that of the "woodbutchers."[12] Here, one aesthetic system slams into the next, or elides with it quite delicately; here an Italian hill town sits on a ski lodge which nestles up to a glass-and-steel office building to turn into a rubble canyon. The *pot au feu* has become a *potpourri* and, in a positive way, this gives a sense of place and multiple meaning so lacking in New Towns. In a negative way, of course, the scheme is a remorseless jumble that makes one

That is, it could incorporate "vest-pocket utopias—Swiss canton, New England village, Dome of the Rock, Place Vendome, Campidoglio, the set pieces of totalistic ideologies, without having to put up with their inherent totalitarianism." The resultant morphology could best be represented in figure-ground city maps which showed, like Nolli's plan, a relation of private to public which was roughly four to one. Modern planning, on the other hand, set monuments in a park, or more likely, in a parking lot, so that the fabric was destroyed and the set piece had nothing with which to contrast.

This urban doctrine of Rowe and others developed piecemeal from many sources. The interest in Hadrian's Villa as a model for urbanism started to be enunciated by Louis Kahn, O.M. Ungers, and Sigfried Giedion: that is, Modernists who were changing their direction. O.M. Ungers and J. Sawade designed a student hostel in 1963 which had the Hadrianic

long for a contrasting order, an easy-going normality. But to stress its positive side and contribution to the theme of this chapter, it shows what participation can do to bring a sense of time and memory to a new city. The construction workers, who were given their head every now and then, created various metaphors —tree, roots, growing wall—which help locate parts of the project with a striking image. The student teams, who laid out the mixed functions, added their skills to those of the designer: the apartments are all different, and the sculptural groups, which they made, provide the anthropomorphic imagery common to traditional building. Seen as a direct result of the student uprisings of May '68, the scheme's excesses have created a reaction and Kroll's team has been dropped by the Catholic university authorities. This is a pity since, given his participatory beliefs and gentle character, Kroll might have finished the scheme in a sympathetic manner.

During the early sixties many architects and theorists started looking at Hadrian's Villa for its morphological implications and its eclecticism, its collage of set pieces and its palimpsest of meaning.[13] What they found to be of interest was the mixture of geometric form and accident, formal set piece and informality, axial planning and the picturesque, foreground and background, monument and infill—in short, the set of dualities which were to be summarized and turned into the theory of "Collage City"

▲ 254 JOHN JOHANSEN
Mummers Theater, Oklahoma City, 1970

▶ 255 JOHN JOHANSEN
Mummers Theater, Oklahoma City, 1970, stage-level plan

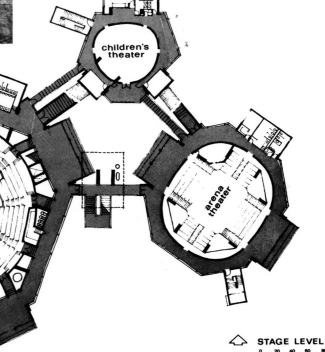

STAGE LEVEL
0 20 40 60 80

by Colin Rowe.[14] The idea of Collage City was dualism itself, an incorporation of opposed qualities which Modern city planning in its utopian, or totalistic phase, had denied. Thus there was a place for utopian, or ideal, urban form, in fragments, set within a background of private buildings, or urban *poché*.

Besides Hadrian's Villa, Giambattista Nolli's plan of Rome (1748) was a model for such urban morphology. As Rowe pointed out, the collage technique had the further advantage of "permitting us the enjoyment of utopian poetics without our being obliged to suffer the embarrassment of utopian politics."[15]

oppositions between monument and infill, and circular public realm and rectilinear background (262). Subsequent influential projects by Ungers continued to develop this dualistic morphology. A scheme for the Tiergarten Museum in West Berlin (1965) introduced the notion of traditional, archetypal patterns—"streets, squares, arcades, corner accents." A study for placing new housing in the old town of Marburg in West Germany resulted in thirteen different models—all variations of the traditional, vertical house without, specifically, copying its style (263). As Ungers pointed out, the identity of old Marburg

257 JOHN JOHANSEN
Johansen House II, Stanfordville, New York, 1974

▼ 258 RALPH ERSKINE
"Byker Wall," Newcastle-upon-Tyne, England, 1972–74, exterior wall

▶ 259 RALPH ERSKINE
"Byker Wall," Newcastle-upon-Tyne, England, 1972–74, garden side

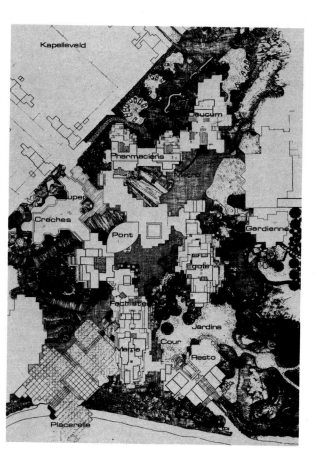

◀ 256 JOHN JOHANSEN
Johansen House II, Stanfordville, New York, 1974, interior

▶ 260 LUCIEN KROLL
AND ATELIER, *Paramedical Faculty Buildings Complex*, University of Louvain, Woluwe, Belgium, 1970–77

▶ 261 LUCIEN KROLL
AND ATELIER, *Paramedical Faculty Buildings Complex*, University of Louvain, Woluwe, Belgium, 1970–77, site plan

consists in the variety and contrast of its house types, and it is this pattern which he has sought to capture in a vertical morphology sympathetic to the context.[16]

Ricardo Bofill and his Taller de Arquitectura have actually built urban schemes which, to a degree, realize aspects of Collage City.[17] Their Barrio Gaudí is composed from sets of housing clusters which form a background around more public places (**264**). Here the neo-Vernacular of pitched roofs and pantiles is used to shape traditional urban space with a difference—the difference being a roof promenade and cheap, concrete-frame construction. But present are the equivalents of the streets, arcades, and squares of old cities, as well as their urban grain.

More recently, Bofill has turned to historicism and the old idea of the palace, specifically Versailles, as a model for public housing. This concept, which the social utopians of the nineteenth century also proposed, produces the ultimate set piece, the "building as monument" favored by Modernism. But the scale of Bofill's Arcades du Lac scheme is so large and flat, and the surface so broken up and ornamental, that the building can also be read as background (**265–266**). This "Versailles for the people" incorporates the expected symmetry and *parterres* of its model, and adds other historical dimensions which root it across time and French culture.[18] Some corners are turned into giant, suggested columns; as in the schemes of Claude-Nicolas Ledoux, these are meant to engage the mind through their amplification. Ceramic and concrete, used in four shades of earth colors, define a vertical morphology which is reminiscent of the traditional French street: large entrance bay, almost an arcade; pronounced *piano nobile* and second floor; and small attic and balustrade. The rhythmical system also recalls Versailles.

Bofill and other Barcelona architects such as Martorell Bohigas Mackay were loosely associated with the Rationalist movement of architecture, a movement started by Aldo Rossi and Leon Krier in the sixties which partly revived Italian Rationalism of the late twenties.[19] This movement was divided between the practice of contextualism, which we will consider shortly, and abstract Modernism, and had centers in Berlin, Paris, New York, Milan, Venice, Rome, Brussels, and Barcelona. With the extraordinary work of Bofill—the giant housing blocks Xanadu (1966–67) in Calpe, Spain, and Walden 7 (1970–75) in Barcelona which were as though lifted out of a city context and stuck like Surrealist *objets trouvés* in a stark, rocky landscape—the movement became a type of Surrationalism. The buildings' simplicity and organizational logic were rational, while their image and scale were surreal. This unlikely compound was quite effective.

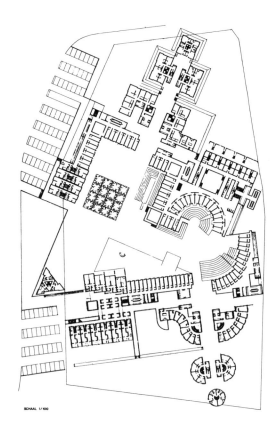

▲ **262** O.M. UNGERS AND J. SAWADE, *Student Hostel Competition Project*, Berlin, West Germany, 1963, plan

▲ **263** O.M. UNGERS *Marburg Housing Project*, West Germany, 1976, axonometrics of four possible models

▼ **264** RICARDO BOFILL AND TALLER DE ARQUITECTURA, *Barrio Gaudí*, Reus, Spain, 1964–70

◀ **265** RICARDO BOFILL AND TALLER DE ARQUI-TECTURA, *Les Arcades du Lac*, Saint-Quentin-en-Yvelines, France, 1975–81

▼ **266** RICARDO BOFILL AND TALLER DE ARQUI-TECTURA, *Les Arcades du Lac*, Saint-Quentin-en-Yvelines, France, 1975–81, facade detail

The most convincing examples of Surrationalism, besides Bofill's architecture, are the projects of OMA (Office for Metropolitan Architecture).[20] Elia and Zoe Zenghelis's Hotel Sphinx, for instance, mixes several urban types with the barely visible image of an animal, perhaps a sphinx (**268**). The legs are escalators, the tails are twin towers, the head that "turns and stares" at important civic events is a health club, the whole animal is a "luxury hotel designed as a model for mass-housing." This might be any one of the Hyatt Hotels, the slick-tech monoliths of Portman which we have looked at, except that it is considerably more colorful and witty. In its mixture of real urban functions and existing urban fantasies it summarizes the current tendencies toward Surrationalism, on both the commercial and artistic planes. Like other anthropomorphic buildings, it animates

potentially overpowering large-scale form. Rem Koolhaas, the ultimate Surrationalist, shows with the designs in his book *Delirious New York* (1978) the poetry behind the mixture of logic and commercial dreams.[21] His rational fantasies consist in taking artificiality, the second nature of the modern city, and its urban congestion to an extreme (**267**). Rationalist grids, skyscrapers, and movement systems are mixed with groundscrapers, buildings with heads, and an architectural shipwreck (symbolizing New York after Modernism dealt it a near-fatal blow). On another level, Koolhaas seeks to revive the tradition of the Chrysler Building, Rockefeller Center, and the Waldorf-Astoria Hotel, all protagonists in the "culture of congestion."

The Rationalists, unlike Surrationalists Bofill and Koolhaas, keep their Surrealist references in the background, as a decoration to sensible rehabilitation schemes. Josef Paul Kleihues, a German Rationalist who has designed several urban block types,[22] will adopt the pyramid form for an old city museum, but underplay the potent imagery with details, such as cross-bracing and half-timbering, that relate to the local vernacular (**269**). Leon Krier will stitch together the medieval and Baroque fabric of a city being destroyed by Modernism and developers with a contextual formal type; but then various Surrealist signs— a hot-air balloon reminiscent of Ivan Leonidov's schemes, a biplane and other twenties allusions—will add a striking contrast (**270**). Other revolutionist images can be found scattered through his drawings, for instance the billowing curtains hanging from a concrete frame indicating the winds of change sweeping through architecture or society. Paintings of the Oath of the Tennis Court, the starting point for the French Revolution of 1789, are a possible reference. Images from De Chirico paintings, which fascinate all the Rationalists, and the line drawings of Le Corbusier and the Constructivists are further sources.[23]

These images are, however, somewhat gratuitous given the Rationalists' basic desire to make a unified harmony out of the city. In his Echternach projects Leon Krier inserts a traditional arcade and circus, using the existing morphology of the eighteenth century to tie the new with the medieval. Height, scale, silhouette, and building materials are all compatible with previous buildings, although accentuated to give a new emphasis to the *res publica*. It is this emphasis which can be thought of as revolutionary in the old European sense of revolution (to revolve back to a better past); inevitably a classicist past as it was in the late eighteenth century.

Leon Krier, in an extraordinary outburst of city drawings reminiscent of Le Corbusier's unsolicited plans, has provided urban icons which are meant to stimulate political, architectural action. He has drawn seductive aerial views of London, Echternach, Rome, Bremen, Barcelona, and Luxembourg which concerned citizens are meant to use against those who would continue comprehensive Modern redevelopment. These views, like eighteenth-century tourist maps, are critical tools, *aide-mémoires* of what the city was, and finally counterschemes to stop that insidious marriage between speculators and Modernists. No urban authority has yet intervened to commission a Krier "mend and modify job," just as no authority commissioned Le Corbusier for thirty years, but his influence has nonetheless been extensive and, like that of ARAU, the Brussels group with whom the Rationalists have teamed up, it has been enough to deflect some of the more destructive plans.

Leon Krier's most poetic intervention in terms of imagery is his modification of the 1748 Nolli plan of Rome, an intervention supported by Mayor Giulio Carlo Argan after the exhibition "Roma Interrotta" (1978), which included eleven other architects' proposals for the city.[24] Krier had reinvented Abbé Laugier's "primitive hut" of columns and triangular roof trusses, but here each column is the size of an eight-story tower, and the pyramidal roof encloses an awesome public realm—a cross between a train shed and an open-air market (**271**). The drawings, when seen collaged into the Roman perspectives of Piranesi, actually stand up to the latter's grand and disturbing images (**272**). The buildings have the breadth of scale and the heavy gestural quality typical of the Roman tradition. Krier's projected buildings consist of three basic types: square, semi-circular, and triangular sheds inserted respectively into the center of Rome, the end of the Piazza Navona, and the open end of the Piazza San Pietro—a triangular wedge thrusting toward St. Peter's Cathedral (and actually a rather Modern completion when compared with those offered by others since 1660). The triangular shed, like the others, is a new social center meant to revive and support a local form of civic organization, the *rione*, an alternative to the centralized bureaucracy, church, and *municipio*. It would have restaurants, clubs, rooms for games, and large top-floor studios for artists. These craftsmen of the new grass-roots democracy would "work on the adornment of their *rione*. Their creative work will naturally spread (in final stages of elaboration) into the square, and for short periods these spaces will be filled with some vast fresco or sculpture before they are taken to their location."[25]

Here we have a typical "vest-pocket utopia," a form of syndicalist organization incorporated into the existing fabric, both formally and politically. The idea, as Krier makes clear, is to revive the *res publica* and create new civic institutions to support it, ones on a par with the seventeenth-century churches of Rome (which would be, ironically, according to Krier, converted back to their origins, into *thermae*!).

If Krier's social idealism is realistic, "embarrassing" (as Rowe would term it), and unrealized, the Rationalists have nonetheless built small, imperfect versions of their white, utopian dreams. Georgia Benamo and Christian de Portzamparc have completed a small urban scheme on the edge of Paris, the Rue des Hautes-Formes (**274**). The scheme inevitably seeks to create "the street, the square, the urban place" with that density or congestion beloved by the Rationalists. Modernist tower and slab blocks are combined into a new type and given a Post-Modern formal treatment with cutout screens *à la* Moore, false hanging arches to signify entry *à la* Venturi, and a variety of window treatment *à la mode*. This last is justified as an attempt to "keep a thousand windows from watching you," the many eyes of the scheme from seeming oppressively large and homogeneous (three types of window are used behind a screen wall). If there are Rationalist doubts concerning the results, they focus on the leaky space, the small size of the piazza and *res publica,* and the rather neutralized relation of solid to void, urban *poché* to monument (the scheme lacks monuments).

Robert Krier, the older brother of Leon, has in a series of drawings and paintings lovingly re-created images of the lost public realm. Focusing most often on the arcaded piazza, his designs recapture the closure and centeredness which are common to most European squares of the past, rendered with a timeless abstraction at once classical and Surrealist. The Krier brothers have revived, or recuperated as they say in Europe, almost all the classical urban forms thrown out by the Modern Movement. Robert Krier has made countless morphological studies of existing historic cities, published in his book *Urban Space*,[26] which show the importance of crescents, arcades, streets, and squares—"universals" that he not surprisingly uses to stitch together the disrupted fabric. In a series of before-and-after drawings, like those of the landscape gardener Humphrey Repton, Krier shows what particular advantage can be had by reinventing and then adding the old elements to a destroyed city center, such as that of Stuttgart (**273**). Other Rationalists, such as Roderigo Pérez de Arce, fill up the empty spaces in the Modern cities of Oscar Niemeyer and Le Corbusier, doubling the density, increasing the "culture of congestion," as Rem Koolhaas terms it. Robert Krier has, with the aid of these designers, reconstructed parts of Berlin using his favorite device of the urban block (**275–**

▼ 267 REM KOOLHAAS
Welfare Palace Hotel Project, 1976–77, painting

▲ 268 ELIA AND ZOE
ZENGHELIS, *Hotel Sphinx
Project*, New York City,
1975, painting

◄ 269 J.P. KLEIHUES
(with R. HAUSER)
Blankenheim Museum,
West Germany, 1976–81,
perspective

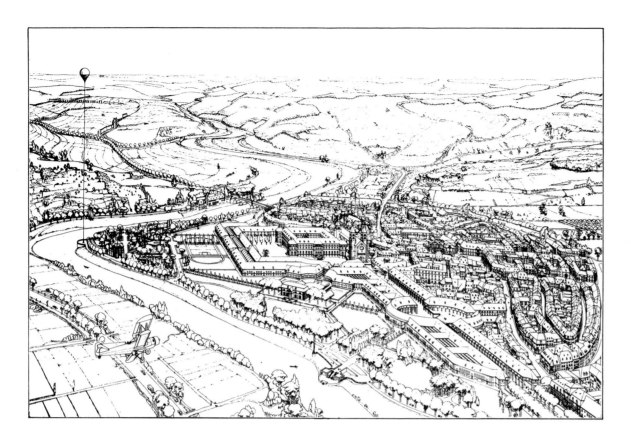

276). Again, the public realm is not as pronounced as he would like it, for economic reasons; but the communal nature of the symbolism and the notion of defensive closure, of a nineteenth-century block, can be felt.

Several of the urban ideas we have looked at come together in the writings of Aldo Rossi. His book *L'Architettura della Città* (1966) and later articles develop notions concerning the importance of memory in the city, and in particular the idea that monuments crystallize this memory. This concept struck at a nerve ending of Modernism, which had attacked the idea of the monument, or wished to turn public housing into monuments (if there had to be some). Rossi, quite polemically, put forward Stalinist monuments as exemplary models to follow—the very sub-classicist piles that were anathema to the Modernists. And as if to make things more contentious, and complex, Rossi himself (and his major apologist Manfredo Tafuri) defends designs which have a minimum of contextual association. They are almost twenties Modernism stripped of all memories save that of this ahistorical movement.

▲ 270 LEON KRIER
Lycée Classique Project,
Echternach, Luxembourg,
1970, aerial perspective

▶ 271 LEON KRIER
*Triangular Civic Building
Project*, Piazza San
Pietro, Rome, Italy, 1977,
perspective

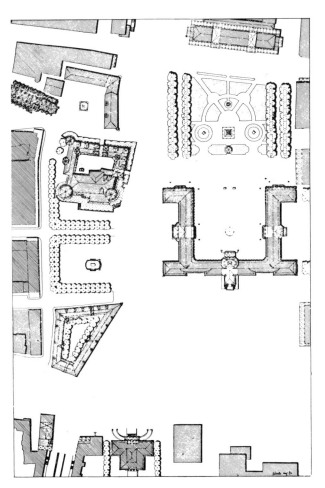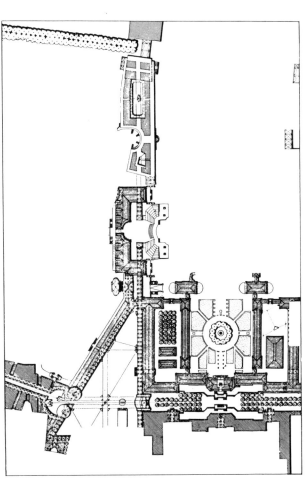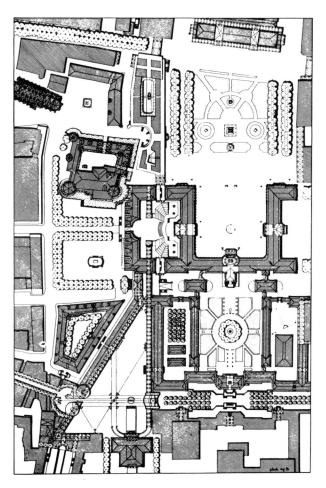

272 LEON KRIER
Semi-circular Civic Building Project, Piazza Navona, Rome, Italy, 1977, perspective

▼ **273** ROB KRIER
Stuttgart Reconstruction Project, plans of present state, proposed additions, and the integration of proposed buildings with the existing environment

◀ 275 ROB KRIER
Ritterstrasse Housing,
Berlin, West Germany,
1978–80, model

▼ 277 ALDO ROSSI
Elementary School Library,
Fagnano Olona, Italy,
1972–76

◀ 274 GEORGIA BENAMO
AND CHRISTIAN DE
PORTZAMPARC, *Rue des
Hautes-Formes*, Paris,
France, 1975–79

▼ 276 ROB KRIER
Ritterstrasse Housing,
Berlin, West Germany,
1978–80, axonometric

Such paradoxes are at the basis of Rossi's approach, and one must thread a way through them with agility to understand his positive contributions.[27] As mentioned, Rossi was instrumental in turning architects' attention back to city morphology and the way in which the city and its monuments form a collective memory. Street, arcade, piazza, and monument: these familiar Rationalist types reappeared in his work along with "the constant elements of architecture"—the column, architrave, hall, roof—that is, Laugier's basic elements. Their reappearance was transformed by new technologies—basically white, planar reinforced concrete—and Rossi's particular, indeed peculiar, fascination with Lombardy farmhouses, barns, and anonymous structures.

Thus, although memory of the traditional city is invoked, it is subtly displaced toward a primitive Modernism. Rossi's contribution to the Gallaratese neighborhood in Milan is a case in point: for him it recalls Italian arcades and the traditional street, whereas for the working-class community it may recall mass housing and the Fascist stripped classi-cism of the thirties. His library for an elementary school in Fagnano Olona recalls the institutional neoclassicism of Ledoux and Boullée on one level, and again unfortunate memories of prison and concentration camp on another (**277**). Rossi's misapprehension of popular codes of architecture mark him as a Late-Modernist, whereas his theory of city memory has contributed to the Post-Modern notion of the contextual city.

All his schemes approach the condition of the grave and the monument; his most influential, for Modena Cemetery, is in fact both a giant mausoleum and an urban landmark (**278**). Laid out as a series of primary elements organized on a grid, adopting an axial approach which focuses on "the house of the dead" and a stark cone-shaped funnel, the cemetery provides a memorable image for death. Black shadows replace windows to create a striking simulacrum of a burnt-out ruin; empty piazzas with long shadows evoke the silent urban spaces and metaphysical loneliness of De Chirico's paintings. The finality of these images might be appropriate to death, although one could argue for the celebration of life in a cemetery. In any case, all Rossi's buildings seem like an illustration of Viennese architect Adolf Loos's statement that architecture resides in the monument and grave, and they depend for their power on the striking incongruity of evoking images of death for life. No doubt these images are so powerful in their reduction to essentials, that, like a bad nightmare, they really do stay in the mind. This unforgettable aspect of Rossi's images must even be granted by the not inconsiderable number of people who actively hate his work.

Rossi's scheme for a floating theater in Venice (281) ties the omnipresent silence of death with more cheerful images of city monuments: we can find the echo of a Renaissance theater (from which it was derived), a medieval flag-topped tower, and the resemblance to a blue dome (it has been moored near the great dome of Santa Maria della Salute). To be able to add a dignified yet modest monument, based as it is on wood frame and scaffolding construction, to this picturesque city is a considerable achievement. As the floating box moves pertly through the canals, it recalls the blue skies of Bellini and the far-off victories of the Venetian pirates—memories which were perhaps in Rossi's mind when he designed it.

The architect whose work summarizes so many of the trends we have discussed in this chapter—the ad-hoc use of various systems past and present, the collage of geometrical set pieces, a contextual approach to urban fabric, and finally city memory—is James Stirling.[28] In his Meineke Strasse Project for Berlin, for instance, he has proposed an ad-hoc attachment to an open space, itself the result of aerial bombardment of a huge parking garage and of Modern planning schemes. Onto this desolate structure Stirling attaches a thin fabric of shops and urban tissue (279–280). He takes the scale and picturesque variety of the remaining houses on the block and manipulates these forms so that they undergo a type of development analogous to the sonata-allegro form in music. Reading from left to right down the street and around the corner, we can see a pattern of introduction, exposition, development, recapitulation, and coda. Bow windows, doorways, and roof exit become the musical themes which are transformed in each section. A thin row of shops only a few feet

▲ 278 ALDO ROSSI
(with G. BRAGHIERI)
Modena Cemetery Competition Project, Italy, 1971, perspective of first design

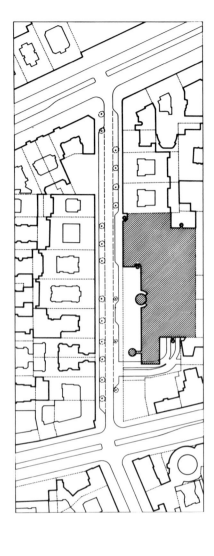

▼ 279   JAMES STIRLING
Meineke Strasse Project,
Berlin, West Germany,
1976, plans of prewar street,
postwar development, and
remedial proposal

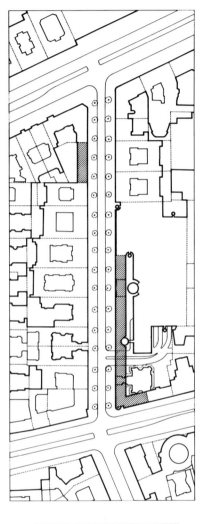

▼ 280   JAMES STIRLING
Meineke Strasse Project,
Berlin, West Germany,
1976, projections of existing
and proposed frontages

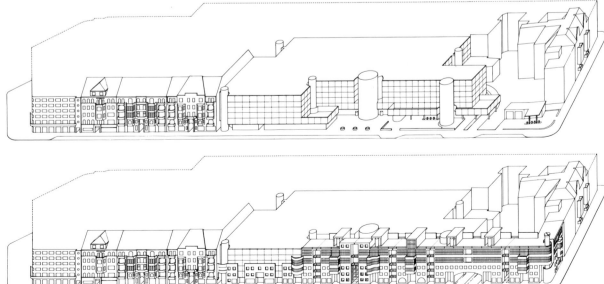

deep, like the attachments onto the wall at the Hrad-cany in Prague, gives way to deeper buildings which allow the garage to play in counterpoint. These themes reach a crescendo with the "hinge" that turns the corner, and then return to a more sedate and contextual rhythm to match that of the adjacent street. Because Stirling is more committed to architecture as a language than many other designers using an ad-hoc aesthetic, his schemes are more highly ordered and syncopated than theirs.

His Staatsgalerie New Building and Chamber Theater in Stuttgart is, like his other German projects, an essay in urban contextualism (**282–283**). The scheme picks up formal cues from the surrounding environment—in this case the height and grain of adjacent buildings, and the basic axial relationships to the main street. From the entrance axis a sequence of space is layered frontally and at right angles to movement; as in a Rationalist building the grid is felt conceptually throughout, although one is forced to move around it in circles and diagonals. Thus a basic dualism is set up between rectilinear and rotational elements. One moves under an entrance arch, both primitive hut and Schinkelesque gateway, but then to left or right off axis. The U-shaped, symmetrical gallery is in front, but one has to approach it diagonally up a ramp; the circular, open-air sculpture court can be reached on axis, but one moves through it on a perimeter, semi-circular ramp. This connects up finally with a walkway into the more domestic urban fabric. In this circuitous way the public is brought informally right into the heart of the museum.

It is an unusual heart, at once familiar like a circular neoclassical museum, and strange, as a dome without a top. Basically, the language is Schinkelesque and as eclectic as was that architect's style, although it is a subdued eclecticism. Barely recognizable Romanesque arches open onto the sculpture court, while slightly Egyptian cornices edge the painting galleries. The references signify museum and art in a stereotypical way—Schinkelesque neoclassicism signifies culture for many Germans—but with a generality and distortion that avoids cliché.

The handling of this language is at once dramatic and easy-going. Several courses of stone are dropped out of the facade to end up on the ground as architectural jokes, seats, and to reveal views; at certain key entrances a Constructivist canopy painted in strong primaries provides a striking contrast to the white and pink masonry background: machine age versus tradition, Modernism versus classicism, progress versus stasis. The outcome is held in balance; neither side is allowed an easy victory. This dualism

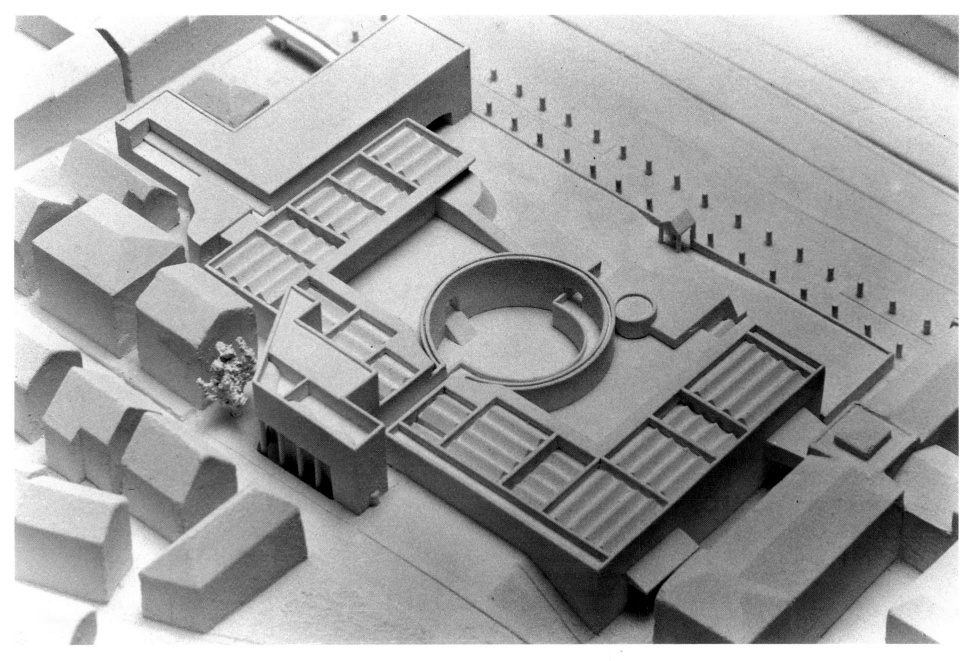

◄ 281 ALDO ROSSI
Teatro del Mondo, Venice,
Italy, 1979

▲ 282 JAMES STIRLING
*Staatsgalerie New Building
and Chamber Theater*, Stuttgart, West Germany,
1977–82, model

extends to the sequence of meanings. The public is
brought into the building informally, as mentioned,
and then given a straightforward chronological
journey through the history of art with no discontinuities. Likewise there is a continuous flow between
new and old buildings, those Stirling has designed
completely and those he has attached onto. In opposition to this ordinariness are the ramps, curves,
views across layered space, and the paradox of the
domeless dome, the inside-out space, the room toward which one moves to find oneself outside, cut off

from urban noise and in touch with sculpture or the
sky. The ideas behind this—the Mandala, the dome
of heaven (the sky), the heart of the city, and the
circular *res publica*—are key ideas of many Post-
Modernists. We have seen the opposition of circle
and square, or foreground and background, not only
in European contextualism inspired by Hadrian, but
also in Charles Moore's Piazza d'Italia. Stirling's
museum is thus another centrifugal center, another
oxymoronic figure which is both open and closed.
Together with its function as a museum and its eclectic existence as a museum-city, it attacks the amnesia
of the recent past and seeks to reestablish the city of
memory as a city of anticipation: for prediction, as
psychologists have rightly shown, is based on memory.

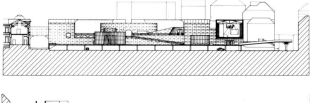

▲ 283 JAMES STIRLING
*Staatsgalerie New Building
and Chamber Theater*, Stuttgart, West Germany,
1977–82, elevation and
cross-section

METAPHOR AND METAPHYSICS
THE QUANDARY OF CONTENT

LIKE ALMOST ALL THE ARTS, EVEN MUSIC, ARCHITECTURE has a representational function. Not only does it express the values (and land values) of a society, but also its ideologies, hopes, fears, religion, social structure, and metaphysics. It may represent these facts and ideas or betray them; it may give the illusion of an unearthly realm (as in a Baroque ceiling) or create in reality an earthly "paradise" (at least New York City's Rockefeller Center and Radio City Music Hall, like a self-fulfilling prophesy, created the ambience and capital gain by which they were later judged). This strange, double aspect of architecture—both to *be* and to *represent* a state of affairs—distinguishes it from other, purely expressive arts such as painting.

Since the late nineteenth century and the growth of Modernism in all fields of art, a more specialized view of the arts has emerged which many people identify with Modernism itself. This is the notion of the specificity of each art. The pure poetry of Stéphane Mallarmé, the pure painting of Piet Mondrian, and the pure architecture of Theo van Doesburg, and later Peter Eisenman, concentrate on those features which are taken to be specific to their medium. All others are rigorously excluded as impure, or belonging to other fields. Photography, it was said, had a monopoly on the representational image and therefore pure representation had to be expunged from art. Theorists and critics, acting like customs inspectors at the Albanian border, told practitioners to jettison all baggage that was not marked "universal" to the field. Thus Modernist architecture concentrated on pure space and form, two of architecture's specific features, and jettisoned ornament, historical allusion, color, metaphor, and representation—to name several of the non-architectural features thrown out.

One might ask why such a Calvinist purging of the field was so successful, given its obvious drawbacks,[1] and two answers suggest themselves. Reductive architecture captured center stage because it was dramatic and new, like a simplified slogan, and also because

society had lost the urgent need for architecture to express an ideology, or religious view. It is the latter quandary which Post-Modernists have faced, and which has led to the traditions with which this chapter is concerned.

The later work of Le Corbusier, particularly at Ronchamp and Chandigarh, incorporated many signs of a cosmic symbolism, both implicitly and explicitly.[2] Paintings on glass, enamel panels, and tapestries alluded, in their subject matter, to the path of the sun, the rhythm of the seasons, and the presence of constant expressive types—male and female, light and darkness. All this cosmic symbolism was conveyed with that heavy, primitive force associated with Le Corbusier's last aesthetic—part Brutalist, part tragic, part a joyful exercise in a collision of geometries **(284)**. A distorted pyramid, a hyperbolic paraboloid inflected toward the path of the sun, various archetypal shapes either collaged onto the surface or cut away from it—the Legislative Assembly Building at Chandigarh was a mixture of metaphysical symbols which both European and Indian could perceive. The only questionable part of this symbolism was its Surrealist nature and its discontinuity from Indian traditions. Like the work of Edwin Lutyens in India, the imposition of alien forms, however convincing as sculpture, has a colonialist ring.

The Post-Modern metaphysical architecture which has developed from Le Corbusier's later work retains this Surrealist and arcane reference. Luis Barragán, Paolo Soleri, and John Hejduk—all really Late-Modernist in their emphasis on pure sculptural form—build up a repertoire of cosmic meanings which are nevertheless hermetic and inaccessible to a wide audience. Roland Coate's work in California is representative of this school.[3] His Alexander House burrows into the side of a hill overlooking a magnificent panorama which includes mountain to one side and ocean to the other **(285–286)**. This underground placement not only protects it from the brush fires that threaten the area, but also roots it firmly and metaphorically within the earth, like a cave. The persistent use of heavy concrete further ties it to the ground, just as masonry has conventionally become a sign of earth. The flat horizontals of the terraces take up the ocean horizon; the primitive columns (one is a meditation center as well as a crow's nest) hold up the sky; pool water, brick, concrete, and grass all take on fundamental attributes. Indeed, Coate connects these images to certain Jungian archetypes—underground, unconscious, etc.—as well as to archetypal Californian experiences—riding along the empty freeways at four in the morning. That other references might be inferred—a German pillbox or bunker, an Aztec altar, a ruined site or burnt house—adds to the above associations rather than runs against them, making the building still more enigmatic as a metaphysical proposition. Finally, the house is reminiscent of a Corbusian roofscape sunk, paradoxically, into the ground.

The metaphysics of traditional architecture were often accessible to the public and shared by it. Greek temple, Gothic cathedral, and Renaissance church may have enunciated unpopular and obscure doctrines, but they nevertheless appealed to a perennial philosophy evolved by many previous cultures. Post-Modernists, by contrast, articulate a diversity of metaphysical propositions which have a narrower base; they choose eclectically from previous systems and focus on single ideas which they present dramatically. Thus the work of James Wines and SITE concentrates on the metaphysics of entropy and "de-architecture"—crumbling, cracking, peeling, or buried facades;[4] Stanley Tigerman represents the ludicrous tendencies of a consumer society with a black humor—his Hot Dog, Daisy, and Animal Crackers Houses, his blown-up suburban house for Best Products, his killing machine for stray dogs, etc.[5] Common to this work and its counterpart in Japan is an explicit, raw symbolism, the architectural equivalent of an advertisement, an image meant to reach a consumer society as forcefully as any one of its clichés. The metaphysics, like those of Andy Warhol, are an ironic acceptance and celebration of consumer madness. Wines and Tigerman, like Warhol, are often accused of producing one-liners—counterclichés which are as easily forgotten as the slogans they celebrate or lampoon. But the results are somewhat more complicated than this.

SITE's Notch Project, with its notch that cracks apart every morning to swallow the customers of Best Products' catalogue showroom, has oxymoronic signs on many levels which turn on the opposition best/worst: the pure facade contrasts with the jagged crack; the forty-five-degree shear lines contrast with the orthogonal grid; the perfect world of Californian shoppers (macadam, cleanliness, order) contrasts with the San Andreas fault always running through their minds (287). These facades which peel away or tilt upward are, paradoxically, carefully constructed (288). Imperfect/perfection is underlined by dumb/wise. The dumb box, which is the Best showroom prototype, is kept ninety percent dumb: no basic changes are made in layout, facade treatment, lettering, brick wall, or parking lot so that the sense of the building type is allowed to predominate. But then one operation is changed: in the Tilt Showroom, for example, the front wall tilts up at an angle to reveal the interior, symbolize entrance, and suggest

that the shoppers might be crushed upon entering. This elementary operation on a dumb box represents a complicated sign: it destroys the pretensions of the merchandise showroom in a violent, willful way, as a child might crush a toy he has found boring. On another level, however, it does produce an effective advertisement and therefore easy accommodation of Best's purposes. These two opposite levels collide in our mind as they do in any joke, especially as we realize that the joke is on us and we have been duped, once again, into consuming a rather shoddy, mass-produced article. SITE's jokes are thus not one-liners, but two-liners—*double-entendres* that force us to look again. Like other forms of low humor—farce, puns, doggerel—they may not provide sustained nourishment, but in a context known for its inflexible humorlessness they do innovate and show a way open for future development (an aspect explored by The Museum of Modern Art, New York, in 1979 in their exhibition on designs for Best Products' showrooms).

Stanley Tigerman's scheme for this exhibition, "The Best Home of All," is an ironic amplification of the standard suburban house (and one he designed for a tract developer some years earlier).[6] It sits in an endless, American prairie grid of other ranch houses,

each with their TV aerials and sub-Frank Lloyd Wright detailing (289). The giant garage door swallows the poor Lilliputian race computerized to consume like zombies; a wholesome Mary Tyler Moore in suggestive slacks acts as the sign of the consumer goodies inside; and a radioactive sunset in the background suggests the hidden price to be paid by a credit-card society. Tigerman allows himself to express in words the hatred he feels toward this society, a hatred more ambiguously stated in the form: "Of course, the very Best thing about their new home lay in its neighborliness, insofar as they had finally found an American symbol right there where they least expected it—at home in the suburban United States of America—and all the snotty bastards in the urban United States were simply green with envy."

Tigerman's project for Pensacola Place, Chicago, is intended as a comment on the "optimism and skepticism" inherent in the linear city (a Modernist archetype meant to usher in an egalitarian society). The project consists of a Post-Modern slab block with ironic, Ionic capitals on the top of each "columnar" shaft of balconies (290). The slab relates to Tigerman's earlier Modernist apartments, with their Chicago frame, and hence to the egalitarianism this structure stands for by convention. It also

▲ 284 LE CORBUSIER
*Legislative Assembly
Building*, Chandigarh,
India, 1953–61

▶ 285 ROLAND COATE
Alexander House,
Montecito, California,
1972–74, aerial view

▼ 286 ROLAND COATE
Alexander House,
Montecito, California,
1972–74, exterior

◀ **287** SITE
Notch Project, Sacramento,
California, 1976–77

▲ **288** SITE
Tilt Showroom, Towson,
Maryland, 1976–78

▼ **289** STANLEY
TIGERMAN, *"The Best
Home of All,"* The Museum
of Modern Art, New York
City, exhibition project,
1979, perspective

relates, however, to the flat horizon of the nearby lake and the funereal imagery of the nearby Graceland cemetery in which Louis Sullivan and Mies van der Rohe are buried. Thus there is an opportunity for a precise hermeneutic metaphysics, as Tigerman describes it: "Now the linear city is in eternal conflict. Its schizophrenia is represented by a utopian optimism mirroring a desired future opposing the ultimate skepticism—knowledge of the finite condition of man."

Obviously such associations are only dimly present in this Ionic slab, and what is more apparent is the classical, tripartite coding of the traditional apartment block, although even this is veiled within the image of balcony and window. Tigerman's metaphysics are represented by metaphors which are only sometimes blatant similes, as in the plan for his Daisy House (**291**), or the side view of his Animal Crackers House (**292–294**). Phallus, buttocks, piano are the similes, but although they are directly stated they may not be perceived because of the abstract, Modernist language or the aerial viewpoint necessary for their perception. Furthermore, they are again tied to more purely architectural features such as windows or doors, and thus have a multivalent role. The Animal Crackers box which gives the house its name is also, according to Tigerman, meant to allude to a calliope and a "Volkswagen backed onto

the property," a shape which resulted from combining two minimum cubes of volume with a continuous curve. This extremely low-budget house of wood and stucco thus turns suburban imagery inside out and amplifies it. Like the iconic architecture of the Las Vegas strip, the house resembles blown-up domestic and food imagery, and like much Tigerman work it is symmetrical about one axis and therefore related to anthropomorphic images.

The argument for anthropomorphism has been put by many Post-Modernists (Yamashita, Moore and Bloomer, myself), as well as by architectural historians such as Vincent Scully, or previously Geoffrey Scott.[7] It rests on the idea that we project bodily states into architectural form, finding a correspondence between our own structure and that of a building—its facade and our face; its columns and our torso or legs; its decoration and our own (eyebrows, lips, and hair to name three ornamental elements). The empathetic projection may be childish or naive, as it often is in the popular American bungalow where these features are exaggerated, or it may be complicated and subliminal, as it is in much classical architecture and the work of Michael Graves. Osamu Ishiyama's Pipe Houses, cheaply assembled from industrial products packaged within sewer pipes, incorporate all sorts of ornamental motifs and mix them with animal and face imagery

(**295–296**). Fanlight, stained glass, and incised waving lines connect the recycled technology to both our body and the historical continuum.[8]

Such anthropomorphism was frowned upon by Modernists (except for Le Corbusier and occasionally Alvar Aalto) but it has since been taken up by Post-Modernists as at least one acceptable subject for iconography. The latter focus on it for the quite obvious reason that it is so universal. Since we are apt to see ourselves in architecture, this projection can be an element in humanizing abstract form and overscaled housing estates. It is also perhaps the most powerful means of gaining the inhabitants' confidence, or engaging the passerby, as an immediate rapport is felt between the inanimate building and

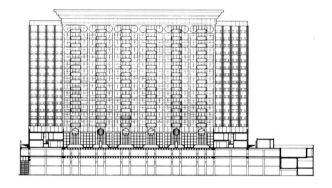

▲ **290** STANLEY TIGERMAN, *Pensacola Place*, Chicago, Illinois, 1979– , elevation/section

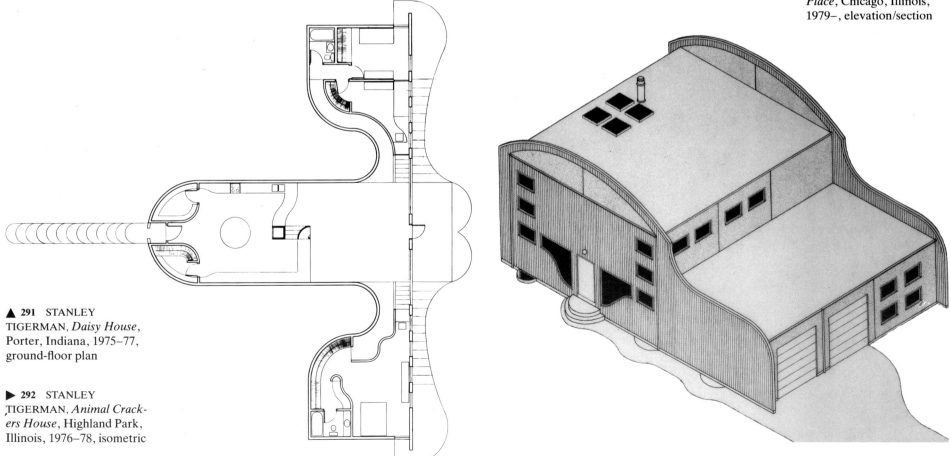

▲ **291** STANLEY TIGERMAN, *Daisy House*, Porter, Indiana, 1975–77, ground-floor plan

▶ **292** STANLEY TIGERMAN, *Animal Crackers House*, Highland Park, Illinois, 1976–78, isometric

our body. Classical architecture recognized this in its exaggeration of columns and moldings, in its profusion of caryatids and sculptural figures, and now Post-Modernists are investing their own buildings with a variety of body images. Robert Venturi's Brant House in Vail, Colorado (1976), resembles a face, as does Takefumi Aida's Nirvana House in Kanagawa, Japan (1972), and my own studio in Cape Cod (**297**). The coding in all three cases is ambiguous, distorted, and combined with other images so that the visage is felt, not seen.

Kazumasa Yamashita, like Tigerman, has experimented with symmetrical structures that explicitly recall animal or human forms. His Face House in Kyoto is so emphatically a face (and one which relates to Mannerist "mouths of Hades") that we cannot see it as anything else (**298**). There it screams with bulging eyes and flaring nostrils, the very symbol of alienation, not welcome. The explicitness short-circuits the very function of anthropomorphism—the empathetic projection—because there is nothing to complete in our mind, no effort is required to fill out the meaning. By contrast, Yamashita has more recently completed another face building which is so

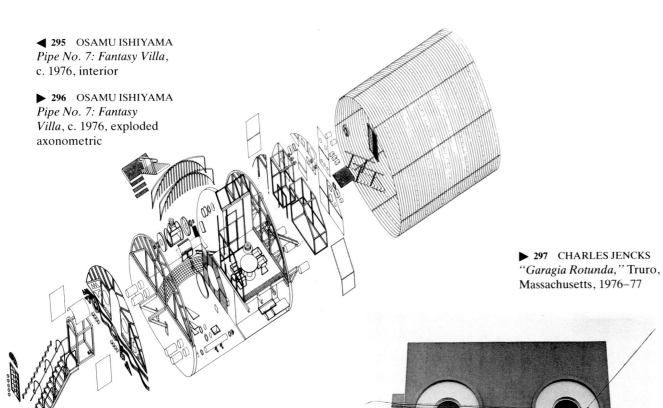

◀ **295** OSAMU ISHIYAMA
Pipe No. 7: Fantasy Villa,
c. 1976, interior

▶ **296** OSAMU ISHIYAMA
*Pipe No. 7: Fantasy
Villa*, c. 1976, exploded
axonometric

▶ **297** CHARLES JENCKS
"Garagia Rotunda," Truro,
Massachusetts, 1976–77

▶ **298** KAZUMASA
YAMASHITA, *Face House*,
Kyoto, Japan, 1974

implicitly coded in plan that the anthropomorphism remains imperceptible (**299–300**). He writes: "I hope you are pleased to find a 'face' in the balcony plan which is not directly expressive." (This was after I had criticized the Kyoto Face House.) "The client who is chief of the company possesses strong dictatorship, and he controls the whole function of the building from the center. To symbolize his dictatorship, I adapted his profile to the design of the office balcony." What we perceive here is the conventional distinction between nature and culture, the curves and right angles, a contrast made more dramatic by the erosion and elision of brick forms.

It is interesting that many Post-Modern architects feel compelled to represent anthropomorphic images, whether for their metaphysical or social implications, or for deep or humorous reasons. Perhaps this is because the content of this imagery is so indisputably shared across all cultures. From 40,000 B.C. to the present the human form has been primary subject matter and so in an age unsure of its metaphysics this becomes a basic foundation, an ultimate truth (like the Vitruvian Man) from which other truths can be generated. Most Post-Modern anthropomorphism (such as that of Graves or Moore) follows the Symbolist injunction of the nineteenth century: "Always suggest and never name an idea." But a case can also be made for literal body images.

If discreetly used only in parts of a building, these can cue the user to the implicit metaphors: the way the "body of the house," the plan, might "have its own life, symmetry and parts," the way views are "framed," the way entrances "welcome and enclose." Effective body imagery is thus a subtle blend of implicit and explicit coding (**301**).

Several architects we have discussed under the Surrational label combine anthropomorphic images with a primitive constructional technique reminiscent of that of ancient Rome. Concrete block wall, archetypal truss, square window, barrel vault—these are the hallmarks of a fundamentalist style coming from the Rationalists, Louis Kahn, and Leon Krier. One

can find these elements in the Surrational skyscrapers of Arquitectonica which perform simple operations on the (giant) step and slab (**302**), in Mark Mack's work in northern California, and in the work of the group Morphosis in southern California. Thom Mayne and Michael Rotundi of Morphosis have designed a primitive barrel vault and set it away from a stepped gable and a sequence of layered space which combines, paradoxically, topiary and high-tech railings (**303**). This fundamentalism is also present in Shin Toki's primitive version of the Mannerist Villa Giulia, Rome (1550–55), which contrasts two discontinuous facades, one of Indian sandstone and one of reinforced concrete (**304**), or in Mario Botta's houses in the Ticino canton of Switzerland, where enclosed concrete blocks in simple forms take on a totemistic aspect (**305**). In Botta's house at Ligornetto, the flat "drawn" facade, with its bands of red and gray cement, defines the edge of the town, and its contrast with nature.[9] A primitive rusticated base, awaiting its *piano nobile*, is meant to be "a sign of the 'wealth' of the poor" and the care they show in building with modest materials, while the hieratic shape, more likely in the shrine of a fundamentalist sect than a house, proclaims a metaphysics beyond any conceivable programmatic requirement. Like T.S. Eliot's Hamlet, a character in search of an object worthy of his malaise, Botta's work evokes a

◀ **299** KAZUMASA
YAMASHITA, *Office Build-
ing*, Tokyo, Japan, 1979,
exterior detail

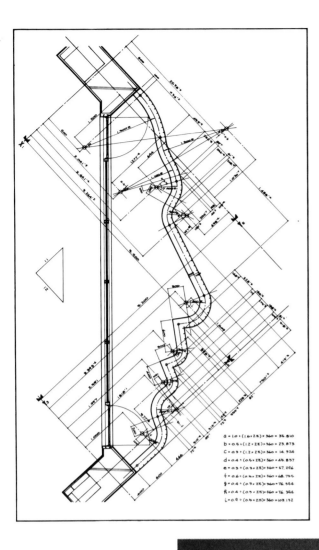

powerful emotion which outdistances the reference. The Metaphysical School of architecture is founded on this disparity.

Minoru Takeyama, in many enigmatic buildings based on fundamental shapes derived from Claude-Nicolas Ledoux, combines this primitive expression with anthropomorphism. His Hotel Beverly Tom is a three-quarter cylinder plus an open, lattice dome—abstract, pure forms which, like Ledoux's Oikema, or Temple Dedicated to Love (1773–79), are actually in the shape of a phallus (**306**). This shape, which is only barely visible, is based on the ancient Shinto sexual symbol, the *Tenri*, which is at times in Japanese life explicitly revealed. The abstract, vertical organization of the hotel, the surrounding gray environment, and the Shinto precedent seem to have led to the use of this symbolism (carried through even in the ashtrays) which is in excess of its referent (hotel function). If society will not provide the building tasks consonant with such cosmic symbols (appropriate for the Washington Monument or Nelson's Column) the Metaphysical School of Japanese architecture will nonetheless continue to provide the symbols.

Arata Isozaki, whose nihilism has already been discussed in relation to the Gunma Museum, has produced several buildings based on the work of Ledoux and other images abstracted from Palladian architecture and the sacred architecture of the Renaissance. His Fujimi Country Club (**307–309**), in the primary shape of a black, silent barrel vault which curves in the form of a question mark, ends with a version of Palladio's Villa Poiana (c.1550). Why, the question mark seems to ask, why Palladio in a Japanese country club? As with any rhetorical question, there is no clearly convincing answer. Isozaki has, however, given some justifications for the form. The acentric columns are a result of concrete technology; the barrel vault is an economic form which sweeps in the view of a pleasant landscape. Finally, since Japan often absorbs Western imagery, it is not surprising to find it dealing with the Post-Modern Classicism of today and the neo-Palladian revival. But these rational explanations only make the absurdities of a question mark more poignant.[10]

The Metaphysical School of Japanese Post-Modernism, with Isozaki as its leader, poses such enigmas in both a logical and absurd form. Mayumi Miyawaki, for instance, has designed a series of defensive buildings in primary colors and forms which turn their backs on the external world and open inward to light, air, and greenery. Miyawaki resorts to such *defensive* architecture—he has built twenty or so "box-buildings" as houses and banks—not only as a "metaphysical shock tactic," but also because the Japanese environment has become so hostile. The concrete box is a defense against noise, pollution, and a terrible view.[11]

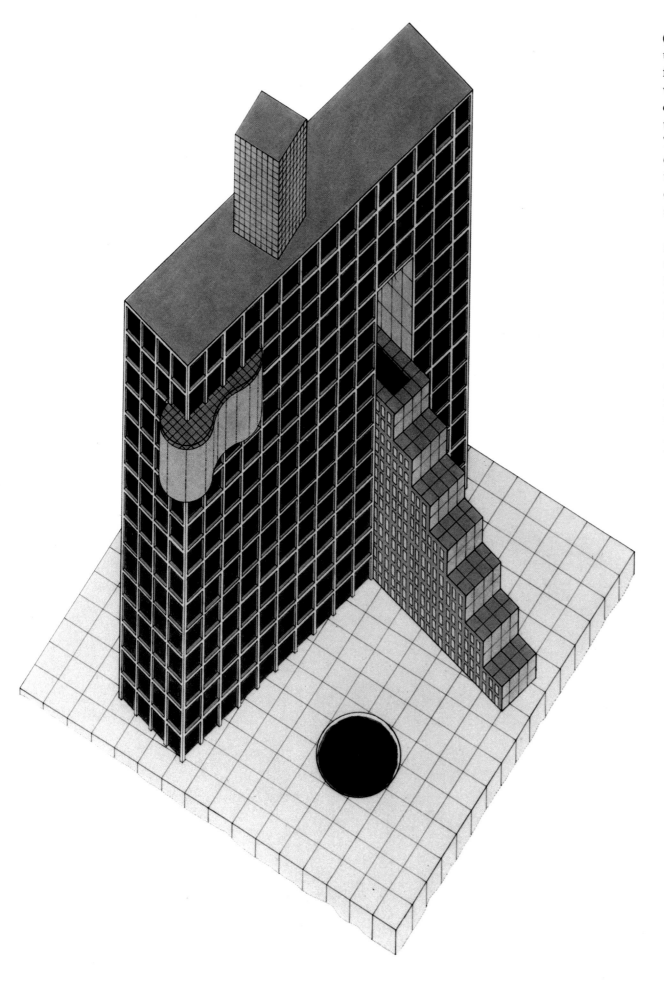

One of his early buildings, the Blue Box House (**310**), perches precariously on the side of a hill amidst urban sprawl and greenery. The outside primary forms exclude contact—except for a small porthole which commands a view of Mount Fuji. Also, one corner of the pure form is violated to allow bamboo trees to penetrate up into an enclosed, interior garden. The interior spaces provide everything that the harsh exterior rejects: complex, flowing geometries, traditional tatami room, lush furnishing, and peaceful, controlled nature. A skylight illuminates the central stairwell, which is designed in opposition to the grid.

Reason and madness, logic and poetry, neutral grid and expressive variation thus oscillate in that dialectic of Surrationalism with which we are now familiar. Hiroshi Hara, another designer of defensive, Platonic boxes, justifies their hieratic space as a reaction against Modernist impersonality. "Homogeneous space tends to atomize human relationships . . . If you agree that homogeneous space is negative and undesirable, then we must somehow regain control of the Post-Modern spatial order . . . A house . . . must possess a strong independent centre. This creates a regular order that is opposed to the surrounding homogeneous space outside."[12] Hara's work, like that of others in the Metaphysical tradi-

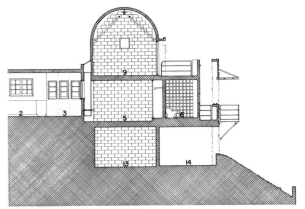

◄ **302** ARQUITECTONICA
"The Palace," Miami, Florida, 1978, axonometric

▲ **303** MORPHOSIS
Flores House, Los Angeles, California, 1979, section

◀ **304** SHIN TOKI
Sanwa Building, Kikuchi,
Japan, 1977

▲ **305** MARIO BOTTA
House at Ligornetto,
Ticino, Switzerland,
1975–76

tion, makes use of strong enclosures, repetitive grids, axial symmetries, mirror images, Palladian motifs, and a religious handling of objects (**311**). In the Hara House, interior volumes are arranged as a series of altars, hieratically fixed on an axis of light which runs down the spine of the building. Semi-circular forms recall the tombs of saints; the silent, pure abstraction creates a place for meditation. Here the outside world has been excluded, and the individual given a psychological shelter which is fundamental to the traditional concept of the house. In this sense, the Metaphysical School has supplied exemplary models of dwellings that relate us to the past.

Takefumi Aida uses highly symbolic forms (such as

▶ **306** MINORU
TAKEYAMA, *Hotel Beverly
Tom*, Hokkaido, Japan,
1973

the truncated pyramid) out of context (for a kindergarten) and justifies such displacements as "a way to expand the metaphysical meaning of architecture."[13] This "expansion" is based partly on shock, on bringing together two seemingly incompatible images such as house and die, or house and steps, and then showing that they have certain features in common (312–314). The House like a Die has a cubic shape and features which run through the numbers one to six; the Stepped-Platform House follows, autocratically, the black-and-white grid and the crowsteps of a gable (which implies that the body of the house is sunk underground). Aida emphasizes the dictatorial logic in all metaphysical architecture: "The architect must always make absolutely subjective judgements in relation to the architectural image that he wants to create. In short, as far as the architectural image is concerned, I intend to make my judgements as autocratic as I can." The autocracy inevitably consists for Aida in reducing architecture to simple archetypal forms—the Platonic solids—but then, unlike a Modernist who might also use this language, in placing them in contrast with the function ("imprison function within innate forms" is another Aida injunction). Every building produced by this method invariably ends up as a place of worship, and it is not surprising that Aida has produced images of himself sitting in worshipful pose in a blank space, lit dramatically from the side like a Mannerist subject lost in deep chiaroscuro.

The space of the Metaphysical School provides a clear antithesis to that of Modernism and Late-Modernism: it is centered, layered, and symbolic rather than neutral and isotropic. Its symbolism may

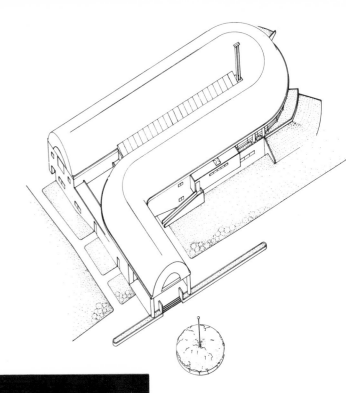

▲ **307** ARATA ISOZAKI *Fujimi Country Club*, Oita, Japan, 1973–74, axonometric

◄ **308** ARATA ISOZAKI *Fujimi Country Club*, Oita, Japan, 1973–74, view from the east

► **309** ARATA ISOZAKI *Fujimi Country Club*, Oita, Japan, 1973–74, interior

be farfetched and consciously inappropriate, as we have seen, but there are certain architects, loosely linked with the School, who try to derive an appropriate symbolism. Kazuhiro Ishii, an architect trained under Charles Moore at Yale, uses a plurality of industrial products to articulate a plurality of meanings and ideologies.[14] His house and clinic, called "54 Windows," incorporates a "large number of differing windows to symbolize a Japanese regionalism" (315–316). We might be skeptical of this, but Ishii insists that Japanese regionalism consists primarily of "excess and display," and so, with his green and orange boxes projecting from the white concrete

► 310 MAYUMI MIYAWAKI, *Blue Box House*, Tokyo, Japan, 1971

▼ 311 HIROSHI HARA *Hara House*, Machida, Japan, 1974, living room viewed from the entrance

◀ **312** TAKEFUMI AIDA
House like a Die, Shizuoka,
Japan, 1974

▼ **313** TAKEFUMI AIDA
Stepped-Platform House,
Kanagawa, Japan, 1976,
elevation

▼ **314** TAKEFUMI AIDA
Stepped-Platform House,
Kanagawa, Japan, 1976,
exterior

frame, he has tried to capture these essentially vulgar qualities. He also argues that the symbols—the die (again), numbers, and color code—relate to regional and popular signs. Clearly they are also adopted for the same metaphysical reasons that Aida uses the die: there is no connection between a house and throwing dice, although there may be a fortuitous similarity between the two in shape and detail. These houses are clear illustrations of the new idiosyncracy: they replace the impersonal images of Modernism with extreme examples of individualism.

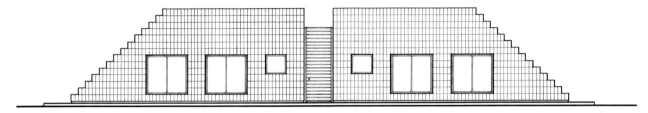

◀ **315** KAZUHIRO ISHII *"54 Windows"* (Soya Clinic and Residence), Kanagawa, Japan, 1975, garden facade

▼ **316** KAZUHIRO ISHII *"54 Windows"* (Soya Clinic and Residence), Kanagawa, Japan, 1975, exploded/cut-away axonometric

▶ **317** MONTA MOZUNA *Anti-Dwelling Box*, Hokkaido, Japan, 1971

The supreme individualist and metaphysician is Monta Mozuna,[15] who takes defensive, boxed architecture into the regions of paradox and black humor. For instance, his Anti-Dwelling Box—a series of three identical boxes telescoped within themselves—does provide a retreat from urban life, but it also gives a repeated series of concrete cages (**317**). The house is for Mozuna's mother (Post-Modernists often experiment on members of the family) and it must be somewhat oppressive with its incessant repetition of the same idiosyncratic box at three scales. It is the mixture of seriousness and black humor which justifies this paradoxical building.

"Usually there are many boxes within a house; for example the television, jewel box, room. In a house, one is always in boxes, between boxes and outside of them. When you have discovered that a house is assembled from a great many boxes, you make a paradox about a house."[16] Mozuna quotes from *Mother Goose* in support of his argument:

> There was a little green house
> And in the little green house
> There was a little brown house
> And in the little brown house
> There was a little yellow house
> And in the little yellow house
> There was a little white house
> And in the little white house
> There was a little heart.

Further justifications (Post-Modernists always like a little "heart" in their centered houses) include the Mandala form, an *imago mundi*, and the notions of miniaturism and the mirror image—all key concepts and forms of Japanese tradition and religion. Indeed,

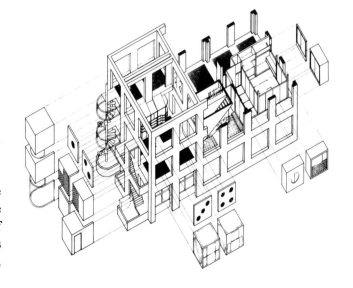

the striking aspect of Mozuna's work is its surplus of metaphysical meanings. He relates his architecture directly to Inca myths, Shintoism, Pythagorean interpretations of the universe, Isaac Asimov's science fiction, Chinese Yin and Yang symbols, the secret ceremonies of the cabala, and Carl Jung's concept of the collective unconscious—to name roughly half the references. This is an inflation of metaphysics. Where the Renaissance signified basically two philosophies in its buildings—Christian theology and Platonic mysticism—Mozuna signifies thirteen. His Heaven Phase House is "based on seven columns positioned on the basis of a projection of the stars in the Great Bear. The architectural spaces are delineated by lines drawn to connect these columns." Demiforms, based on the Yin/Yang duality, generate the living and private areas, the skylights, the half-arched bridge and half-sunburst (**318**). Half a five-pointed

star creates the staircase. As in John Hejduk's One-Half House (**124**) we might miss these demi-forms and their significance because they are absorbed into the geometry in an abstract way.

Mozuna's Yin-Yang House, an addition to an existing building, is more explicit in its cosmic symbolism (**319–320**). We can read the Yin/Yang double-comma form in parts of the living room, with its curved projection and ribbon window. Again, paradox and erosion are used rhetorically. The supporting column is only half supporting (and the other half is hidden behind opaque glass); an eroded section of the old building is projected through the new one to end as a rubble ruin; beams turn into arches; demi-forms abound. The new block is "designed on the basis of the eighteen phases of the moon known to Oriental philosophy. In this willful design, the north facade represents the full moon; and the progression

moves from old to new to reach the south facade, which represents the dark, unexplored side of the moon.'' Not for nothing does Mozuna prefer esoteric Buddhism to the more accessible varieties. Most of his schemes, such as the Mirror House, highlight the related notions of twins, inversion, anastrophe, and mirror reversal—figures we have seen in Late- and Post-Modernism alike (**321**). Others, such as the Okawa House (1974), are historicist parodies which telescope images, here from Brunelleschi and Michelangelo.

Mozuna's Zen Temple uses all these devices—twins, mirrors, historicist parody of East and West—to create a hieratic image which is, for a change, appropriate (**322–323**). We proceed through an almost traditional gate (made different by being a combined beam-column with Yin/Yang symbol), across a bridge, past ruined columns, and up steps to a giant

▲ **319** MONTA MOZUNA
Yin-Yang House, Hokkaido, Japan, 1977

▲ **320** MONTA MOZUNA
Yin-Yang House, Hokkaido, Japan, 1977, conceptual axonometric

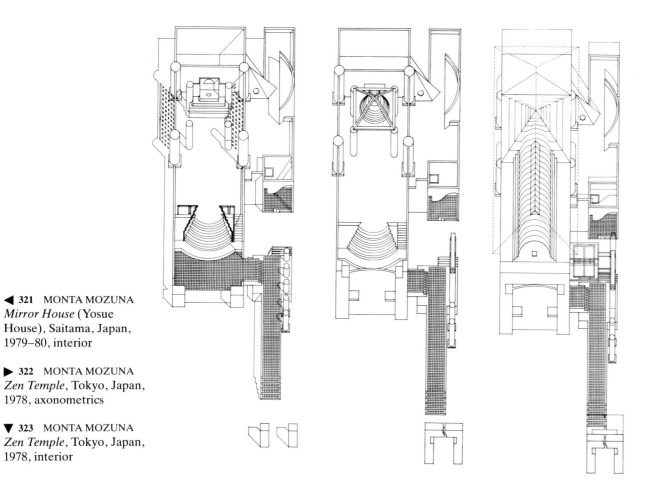

◀ **321** MONTA MOZUNA
Mirror House (Yosue House), Saitama, Japan, 1979–80, interior

▶ **322** MONTA MOZUNA
Zen Temple, Tokyo, Japan, 1978, axonometrics

▼ **323** MONTA MOZUNA
Zen Temple, Tokyo, Japan, 1978, interior

altar with a statue of Buddha. This is placed on the axis of a barrel vault (with Gothic point) and under a pyramid (which has a "right and wrong" side, like the Egg Dome). Further tricks—the irrational grid ("magic square planning") and twin mirrors (the Yin/Yangs)—are apparent, together with a long list of cosmological symbols culled from Vitruvius, Alberti, the I-Ching, "Abhidharma-Kosha-shastra, and so on."

We might, on first acquaintance, wish to criticize this kind of pluralism, a confusing amalgam that never asks us to believe anything with finality. But then we might also applaud Mozuna's courage in attempting to represent our present uncertainty and to generate an absolute architecture from it, one whose rigor consists in the geometricization of eclectically chosen cosmologies. Where other architects would hide their agnosticism behind a technological neutrality or social *bonhomie*, Mozuna wishes to insist that architecture always has a metaphysical role, even when the metaphysics are as confused as they are today. Thus he suggests that when the universe finally gives up her secrets she will turn out to be a pluriverse.

POST-MODERN SPACE
LAYERING, ELISION, AND SURPRISE

THERE ARE TWO BASIC IDEAS OF MODERNIST SPACE ON which Post-Modernists have built, and to which they have also reacted. The first, articulated by Sigfried Giedion in *Space, Time and Architecture* (1941), developed from nineteenth-century Germanic theories of space and from studies of the actual practice of Francesco Borromini, Guarino Guarini, and Balthasar Neumann in the seventeenth and eighteenth centuries.[1] It focused on the notion of spatial interpenetration—the way two or more volumes could overlap, large glazed areas could unite previously separated areas, and planes of architecture could slide by each other, producing continuous flowing movement. From Frederick Kiesler's and Theo van Doesburg's abstract "planes in space" formulated in the twenties to New York City's Rockefeller Center and the suburban house uniting inside and out, there has been a steady development of the idea of interpenetration. The negative results of this idea, the isolated monument or city in the park, have already been discussed in chapter 8.

The other, related notion of Modernist space developed from the Chicago frame and Le Corbusier's Domino block,[2] and resulted in the extreme isotropic space of Late-Modernism. Post-Modernists have clearly reacted against this, seeking to define "place" rather than abstract space and to establish ambiguity, variety, and surprise rather than the predictability of the Chicago office floor. But even in this essential rejection of homogeneous space, there have been certain carry-overs from Modernism: in particular some spatial ideas of Frank Lloyd Wright and Le Corbusier—notably layered, shallow space—

have been developed by Post-Modernists.[3] Interpenetration and layered space, two rhetorical figures of Modernism, are used by Post-Modernists to define a new kind of ambiguous space which is mysterious, complex, and full of surprises.

THE SHIFTED AXIS

ONE OF THE FIRST ARCHITECTS TO CONVENTIONALIZE this ambiguous space was Robert Venturi. In a house for his mother in Chestnut Hill (**324**) he made use of the shifted axis, a motif which was to become common in subsequent work by Robert Stern, Thomas Gordon Smith, and others. The shifted axis was a standard form in seventeenth-century French hôtels designed on odd-shaped plots, where it mediated between two symmetrical fronts—one on the entry court and one on the garden side—which were offset with respect to each other. François Mansart and Jean Courtonne (Hôtel de Matignon, 1622) absorbed the shifted axis within primary, ideal forms, while much later Edwin Lutyens, in his Folly Farm (1906), twisted the form itself to indicate the shift (**325**). It is this twisted oval, or distorted ellipse, with entry and exit at opposite corners, which Venturi and others have developed. In the Vanna Venturi House the fragmented oval is combined with two other Post-Modern spatial motifs: the skew, or wall placed diagonally to the frontal plane, and the reverse perspective, or here the stairway which gets *wider* as it recedes. The collision, or juxtaposition, of shifted entry, stair, and fireplace—all demi-forms—and the presence of so many ambiguous spatial devices make this the seminal plan of Post-Modernism. On the outside of the house these surprising distortions are indicated by another Post-Modern convention: asymmetrical symmetry.[4]

Some ten years later, in his Lang and Westchester Houses, Robert Stern used the shifted axis with a sequence of spaces layered at right angles to movement (**326–327**). In the case of the Westchester House, these devices make penetration into the heart of the house, the living room, more dramatic. The constant use of back lighting, and punched-out walls with indirect lighting spilling down behind them, adds to the sense of excitement. This use of layering, lighting, and shifted axes is reminiscent of Lutyens's spatial

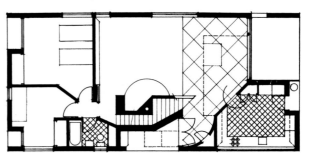

◀ **324** ROBERT VENTURI
Vanna Venturi House,
Chestnut Hill, Pennsylvania,
1962, ground-floor plan

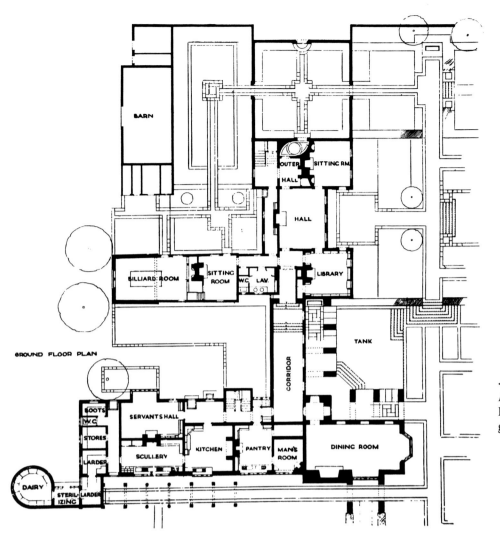

GROUND FLOOR PLAN

◀ **325** EDWIN LUTYENS
Folly Farm, Sulhampstead, Berkshire, England, 1906, ground-floor plan

▼ **326** ROBERT A.M. STERN AND JOHN S. HAGMANN, *Westchester House*, Armonk, New York, 1975, interior

Michael Graves, who has studied Raphael's Villa Madama, Rome (1517), as well as Courtonne's hôtels, shifts the axis, by erosion, in his Kalko House (**329**). The Villa Madama provides the model for the central aedicule which is framed on axis, between eroded pillars.[6] Once through this gate, however, the space widens in reverse perspective and, because the right-hand garage is only two bays, spills to the right, giving a bent if not shifted axis. After one proceeds on the major axis through the asymmetrical symmetry of the house, this axis is again bent on the garden side, and again to the right as the pergola is set against trees. The asymmetrical symmetry of the facades forms a cue to these bent axes and erosions. Nature and building are equated by eroding first one then the other, by making them figure and ground in turn. This idea, also borrowed from the Villa Madama, is carried through with a mixture of ideal, classical forms and Post-Modern demi-forms.

ELISION AND LAYERING

OBVIOUSLY THE COLLISION OF CLASSICAL FORMS IN the Kalko House is meant to recall a more harmonious past, while at the same time throwing this into doubt, or at least combining it with a Modern dynamism. Asymmetrical symmetry is a natural consequence of such juxtapositions, as is the rhetorical figure of elision. We can find many elisions in the later work of Alvar Aalto and the early work of Robert

surprises, which Stern was studying at the time. The omnipresent demi-forms—above all unfinished curves —and ambiguous zoning make this another key example of Post-Modern space.[5]

A third work which uses the shifted axis, here with more classical, completed forms, is Thomas Gordon Smith's Matthews Street House, unfortunately not built (**328**). As the plan makes clear, the shifted axis mediates between semi-public living room and more private back garden—a rather classical, eighteenth-century role for it to play. However, it is also used to dramatize the distinctions between formality and informality, the public Michelangelesque front and stucco behind. Another Post-Modern device, the asymmetrical symmetry of the cross-axes (which always focus to the right of movement through the building), is used for pragmatic reasons—there is not much space on this suburban lot, and the view to the north is not worth seeing. All Smith's plans have this elegant mixture of the practical and the grandiose, the cheapskate and the pretentious—a mixture which is conventional in San Francisco, particularly in the work of the Newsom brothers and Bernard Maybeck (whom Smith admires).

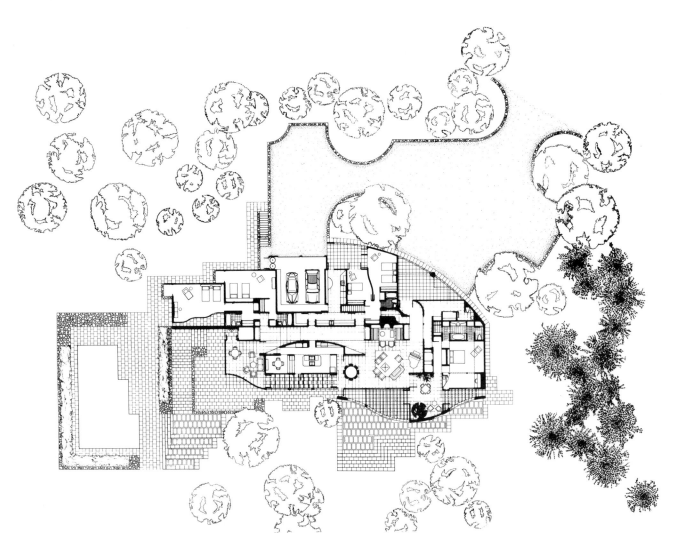

Venturi (the latter's Millard Meiss House, 1962, elides different pitched roofs, facade, and curved wall, etc.), but the most dramatic case of eliding spaces, and hence one of the most ambiguous examples of Post-Modern spatial layering is Charles Moore and William Turnbull's Faculty Club for the University of California at Santa Barbara (**330–331**). Here, various traditional, Modern, and kitsch elements are collaged onto a white, abstract space which has punched-out holes, bridges on the diagonal, and a skew of space expressed also by the roof structure. It is a very difficult space to comprehend in plan, and a very mysterious one to experience. The sense of mystery is heightened not only by the skews and diagonals but also, more importantly, by the layering. Inside and outside screens are syncopated with respect to each other so that space seems to flow indefinitely. The boundaries or edges are left undefined, just as one zone interpenetrates another, so canceling a rational perception of order.

If the business world is well defined spatially and temporally, then the spiritual world—and today ironically the restaurant and entertainment worlds—are not so defined. They consist, in the words of the social anthropologist Edmund Leach, in *liminal* qualities—qualities which elide opposites or are set in between customary categories or social activities.[7] In Moore and Turnbull's Faculty Club the dining

▲ **327** ROBERT A.M. STERN AND JOHN S. HAGMANN, *Westchester House*, Armonk, New York, 1975, ground-floor plan

▲ **328** THOMAS GORDON SMITH, *Matthews Street House Project*, San Francisco, California, 1978, ground-floor plan

area is, by definition, an elision of formal and informal, neon banners and circulation space, functional time (to eat) and unmarked time (to converse). Liminal, in-between space has, as we shall see, been taken from religious architecture and applied to many secular commissions in order to make them appear more mysterious.

◀ **329** MICHAEL GRAVES
Kalko House, Green Brook,
New Jersey, 1978, model

▲ **330** MLTW/MOORE
TURNBULL, *Faculty Club*,
University of California at
Santa Barbara, California,
1966–68, interior

◀ **331** MLTW/MOORE
TURNBULL, *Faculty Club*,
University of California at
Santa Barbara, California,
1966–68, ground-floor plan

▼ **332** CHARLES MOORE
Moore House, Orinda, California, 1962, isometric

Indeed, one of the early uses of liminal space was by Louis Kahn in his Unitarian Church in Rochester, New York (1959–67), which has an in-between space wrapped around a central communal area. A more influential extension of the same idea is the plan of his Goldenberg House in Rydal, Pennsylvania (1959), where skewed space spins around a central aedicule. It is this idea which Charles Moore has developed into his chief motif, and it has hence become one of the most repeated spatial ideas of Post-Modernism.[8] We can follow its development from the Goldenberg House through all of Moore's work to the work of his students at Yale, and to West Coast designers such as Eugene Kupper, Frank Gehry, Frederick Fisher, and Thom Mayne.

One of Moore's first aedicular works was a house for himself near San Francisco Bay (**332**). Here, the notion of the aedicule—the little house or shrine—was adapted from many sources: an essay by Sir John Summerson on the aedicules covering Gothic saints ("Heavenly Mansions," 1949); the aedicular breakfast parlor of Sir John Soane's house in Lincoln's Inn Fields, London (1812–13)—a key work for Post-Modernists because of its layered, shallow space; and the four-poster bed. In his Orinda house, Moore sets

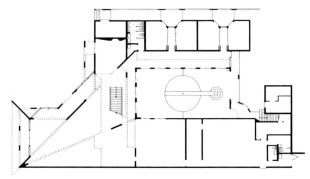

two aedicules so that their vaults, on the skew, overlap and fit into a common, flat skylight.[9] One aedicule is over the living area, giving it focus and a diffused white light, while the other dramatizes an oversized sunken bath and shower, "a celebration of the act of bathing here liberated from the cramped conventional bathroom." The two white shrines, with their ten-foot-high Tuscan columns (bought from a demolition site), sit in a darkened, barn-like space making one large room into many different places. These ideas of place-making were developed further, as we have seen, in Moore's Sea Ranch Condominiums, and then in his own converted house in New Haven (**333**–**334**). Here, the aedicules have become tubes of space

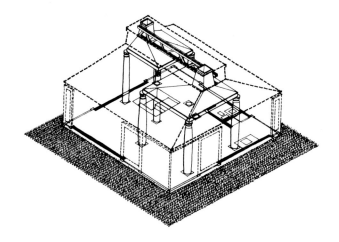

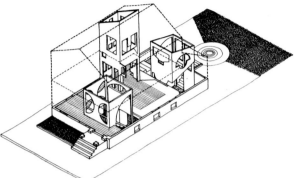

▼ 333 CHARLES MOORE
Moore House, New Haven,
Connecticut, 1967,
isometric

▶ 334 CHARLES MOORE
Moore House, New Haven,
Connecticut, 1967, kitchen
aedicule ("Ethel")

▼ 335 MLTW/TURNBULL
ASSOCIATES, *Zimmermann
House*, Fairfax County, Vir-
ginia, 1975, exterior

uniting different levels of the 1860 clapboard house.
They are given names—"Howard, Berengaria and
Ethel . . . to help increase their presence" or different character.[10] Each square tube is made by a
double layer of plywood which is then cut away and
painted in different colors to accentuate the layering.
With these interesting screens of color, and demi-
forms, Moore translates the tightly layered space of
Le Corbusier into a Post-Modern collage of vibrant
colors and both popular and historicist symbols.
Like Sir John Soane's house, Moore's becomes a
symbol-thicket replete with memorabilia, fragments,
toys, bric-à-brac, and jokes (for example, jacks used
above column capitals as double capitals).

The notion of screened, layered space was inherent
in Louis Kahn's "wrap-around-ruins" which he used
in the Assembly Hall in Dacca (designed 1962).
Alvar Aalto also used tightly layered skins at his
Imatra church (1957–59). But again it was Moore,
who acknowledges these precedents, who developed
them into a distinctive style. His Tempchin House
(1968–69), Klotz House (1967–70), and Koizim
House (1969–71) established the cutout screen and
aedicule as conventional devices of Post-Modernism.

William Turnbull, formerly a partner of Moore,
took these ideas in a different direction with his
"porch-house" for the Zimmermanns (**335–336**).[11]
Here, the aedicule or cutout tube of space which
surrounds the house is made from redwood lattice,
while the interior cubes of space are more formal
and painted white. This inversion of Moore's usage—
turning the aedicule inside out or wrapping it around
the major building—is an idea Frank Gehry used on
his own house, again with skewed windows (**360–
363**). The Zimmermanns wanted this duality—inside
bright, outside dark—as well as something that
would parallel grand Virginia porch-houses, without
recalling them specifically. Here, the surrounding
porch with its lattice and large holes cut out to
frame views is a Post-Modern equivalent to the grand
colonnade: it syncopates nicely with the openings
and windows behind, as the plan reveals. A central
skylight over a tube of space containing a skewed
stair and bridge shows the Moore convention while
the intersection of this tube with fireplace and stair
derives from Venturi. All in all, the house is a mas-
terly summing up of the elisions, screens, and aedicules which continue to form the mysterious space of
Post-Modernism.

SKEWS AND DIAGONALS

DURING THE TWENTIES CONSTRUCTIVIST DESIGNERS IN Russia introduced an obsessive diagonalism into the square world of bourgeois architecture. Diagonals in the graphics of El Lissitzky and Alexander Rodchenko, cantilevers at an angle in the architecture of Vladimir Tatlin, Nikolai Ladovsky, and above all Konstantin Melnikov, were meant to introduce dynamism, progress, and dialectic to the previously stable world of Renaissance architecture. Actually, that stability had already been shaken two hundred or more years previously by Late-Baroque architecture —the implied diagonals of Borromini and the explicit ones of Carlo Fontana, Johann Fischer von Erlach, Germain Boffrand, and Filippo Juvarra. Indeed, the grand palaces of Boffrand (La Malgrange, 1712), and Juvarra (Stupinigi, 1729–33—a small Versailles) incorporated pure forms on occasionally dissonant angles (**337**). At La Malgrange, fragmented *poché* fills in between the pure forms, and the axiality inherent in circle, rectangle, and oval is broken by the asymmetrical entries to each wing of the St. Andrew's cross. This dynamism of plan was taken up by Claude-Nicolas Ledoux in the eighteenth century, and then later, as mentioned, it was fetishized by the Constructivists, but in section and elevation as well as in plan. Scandinavian designers softened the dynamism inherent in the abrupt diagonal, took away its revolutionary impact, and made it more ironically awkward. For example, Gunnar Asplund's Villa Snellman (**338**) skews two grids rather than colliding them on the diagonal, and countless Aalto buildings and projects (Bremen apartments, 1958–62; Wolfsburg Cultural Center, 1958–62; Seinäjoki Theater project, 1968–69) explore the possibilities of this planning idea. Basically, it compresses space, where the two grids start to pinch each other, and gives not unpleasant feelings of tension, grating, sharpness, movement, and awkwardness where the two systems meet at a dissonant angle.

As we have seen in the chapter on twenties revivalism, diagonal rotation and skewed grids are common to Late-Modernists such as John Hejduk and Richard Meier. Indeed, C. Ray Smith in his book *Supermannerism* called the sixties "the decade of the diagonal" and illustrated some of the "diagonalosis" produced (especially in work by Moore, Hardy Holzman Pfeiffer, and Walter Netsch).[12] Except for Moore's work, however, most of this architecture is closer to the clear juxtapositions of the Constructivists than to the more ambiguous space and angles of Post-Modernists. Although Robert Venturi warped stairs, zigzagged corner windows, shifted axes, and skewed space in the plan of his Brant House (**339**), it was

Charles Moore who pushed the idea of skewed space a little further in his Klotz and Stern Houses (**340–341**).[13] In the latter, two gallery-rooms are skewed at an acute angle—like a St. Andrew's cross—thereby creating dissonance. The galleries expand upward and sideways to become usable rooms and afford diverging perspectives. At the main point of collision between the galleries, the space is partly joined and partly separated (by walls) and lit from the sides. One exciting aspect of this space is its long, thin proportions—the galleries are over one hundred feet in length. Another interesting aspect is the collision of two clearly distinct frames of reference giving us the equivalence of a simultaneous view down two telescopes. Space drops off or jumps up at the end of these views, while movement is implied by the ambiguous edges and directed by the two bowling-alley tubes of space. These could be corridors except that contrast is provided by "places," which are closed off and given symbolic accentuation by means of color and shape.

Michael Graves also collides grids at an acute angle in his Mezzo House Project (1973) and his Newark Museum Carriage House renovation, although in the latter the grids are fragments of wall, topiary, and stairs—not tubes of space (**342**). The influence of

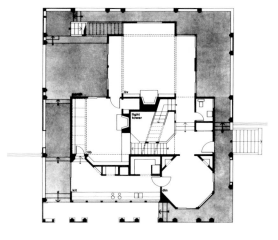

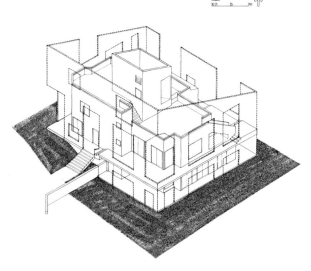

◀ **336** MLTW/TURNBULL ASSOCIATES, *Zimmermann House*, Fairfax County, Virginia, 1975, ground-floor plan and cutaway isometric

▼ **337** GERMAIN BOFFRAND, *La Malgrange*, Nancy, France, 1712, plan of second project

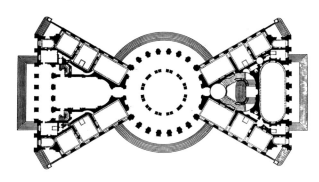

▼ **338** GUNNAR ASPLUND *Villa Snellman*, Djursholm, Sweden, 1917–18, ground-floor plan

▼ **339** VENTURI AND RAUCH, *Brant House*, Greenwich, Connecticut, 1971–73, ground-floor plan

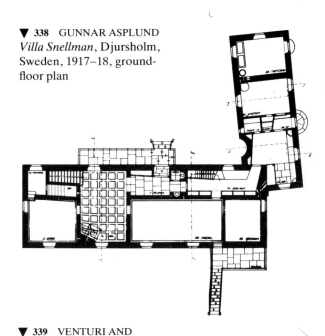

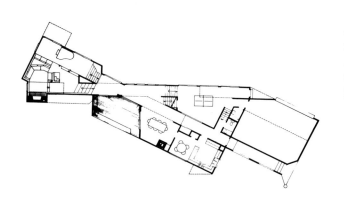

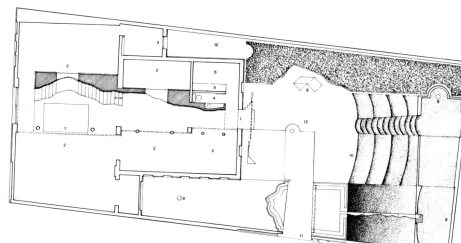

◀ 341 CHARLES W. MOORE ASSOCIATES, *Stern House*, Woodbridge, Connecticut, 1970, ground-floor plan

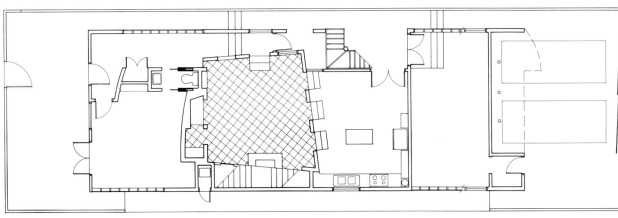

▲ 342 MICHAEL GRAVES *Newark Museum Carriage House*, Newark, New Jersey, 1975, ground-floor plan

◀ 343 FREDERICK FISHER *Caplin House*, Venice, California, 1979, site plan

▼ 344 FREDERICK FISHER *Caplin House*, Venice, California, 1979, interior

1 Entrance
2 Gallery
3 Office
4 Toilet
5 Kitchen
6 Coats
7 Existing hoist
8 Entrance from present museum
9 Sculpture
10 Amphitheater
11 Entrance from museum garden
12 Terrace
13 Open to below
14 Mechanical

GROUND FLOOR

Asplund's Villa Snellman is clear: here, skewing grids slightly compress space and give, again, a dissonance and pleasant uneasiness. These feelings are heightened by characteristic Gravesian motifs—positive/negative reversals of building and landscape and pure volumes which are eroded (as if a Cubist had torn Platonic shapes apart and scattered their ripped fragments five degrees off the grid). Such warped grids in the Late-Modern work of Philip Johnson (his Pennzoil Place trapezoids) and of Richard Meier have already been discussed. If the sixties was the "decade of the diagonal," then the seventies was the "decade of the skewed grid" (although it must be remembered that there are always *many* fashionable shapes around).

In any case, skews certainly abound in plan, section, and elevation, as if some international earthquake had suddenly sent the right-angled world into partial shear. By 1979, in Los Angeles, skewed grids, reverse perspectives, and diagonals were reverberating through the houses of Frank Gehry and Frederick Fisher, causing just enough distortion to keep one's teeth grating and one's body slightly off balance. In Fisher's Caplin House (**343–344**) a barrel vault is distorted so that the roof rolls toward the Pacific Ocean (according to the architect, like a wave). Symmetrical stairs are set *just* askew and then differentiated in size; punched-out walls and exposed

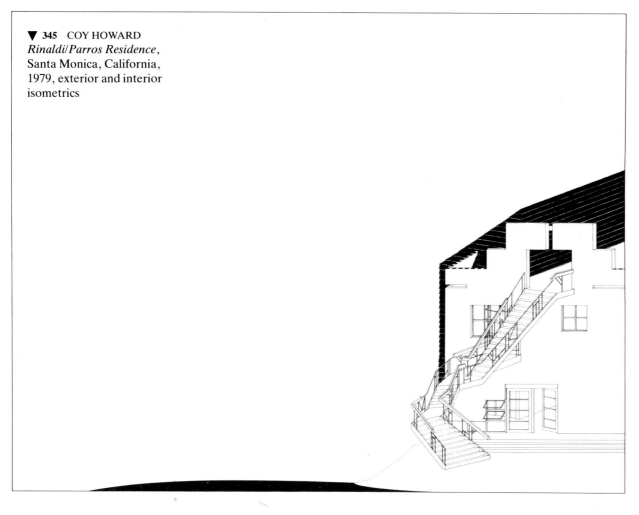

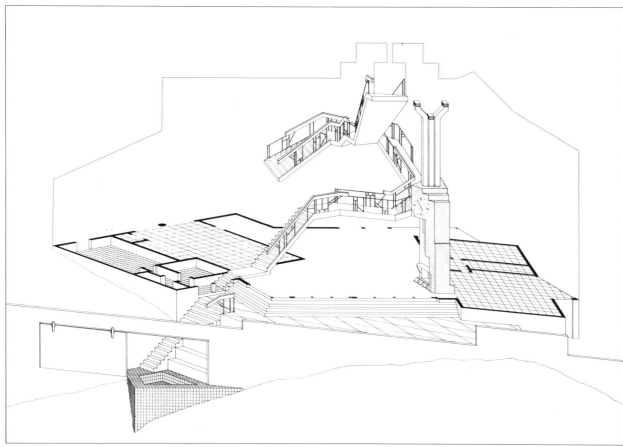

funk materials (chain link and industrial pipe) take the place of the traditional forms one expects to find. It is all slightly "off"—like the plan, a very modest tilt in reality. Coy Howard, another West Coast designer, takes the skew and reverse perspective stair much further in his Rinaldi/Parros Residence, which perches uneasily on the side of a mountain in Santa Monica (**345**). "The stair, like a country path, begins in a clearing at the entry court, winds its way up, on top of, and through the house, ricochets off major features such as the quilted stainless steel 'Grandfather's Clock' fireplace, and halts at the tile pool, providing a selected view of the distant ocean."[14] The formal complexity and symbolic collage are characteristic of Post-Modern space.

POSITIVE/NEGATIVE REVERSALS

IN HIS BOOK *Complexity and Contradiction in Architecture* (1966), Robert Venturi included a chapter concerning the various contradictions which can exist between "the Inside and the Outside" of a building, discrepancies which he found particularly in Late-Baroque architecture. The fact that inside and outside pressures on a building are often different and that traditional, as opposed to Modernist, architects often mediated this difference with "residual," or left-over, or *poché*, or layered, or "lined" space, were lessons insisted on by Venturi. A minor point he touched on was the way exterior, urban space can be considered dominant over interior space and functions. This later became, as we have seen in the chapter on urbanism, a seminal idea of the Krier brothers, Colin Rowe, and the contextualists. For architects such as Michael Graves, this notion led to an ambiguity

▼ 346 VENTURI AND SHORT, *North Penn Visiting Nurses Association Headquarters Building*, North Pennsylvania, 1960, ground-floor plan

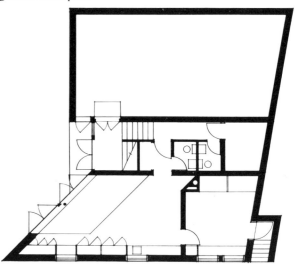

between, and sometimes reversal of, positive and negative space, solid and void. We have seen this same ambiguity in Richard Meier's exquisite plans.

Post-Modernists have looked to such urban precedents as Filippo Raguzzini's Piazza S. Ignazio in Rome (1727–28) in which exterior space is molded into a series of overlapping ovals which focus in a theatrical perspective on the church of S. Ignazio.[15] The gentle curves of these middle-class residential buildings were created not as a requirement of the housing itself, but to focus the piazza and church. Thus space is positive and building volume and function are negative (or left over). One does of course *read* the volumes as positive and the space as negative, and this causes the reversal, or double meaning, that Post-Modernists find interesting.

Venturi cites as another example of this ambiguity Lutyens's Grey Walls (1900), although his own nurses' building is a case in point (**346**). Here, the architecture is designed from the outside in so that the building has a flat street facade, and then a skewed corner which helps to complete the positive space of the parking lot and turn-around for cars. Positive space appears to have molded the negative building, at least in this plan, while what we actually perceive is an equilibrium between building and space.

Michael Graves's first significant Post-Modern work, the Crooks House Project (1976), takes these positive/negative reversals much further—to the point where the topiary itself becomes the building form and the architectural structure is fragmented and exploded apart to articulate public front, parking space, and ceremonial garden. The topiary can be seen positively as voussoirs and keystones skewed to the left and eroded to the right, while the negative space this leaves is an Art Deco stagger, one side of which is the building (**347**). Fragments of Post-Modern Classicism ripple across the public front, and peel away to leave further, conceptual layers (of building and of implied, tight space). The building explodes with fragmented signs: demi-moldings; uncompleted pure forms; a triangular hole cut in the topiary, as in the Treasury of Atreus, Mycenae, 1400 B.C.; the building skew and topiary skew, together forming a broken pediment (which lies down!); and a partial shifted axial entrance which disciplines the pitched-roof skylights. In this scheme Graves achieves a positive/negative reversal between building and landscape: "While privacy is accomplished by isolation [in the center of the lot] in the surrounding tract houses, the Crooks House derives its privacy by treating the major formal gestures as fragments of a larger organisation, thereby setting up a dependence of object and landscape. Rather than a single centre, a succession of centres is produced both in the building and in the

▲ **347** MICHAEL GRAVES
Crooks House Project, Fort Wayne, Indiana, 1976, site plan and axonometric

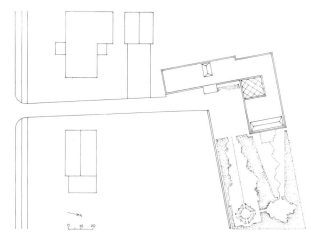

▲ 348 MICHAEL GRAVES
Warehouse Conversion: Private Residence, Princeton,
New Jersey, 1977, site plan

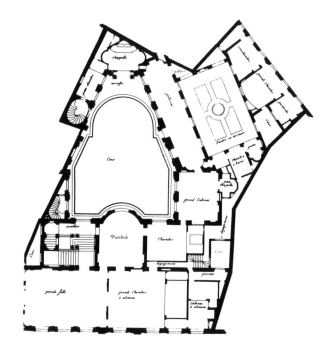

▲ 349 ANTOINE LE
PAUTRE, *Hôtel de Beauvais*,
Paris, France, 1652–55,
first-floor plan

▶ 350 THOMAS GORDON
SMITH, *Richard Long House
Project*, Carson City,
Nevada, 1978, aerial perspective and ground- and
first-floor plans

BIRDS EYE VIEW FROM SOUTH

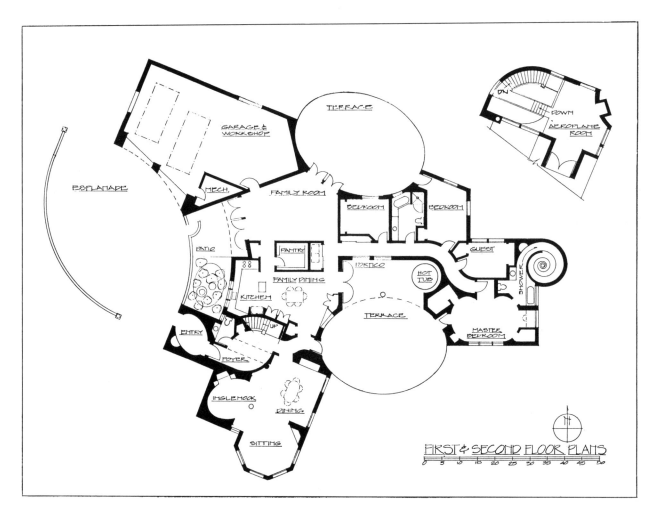

FIRST & SECOND FLOOR PLANS

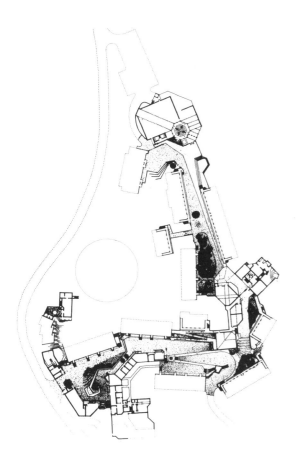

▲ **351** MLTW/MOORE TURNBULL, *Kresge College*, University of California at Santa Cruz, California, 1965–74, site plan

▼ **352** MLTW/MOORE TURNBULL, *Kresge College*, University of California at Santa Cruz, California, 1965–74, triumphal arch

▲ **353** MLTW/MOORE TURNBULL, *Kresge College*, University of California at Santa Cruz, California, 1965–74, colonnades

landscape. These centres are limited and can be understood as a spatial continuum [running from public to private]."[16] Here we have the spatial flow of Modernism combined with the centeredness of traditional space, tightly layered spaces combined with shifted axes, skews, demi-forms, and reverse perspectives.

Subsequent topiary/building projects of Graves developed these positive/negative reversals in different ways: the Plocek, or "Keystone," House in Warren Township, New Jersey (1977), skewed and shifted the processional route through landscape/ building, while the warehouse conversion for Graves himself (1977) placed the reversals in figure/ground, rough/smooth, and building/parking-lot opposition **(348)**.

DEMI-FORMS AND STRUCTURED SURPRISE

THROUGHOUT THIS STUDY OF POST-MODERNISM WE have looked at the related notions of fragments, bricolage, ad hocism, juxtaposition, collage, and their corresponding rhetorical figure of the demi-form. The urbanist and semantic justifications for the emergence of such forms have been stressed, but there are also more purely rhetorical reasons: demi-forms in their incompletion force the viewer not only to add on the missing parts—complete the eroded figure, or ellipsis—but also to transform them in his mind. It

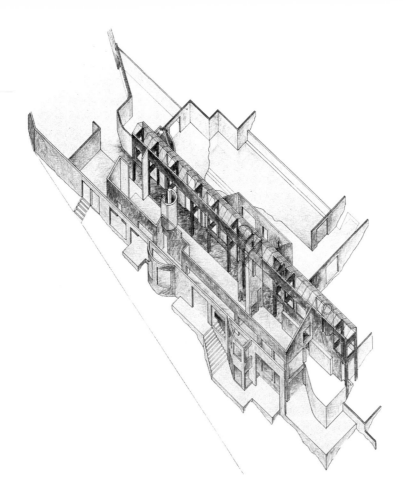

is this active involvement on the part of the viewer which is the persuasive part—its impulse. We have seen that Hadrian's Villa was composed as a collage of pure forms—circle, square, and their derivatives— and we recall that Charles Moore wrote about the way these are used to *transform* previously existing architecture.[17] An important model for Post-Modern space is Antoine Le Pautre's Hôtel de Beauvais (1652–55), which also contains a Baroque transformation and juxtaposition of pure forms **(349)**. As Colin Rowe has argued, its "free plan" is the reverse of Le Corbusier's because the stability of its image is created by a strong internal space, not a strong external envelope: " . . . the built solid [of the Hôtel] scarcely divulges itself . . . while unbuilt space (courtyard) assumes the directive role, becomes the predominant idea. . . . "[18] Here we have both the equality of solid and void that Graves uses and an ad-hoc juxtaposition of pure shapes. It is precisely this ad-hoc juxtaposition which Post-Modernists have now applied to demi-forms.

Richard Weinstein uses a juxtaposition of demiforms in the plans of his Bernstein House in Montreal (1972–73), while Thomas Gordon Smith, following Venturi *et al.*, turns this rhetorical device into a most lyrical tool **(350)**. In his Richard Long House, freeflowing Baroque and Modern curves leap across

▶ **354** EUGENE KUPPER
Nilsson House, Bel Air,
California, 1976–79, axonometric

▼ **355** EUGENE KUPPER
Nilsson House, Bel Air,
California, 1976–79,
interior

◀ **356** EUGENE KUPPER
Nilsson House, Bel Air,
California, 1976–79,
exterior

space—leaving breathtaking gaps to be filled in—or tear into each other, colliding, intersecting, sometimes merging playfully or with tension. Not one, but three shifted axes mark the entrance, while oval terraces, a favorite Baroque motif, erode the volumes toward the view—the rolling hills which are recalled in the undulating roof forms. The interpenetrating ovoids characteristic of the work of Kilian Ignaz Dientzenhofer (1689–1751) are recalled in the dumbbell plan of the bedroom, while the shower is in the form of an iconic volute. Both these rooms incorporate a phallic shape (but only implicitly, according to Smith).[19] At least half of the forms of the Long House are demi-forms—eroded or left unfinished—which are clear enough to demand that we mentally complete them. As we traverse the plan, we can see that the demi-forms lead us to the two explosions of space—the ovals, which are half inside the court and half outside, half embraced like a traditional plan and half open like a Modern one. This sequence is a carefully orchestrated variation of themes (or half-themes): that is, a sequence of structural surprises.

One of the most elaborate examples of such space

to have been built is Moore and Turnbull's Kresge College dormitories (**351–353**). Since I have written about these elsewhere as an example of Post-Modern space, the distinctive features will only be mentioned, not analyzed.[20] Firstly, the plan meanders on an L-shape, through a redwood forest, uniting different, highly symbolic "places." Skews, reverse perspectives, syncopated colonnades, and bright colors (behind white cutouts) orchestrate the sequence and give it variety. As opposed to a comparable Modernist university plan, such as Mies van der Rohe's Illinois Institute of Technology, the grids are inflected and punctuated with surprising elements—"monuments" to *trivial* functions, such as the laundromat, as well as monuments to significant functions (the assembly hall and mailbox area are the two foci at either end of the route). As one turns a corner, a triumphal arch is suddenly revealed (**352**); as one begins to understand the complex syncopations of the colonnades, suddenly they are broken—the ends are left empty, the rhythms unfinished (**353**). These surprises are well prepared for by similar themes stated earlier, and in that sense are structured.

A Modern or Late-Modern space might, if isotropic, be known at a glance. In the typical open office building, such as Norman Foster's Willis Faber Dumas building, we can take in the whole *and* see the edges (**150**). Even in Mies's Illinois Institute of Technology, where planes overlap, we can infer the whole from the part, and we know that the scheme is disciplined by the grid. In Post-Modern space, because it is transformational, we cannot infer the whole from the part, nor, because it is ambiguously layered, can we see the edges. These aspects heighten the drama by increasing our expectation of finding something unexpected.

Eugene Kupper's house for the singer Harry Nilsson uses several of these devices to create surprise (**354–356**). The exterior states the theme of an extruded aedicule—or spine—in an understated way. The earth colors, and sliding contours of layered space, are understated metaphors of the hilly site. (Like Frank Lloyd Wright's Ennis House of 1924 and Falling Water of 1935, which influenced the plan, walls of shallow space cascade along contours and open up to the view.) Both understatements

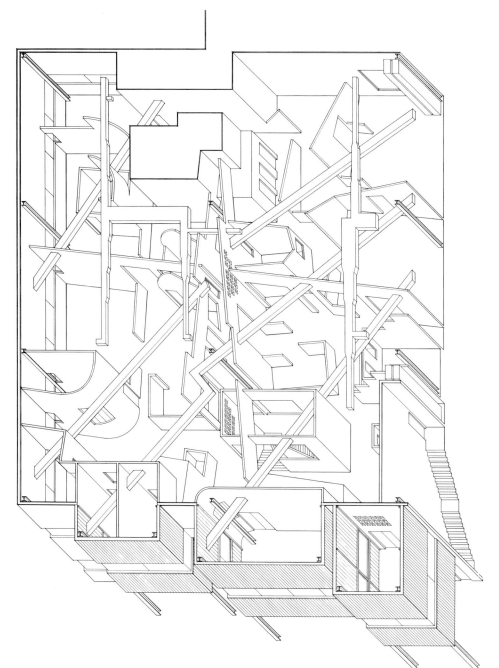

plicated Post-Modern space with a *Late-Modern use of industrial materials*. Like Eisenman, who also is not interested in semantics and symbolism, Gehry complicates space as an end in itself until it reaches the point of becoming symbolic of itself. This system is self-referential, like any aesthetic system, calling attention to itself on the level of rhetoric, not function.[21] Gehry's Mid-Atlantic Toyota Distributorship Offices use the by now (1978) conventional skewed grids and reverse perspective to create a highly ambiguous and zany interior (**357–359**). Heating ducts smash (or thread) through walls (or cutouts); pink partitions slide off at an angle and bisect other planes of space which themselves zoom off in another direction. The effect, as one looks through a sequence of five or six cutout holes, is as ambiguous as a Chinese garden. Is it ad hocism, Late-Modernism, Post-Modernism, punk, the "cheapskate aesthetic" (another Gehry claim), cutouts *à la* Moore, sadomasochism, accidentalism—or even "architecture"? Labels are hard to apply, partly because too many fit. The chain link (strewn around as though it were a fetish) with its unfortunate overtones of brutality, cheapness, and boredom, mark the work as sadomasochistic, and Gehry's extraordinary *succès d'estime* with architectural critics shows that such signs are as greatly appreciated in the architectural world as in the musical one. But this Punk exaggeration is mediated, as Gehry notes, by understatement, by hiding, by making "an invisible architecture."[22] ("The trick is not to show all your cards at once.") Only slowly are the (fortuitous?) semantic overtones recognized, and one realizes that these offices for a *Japanese car company* are appropriately themed in a utilitarian and delicate filigree of space. The most clear aspect is that the Post-

◀ 357 FRANK O. GEHRY AND ASSOCIATES, *Mid-Atlantic Toyota Distributorship Offices*, Glen Burnie, Maryland, 1978, cutaway axonometric

▼ 358 FRANK O. GEHRY AND ASSOCIATES, *Mid-Atlantic Toyota Distributorship Offices*, Glen Burnie, Maryland, 1978, interior

prepare one for the interior space which is a long, linear spine of H-frames—a public corridor as it were —which opens off into more private, surprising areas. (One unfortunate surprise is that the spine ends in a shower which affords views for and of the singer himself.) The tightly layered space descends to the right, and toward a dramatic view over Los Angeles. A center here also focuses on the hearth, the traditional heart of family life—and then opens down the minor spine to the other center, the dining table. This minor spine, which has a low ceiling, spills down over the carpet to the grass carpet outside, another surprise and a very pleasing *trompe l'oeil*. As the axonometric reveals, a basic duality is set up between the gridded spine and the attached spaces, between syncopated order and surprise.

Frank Gehry, with whom Kupper worked on the Concord Pavilion (1975), has also developed a com-

Modern spatial devices—demi-forms and elaborated confusion—are taken to a frenetic extreme, while the liminal elements are used most inappropriately (and surprisingly) for the well-ordered life of business.

Frank Gehry's converted house for himself uses many of these devices in a less aesthetic but more appropriate way (**360–363**). A twenties salmon pink house is wrapped around, and punctuated by, corrugated metal and chain link. Various parts are ripped away: studs and foundations are exposed to indicate the "reality" of construction and bring this to attention. Windows are centered and the grid is twisted and warped and skewed to undermine the right-angled world and relate to the Ron Davis painting on view (both Gehry and Davis were already "into skews" before they collaborated on the Davis House in 1977). Glass planes head toward each other at the corner—one gives way and the other

▼ **359** FRANK O. GEHRY AND ASSOCIATES, *Mid-Atlantic Toyota Distributorship Offices*, Glen Burnie, Maryland, 1978, interior

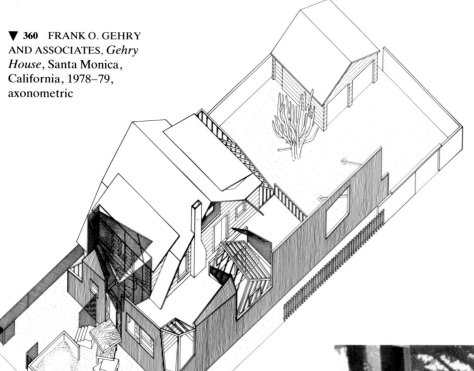

▼ **360** FRANK O. GEHRY AND ASSOCIATES, *Gehry House*, Santa Monica, California, 1978–79, axonometric

▼ **361** FRANK O. GEHRY AND ASSOCIATES, *Gehry House*, Santa Monica, California, 1978–79, interior

slides past in a botched critique of the "perfect" Modernist corner of Mies van der Rohe. New confronts old, especially in the kitchen, where the traditional ornament, wood siding, and window panes give the scale and meaning lacking in Late-Modern buildings. But the virtue of the space and its layering consists mainly in its orchestration of a series of surprising views. New frames old, or vice-versa; new erodes old, or vice-versa; high collides with low and refinement with Punk, or vice-versa. When one is outside the original house and walking on black tar, one is in fact inside the kitchen of the new house. When one looks through the living room studs to the sunken aedicule—a "primitive hut"—one is still inside the building. All boundaries are broken and the border lines are literally transgressed.

It is this transgression and elision of elements to

▼ **362** FRANK O. GEHRY AND ASSOCIATES, *Gehry House*, Santa Monica, California, 1978–79, kitchen

create an experience that is at once mysterious and full of surprises which relates Post-Modern space to religious and mystical space. To a certain extent, all art and architecture, motivated as it is to stimulate the spirit, is a spiritual activity and involves the suspension of normal categories of experience. Post-Modern space, and indeed the metaphysical architecture discussed previously, provides the equivalent of a liminal experience without, necessarily, finding confirmation in the building tasks which have led to this in the past. Surely the ultimate paradox and strength of Post-Modernism is its adamant refusal to give up the imperatives of the spirit at a time when all systems of spiritual expression have been cast into doubt.

▼ 363 FRANK O. GEHRY AND ASSOCIATES, *Gehry House*, Santa Monica, California, 1978–79, exterior

FRED BURNS, *Own House*, Belfast, Maine, c. 1941–77, exterior detail

Alternatives

INTRODUCTION

"ALTERNATIVES" CAN MEAN TOO MANY THINGS. DEPENDING upon viewpoint, there can be many different technological, aesthetic, social, or political ways to skin the same architectural cat. Throughout architectural history, and particularly within the last two decades, a genre of graphic, conceptual architecture has flourished; much of this has been alternative in the absolute sense that it was never meant to be (or could not be) built, but rather aimed to offer up speculations, elaborate conceits, or provocations. (The work of the English group Archigram, or Claes Oldenburg's *Proposals for Monuments and Buildings* series, has perhaps been more effective for being unbuilt.)[1] Yet, also in the recent past, amateurs and others outside the design professions have increasingly been building alternatives to both conceptual and conventional architecture. The following chapters deal almost exclusively with *built* examples of such outsiders' architecture. It is not an arbitrary criterion, since this kind of alternative architecture happens to be short on theory but long on practice. (And since much of it resulted from designing-by-doing, drawings illustrating it were usually made *after* construction.)

Registered architects, to their sincere regret, are responsible for only a minuscule percentage of the built environment, but the rest is not necessarily alternative architecture. Most commercial construction makes no claim to be architecture at all. Falling somewhere between traditional vernacular and do-it-yourself utility, the alternatives, first exemplified by the commune Drop City, were unprecedented in that new ways of building and living seemed to have been invented or discovered for each other, simultaneously.

This sets our chronology, beginning about 1965 and continuing through the seventies. Its scope takes in the alternative subcultures active in the same period. My first two chapters span the commune movement from which much alternative architecture was disseminated; subsequent net shifts of emphasis and theme can be followed in the genealogical chart provided (see page 221), although obviously such diagrammatic organization is of arguable value. For reference to these phenomena or episodes I keep a consistent terminology even if it, too, is not always or entirely satisfactory. The problem with the term *counterculture* is that it is defined by its opposite, but I employ it in the historical sense of Theodore Roszak's *The Making of a Counter Culture*;[2] for background see this and other contemporary accounts. The term *mainstream* seems preferable to monoculture for the social and architectural data to which any culture-within-a-culture might be alternative. *Life-style* is, today, a word over-used for individuals' cultural surrogates, but must be more than personal habits or outlook to be meaningful. (The anthropologists' *genre de vie* or *modus vivendi* are more exact, but by the same token the term *life-style* is not bound to the social sciences and, if an indiscriminate cliché, is at least in English.) Although the architecture discussed within these chapters is current inasmuch as its incidence is still influential, some years have distanced us from the events or spirit circumscribing its origins. Present detachment may even help put them into perspective. To my knowledge, the architectural history and, to a lesser degree, the language of alternatives have not been compiled before in this form.

The times, Bob Dylan sang, were a-changing, certainly, but in what direction? As in an earlier revolutionary moment, "It was the best of times, it was the worst of times."[3] It was the age of creative surges in many arts, it was the age of crazes now forgotten; it was the epoch of belief in dream futures, it was the epoch of cynicism about itself; it was the season of Human Be-Ins and Flower Power, it was the season of police repression and race riots; it was the spring of euphoric Peace and Love, it was the winter of anti-war and political despair. The violent contrasts of the late sixties—in the Paris of student *manifestations*, in swinging London, and in Vietnam no less than in the America of Woodstock Nation—left open wounds and a sense of something momentous, climactic, having happened. Its complexity and contradictions may not have been legible in its alternative architecture, but that architecture's content was, in a way, change itself. It was not about stylistic change. Any new style is a tentative successor to whatever is extant, and architectural history—made by architectural historians—"alternates" in such cycles. This Alternatives section is about parallel architectures, not a progression of styles chronological or individual.

There was also a geographical component of change. Examples come from Europe, Canada, and America, but especially its Southwest and West Coast, for there the narrative begins. This, I believe, was because the stirrings of the counterculture corresponded in place as well as time with a larger redirection of American energies during the sixties from the rest of the country to what has been dubbed the Sun Belt. This stretches from California down into Arizona, thence through Texas and the "New South" to Florida. As Pittsburgh's steel mills, Detroit's automobile plants, and Chicago's manufacturing were supplanted by new industrial technologies—electronics in northern California's "Silicon Valley," aerospace in Seattle, Houston, and Cape Canaveral—wealth and workers flowed into the Sun Belt,

in the middle of which, Texas, a new financial nexus was centered on oil. Not unconnected with this national economic displacement, the political power base also switched from the old Eastern establishment. After John Fitzgerald Kennedy was assassinated in Dallas and Robert Francis Kennedy in Los Angeles, the next four Presidents all hailed from the Sun Belt: Johnson, Nixon, Carter, and Reagan. Under Nixon, Presidential palaces at San Clemente and Key Biscayne marked the western and southern reaches of the Belt, and all the President's men came from there too. Even organized crime migrated westward to the rich pickings of Las Vegas, from which Yale architectural students began to learn rather than from European Grand Tours. So the alternative architecture movement quite physically followed the same

demographic pattern, and I have prepared a map (**364**) to suggest how they coincided.

THE ROLE OF OUTSIDERS

WHEN A MEMBER OF THE COLORADO COMMUNE LIBRE avowed, "We are trying to subvert the building industry in its present form,"[4] this *was* an idle threat. The commune builders may have hoped to set an example by their isolated independence, but any effect they had on conventional architecture was not on a material plane. The role played by alternative architecture—stimulating or acting as a sounding board for mainstream ideas and issues—was one laid upon it by mainstream designers and critics themselves, and therefore subject to their own interests and misconceptions. For instance, because it was popularly

▼ **364** Map showing the westward migration of alternative architectures, 1960–80

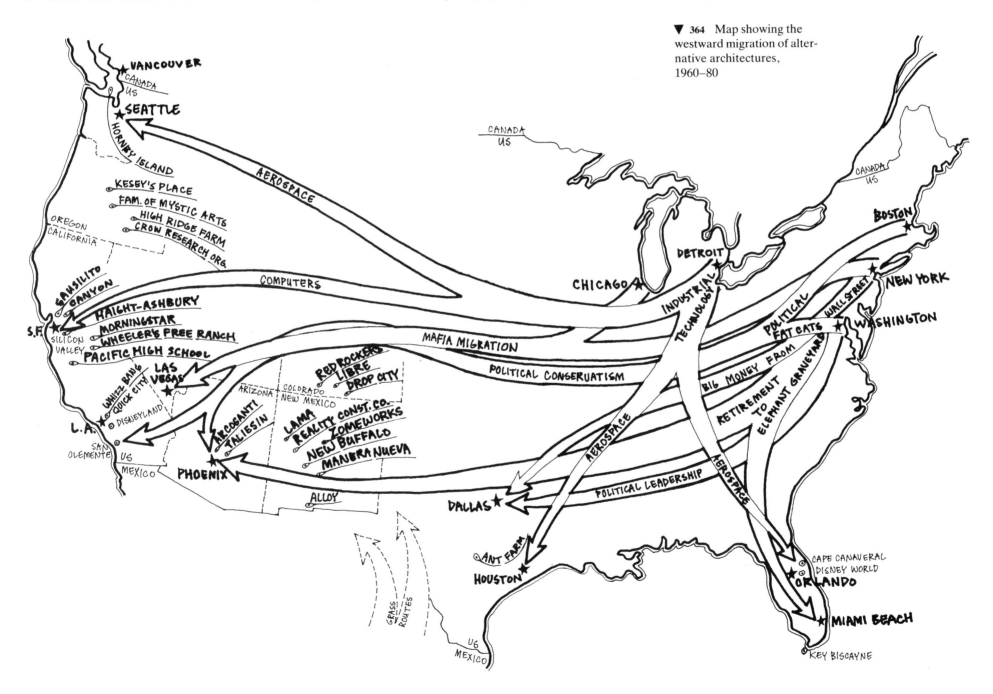

supposed that the commune movement was in passive revolt against technology (Roszak's *The Making of a Counter Culture* is subtitled "Reflections on the Technocratic Society and Its Youthful Opposition"), alternative architecture was not looked to for advanced building techniques. Instead, what was expected was found: vernacular revival, simplified self-build, and low-gain energy systems—all on the de-industrialized model of an "underdeveloped country" of communes.

Simply to describe the adobe pueblo of the New Buffalo commune—with its primitive farming and building methods learned from local aboriginal tribes—might make it seem as though these White Anglo-Saxon Protestant dropouts were playing at being Red Indians. There was more to it than that for them, but their endeavor was also taken seriously as living out a yearning attributable to many professional architects and planners: vernacular nostalgia. Demonstrable connections between natural environment, built habitat, and human culture had been lost to modern housing, but could still be found in remote indigenous preserves. As far back as 1959 Ralph Erskine reported to the C.I.A.M. Congress (convened by Team Ten urbanists) on living in the sub-Arctic tundra, while Herman Haan presented vernacular studies from the Sahara.[5] Aldo van Eyck, also a Team Ten member, had to dwell among the Dogon tribe of West Africa in order to experience "Meaning in Architecture."[6]

In addition to vernacular nostalgia, a guilty social conscience afflicted many liberals among architects and planners of the sixties. While they agonized over accusations of professional elitism, and began advocating community activism over imposed housing policies, and as their ideal tower blocks came tumbling down, they looked approvingly on alternative efforts. Here was participatory design, communal self-determination. As astutely noted: "The reason for the recent popularity of barriadas in architectural circles is that they dramatize in a non-romantic way the opportunity for determining one's own way of life and life style. Many other examples of this individual initiative could be given in the West, from the 'self-build' groups in England to 'Drop City' in America. . . ."[7] This commentator could lump together South American barriadas with North American communes to make the point that both were self-built and designed by their unschooled inhabitants, in defiance of authority. However, differences of intent must also bear upon this Alternatives section. The American communes were built by middle-class exiles from the cities, prepared to de-culture themselves through new environments. The barriadas were built by peasants coming *to* the cities, on whose

outskirts they "squatted" while trying to work *into* industrialized urban society, with all its material benefits. As these accrued, the original makeshift houses were improved until they achieved the desired image, and economic reality, of middle-class respectability; and the barriadas—once politically unified by community action—became new suburbs. Whereas barriada architecture strove to replicate suburban norms, commune architecture opposed them with alternative forms, even if the building processes were similarly self-initiated in each case. For this reason, barriadas will not be pursued further as a subset of Alternatives, but communes will be.

It was only by taking aspects of commune architecture out of context that it could be made relevant to current concerns of mainstream professionals. That historical context, for those new forms, could itself be misinterpreted. In a talk given in 1971, Anatole Kopp assumed the commune movement to have been escapist, and faulted its architecture for it: "Some people . . . take refuge in a new utopia: they think that if they change their own way of living they will gradually change society, they form communes . . . and some, in America at least, even imagine an architecture adapted to their needs . . . I don't believe in the possibility of making small islands of independent life, and even less in the possibility of structuring them and giving them real architectural expression."[8] Kopp's model was the Old Left theory of buildings as social condensers, which both mold and mirror the new society. Thus, "there cannot be a really *new* architecture, a *revolutionary* architecture except in the context of total social upheaval," as in Russian Constructivism.[9] Yet even if the convulsions of 1968 rated as such a social upheaval, the apolitical counterculture furnished no coherent ideology for either its social or architectural experiments. Alternative forms bore no inbuilt revolutionary symbolism, as witnessed by the ease with which domes, solar energy, and handmade houses were co-opted into mainstream acceptability. Indeed, the language of alternative architecture seemed, to arbiters of style, more like the new pluralist freedom of progressive designers in the sixties: inclusivist and anti-purist rather than ideologically consistent. The *funk aesthetic*, as I call the underground version of pluralism, was, however, as much a builders' as a designers' mode, taken beyond the drawing board into the building's construction and use.

Since their responses to alternative architecture tell us more about mainstream architects and critics than about the alternatives themselves, it is worth questioning at least one critical premise. Was alternative architecture really an anti-technological refutation of "the scientific world-view of the Western

tradition," from which, Roszak maintained, the counterculture had dropped out? There is considerable evidence to the contrary. While rural simplicity characterized agrarian communes, and raw materials or junk replaced industrial building technology, a few quotes suggest that it was not that simple. The founder of Lama, expounding his commune's spiritual awareness, added offhandedly: "We've been talking about putting in a computer terminal here—a kind of group mind to serve as a storage bank of all the minds in all the communes and what they're learning."[10] The commune of Libre wanted one too: "With a computer we could do everything. We could be doctors, physicists . . . Renaissance men!"[11] And from Drop City went up the feverish cry: "We want videotape recorders and cameras and strobes—hundreds of them—and tape decks and amps and echo chambers and everything . . . we want an atomic reactor."[12]

Although this does not demand to be taken so literally, it is indicative of the communes' thinking. Apparently technology was not entirely anathema, especially cybernetics, media, and other software as art, play, or tools. Alternative designers were too much "technocracy's children" (Roszak) not to take along their infatuation with creative science and invention, if not the industrial system. In fact, far from initial distrust of high technology, over-enthusiasm for it and its liberating potential marked the earliest commune-building phase, much inspired by Buckminster Fuller. (He, before becoming godfather to Drop City, had already been taken up by Archigram and other avant-gardists on a conceptual level.) Only later did the counterculture find its own balance with handmade houses and alternative technologies.

This survey can only skirt the vast pool of information on alternative energy. As for geodesics and zonahedra, I refer to these in the terminology habitual to their designers. Terms like *rhombicosadodecahedron* are not jargon—intended to impress, mystify, or exclude the uninitiated—but are as geometrically specific as *cube*. Their difficulty lies in being less familiar, yet I can only hope readers will accept them as they would *pediment* or *groin vault* in other architectures. Alternative design has been somewhat abused by coverage at the opposite extreme of too loosely blanketing polyhedral buildings as domes when they were not. Less-technical terminology can be more sensitive and, when dealing with the vagaries of style, calls for further explanation.

THE FUNK AESTHETIC

I FREELY USE THE TERMS FUNK OR FUNKY FOR OBservable visual or methodological elements common to many of the examples of alternative design given here. The terminology fits insofar as it was understood in the counterculture of the late sixties, even though the words remained largely undefined. By the time Bill Voyd of Drop City wrote his article on Funk Architecture (1971) there were already musical associations with Funky Blues, and a dance, The Funky Chicken. Tom Wolfe had also applied the word to codes of dress in "Funky Chic." In the cradle of the counterculture, San Francisco, an exhibition of Funk Art was held as early as 1967; the catalogue contained an introductory essay by the art historian Peter Selz, to whose "Notes on Funk" I am indebted.

Selz confirms that Funk was San Francisco's artistic alternative to both the rarified, intellectualized Minimalism of New York and the cultural consumerism of the Los Angeles art market. Like the anti-formalism of San Francisco Beat poets during the fifties, Funk Art began as an irreverent gesture toward free association, brash juxtapositions, and dark satirical humor. Following the self-parody of ceramicists making useless pots, a number of local artists in the sixties took to constructing *outre* sculptures of wood, metal, plastics, fabrics, clay, and other materials of unlikely kinship. Although three-dimensional, these were often polychromed like paintings. They were rarely altogether abstract *or* figurative, vaguely perverse, and usually given suggestive titles. "Funk Art is hot rather than cool," contends Selz, "it is sensuous, and frequently it is quite ugly and ungainly." When he says, "Its subliminal post-Freudian imagery often suggests erotic and scatological forms and relationships," he could almost have been referring to Drop City—created as "an elaborate dropping"—or the testicular protuberances of the House of the Century by the Ant Farm design group.

Selz's chosen precursors of Funk Art encompass Lewis Carroll's "Jabberwocky," Alfred Jarry's *Ubu Roi*, and the Theater of the Absurd generally, as well as Marcel Duchamp's self-imposed "tastelessness" and Dada and Surrealism generally. Early Pop Art contributed to the tradition, yet Funk differs in not merely accepting "the vulgarity of the contemporary man-made environment"[13] but in transforming its subject matter. (Architectural instances of this might be the use of junked-automobile tops for the roofs of domes or zomes at Drop City and other communes, or Ant Farm's rituals of, and monuments to, American Kar Kulture.) However, while Selz offered valuable characterizations of the essence of Funk in the art he gathered for exhibition, the artists themselves resisted verbal commitment. "When you see it, you know it," they equivocated.[14] This was like "The Unspoken Thing" among the Pranksters, Ken Kesey's embryonic hippies,[15] and like evasive reticence in the counterculture about articulating what was an ineffable attitude or quality of experience. So if, for them, art and life-style were one, then there could be no special aesthetic terminology, and in neither art nor life was Funk dissected.

What is fairly certain, though, is that the word no longer conformed to its traditional dictionary definitions: "to flinch, shrink back, or be afraid" as a verb, or, as a noun, the abject state of being "in a funk." Such usage, once prevalent in English literature and speech, is mentioned only as a reminder that the words now connote just the opposite. With its etymology reversed, like the counterculture term *freak*, funky is *not* fearful, but defiant, undeterred. (This may have first been borrowed from another subculture: since the twenties, the Blues sound of black jazz bands marching in funerals was *funky*, i.e., brave, unsophisticated, but soulful.) "Funk objects, which are loud, unashamed, and free" (Selz), can be disconcerting in their candidness and, if accepted with all their honest imperfections, can have a bold, raw kind of beauty.

It is not so much that Funk's lack of semantic precision lends it sublime ambiguity, but that its lack of conceptual idealization was natural to an alternative design aesthetic. The counterculture had its conventional wisdom too, one nugget of which was "For waiting to do it perfect, it never gets done."[16] The naive and audacious Drop Cities of alternative America would never have been begun if their builders had been intimidated by poor prospects for accomplishment or deficiencies in skill, experience, and systematic direction; the whole movement was an amateur affair. Funkily unafraid, they went ahead regardless, and if the millennium did not arrive, well, that had not been their goal. What did result, tangibly, was new architecture. The uninhibited effort is doubtless still being made, in ways as yet undocumented.

THE COMMUNE BUILDERS

DROP CITY WAS NOT REALLY TYPICAL OF SELF-BUILT alternative settlements in the American Southwest, although it shared certain characteristics with some of them, but it was the first. To an arid, windswept goat pasture near Trinidad, Colorado, came two or three former art students from the University of Kansas. In early 1965 they purchased five or six acres. They already had in mind an image of A-frame architecture, but then they heard a talk by Buckminster Fuller. Thereafter, "it was obvious," affirmed the commune's chronicler Peter Rabbit, "that Drop City should be geodesic domes."[1] Enthusiasm aside, none of the Droppers (as they called themselves) then fully understood the technical geometry of geodesics, and the model they copied turned out to be a dodecahedral dome instead (**365**). Eighteen feet in diameter, it was constructed of scrap timber, fenestrated with automobile windshields, waterproofed in tar paper, and painted sky blue. Their second dome, used as a kitchen to the first, was of roughly the same construction and size, yet a true geodesic.

So Drop City grew, adding several more small dwelling domes, a thirty-foot-diameter domical workshop, and a forty-foot theater dome, all geodesic, by 1966. In April of that year, Steve Baer became involved. Baer was not a resident member but an unconventional designer living nearby who had been intellectually intrigued by geodesic and other geometries since 1963 through Fuller's books, Keith Critchlow's work in London,[2] and recondite mathematical papers. By inventing an architecture based on these geometries, he wanted not only to explore abstract topologies, but also alternatives to what he saw as overly traditional, expensive, and restrictive status-quo construction, which perverted technology and wasted resources.

Baer's geometrical investigations crystallized into the architectural applications of zonahedra. These derive from semi-regular Archimedian solids, some of whose polygonal facets have parallel sides—unlike triangulated geodesics—and so can be distended by changing side lengths without affecting angles.[3] Baer's first Drop City design, an asymmetrical zonahedron (**366**), proffered a more flexible alternative to the geodesic dome, which must always be a portion of a sphere and thus have a circular floor and radial symmetry. To object that the fourteen-by-twenty-seven-foot space of Baer's "stretched" dome could be more easily approximated with rectilinear geometry and traditional building methods would be to miss the experimental point. Baer and his crew prefabricated panels of sheet metal cut from the tops of junked cars; the resultant structure, known as the Cartop Dome, cost about fifteen dollars and took two-and-a-half days to erect, from the commencement of foundations to the Droppers moving in. The steel skin had no internal supports, frame, or bracing other than integral folds in the metal.

By autumn 1966 Drop City had outgrown its kitch-

▶ **365** *Dodecahedral Dome*, Drop City, Colorado, 1965. The structure to the right is a solar collector, built later

en dome. Baer's next design, for a larger and more versatile communal facility, showed another advantage over geodesic domes, which cannot be joined to each other with any geometric grace. His three intersecting rhombicosadodecahedra (367), however, could be joined very neatly, and the resultant interior, while spatially unified, implied places for separate activities in the three lobes—each thirty-five feet in diameter—and in the open loft over their common intersection. In addition to the kitchen there was an eating area, a sort of lounge, a library, toilets and storage enclosed below the loft, workshops, and a washing machine: the whole a community center called the Complex (368). Externally, it too was clad in cartops, this time left in their original colors, direct from the dead hand of Detroit, with the joints between the panels crudely sealed in thick black tar, which out-

that counterculture architecture was not necessarily without its architects (even though Drop City figures among *vernacular* studies in Paul Oliver's *Shelter and Society*). On the other hand, while Baer freely traded his designs for the opportunity afforded, the relationship was never that of architect to client. Baer learned from Drop City, tempering his pristine polyhedral geometries with the salvage ethic and funk aesthetic of the Droppers' building methods and social needs. And where the Droppers had attempted a solar cooker—a splendid-looking antler-like assemblage of rear-view mirrors to focus the sun's rays—Baer undertook to make such artful and well-meant gestures actually work. Others joined him to become itinerant, architectural Johnny Appleseeds and wandering alternative-energy tinkers, dropping their designs at several more Southwestern communes.

nor waterproof, and eventually had to be shingled, effacing the clean-edged faceting.) The panels required five weeks to prefabricate but only three days to bolt together on site. At Manera Nueva, Baer extended the clustering potential of zonahedra, and repeated the garnet-crystal form of Drop City's Cartop Dome as a module in a fourfold asymmetrical complex, armored in overlapping cartops (370). Another zonahedron was constructed of kaleidoscopic panels reinforced with beer cans.

Drawing upon their Drop City experience, Libre also built geodesics: a forty-foot-diameter communal kitchen and workshop (ceramics, wood-working, jewelry, sewing, welding) adjacent to a twenty-two-foot bedroom dome (371), among others. Another house had a heavy, earthbound structure of stacked railway ties for its polygonally planned lower floor,

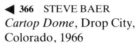

◀ 366 STEVE BAER *Cartop Dome*, Drop City, Colorado, 1966

▶ 367 STEVE BAER *The Complex*, Drop City, Colorado, 1966, roof plan

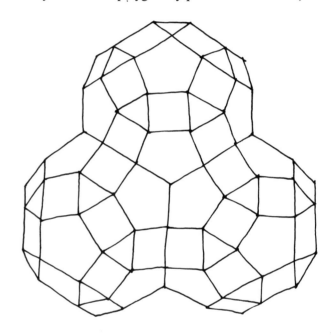

lined the patchwork of shapes like an impossibly crude Mondrian. The Complex gave Drop City (and to some degree the whole commune movement) its most familiar, photogenic, iconic image, reproduced in many publications—underground, overground, and architectural. In an architectural context, Drop City—and the existence of an alternative architecture discovered in it—triggered topical dialogues about ecological accountability, junk architecture, ad-hocist improvisation, and other associations not necessarily intended by its builders. European magazines especially, sufficiently removed from the American scene to idealize it, superimposed their own interpretations on these "coupoles géodesiques pour l'habitat hippie" or "Drop City: Le Cathedrali della protesta."[4]

Baer's design contributions to Drop City—and, later, to other communes—showed, on the one hand,

Due to an increasingly disruptive influx of gawking tourists, journalists, photographers, and sociologists, as well as new arrivals dropping in uninvited to seek counterculture sanctuary and free lunches, most of the "old" Droppers felt themselves forced to move on. One faction, spearheaded by the indomitable Peter Rabbit, trekked sixty miles over the proverbial next mountain, like many Colorado pioneers before them, to greener and more inaccessible pastures, three hundred and sixty acres at an altitude of nine thousand feet. They founded a new commune, Libre, in June 1968. Another splinter group moved south to Placitas, New Mexico, joining a commune called Manera Nueva. For both of these venues, Steve Baer again designed virtuoso structures. Peter Rabbit's house at Libre, a "four-fused exploded rhombic dodecahedron" (369) was covered not in cartops but in fiberboard. (This proved neither strong enough

capped with an airy, silver-painted dome for sleeping. "A house form which echoes the mountain peaks" had pyramidal roofs over four equal areas for living room, kitchen, workshop, and children's room, with two lofts above. Still another was built around a twenty-nine-ton boulder, on which rested eight "spokes" radiating from it to posts. There was also an adobe, an A-frame, and a cement-shell house. By 1973, when Libre had already lasted longer than its parent Drop City, and had a dozen or so dwellings completed, this second-generation commune seemed to have achieved sequestered freedom both from the outside (Libre means free in Spanish) and freedom of individual expression in its architectural variety. Although "no one is a trained architect or construction engineer," and "no one at Libre has any money," yet, "the house builds itself," members claimed.[5] A visitor was moved to remark: "Libre was an artistic

statement, and the medium through which it conveyed its image of the future was architecture."[6]

Libre's character as an artists' commune was carried over from Drop City, as were a number of the
characters involved. The artists who founded Drop
City did paintings, some of which ended up as table-
tops for the dining room of the Complex (**372**), or
panels lining the inside of the Cartop Dome (**373**);
moreover, the multicolored domes were paintings
themselves. The commune was both object and event,
"with no distinction between art and life."[7] The
charter members had done impromptu Happenings,
called Droppings, in their University of Kansas days,
held a Joy Festival at Drop City, and put a multimedia road show on tour to spread their message and
finance their commune. Their attitude that "Drop
City is conceived as an elaborate dropping" promised
no more permanence than a Happening; it never
became, socially, an established community, yet the
artistic statement had been made. After Drop City
had been disbanded as a commune in the autumn of
1969, its counterculture reputation still attracted
fledgling dropouts to what had become instead a
decompression chamber or halfway house. Many
paused to wonder at the derelict domes (**374–375**)
and the legendary lost tribe which once raised them.

Although the apparently spontaneous, intuitive
environmental design which sympathetic outsiders
(especially architects) saw in Drop City, Libre, and
Manera Nueva could be attributed to the art back-
grounds of the communards and the supplementary
role of Steve Baer, other communes also sought an
architecture as radical as the social alternatives sheltered within—indeed, an architecture which symbolized as well as sheltered. Architecture, historically,
has purveyed cultural values, and it may seem extraordinary that a subsociety as volatile, dispersed,
and unstable as the commune movement should
produce its own architecture, especially in only a
few years. Some builders were no doubt negatively
motivated to reject the architectural norms of the
society they had left behind, as in the original Droppers' impulse to construct A-frames as an alternative
to suburban boxes. With the geodesic dome, however, communes chose by simultaneous consensus a
shape meaningful to them ideologically; what they
thought the form language of the dome could say to
or about them will be considered in the next chapter.

Another quite different iconological source was cul-
tivated by those communes more committed to back-
to-the-land agrarianism: American Indian architecture. Such communes were particularly numerous

in marginally arable northern New Mexico (the
1970 Census estimated their combined population at
between five hundred and one thousand)[8] with an
epicenter at Taos, whose ancient Hopi pueblo was still
inhabited (**376**). Earliest of these communes was New
Buffalo, founded in the summer of 1967 and named
from the buffalo which had provided food, clothing,
fuel, and shelter for the Plains Indians; so would the
community take care of all the needs of its members.
In attempting agricultural self-sufficiency (unlike
Drop City), the New Buffalo communards consulted
the local Hopi Indians not only on how to plant corn
but even on how to do the Corn Dance which sanc-
tified their efforts, and they also maintained the regional Indian diet. Architecturally, too, they imitated
the Indian manner of building, using available materials like sun-dried mud-brick adobe from the
good earth itself (**377**) to suit the locale and their
limited budget. In a semi-sunken, skylit space called
the Circle (**378**)—corresponding to the ceremonial
room, or *kiva*, of Hopi pueblos—they practiced rites
of the Native American Church and held other communal gatherings. Adjoining this was the more casual
social focus of the kitchen, with a bathroom behind. Flanking wings contained individual dwelling
rooms, each ten by twelve feet, with authentic dirt
floors and sod roofs supported by log beams. These
rooms, twelve in all, opened onto an outdoor plaza,
pueblo-like, enclosed on three sides. The whole New
Buffalo pueblo cost only two hundred dollars. Before completing it they lived in tipis, which continued
to serve as summer quarters.

The tipi in fact became the standard tent of the
counterculture (**379**), accommodating the new nomadism, although the twenty-foot-long poles of the

◀ **370** STEVE BAER
Garnet-Crystal Dome,
Manera Nueva, New Mexico, 1968

▼ **371** *Geodesic Domes*,
Libre, Colorado, 1968

Plains Indians' buffalo-hide tipis were dragged behind their ponies, not loaded into psychedelic vans. "Tipis are cheap and portable," as *The Whole Earth Catalog* endorsed them. "To live in one involves intimate familiarity with fire, earth, sky, and roundness . . . you can appreciate the elegant design of the tipi and the completeness of the culture that produced it." Other Indian forms were similarly annexed. The Family of the Mystic Arts, in Oregon, all lived in a large, log-walled hexagon, its floor below grade, very like Western Indian earth lodges even to the smoke hole over the open stone fireplace in the center. Around half the inside perimeter ran two tiers of sleeping berths for twenty to thirty people, separated by curtains, bookcases, or personal storage partitions adjustable according to need. On the other side, slightly raised, was a kitchen and dining platform. During the summer many members here too dispersed to tipis, just as the Indians had only wintered together in their clan house. Adaptations of the Navajo Indians' hogans, smaller but equivalent in shape and construction (earth walls supported by timbers) and also partaking of a roughcast, earthy, even troglodyte vernacular, vied with basic adobe in the Southwest. Four miles from New Buffalo were Reality Construction Company,

◀ **372** *Painting*, Drop City,
Colorado, 1965–68

▲ **373** *Painting*, Drop City,
Colorado, 1965–68

◀ 374 STEVE BAER
The Complex, Drop City, Colorado, 1966, exterior after abandonment, photographed 1974

▼ 375 *Geodesic Dome*, Drop City, Colorado, c. 1965, exterior after abandonment, photographed c. 1973

▶ 376 *Hopi Pueblo*, Taos, New Mexico

with one adobe rectangle of ten rooms and a communal kitchen, and Morningstar East, with a twelve-room pueblo and a kiva entered authentically from above, the ladder's rungs representing world stages in Hopi cosmology. By avoiding high technology, private ownership, and the material comforts to which most of these formerly urban Americans had been bred, in favor of the spiritual rewards of kinship with nature and each other which they believed the native Americans had found, the farming communes hoped to regain a state of aboriginal grace. As they identified with an Indian cultural model, so the architecture which went with it was an outward sign of that grace.

Only nine miles from New Buffalo was Lama, a commune whose physical style combined Indian-inspired architecture with the geometrics of Steve Baer. Like New Buffalo, Lama was guided by "consultants" from the Taos pueblo; and Lama's main building, the Center (**380–381, 383**), is of adobe construction, with characteristic protruding beam ends. But the dome over the middle is a zonahedron, designed by Baer and erected by helpers from Drop City. It was the commune's leading light, Steve Durkee, who actually coined the term *zome* for such zonahedral domes, and Lama Foundation which published Baer's seminal *Dome Cookbook* on them. Although Durkee collaborated with Baer on design, and had himself been a Pop, environmental, and media artist in New York,[9] the community he set up here is not an artists' colony. Nor is it a farming commune like New Buffalo (both began life at the same time, June 1967) but rather a School for Basic Studies of those spiritual disciplines relevant to the "self-actualization" of each resident. Selected for membership by the others and limited to about twenty-five, the residents follow a daily routine of work and various religious exercises, yet without adherence to denominational dogmas or the authority of any one guru. The foundation took its name from a deserted local village, Lama, prosaically meaning *red mud* in Spanish—but also *teacher* in Tibetan, thus the community itself teaches.

Durkee had initially envisaged a large geodesic dome encircled by smaller ones. But as Lama developed—being well-funded, smoothly organized, and consequently longer-lived than most—its architectural parlance became a composite as syncretic as its inclusive religious philosophy encompassing Eastern and Western, individual enlightenment and mass communion. The changes are more literally rung on Lama's version of church bells or prayer gongs—two empty pressurized-gas cylinders and the flared rocket nozzle of an ICBM found in a junkyard (where else but in America?)—calling members to the domed Center for, say, Sufi dervish-dancing on Sundays. Under the rhomboidal panels and diamond skylights of Baer's peaked zome, the floor's octagonal shape is echoed by a gaping God's-eye window. In one adobe wing is a Japanese tub large enough for everyone, surrounded by an indoor garden. The other wing contains a windowless meditation room and a library. Exterior massing, spreading its low adobe wings in symmetrical repose (**383**), is detailed with care and perhaps with cosmological or meditational patterns to be discovered in the windowpanes.

Communal meals take place in a separate two-story wooden building, again octagonal in plan and topped by a Baer-designed zome. A dumbwaiter rises from the kitchen below, through the floor of the dining level above, and indeed right through the center of the table. Residents also live in separate structures including six A-frames (each eight-by-ten feet with a sleeping loft, each subtly different), a six-person dormitory, three eneacontrahedron-roofed houses designed by Baer, in addition to a barn, an A-frame outhouse, goathouse, doghouse, and, as a greenhouse, a solar-heated "grow-hole." Speaking of his urban past, Steve Durkee recalled: "We had always sought to fit our communal lives into physical

forms that were unfit to contain them." Making alternative arrangements for Lama was important for that reason, or because, as Barbara Durkee said, "We praise God by building domes." Lama's architecture may be, broadly, a cross between Drop City and New Buffalo, but its standard of craftsmanship is far superior to either. With naturally finished, milled lumber and fitted glazing rather than cartops and windshields, the zomes redeem their mathematical lucidity. The same observer who had acclaimed Libre conceded of Lama: "The buildings are the finest examples of contemporary communal architecture in America." They are enhanced, of course, by their wooded mountainside setting with its one-hundred-and-fifty-mile views over the primeval Sangre de Cristo range, and are perhaps worthier of it than nearby Red Mud, New Mexico.

OPEN LAND, OPEN PLAN

A GEOGRAPHICAL CONSTELLATION OF SOUTHWESTERN communes could be grouped by amalgamating those of northern New Mexico, having their focus at Taos—New Buffalo, Morningstar East, Reality, Lorien, Tawapa, Manera Nueva, Lama—with Drop City, Libre, and Red Rockers across the arbitrary state line in southern Colorado. Other local clusters appeared in Oregon and northern California on the West Coast, in the Hudson River Valley and New England—especially Vermont—in the East, and were scattered elsewhere to a total number of American communes reliably estimated to be from two to three thousand,[10] all between 1965 and 1970. How communes may be defined and accounted for as a symptom of the times is best left to the exhaustive literature available. It should be reemphasized here, however, that the great variety of their alternatives contradicts the Peace-and-Love stereotype.

Communes based on farming, spiritual self-awareness, and life-style-as-art have so far been surveyed. Self-sufficiency could be other than agricultural, as at Twin Oaks, Virginia, a manufacturing collective governed by the behaviorist principles of B. F. Skinner's *Walden Two*; and self-awareness could be pursued, not only through religious teachings, but through psycho-sexual liberation, as in Harrad West's group marriage in Berkeley, California, or at Arrakis, a rural New York commune of professional psychologists living in perpetual, marathon group therapy. More extroverted, ambulatory communes plied the counterculture itself with design services, like Zomeworks, or did good works like Hog Farm, or disseminated information tools like *The Whole Earth Catalog*.

A "community in print," the *Catalog*'s communications network and clearinghouse of survival skills kept the communes informed, not least of each other's existence, particularly in the Southwest. Its prime mover and editor, Stewart Brand, had been one of Ken Kesey's Pranksters—the early sixties proto-commune—and before that a biochemist. So it was as a biological metaphor that he saw the communes *evolving*, each in its way re-inventing culture. Since, "the main design element of evolution is variability," and the number of variables proportional to the chances of workable mutations, then: "the more communes the better. Big ones, little ones, urban, rural . . ."[11] Design—choice preempting random chance—becomes an evolutionary tool, but requires data never learned in middle-class homes and schools.

As it happened, new architecture in many communes was either not required pragmatically or, if built, not very interesting. To an outsider, one of the buildings at Twin Oaks "looked like a summer camp rec hall," another "reminded me of an airplane hangar"; in a third, "the room looked like a firehouse."[12] Perhaps too true to their utilitarianism, Twin Oaks' members lived in rooms ranged in rows on either side of their factory work space, with concrete floors underfoot and fluorescent lighting overhead. In the Southwest, not only were there usually no preexisting buildings for communes to use, but those they built seem to have been about architectural meanings as well as functions. However, this did not extend to site planning; so even if there is no "typical" counterculture commune, they all still contrast with previous intentional communities in respect to the spatial relationships between buildings, or group form.

Utopian schemes of the nineteenth century, and earlier, were often accompanied by city plans neatly diagramming their structured societies, as in the French social theorist Charles Fourier's Phalansteries or Robert Owen's New Harmony, Indiana, a quadrangle one thousand feet on a side, "so regulated [as] to form . . . greater physical, moral, and intellectual advantages than have ever yet been realized in any age or country."[13] The Drop Cities of Aquarian America, rather than idealizing a system of social engineering into which individuals were to fit, took their identity from the proclivities of their members, and have not generally been regulated at all. New Buffalo might seem an exception, planned as it was around a public plaza, yet because it merely emulated the Indian community which evolved that form and its signification, it proves the rule. A pervasive myth of idealistic Americans, "from Thomas Jefferson to Frank Lloyd Wright,"[14] urged the promised land of a utopian society, and an architecture for it, without cities.

◀ 377 *Main Building*, New Buffalo, New Mexico, 1967, exterior detail

▶ 378 *The Circle*, New Buffalo, New Mexico, 1967, interior

▼ 379 *Tipi*, Whiz Bang Quick City East, New York, 1972

hopefuls fled the great British recession. A newspaper report of August, 1981, gave the more-or-less permanent population as fifty adults and twenty children. And although its chosen "architecture" is the North American Indian tipi, the encampment is also a rarity in being far from the American continent and ethos.

An earlier open-land commune was Morningstar West in California. As with many other communes, land was purchased by a wealthy benefactor, in

These were urban folk, after all, who went back to the land. Even the Woodstock Festival—an "instant city" of five hundred thousand souls—was advertised as a *nature* trip: "Three days of peace and music. Hundreds of acres to roam on or walk around without seeing a skyscraper or traffic light. Fly a kite, sun yourself. Cook your own food and breathe unspoiled air."[15] Fly a kite, indeed, with half a million other people? That this densely packed brotherhood would seem preferable to the urban structure represented by "a traffic light" had been prophesied by Marshall McLuhan, whose Global Village conceptually nullified quantitative physical space.[16]

Longer-term versions of the Woodstock environmental Happening were the open-land communes. One of them, dating back to the early seventies, originated as refugees from the city set up tipis in the green havens of a remote Welsh valley somewhere near Llandeilo, Dyfed. Somebody bought forty acres. Lack of electricity, plumbing, or other modern conveniences made the resident feel "close to the earth and nature," while another complained: "Hundreds of people are passing through and we have to conserve the limited land we have," obliging prospective settlers to bring their own shelter and fend for themselves. In this, the "tipi village" (otherwise nameless) typifies open-land communes, but it is atypical in that it has continued to exist and even grow, as more

Morningstar's case Lou Gottlieb, who opened it to anyone in 1966. (Unlike Britain, America has firm trespass laws which prosecute squatters.) Despite Gottlieb's expressed belief that "the land selects the people," natural selection failed to prevent the overpopulated thirty-two-acre tract from becoming a rural slum of tipis and vans parked indifferently on it. Nor did his act of deeding the land to God (mythical frontier America had always been God's country) prevent the county health department from bulldozing everyone off it. This is one extreme; the other is that pre-industrial Jeffersonian tradition of the lone, self-reliant home in the clearing or Henry David Thoreau's log cabin by the pond, revivified by the post-industrial ex-urban communes. Between these poles, alternative townplanning had no compelling rationale. Libre, for instance, instituted an extraordinary rule for a *commune*: "No house shall be built within sight of any other house" (**382**).

Libre did not even undertake a focal community building, like the Complex at Drop City, the Circle at New Buffalo, or the Center at Lama. As a second-generation commune, Libre had learned the hard lessons of open-endedness. In an over-compensating reaction, the very word commune was protested against: "We are not a commune. We are a community" (Libre member).[17] "We're not a commune. Communes don't work—we're a village!"

(Manera Nueva member).[18] "We don't want a commune, we want a community" (Ex-Prankster).[19]

Two types of communes, open and closed, suggest themselves. Although the structured order of Lama or the regimentation of Twin Oaks prospered simultaneously with amorphous open communes, some went through open and closed *phases*.

New Buffalo, a case in point, underwent a crisis in March 1969 over the open vs closed issue. The commune had been inundated by new arrivals—known as Apaches in New Buffalo's Indian frame of reference—who "joined" by appropriating living space. Although older members argued that the *land* could only support a limited population, they expressed the threat to social stability in architectural terms: the increased numbers could no longer all meet in the Circle, or eat together around the communal table. Most of the "Apaches" did voluntarily depart after a collective appeal, but the permanent residents had been reluctant to defend their property rights or invoke coercive authority, since disenchantment with such a value system had led *them* to New Buffalo. Yet to remain an open commune would probably have been to incur the irreversible fate of Drop City.

Whereas disavowal of unconscionable rules, or submission to rule by a charismatic leader, as in many nineteenth-century utopian sects, made open communes vulnerable, their vitality or at least initial momentum sustained them. Another biological proverb from Stewart Brand had it: "The flow of energy through a system tends to organize that system." He might have added, "for a time." This partly accounts for the explosive proliferation of early commune architecture. As the activity of building gave purposeful direction,[20] so the buildings themselves broadcast a group identity more often emblematic than actual. This may also be why the architecture of any one commune did not particularize, with any iconographic precision, its own special preoccupation. Few communes displayed unique house styles, and many with similar architecture were of quite different persuasions. As these fluctuated with the turnover of residents, so did the overall character of an open commune, even if—like a rock band—it kept the same name. The architectural imagery, too, stayed constant, while members joined or left at will.

Within open communes, the first phase was often marked by unstructured but eagerly embraced togetherness in living arrangements. This tribal socialization was more a practical architectural determinant than farming, art, religion, etc., and was reflected in open-plan interiors, as with the Family of the Mystic Arts already cited. Sometimes, as when the unitary volume of a geodesic dome signified a single communal house, open planning had its external coun-

terform. In 1970 the Red Rockers, settling among the red rocks of southern Colorado, built the largest such living dome **(384)**, with a diameter of sixty feet, because, "We like living together 'in a heap' with one kitchen and lots of shared space . . . We wanted our home to have a structural bias against individualism and for communism . . . There's no point in building revolutionary structures to shelter reactionary

▲ **380** STEVE BAER AND STEVE DURKEE, *The Center*, Lama, New Mexico, 1967, exterior detail

▼ **381** STEVE BAER AND STEVE DURKEE, *The Center*, Lama, New Mexico, 1967, roof plan and elevation

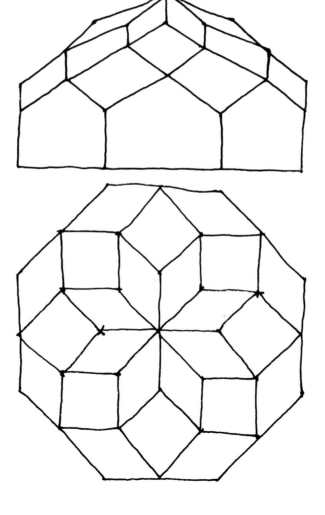

life-styles."[21] The hemispherical interior space was minimally subdivided by horizontal levels, rather than vertical partitions **(385)**, with a sleeping loft or mezzanine extending around three-quarters of the circumference. However, within three years the Red Rockers had adjusted their mix of community and privacy, converting the loft into work space, still using the dome for eating and meeting but now dwelling in smaller shelters outside. This progression, from open-plan communes to communities recognizing a need for personal space, recurred almost invariably. Yet it is both remarkable and instructive that the first phase happened at all. Although their open planning might seem as casual and unconsidered as the communes themselves, it infers a more positive lesson upon examination.

It is not really the same as Le Corbusier's "plan libre," Mies van der Rohe's "universal space," or Frank Lloyd Wright's "open plan."[22] Wright, especially, hoped to free the Victorian house from the specialized "boxes" of its dining, sitting, drawing, music, smoking, and sewing rooms, each with a familial role or social function: private for individual members or public for entertaining. As Wright's Prairie House devolved into the suburban American "ranch," only the *degree* of compartmentalization was mitigated; the *kind* of zoned space remained, deformalized for the modern nuclear family. (The TV set replaced the Wrightian hearth; family unity was addressed, unabashedly, in family rooms; the housewife was relegated to the kitchen but placated with electric servants, gadgets to call her own; the bathroom became a sanctuary of sanitized privacy; and only in the living room was a showcase of acquired possessions on public display through the picture window.) Reintroduction of true open planning had to await alternatives to that kind of family. Open communes were, if anything, non-kinship families, sharing the upbringing of all their children, not bifurcating work and play, and bathing socially. They dined together as an extended family occasion which, in conventional households, is reserved for the annual Thanksgiving feast. If architecture is the social art, then theirs was as much a domestic architecture as that of Middle America: a house is a home is a family. Yet since most communards had grown up in a nuclear family environment, they must have had to decondition themselves sufficiently to collectivize "a larger and more populous house."[23]

This was germane to a new interest in "proxemics" —relationships between humans and space—current among architects and planners at about the same time as the communal experiments. *Community and Privacy* by Serge Chermayeff and Christopher Alexander (1965) called for housing designs which would be insulated against external incursions. Amos Rapoport's incisive *House Form and Culture* (1969) analyzed indigenous cultural determinants of social space, and although he could conclude with a sketchy delineation of how Western popular culture relates to its residential architecture—and "why the 'open plan,' so beloved of architects, has never really been accepted by the public"—his anthropological approach was not applicable to the nebulous values of a counterculture. In *The Hidden Dimension: Man's Use of Space in Public and Private* (1966), Edward T. Hall reminded readers that the nuclear family is a fairly recent development, and with it the compartmentalized house. As the house's "fixed-feature" spaces consolidated physical segregation of both activities and persons within, the nuclear family began to compensate for other forms of social intercourse, redirecting loyalties and manners to private lives in private homes, and to individual possession of space as if property. It may not have been easy for communes to divest themselves of this ingrained, subconscious "hidden" cultural dimension, yet those that survived the claustrophobic frictions of their open plans ("We all live in a yellow submarine") usually moved on to phase two counterculture communities; veterans rarely returned to nuclear family forms.

Hall had compared ethological studies of animal societies—most notably Calhoun's "behavioral sink" experiments with overcrowding stresses among rats—to regulatory mechanisms of territoriality,

body space or distancing, and hierarchical pecking orders in human cultures. More mischievous was the direct analogy drawn between ethology and housing in Oscar Newman's *Defensible Space* (1973). As a "territorial imperative" was alleged to enforce an *instinctual* need to defend architectural turf, Newman advocated that design *encourage* this in the no-man's land of public space in, say, high-rise blocks of flats. Some architects and planners gratefully seized upon the new functionalism of the book's behavioralist guidelines; others objected on moral, philosophical, or sociological grounds. The qualm was not that Newman chose data based on the induced space deprivation of rodent populations—rather than empirical evidence from the voluntary associations of the commune experience—but that implicit in his planning recommendations was the old premise that environment influences social conduct, not the reverse. Architects have long believed that *if* man is a creature of his environment, then this can and ought to be transformed for his best interests, as defined by those architects. This *imposes* design upon the anonymous clients of mass housing, unlike the self-determination of communards. The latter, who had no blueprint for social order and held "raised consciousness" more important than changing the world, still assumed creative responsibility for their own environments.

While the governmental or commercial architectural establishment does not, or cannot, design for living outside the statistical averages of the nuclear family, nor cater for ethnic minorities, single parents,

▲ **382** *Libre*, Colorado, 1968–73, aerial perspective

▼ **383** STEVE BAER AND STEVE DURKEE, *The Center*, Lama, New Mexico, 1967

or even flat-sharing, the alternatives for those excluded from the housing market must lie in making their own homes. Communes no longer command the celebrity or notoriety of a movement—perhaps as much sponsored by sensationalistic media as symptomatic of the youthful spirit of 1968—but there are still many of them, surviving or new, perhaps in a lower key now, without distinctive names or architecture. In Europe, where communes had never been predominantly rural as in North America, existing urban architecture inhibited chances and choices of adaptation to communal needs. For example, a converted factory served as the setting in Templehof, West Berlin. In Europe, however, the squatter movement has been both more active and more political than in North America, from the first organized occupation of vacant property in London, 1968, continuously through to squatters' demonstrations in Amsterdam at the time of this writing, May 1980. Occasionally squatters have been able to foster communities around themselves, as in London's Tolmers Village for some years, or Christiana Free City in Copenhagen (386), "Europe's longest running and largest squat."[24]

Christiana began when homeless activists "liberated" the 50 acres and 157 buildings of an old military base vacated by the Danish Ministry of Defense in 1971. As is often the case, the squatters have since attained the official but insecure status of being "tolerated," surviving only on sufferance of the political equipoise between opponents (including the Mayor of Copenhagen) and partisans on the city council (one of whom lives at Christiana). Within, the Free City functions as an autonomous village— not far from the center of a great capital—providing its own public services, such as street cleaning, soup kitchens, and a hospital. Such municipal employment supports perhaps one-third of the population, which now numbers about a thousand; another third of them work in Copenhagen, so the community is linked to the mainstream as well as to an alternative economy of barter with rural communes for food. It has craft workshops, a bicycle factory, and no cars. Former barracks of institutional brick have been gaily decorated and converted into flats and rather chic artists' studios; some new houses have even been built on stilts over a nearby lake.

Still, architectural development was limited here, as opposed to the rural American communes which could build from scratch, yet the bucolic life attracted Europeans for other reasons. One compromise is Findhorn, occupying a converted country hotel in Scotland. Another, Redfield in Buckinghamshire, England, uses an existing country house. Redfield is a handsome, century-old, fifty-room stately home into which seventeen adults and twelve children moved at the beginning of 1978. The group—including ex-squatters and one initiator of the project formerly active in Danish communes—was modest in size compared to Christiana Free City, but equivalent to most North American communes. Redfield was purchased in common as a housing cooperative, and although the building is subdivided into living units,[25] residents share cooking, maintenance, and more convivial

▲ 384 RED ROCKERS
Communal Dome, Red Rock, Colorado, 1970

activities. They run a study center (teaching courses in, among other alternatives, communes), and raise much of their own food in the estate's gardens, orchards, and greenhouses. The old physical arrangements are well suited to Redfield's new uses; it may be a portent that its formal architecture, and the manorial style of class, cultural, and family life that went with it, should yield to new social arrangements. However, Redfield did not apply even cosmetic redecoration to its adopted environment, as did Christiana. A new architecture is not a necessary and sufficient communal condition, but when attempted afresh, it can extemporize its own iconography with considerable consistency, as in the geodesic domes to be examined next.

▲ 385 RED ROCKERS
Communal Dome, Red Rock, Colorado, 1970, interior

◀ 386 *Café*, Christiana Free City, Copenhagen, Denmark, c. 1971

GREAT CIRCLES

IN TERMS OF THEIR ARCHITECTURAL "BRIEF," THE COMmune builders' enthusiasm for geodesic domes is understandable enough. Externally, a sphere stands discrete and visually self-contained in the landscape, like the isolated country homestead of American myth, while the lack of spatial relatedness between such freestanding geometric objects also suited the communes' indifference to planning ensembles. Inside, that insistent sphericality might seem restrictive, yet the same quality of pure Platonic abstraction offered a neutral volume available for various unforeseen purposes, without nuclear family associations. As a dome dweller at Libre recounted: "The dome seemed especially fit for changes, being an empty unimposing shell. In fact, for years the interior design has never settled in: each month it changes, may never stop shifting as new needs arise, new images are launched" (387).[1] The dome's imagery, more generalized as standard commune architecture than specific to any commune, was elastic enough to cover the self-styled social-revolutionary Red Rockers as well as the Ananda Meditation Retreat and Spiritual Community in California (388).

Ananda's first dome had been built by its resident Swami (who saw in geodesics the Lotus of a Thousand Petals) from mail-order do-it-yourself plans procured through the May 1966 issue of *Popular Science* magazine. Prior to this, the requisite dimensions of a geodesic dome's structural members had not been publicly accessible.[2] (As noted, the founders of Drop City had some difficulty getting it right in 1965.) So although geodesic domes were invested with counterculture meanings and applied to counterculture uses (the *Popular Science* plans were supposed to make a small "greenhouse or swimming-pool cover"), the geometry first had to be demystified for untutored alternative builders. A *Popular Science* Sun Dome was also the novice essay of Lloyd Kahn, who was to make amateur dome-building feasible if not foolproof and, to many, practically irresistible. The example of *The Whole Earth Catalog* encouraged Kahn to publish, and the

Catalog in fact lent its printing facilities.

His two data-packed and proselytizing *Domebooks* were the outcome of design-testing seventeen domes (1969–71) at Pacific High School, a Summerhill-type "free school" in the Santa Cruz Mountains of California which became a commune of sorts when the sixty students and staff decided to live in rather than commute.[3] They therefore needed places to live and something educational to do. With local enthusiast Lloyd Kahn, joined by designer Jay Baldwin and others, some from Ananda, they built domes. Like Steve Baer's Zomeworks, they operated outside the architectural profession and building industry, and made what had begun at Pacific as teenagers' therapy into a field laboratory of geodesics, and an energetic, purposeful commune. Just as, "No plans were ever drawn for our domes, only a few sketches," so were, "things moving along of their own accord, no one directing. When I look back I see that what happened was a community forming itself, created with no real plan other than the need to live together."[4]

The basic Pacific dome (389), the first seven of which were built in three lively months, had a diameter of twenty-four feet and a timber skeleton sheathed with triangular plywood panels. Initially some panels were left transparent as windows, like holes cut in conventional walls, but it was the students themselves who conceived the long arcs of continuous fenestration running over the convex surface to follow the path of the sun. (This was taken up in many later domes, for example, Red Rockers'.) The builder-inhabitants of each dome found their preferred ways of inserting doors into a hemisphere—sometimes by cunningly hinged triangles—and siting domes on Pacific's hilly terrain, sometimes resolving both problems by a trapdoor entered from below, on the downhill slope. Each dome had to be supported underneath, its polygonal floor structured, and its living space used, sometimes with lofts exploiting the headroom above. The constructional lore vented in *Domebook One* aided readers, who then built their own domes, and their new discoveries, reported in *Domebook Two*, then spurred still more readers to further experiments.

Meanwhile, at Pacific High School, the geodesic theme was varied to explore domes of more or fewer facets, geometries based on icosahedra or octahedra, and the several possible truncations of spheres into domes. This was taken to Baroque extremes in two elliptical domes. Deciding that the floor platform he had already built would allow too small a hemisphere, Peter Calthorpe mathematically warped the geodesic geometry into an egg shape which, using the same circular base, gave greater height. Unlike this first ellipsoid, having its long axis vertical, the second was oriented with that axis slantwise to the ground, so the dome's truncating floor was an ellipse, and its halved volume asymmetrical (**390**). Both domes were still geodesic, but parlayed into unexpected transformations.

Both Egg Domes, also, had skeletons whose skins were sprayed with polyurethane foam. Lloyd Kahn would later say of Pacific that their main work had been the trial of new materials for domes. Certainly at the time he put great faith in Space Age plastics—flexible vinyls or unbreakable perspex in place of glazing, for instance, or silicon sealants to waterproof the countless joints between panels of "all-roof" domes—as if these modern chemical miracles might circumvent traditional architectural detailing and specialist builders' crafts, and so make for truly do-it-yourself domes. Two more at Pacific (**391**) were of lightweight sheet aluminum, so thin that only folds across the panels gave them sufficient rigidity, without any framing structure (like Baer's Cartop Dome, but even more minimal). Seams were sealed with neoprene tape, and insulation was urethane or styrofoam: another concatenation of hydrocarbons.

As Pacific investigated other materials and methods, three of their domes departed from geodesics. For a small "Pod" dwelling dome (**392**), wedge-shaped segments of plywood—affixed at their bases around the circumference—were bent inward to their common apex, and there topped with a bubble skylight. For a communal bathhouse, a government-surplus Radome was bought, and its prefabricated fiber-glass panels bolted together into a translucent sphere; the sun coming through this made for very pleasant bathing in the large stainless-steel tub, formerly a therapeutic whirlpool from a hospital. (Thus Pacific too could expropriate technological wastage, although intercepting discards before they became the junk beloved of Drop City.) Then, for a latrine adjacent to the bathhouse, they tried a dome in thin-shelled ferrocement (**393–394**). Strong, waterproof, cheap in materials but labor-intensive, the technique had already been pioneered in ferrocement boats and the inverted hulls of several domes elsewhere.[5] Pacific's refinements used the seamless plasticity of the cement to flare a canopy over the door and form pockets from which plants grew out of the shell itself.

Returning to a true geodesic dome (**395–396**), Jay Baldwin matched its efficient structural geometry with high-tech materials. Twenty feet in diameter, it was first framed in tubular metal alloy (rigid electrical conduit); then in the triangles between the tubes were fixed pneumatic "pillows" of transparent vinyl. These triangular pillows, inflated with nitrogen (to avoid the condensation of water vapor in ordinary

air), afforded insulation while retaining transparency, so the unobtrusive enclosing hemisphere interfered very little with a sense of living virtually outdoors, yet sheltered. This concept of a semi-permeable geodesic membrane as a selective "environmental valve"—letting in what is wanted, such as light or view, and keeping out what is not, such as cold or rain—originated with Buckminster Fuller two decades earlier. Appropriately it came full circle when, in 1970, Baldwin delivered a commissioned copy of his Tube-Frame-and-Pillow Dome to Fuller across the continent in Maine. And while the putative hippies of Pacific High talked spherical trigonometry and compared notes on manufacturers' specifications more than did the junk architects of Drop City, *Domebook One* spoke for both design camps in its dedication: "We were largely inspired by R. Buckminster Fuller."

▲ **387** *Geodesic Dome*, Libre, Colorado, 1968, interior

◄ **388** *Temple Dome*, Ananda, California, 1966, interior

▼ 389 LLOYD KAHN
Geodesic Dome, Pacific
High School, Santa Cruz
Mountains, California,
1969

Fuller directly influenced, among innumerable others, each of the principal pioneers in the new design frontier of the American West. For Lloyd Kahn (in 1968 at Big Sur Hot Springs, California) and the first-generation Droppers (in 1965 at Boulder, Colorado), public lectures by Fuller were turning points. (Fuller in turn recognized Drop City with an impromptu Dymaxion Award in 1966.) Jay Baldwin had been a teaching colleague of Fuller at Southern Illinois University immediately before Baldwin joined Pacific High School, and Steve Durkee had extensive contact with Fuller (1965–66) prior to founding Libre. Steve Baer's involvement dates from 1963, and Stewart Brand, founder-editor of *The Whole Earth Catalog*, said simply: "The insights of Buckminster Fuller are what initiated this catalog," whose whole-earth logo, the first full portrait of the planet photographed from outer space, corresponded to Fuller's design strategy for that whole system. It was not just the geodesic dome (which Fuller did not, strictly speaking, invent) but the very wholeness of his world view, his unique cosmology, which inspired them, although not always unreservedly. Fuller's thinking is impossible to summarize, and his idiosyncratic

verbiage, with its neologisms and non-linear logic, can appear impenetrable. (Even that may have impressed some auditors as arcane, oracular, or metaphysical.) Yet he already had a cult following among architecture students, and now reached a mass youth audience. Seeming to them an elder sage, prophet for the times, and philosopher of ecology and transcendental science, he in turn had great respect and hope for the young. Like them, he had no use for politicians, nationalism, specialists, or the profit motive, and had himself "dropped out" in 1927.

As an alternative designer in his own terms, Fuller was to orthodox Modernism of the late twenties and thirties rather as the commune builders were to American mainstream architecture of the late sixties. "The Bauhaus international school," Fuller criticized, "never went back of the wall surface to look at the plumbing";[6] what it did was literally whitewash woolly technological thinking with a superficial "garmentation" of style. The Modernists' machine aesthetic visually symbolized and glorified its received hardware without understanding its mechanics or exploiting it for domestic creature comforts. The telling difference is between the reductive abstraction of Mies van der Rohe's "Less is more," and Fuller's "Do more with less," i.e., get more efficient design performance. Fuller's first Dymaxion House of 1927 projected an environmental package as advanced technologically, as readily mass-produced, and as economically accessible to the American family as the Model-T Ford, and with perhaps as much power for social transformation. It was to be an alternative to the one-off styling exercises commissioned from architects, but when Fuller offered his patent rights in 1928 to the American Institute of Architects, that body rejected the whole idea with understandable protestations.[7]

The Dymaxion's hexagonal floor and roof decks both hung by tensioned cables from a central duralumin mast, which integrated structural support and services. "The formal qualities of this design are not remarkable," comments Reyner Banham, "except in their invisibly radical mobilization of industrial technology."[8] It might even be considered, so far as public taste and cultural symbolism were concerned, an aesthetically value-free and styleless "un-house" (like Banham's own Un-House of 1965). The second Dymaxion House, of 1946, assumed a more resonant form in that it looked like a dome. This, however, was only the result of streamlining it against wind resistance and consequent heat losses on the lee side. It retained, most importantly, the central core—unlike the geodesic dome with its environmental controls in its skin, enclosing only a void. It incorporated many improvements, such as Fuller's Dy-

maxion Bathroom of 1937 (he meant what he said about the plumbing!),but in concept was diagrammatically much akin to its predecessor of seventeen years before, now upgraded to a par with aeronautical rather than automotive construction. Usually known as the Wichita House after Beech Aircraft's factory in Wichita, Kansas, where the prototype was manufactured, Fuller's Mark II Dymaxion was to have provided new housing and jobs from plants tooled up for wartime mass production, as a spin-off of wartime technology, and for a postwar market. Only when this market failed to respond did Fuller, in the late forties, turn to geodesic domes (**398**). These did prove successful as industrialized architecture in the fifties (and only then, incidentally, did professional designers accept Fuller as other than a brilliant crackpot). It must be stressed, though, that the high structural technology and prefabrication of geodesics were first and most commercially suited to non-domestic and especially military uses, not to single-family houses as were the Dymaxions.

In the Dymaxions Fuller had set out to redesign a technologically ideal home; contrariwise the geodesic dome had no such program and came about as Fuller, a polymath, brought together engineering, geometry, cartography, and even navigation. A *geodesic* is literally an earth line, the shortest distance between two points on the terrestrial globe or any sphere. Extended into circumferences, geodesics also define the largest circles on a spherical surface, yet the great circle routes of ships and aircraft follow the shortest courses. Structurally, such lines must transmit forces most directly across a spherical dome. Certain configurations of geodesics, approximating the edges of certain semi-regular polyhedra, make up a network of triangles. The triangle is the simplest stable, closed, planar shape, while the sphere encloses the greatest volume for the least surface area of any three-dimensional solid. Nearly spherical domes, structured with triangular panels or nearly geodesic straight members, can therefore be very strong for their weight. To Fuller they seemed working models of "synergy": whole systems which are more efficient than the sums of their parts. Far from conceiving of geodesic domes as homes, Fuller researched them as pure structure, and only when uses came to be suggested did his designs tend toward considerable spans, since the bigger the dome the better its ratio of material to performance, or economy of means. His proposal for an "environmental valve" two miles in diameter, over midtown Manhattan, would envelop its own microclimate, since any dome's shape generates regular air currents within. Among the thousand or so geodesic domes actually built by 1959, spans of several hundred feet were typical. In 1967, at the Montreal World's Fair (**397**), such a dome served as the U.S. Pavilion (and perhaps as a gentle riposte to the American Institute of Architects and Mies van der Rohe, whose Seagram Building contained no more volume but weighed a great deal more). And simultaneous with Fuller's legitimization by official patronage, smaller progeny of his dome were being hand built by a new generation of North American alternative designers.

THE CULT OF THE DOME

THE COMMUNES, FROM DROP CITY ONWARD, LOOKED to Fuller's dome more for its image than for its efficiency. It may even have been the relative *stylelessness* of the geodesic that made it an apt blank recipient of the counterculture's aspirations; more traditional domes had never been so neutral. As an historically loaded archetype, the ubiquitous dome has had many notional meanings in the public, monumental, and institutional architecture of as many cultures. One of the most pregnant forms in world architecture, reinvented over and over, it has endured for at least two millennia. It can be a solid convex mound like the Buddhist stupa, or a pure negative concavity like a Mycenaean tomb chamber, or more usually both an external landmark and interior space at once. In religious architecture the dome has been *axis mundi* and canopy of Heaven, from the Pantheon with its skylight of the gods, to St. Peter's, a later Rome's own Dome of the Rock. It satisfied Islamic and Byzantine creeds as well as the ideal central-plan church of Renaissance Humanism. As classicism spanned religious and temporal architecture with domes, its civic symbolism begat the U.S. Capitol, which begat kindred state capitols, which begat county courthouses and city halls—the culture to which the communes were counter.

These domes embodied vested authority, seats of governance, and a perennial order as firm and imposing as the buildings themselves. Inasmuch as the communes had rejected these values, their choice of the generic dome—with such conventional overtones—seems ironic, and would be doubly so if they had intended to borrow that form and then invert its associations, reorienting them toward their own anarchic, indeterminate communities. There is, however, no evidence for this. Instead, an alternative history of domes was more attractive to them: domical vernacular shelters. *Domebook Two* is prefaced: "This is the story of a new indigenous architecture," although again, it was wishful thinking to expect built form alone to confer cultural identity. Still, the vernacular tradition is even older than that of upper-case Architecture, and more like the communal case in being primarily domestic.

► **390** PETER CALTHORPE, *Egg Dome*, Pacific High School, Santa Cruz Mountains, California, 1970

▼ **391** LLOYD KAHN *Aluminum Dome*, Pacific High School, Santa Cruz Mountains, California, 1971

Vernacular house design is also endowed with cultural and religious symbolism—in a more intimate and less authoritarian way than the codifications of church and state architecture—and so alternative builders were drawn to it in their search for significant form. They intuited a free allusion between their geodesic domes (given meaning by Fuller's cosmology) and vernacular, domestic domes (given meaning by tribal cosmologies). Common to both was the "geomancy"—magic geometry—by which architecture and cosmic environment were interrelated, either through scientific or mythic universals. This allusive conjunction was further sharpened when the counterculture began attributing to itself a "new tribalism." The stage had been set for the communal domes of 1965 and afterward by

three books of the period. Bernard Rudofsky's *Architecture Without Architects* (1964) illustrated the conical *trulli* of the Apulia region of Italy, Arab umbrella vaults, African thatched huts, and other conical vernacular house types. Buckminster Fuller's *Ideas and Integrities* (1963) contained a chapter entitled "Domes—Their Long History and Recent Developments" which imagined early domes as nomadic shelters and the ancestral "primitive hut" as an igloo. Marshall McLuhan's *Understanding Media* (1964) pronounced categorically that tribal, nomadic peoples live in round houses. "Men live in round houses," explained McLuhan in his chapter on housing, "until they become sedentary and specialized in their work organization. Anthropologists have often noted this change from round to square without

▶ 392 MARTIN BARTLETT
"Pod" Dome, Pacific High
School, Santa Cruz Moun-
tains, California, 1970

The sky is round, and I have heard that the earth is
round like a ball, and so are all the stars. The wind,
in its greatest power, whirls. Birds make their nests
in circles, for theirs is the same religion as ours. The
sun comes forth and goes down again in a circle. The
moon does the same, and both always come back
again to where they were. The life of man is a circle
from childhood to childhood, and so it is in everything where power moves. Our tipis were round like
the nests of birds and these were always set in a
circle . . . But the whitemen have put us in these
square boxes. Our power is gone and we are dy-
ing . . ."[10] Well before the round tipis, kivas, and
hogans of the Indians were transcribed into a new
tribal vernacular, the "square boxes of the whitemen" had been a target of internal dissatisfaction, at
least since the fifties, when subcultural argot attached
much pejoration to the term *square*.[11] A song by

knowing its cause." Anthropologists would probably
dispute McLuhan's cause, and the plain fact can
be gleaned from Rudofsky's cursory visual survey
that some tribal nomads live in round houses while
others do not. The point, though, is that although
McLuhan's elisions and sweeping generalizations
might invalidate his theories, he was nevertheless a
household name in the sixties. Since then the currency
of his catch phrases has declined sharply (Marshall
who?), yet counterculture sympathizers at the time
were most receptive, and accepted that: "The square
room or house speaks the language of the sedentary
specialist, while the round hut or igloo, like the
conical wigwam, tells of the integral nomadic ways of
food-gathering communities." This was then echoed
by the "re-tribalized" youth of domed, itinerant communes like Drop City: "To live in a dome is—psy-
chologically—to be in closer harmony with natural
structure . . . Corners constrict the mind . . .
Domes carry the values of the community into the
outer world." Or from Libre: "Build circular musical
structures and help destroy rational box-reality."[9]

McLuhan distinguished between the housing of
Western man, whose linear logic "tends to restrict
and enclose space and to separate functions," and
that of pre-literate, pre-industrial tribal man, which
extends his own sensorium to the cosmos through
the continuity of circular forms. *Domebook Two*,
among other alternative publications, quoted extensively from the biography of Black Elk, a van-
quished Sioux Indian at the violent intersection of
these two cultures: "You have noticed that everything an Indian does is in a circle, and that is because
the Power of the World always works in circles, and
everything tries to be round . . . This knowledge
came to us from the outer world with our religion.

▲ 393 LLOYD KAHN
Ferrocement Dome, Pacific
High School, Santa Cruz
Mountains, California,
1971, exterior under con-
struction. On the right is
the fiber-glass bathhouse
dome

▶ 394 LLOYD KAHN
Ferrocement Dome, Pacific
High School, Santa Cruz
Mountains, California, 1971,
exterior completed

Pete Seeger summed up suburbia: "Boxes, little boxes, all made out of ticky-tack and they all look just the same." The costive rectilinearity of postwar American Modernism (out of the International Style by Mies van der Rohe) was seen by some to equate the endless, homogenizing, graph-paper facades of corporate offices with the oppressive conformity of gray flannel organization men, the consumer mentality of Madison Avenue, and the anonymous urban environs of the Lonely Crowd. While professional tastemakers lauded that same architecture as sublime elegance, those alienated from it had somewhat desperate recourse to geodesic domes—whose virtues were justified, if not by abstract aesthetics, then by texts from the curious threesome of Buckminster Fuller, Marshall McLuhan, and Black Elk.

The contrived cultishness surrounding the dome to an extent overtook reasoned evaluation of it as habitable architecture. The more extreme cultists forged an ersatz folk architecture without its common sense and took Fuller as a geodesic guru without his hard science. The well-intentioned Lloyd Kahn suffered such excesses from the fringe elements of his own alternative following. He recollects a visitation from a fey creature calling herself "The Ice Cream Fairy," whose Merry Fairy Dairies were to be domes because: "She says they don't offer as much wind resistance as sharp-angled buildings, which slow down the earth's rotation." Excerpts from three letters to *Domebook Two* follow: "Living in a spherical single unit home makes us wholer people . . . [but] In the future we've decided not to live in a metal frame or metal skinned dome. Both my wife and I feel that the metal steals vibrations from us and creates an artificial magnetic field around us . . ."; "Sitting in the middle of the dome in summer is like being at the centre of the universe. I feel infinitely large and small at the same time; unity of all things is apparent"; "Living in the dome was an unending education in planetary consciousness . . . Lying on your back, the translucent skin of your dome registers each energy transformation of the cosmic lightshow. Like a giant retina, the dome scans the heavens. Now it is a tympanic membrane transducing rain into rhythmic meaning. You merge with the dome; its skin becomes your skin . . ."[12]

This breathless hyperbole expanded on certain individuals' subjective experience of the dome; from others was elicited a more social pattern of meaning. "All those triangle sections coming together to make a single dome, a self-supporting thing. It's like a community can be," said a member of Drop City. Another communard independently hit upon the same simile: "The commune is like a geodesic sphere

of many facets . . ."[13] Steve Baer suggested that the shape of the zome, polyhedral cousin to the dome, prefigured a "new society—load sharing, intelligently put together, one that will someday reveal the load-bearing pillars of today's arrangements as totally unnecessary."[14] Such structural symbolism was probably arrived at after the designed fact, yet is not unlike the interpretations of architectural historians who see, say, in classical Greek colonnades the ideological structure of the polis (interchangeable pillars of society, democratically and equitably upholding the public edifice, etc.), or medieval feudal hierarchy programmed in Gothic rose windows. "It's like a community can be."

THE DOME CO-OPTED

GEODESIC DOMES HAD BEEN ON THE CONSUMER MARKET since the late fifties as prefab kits, manufactured by the Pease Woodworking Company and a few other franchise holders licensed under Fuller's 1954 patents. These were not environmentally controlled dwelling packages like the Dymaxions of 1927 and 1946, but basic shells of timber-framed plywood panels to be assembled and used for any purpose, including housing. (Fuller himself dwelt, at Southern Illinois University, in a Pease Dome [**399**]. Its interior was extremely conventional.) Domes could also be homemade from the *Popular Science* blueprint of 1966. But it was only in the early seventies that domestic dome building rather suddenly escalated into a mainstream vogue.

Time magazine featured a "Boom in Dome Homes" in its Modern Living section, March 1, 1971; "A Mushrooming of Domes" enlivened the pages of *Life*, July 14, 1972; *Popular Science* trumpeted "The Great Dome Boom is On" in its February 1972 issue, and later that year returned as a do-it-yourself source with new plans for a twenty-four-foot-diameter improvement on its Sun Dome, now with proper windows and doors. Many more kit-producing firms and specialized contractors arose to service the demand. Cathedralite Domes came in three

sizes. Five hundred Dyna-Dome kits had been sold by 1971, and one hundred more built under the supervision of the firm's capable founder, Bill Woods. At Lake Havasu City, Arizona, Dyna-Dome components were fastened into an eighty-foot-diameter church (**400**) by the parishioners themselves; and a full sphere (**401**)—forty feet in diameter, impaled on a supporting shaft—contained a bar, restaurant, and real-estate office, advertising this private developer's new town, whose other novelties included London Bridge transplanted to the desert. But most of the fashionable geodesics were residential, sometimes multiple domes: two for a house in Phoenix, Arizona; four as a house in the suburbs of Chicago; and another four by Envirotecture for a house near San Diego, California (**402**). All were plywood, often identical to the Pease Domes for which, over the past decade and a half, there had been only limited demand.

What had happened to make domes newly acceptable was, ironically, their appearance in alternative architecture. Intensive media coverage of the Flower Power Movement had made communal and rock-festival domes familiar; artful photo-journalists flattered them with wide-angle lenses; the *Domebooks* of 1970–71 and manuals made them seem buildable even by feckless hippies. This much is undisputed by all the articles mentioned above, such as *Popular Science*: "Domes gained much of their momentum in counter-culture communes . . . Now domes are mushrooming into suburbia, and gaining popularity as vacation housing and second homes." For the purposes of the leisured good life, domes had a welcome novelty value like A-frames or chalets, so the form alone could be taken without the indelible taint of a counterculture which middle-class dome owners would strenuously disavow.

◀ **395** JAY BALDWIN
Tube-Frame-and-Pillow-Dome, Pacific High School, Santa Cruz Mountains, California, 1970

▲ **396** JAY BALDWIN
Tube-Frame-and-Pillow-Dome, Pacific High School, Santa Cruz Mountains, California, 1970, interior. Buckminster Fuller is on the right of the photograph

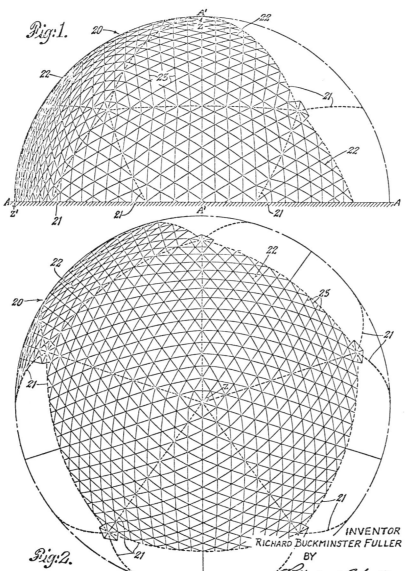

June 29, 1954   R. B. FULLER   2,682,235

BUILDING CONSTRUCTION

Filed Dec. 12, 1951   6 Sheets—Sheet 1

Fig:1.

Fig:2.

INVENTOR
RICHARD BUCKMINSTER FULLER
BY

ATTORNEY

◀ **397** BUCKMINSTER FULLER, *U.S. Pavilion,* Expo '67, Montreal, Canada, 1967

▶ **398** BUCKMINSTER FULLER, *Geodesic Dome,* elevation and roof plan submitted to the United States Patent Office, December 12, 1951, and granted June 29, 1954

▼ **399** BUCKMINSTER FULLER AND PEASE WOODWORKING COMPANY, *Fuller Home,* University of Southern Illinois, Carbondale, Illinois, 1960

ecutives. In the Beatnik-to-banker cycle, the banker's sandals might be imported, his turtleneck sweater more expensive—but so was his dome, now a respectable, even faddish, status symbol, and rather characterless. However, this process of assimilation does admit new forms to the mass culture's repertoire of residential choices, in a way more mundane but likelier than the form-giving of architects or the will-to-form of some technological *Zeitgeist.*

Radical chic—liberals patronizing subcultural radicalism—was not a major factor in the dome fad, although token domes were sometimes commissioned by rock stars like Paul Kantner and Grace Slick (**404**). When schooled architects were thus entrusted with a client's dome, it could be treated as an interior design job within the given shell. A typical case, in Chatham, New York (**405–407**), was an executive's weekend country refuge from her Manhattan town house and workplace in Rockefeller Center. Within a standard Pease-type prefab the designer indulged the stylistic clichés of the time, 1971–72, all mannered details and cantilevers. Nevertheless, the dome was hand built by the designer, the client, and their friends, and an attempt was made to respect its own spatiality.

In their wholesale popularization, however, domes were more frequently brought into consonance with a middle-class image of The House. Upon the blank exterior could be imprinted domestic insignia—such as the Colonial shutters, shingles, and Palladian door surrounds, flanked by carriage lamps, added to one Pease Dome in Vermont. These symbolic fixtures of "personalized conformity," often applied to other house shapes, looked only slightly more risible on a dome. What with word plays on domicile, domestic, and home-dome, the hemispherical form itself seemed no great impediment to full residential adoption. Yet *inside* the problem was, as *Life* magazine phrased it, "Room galore but hard to subdivide." The hemispherical volume may have befitted open commune living, but not the nuclear family with its cultural requirements of private and differentiated spaces. This necessitated either multiple domes to segregate activities, or the partitioning of a single dome into private pie-slice rooms. Since geodesics cannot be easily clustered, nor their "room galore" easily subdivided, neither expedient worked very well architecturally, and eventually the boom faded as the mainstream acceded to the dome's disadvantages. For other reasons, the counterculture did so too.

The cross-cultural gap, on the other hand, was not abysmal. The same virtues which recommended the dome as an anti-urban alternative—economy of means, freestanding independence, and unitary image of the family house (**403**)—were traditionally American and common to both the dome cult and the popular boom. Moreover, the process by which subcultural, non-conformist, or even protest styles are assimilated into mainstream usage has often been rehearsed before in the history of taste. For instance, in the fifties, women informally dressed, without lipstick, foundation garments, or artificially curled hair, were taken for Beatniks, as were men with facial whiskers. In the sixties, however, the same sartorial cues might have denoted suburban matrons and ex-

▶ **400** BILL WOODS *Church Dome,* Lake Havasu City, Arizona, 1972, interior under construction

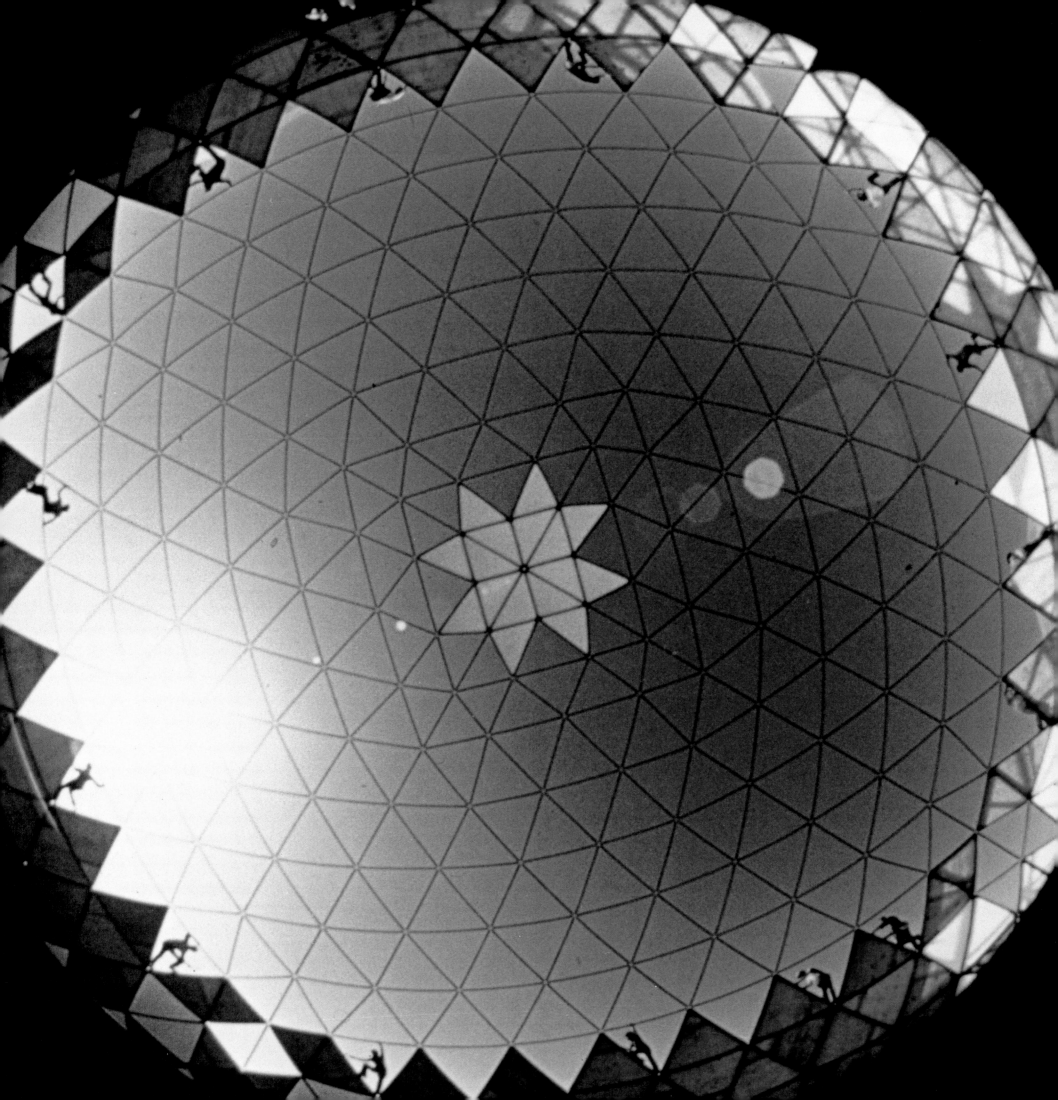

◄ 401 BILL WOODS
Spherical Dome, Lake
Havasu City, Arizona, 1972

▼ 402 ENVIROTECTURE
Four-Dome Residence, San
Diego, California, c. 1973,
exterior under construction

pressed, that the reinforcing of a ferrocement dome for the Zeiss Planetarium, Jena, East Germany (**408**), had first used geodesic structural geometry as early as 1922; this historical footnote was now brought to the fore in *Shelter*.[15] Inevitably, "Bucky's" moral authority was questioned, along with the authorship of his patented dome, which had to be reassessed as counterculture housing. Fuller's message now seemed addressed to the other side, the technocracy with its architects plugged into computer terminals. In fairness to Fuller, it should be remembered that *he* never thought of geodesics as *alternative* architecture, but on the contrary as the next progressive development of building in a technological civilization.

Even Fuller's design philosophy of maximum efficiency, "Do more with less," had to be rebutted. Now Kahn advised: "Don't worry about how much your building weighs, it doesn't have to fly." At the

THE DOME RECANTED

THE SEEDS OF DOUBT WERE ALREADY SPROUTING between the lines of the 1971 *Domebook Two*. In 1973, Lloyd Kahn's next alternative guidebook, *Shelter*, subsumed "Domebook Three" but also contained other kinds of hand-built housing, and a revised editorial position on domes. Popularized domes had lost much ideological potency, freshness, and exclusivity, yet Kahn based his recantation on personal experience of designing, building, and living in them over four years. He and many other dome builders came to conclusions they might logically have reached earlier, except for the overriding appeal of domes as a ready-made alternative architecture, and the need to find out empirically for themselves. One verdict was that geodesic structures, with their high tolerances and repetitive parts, really did work better for industrial mass production than for handicraft. A contributor to "Domebook Three" adjudged that after skillfully and painstakingly dowelling logs together to make his geodesic home in British Columbia, he might as well have made it some other more complicated, personal, or rustic form. If, as he said, domes were best "stamped out by machine" like cars, they could never be Kahn's hoped-for "new vernacular."

The moment of Kahn's final conversion was May 1972 at a Massachusetts Institute of Technology conference on "Responsive Housebuilding Technology." He was disconcerted to learn what the Institute's architectural students and staff meant by that title: automatic design response by the robot sensors of computer technology. (Their cybernetic studies were published by MIT Press in Nicholas Negroponte's *The Architecture Machine;* Kahn's own response was an essay, "Smart But Not Wise," in

Shelter.) Architects generally, it seemed to him, wooed oversophisticated technology not wisely but too well—as if to be requited by some housing breakthrough. He had himself been seduced by geodesics, although he now regretted making them "look too easy, too much like a breakthrough solution, too exciting." And in denouncing Le Corbusier's "Machine for Living," Kahn put Buckminster Fuller in the same sentence.

It had been known, but played down if not sup-

time of his initial conversion, by Fuller, to domes, Kahn had been building a house in Big Sur out of timbers from an old redwood bridge. Some of the house beams were twenty inches thick. His first dome employed the same material, but reduced to spidery filaments. By 1973 Kahn was favorably reconsidering his hardy local tradition of rough, heavy, redwood vernacular, and urging others to do likewise.

In *Domebook One,* Kahn had promised: "New materials, partially a fall-out from the space program,

▶ **403** *Home Dome*, Santa Barbara, California, 1973

tions from its formalized vocabulary and syntax while, on the other, tied to an existing technology often quite beyond the architect's control or even competence. But Funk was the inevitable architectural style for an alternative life-style that was itself "loose-fit" and funky. When geodesics or zonahedra were made of vulgar, garish multicolored cartops ("We find what we use and use what we find"), it was the outrageous clash between sophisticated geometries and junk which expressed this architecture's funkiness. But in the end it was the domes and zomes that had to go. They leaked, and did not last very long—but then neither did the communes. Lloyd Kahn revisited Pacific High and found its failed domes "depressing in decay." Peter Rabbit revisited the ruins of Drop City, which had been built of scrounged materials, and was undismayed: "I guess we'll go down there and scrounge." The cycle goes on.

are now available to everyone . . . These are needed to make domes work." After four years of trying to seal hundreds of homemade domes, those amazing new plastic compounds obviously did not work—or, if they did, their unpleasantness was not worth it. Urethane foam, while liberating constructive possibilities, also sustained particularly noxious industrial pollution in its manufacture, required the wearing of poison gas masks for its application, and rapidly deteriorated into horrid toxic-looking colors, if it had not already caught fire, releasing cyanide fumes. No plastic aged gracefully, and Kahn, like others, decided he preferred the peerless clarity of ordinary glass to shatterproof perspex.

In the last analysis, the recantation of the dome was an aesthetic imperative. This is a question of intent, not taste. The dome builders of Pacific High School and the Southwestern communes had always judged methods and materials, even junk, by their architectural effects; Fuller's design criteria were not aesthetic at all in their intent.[16] More especially, the disillusionment with domes vindicated the Funk Aesthetic of Drop City over, say, the Fulleresque ethic of Jay Baldwin at Pacific High School. For the wages of Funk are leaks, if the dome demands a precision its builders neither command nor desire. Funk is not antitechnological so much as permissive in allowances for limitations, margins of error. Neither is Funk short for *functional* in the Modernist usage; that style had been, on the one hand, quite intolerant of devia-

▲ **404** ROY BUCKMAN
Jefferson Starship Dome

▶ **405** WILLIAM CHAITKIN
Dixie Martin's Dome,
Chatham, New York, 1971–
72, exterior

▼ **406** WILLIAM CHAITKIN
Dixie Martin's Dome,
Chatham, New York, 1971–
72, exterior detail

▲ **407** WILLIAM CHAITKIN
Dixie Martin's Dome,
Chatham, New York, 1971–
72, interior view from loft

▲ **408** WALTER BAUERS-
FELD, *Planetarium Dome*,
Carl Zeiss Optical Works,
Jena, East Germany, 1922,
exterior under construction

HANDMADES

THE SELF-BUILT SHELTER IS OLDER THAN CIVILIZATION—which is historically defined as the creation of cities—and survives today despite, or because of, urbanization. The do-it-yourself urge—if not the necessity—still exists in industrialized societies. Its manifestation in North America is particularly rural, freestanding, and private. In the New World, where Western civilization arrived only a few centuries ago, cultural memories of homesteading settlers are fresh. The log-cabin tradition is not only a national heritage but is also positively valued as mythical freedom from, and disavowal of, urban constraints. Yet although each year more than one hundred and fifty thousand American families build homes for themselves, either directly or as their own contractors—accounting for twenty percent of all new single-family dwellings[1]—few deviate from prepackaged norms. So, whether self-built, spec-built, or architect-designed, the standard detached home is rarely personalized by more than pink plastic flamingos on the lawn, or other North American equivalents to British garden rockeries and conclaves of gnomes. The most common exceptions to this conformity exist in commercial roadside architecture: deliberately eye-catching (iconic hot-dog stands, etc.) but hardly expressive of individual domestic values.

Outside the mainstream, back-to-the-land movements recapitulated the homesteading experience with more conviction than did Middle America's ranch houses (or Prairie Houses), and less reliance on either professional designers or builders. The handmade house became a concern of the counterculture in the seventies, although it had been present throughout the sixties and was granted prominence only when it seemed to supersede the devolving commune as a focus of architectural energies. As the light of the Aquarian dawn was diffused, its most extroverted, experimental activity was redirected toward more modest, personal, pragmatic projects. Alternative self-built and self-designed houses no longer necessarily communicate group unity, and many builder-designers do not identify with a counterculture at all. Handmades therefore adhere to their own requirements, not only of smaller-scale social units, but also of architectural self-expression. Nonetheless, the communes too had been hand built and rural, and many themes were carried over from their architecture, such as vernacular models and, as observed, domes. A new influence, though, was the example of a few inner-directed architectural craftsmen, who were marginal to both mainstream and counterculture.

ECCENTRIC ANTECEDENTS

THE YOUNG, NEW GENERATION OF BUILDER-DESIGNERS took liberating cues from the old, since those uninhibited originals had undertaken their strange and spectacular backyard monuments late in life and were elderly by the time they finished, if ever. Despite claims on their behalf to folk-art populism, they were the ruggedest of individualists, and despite attributions of a "primitivism of the subconscious" they knew what they were doing and why. It was precisely in their individuality that the self-build lesson lay: they were the great solitaries. They were not, however, alienated or misanthropic: "I live alone, but I like everybody," attested Fred Burns, a Maine fisherman who cobbled together a house of driftwood (**409**) and decorated it with "all the paint I could find."[2] Articulate, opinionated, and vocal, Art Beal, on the opposite coast near Big Sur, California, created a hillside castle of junk and abalone shells, and remained "the biggest revolutionist that ever put on a pair of shoes" at the age of seventy-seven.[3] Beal calls himself "Capt. Nitwit" and "Dr. Tinkerpaw"; another architectural scavenger's apt pseudonym is I. Pullem, whose collage house is in North Carolina (**410**). An American Indian who goes by the resounding name of Rolling Thunder has recently built a roadside attraction near Thunder Mountain, Nevada (**411**). It is a protest—a display of bones is labeled (White Man's) "Promises"—but didactic content notwithstanding, his forms bear an uncanny family resemblance to naive sculpture and architecture, such as Samuel Dinsmoor's "Garden of Eden" in Kansas (c. 1900), rather than to tribal styles.

These intense, imaginative follies are highly eclectic, combining miscellaneous materials and referential forms with innocent abandon. Boyce Luther Gulley (1883–1945) lived alone in the desert near Phoenix, Arizona, building a fantasia of Mexican/Indian adobe embellished with "medieval" turrets, and with a pair of romantically ruined, classically fluted columns flanking the entrance (**412**). Yet the Old Masters of the packrat and magpie sensibility must be Simon Rodia and Clarence Schmidt. For geographical symmetry, Rodia worked in the West of the United States and Schmidt in the East; chronologically Schmidt began just before Rodia left off. Both excelled in functionless constructions of remarkable size and complexity. Even if not for their combined effect upon hand builders, they would repay review as alternative architects themselves.

The Rodia site (413) is a right-angled triangle, bounded on its longer sides by a street and a railway. It had been the yard of Rodia's house, which stood, before burning down, on the shortest side. Between sixty and one hundred feet high, three slim, conical, openwork spires dominate: the tallest stands free, while the second is linked by a filigree flying buttress to the third and shortest (416). The plot is enclosed by a scalloped wall; when its cement was wet Rodia incised ornamental patterns, left impressions of his tools, other objects, and handprints, and inset colored stones, seashells, cups, and saucers (414). Around the spires mingle five shorter ones (no more than forty feet tall), arches, benches, gazebos, and fountains, all clad in a rich mosaic of broken tiles, bottle bottoms, and more seashells—seventy-five thousand, someone has reckoned.

Simon Rodia (415), born in Rome in 1879, emigrated to America in about 1889, eventually settling

▼ 409 FRED BURNS
Own House, Belfast, Maine, c. 1941–77, exterior detail

in a nondescript lumpen suburb of Los Angeles called Watts. (The place has been better known since 1965 for the first of the long hot summer race riots than for the Watts Towers.) The Towers are thus far unique among architectural eccentricities in having an urban, or almost urban, setting. Rodia did not begin building until his forty-second year, in 1921. Thereafter he labored, single-handed, for thirty-three years. After they were completed in 1954, he simply moved away and never saw them again.

Whether or not his masterwork is "without a doubt, the largest structure ever achieved by one man,"[4] or contains "the longest and thinnest reinforced concrete columns in the world," the structural accomplishment alone is inestimable. A tenuous web of salvaged pipe, reinforcing bars, and steel bed frames—wedged under the adjacent railway track and levered into the desired curves—was erected without scaffolding or mechanical hoisting equipment, wired together without bolts, rivets, or welds, and bonded in cement encrusted top-to-bottom with tilework and *rocaille*. Of the odd jobs Rodia held in his obscure early life, that of roofer or telephone lineman may have indurated him to working at heights, but his later trade as a tile setter was more applicable

▲ **410** I. PULLEM
Own House, North Carolina

▶ **411** ROLLING THUNDER, *Own House*, Thunder Mountain, Nevada, exterior photographed 1978

◄ **412** BOYCE LUTHER GULLY, *Own House*, Phoenix, Arizona, c. 1927–45

aesthetically. While subsequent acclaim has drawn inevitable comparisons with the kaleidoscopic tiled surfaces of the Catalan architect Antoni Gaudí (whose own fanciful architecture has enjoyed a recent favorable reappraisal), Rodia received scant education and was indebted, if at all, only to the shellwork grottos and wrought-iron outdoor shrines of Latin popular culture.

The Watts Towers only acquired their due publicity when threatened with demolition by municipal authorities in 1957 as "unsafe eyesores." Defenders rallied with legal delays until 1959, when the issue was forced by a structural test of the tallest spire. It refused to be pulled down, in a vindication of intuitive engineering (reminiscent of Frank Lloyd Wright's triumphs over bureaucratic building commissioners and earthquakes). Yet, when during the campaign to save his creations Simon Rodia was discovered living elsewhere in California, he made little comment except: "If your mother dies and you have loved her very much, maybe you don't speak of her."[5] The Watts Towers had "died" for him when he finished them.

On the other hand, Rodia did say he had wanted to do "something big" like other Italians who had come to America. Just as Columbus had first claimed the continent's eastern edge, so Rodia marked its westernmost extension. Although he meant to leave some token behind, in gratitude to his country of adoption and the "nice people" who lived there, this does not fully explain his impulse in 1921 or the form it took.[6] It does, however, accord with the similarly general intentions behind the similarly grand gesture of Clarence Schmidt. "It's a dedication on my part," said Schmidt. "It isn't what it's made of, it's what it signifies. This is going to make history," and, "I'd lay down my life for art."[7] He did, building for decades with compulsive energy and manic native talent in the Catskill Mountains near Woodstock, New York. His construction was "like a child" to him, as Rodia's had been a mother.

Clarence Schmidt looked the part of prophet and mad mountain hermit, with a full white beard like Rip van Winkle, an earlier legend linked with the Catskills. The 1969 Woodstock Festival became a later myth of the genius loci, and Schmidt's artistic efforts climaxed simultaneously with it. Born in New York City in 1897, he had established Woodstock residency by 1940, and found employment building drystone walls. His masonry skills would support his own constructions more literally in the retaining walls of the house and terraced garden he built on the slopes of Ohayo Mountain. In about 1948, when Schmidt was fifty-one, his vision grew expansive and his mountainside burgeoned.

After Schmidt devoted himself full time to what is best known, and described, as his House of Mirrors (**417–418**), the original one-room cabin proliferated into a seven-tiered wooden ziggurat of some thirty-five rooms around an inner sanctum. Its exterior was composed—if that is the word—of mismatched windows, salvaged siding, and scrounged timbers, framing balconies, and enclosing galleries. Inside, nominal rooms were no more habitable or purposeful than Rodia's range of towers. They spread in all directions, dense with plastic flowers, defunct TV sets, and Christmas tree lights. Real trees too were encompassed by the quasi-organic growth, so the annex he called his tree house merely used their trunks for

◀ **413** SIMON RODIA
Watts Towers, Los Angeles,
California, c. 1921–54

▼ **414** SIMON RODIA
Watts Towers, Los Angeles,
California, c. 1921–54,
detail of enclosing wall

▲ **415** Photograph of
Simon Rodia in Watts
Towers

▼ **416** SIMON RODIA
Watts Towers, Los Angeles,
California, c. 1921–54, view
of the three tallest towers

living corner posts as it rose in three stories from the ground. The roof garden, more a sculpture garden than a horticultural one, rambled from the house-top to the road behind, overspilling Schmidt's property lines until irate neighbors restrained its further development. Alleyways and outdoor stairs extending from the house and meandering around the five-acre site were also arrayed with a vast inventory of advertising signs, bathtubs, bedsteads, beer cans, bicycle wheels, car parts, milk churns, and so on. Unlike the haphazard roof garden, some of these found objects were arranged into totemic groupings designating "shrines."

Simon Rodia, with his overall form language (Pop Art Nouveau? Los Angeles Gothic?), his uniformly scaled structural vocabulary, and aggregate surface treatment, may seem a high purist compared to Schmidt. Yet this is perhaps not so much due to personal stylistic or methodological differences as to the fact that Rodia's environmental design appears more consistent in its abstraction, while Schmidt's could be representational. Subject matter adds legibility to the abrupt formalistic juxtapositions. His shrines often

had themes and even titles: Cinderella, Cleopatra, Homer, The Four-Headed Indian. Their figurative imagery was readily facilitated by the many shop-window dummies, plastic dolls, and rubber face masks Schmidt incorporated. "Thus the Red Cross (Hope)" is a tableau of pleading hands. Dolls suspended in trees symbolize sixties astronauts. Headless dolls with twigs sprouting from their necks recall the paintings of Hieronymus Bosch; disembodied faces merge as in an Auguste Rodin sculpture. Some shrines relate to each other, as in the series on American Presidents: Washington the father, and the crucified Kennedy (any pseudo-religious character of these shrines was secularized through Schmidt's atheism). More than one centers on photographs of Schmidt himself.

"Sometimes the frame is better than the picture," Schmidt noted of the ambiguities between form and content. Still, at least by 1967 when the Ohayo Mountain complex reached saturation, a leitmotif of reflectivity had effectively unified it. Schmidt had always favored mirrors in his junk collecting—they both brightened and complicated the labyrinthian spaces

of the house—and had often mummified his fetish-objects in silver foil (originally gum or candy wrappers). Tar, applied to walls for waterproofing, was embedded with shards of glass and crinkly tinfoil. In his mature phase, Schmidt wrapped whole trees in it, each branch separately, as well as cobweb skeins of twine strung between shiny hubcaps and pie tins, supplementing all this with liberal coats of aluminum paint and, of course, more mirrors and fragments of mirrors. Reflected light fascinated him; and his manipulation of it was one means whereby his funky *Gesamtkunstwerk*, inside and out, integrated architecture, sculpture, and color no less than Rodia's Watts Towers.

Unlike the Towers, Schmidt's *magnum opus* survives only on emulsion. At the beginning of 1968, the House of Mirrors burned completely. Schmidt moved into his car, which became the basis for a new house, called the Mark II, when he built three rooms atop it. Soon he began transforming its environs into a Silver Forest, whose paths wound through it like the corridors of the former house, and continued the theme of foil-wrapping branches and pathside objects. At the end of 1971, the Mark II house also caught fire.

Again Schmidt attempted renewal, but his health failed. Aged about seventy-five, he was confined to a nursing home.

Schmidt has been institutionalized in other senses too. The first published material on him dates from 1963, to be followed by numerous magazine articles and monographs. As Rodia's work had been likened to Gaudí's, so was Schmidt's to the Palais Idéal (1879–1912) of "Facteur" Ferdinand Cheval. Cheval, in turn, had only been discovered posthumously in 1929, and embraced by the Surrealists in the thirties. Analogously, Clarence Schmidt was courted by the counterculture of the sixties, and visited by leading personalities including Bob Dylan, Joan Baez, and Dr. Timothy Leary. Films documented the House of Mirrors, and songs were written in its honor, abetted by its proximity to Woodstock and its do-your-own-thing ethic. Unlike Rodia or Cheval, Schmidt's self-consciousness might be qualified by the paradox that his late "style"—especially of the four years between the fires—was executed to an extent in the light of adulatory attention, as had been the reciprocal case of the naïve painter, "Douanier" Henri Rousseau.

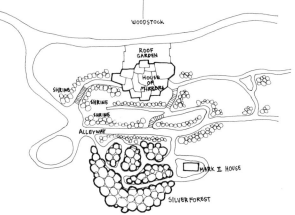

Art dealers and collectors patronized Schmidt, museum curators exhibited his folk sculpture, and theorists invoked it in sixties terms of popular grass-roots culture, mixed or multimedia, Assemblage, *objets trouvés*, *l'art brut* of Jean Dubuffet, the environmental happenings of Allan Kaprow, Kurt Schwitters's *Merzbau*, junk constructions by Tinguely *et al.*, and ad hocism. ("Everything is ad-lib," Schmidt said, if not ad hoc.) Conversely, British art critic Robert Melville confides: "There is no telling how much

Clarence knows about avant-garde art movements. I suspect that he has had more influence on neo-Dada and assemblage sculpture than any of the earlier movements have had on him—he talked and acted like one of nature's Dadaists." Beyond interpretation, Melville also notes: "His example started a craze, not only in Woodstock but much further afield, for houses that look eccentric and home-made: the results are often amusing, inventive, tastefully mock-primitive and even beautiful . . . " This is seconded by advocates like Tony Dugdale calling Schmidt "the seminal figure of the grass roots builder movement."[8]

HOUSECRAFT

ROBERT HANEY AND DAVID BALLANTINE PREFACED their 1974 *Woodstock Handmade Houses* with an acknowledgment of Schmidt's inspiration to local

▲ **420** *Adobe-making*

◄ **421** *Handmade House*, Woodstock, New York, photographed by Robert Haney for the book *Woodstock Handmade Houses* (1974)

► **422** WAITE *Engineer's House*, California, photographed by Barry Shapiro for the book *Handmade Houses* (1973)

brick, for instance, was native to the Southwestern United States where, in back-to-nature communes, children of the Atomic Age had already dug it, anachronistically, from the all-providing earth, while wearing no clothes to be muddied (**420**). Now an adobe revival afforded stylish, comfortable, private homes of the same material in the same region.

Since, however, as Rudofsky had put it, "the vernacular's unfortunate weakness is constancy," and since the stasis of a culture-bound architecture was not binding upon individual modern hand builders, the old methods could be mixed with upgraded technologies or geometries. Thus a Woodstock "saltbox" wears a fashionable geodesic hat, both shingled traditionally (**421**); a California log cabin sports a hyperbolic paraboloid roof, hand built by a retired engineer (**422**). Materials could be recycled

alternative builders, but publication of the book itself may as well have been inspired by the success of *Handmade Houses: A Guide to the Woodbutcher's Art,* brought out by Art Boedicke and Barry Shapiro the previous year (**419**). Haney/Ballantine closely followed the Boedicke/Shapiro format, and both appealed to vicarious armchair dreamhouse-builders. It may be unfair to dismiss these as coffee-table companion volumes, by dint of their "sophisticated and affluent"[9] reading market; yet Boedicke's encouraging sentiments and Shapiro's seductive color photography seem to be at the expense of information, either technical or historical. (They also respect the modesty and privacy of the owner-builders.) In the same category was Bernard Rudofsky's *Architecture without Architects* which, back in 1964, had opened many eyes to vernacular inspirations, without substantiating their cultural context, nor did his 1977

sequel *The Prodigious Builders*.[10] The year 1977 also saw a Boedicke/Shapiro sequel, *The Craftsman Builder,* in the same vein.

Equally influential, yet much more informative, was *Shelter*, published the same year as the first *Handmade Houses* (1973). Edited by Lloyd Kahn, with the thoroughgoing intelligence which recommended the *Domebooks*, but now driven by a new search for alternatives to the domes with which he was now dissatisfied, *Shelter* presented a heady compendium of vernacular solutions interspersed with building techniques applicable to various environments, available materials, and habitation requirements. *Shelter*'s exemplars were not designed by exotic eccentrics, but by the anonymous craftsmen of indigenous cultures. Being both natural and functional, pre-industrial building techniques retained their validity, but had to be re-learned. Adobe mud

from other buildings or appropriated from industrialization itself—hence Hawaiian tree houses (**423**) of palm leaves and polythene, bamboo and nylon rope ladders. Disparate windows and doors (**424**), especially, were combined anew by this more catholic tolerance of mixed metaphors.

Some of the technical sources offered in *Shelter* duplicated those of *The Whole Earth Catalog*—no longer being published—but added works then in progress; for a great many handmades were being built. The main thrust seemed to be in timber construction, a whole genre of the woodbutcher's art. The original *Handmade Houses* covered the West Coast; *Woodstock Handmade Houses* concentrated on the East. Although the provenance of handmades was widespread, certain favored pockets formed. One was an anarchic collection of bizarre domiciles at Canyon, California, in the Berkeley Hills. Here Barry

Smith's open plan nestled under its hyperbolic paraboloid. It had no walls, but extraordinary plumbing: an outdoor self-heated bath, and sink fittings in exaggerated profusion. But about 1967 Canyon suffered media exposure and subsequent cleanup by order. Many refugees fled northward, but in 1972 another official crackdown put pressure on all northern California. Oregon State had a standing policy of discouraging newcomers, and so it was up into Canada that the Western Movement—seeking *Lebensraum*—deflected.

British Columbia is twice the size of California, with only one-tenth the population, attracting American war-evaders, British dropouts, and young, skilled, solvent Canadians. Vancouver hosted a United Nations Habitat Conference—on alternatives—in 1976, but even that city had summarily cleared its own self-built squatter settlement from nearby harbor mudflats in 1971. North of Vancouver, though, close enough for exurban flight but beyond the range of building regulations, lay twelve-mile-square Hornby Island, and here hand builders foregathered, joined by veterans like Tim Biggin from Canyon and Tom Burrows from the Vancouver mudflats. The "Hornby style," which developed fully, under propitious conditions, makes for a valuable case study, as in fact undertaken by Boh Helliwell and Michael McNamara for *Architectural Design* magazine, July 1978.

The island is indeed a woodbutcher's earthly paradise. It is so situated that the surrounding straits provide building materials, not only driftwood but giant pre-felled pines. Escaped from the floating booms of one of the world's major timber-producing areas, these beach-logs fetch up on Hornby, like the builders themselves. Large enough for structural members, they are often interestingly sculpted by natural forces into the bargain. A single such beam, balanced on a twisted, trunk-like post, supports Lloyd House's Leaf Retreat, built in 1970. Monolithic wooden arches are frequently used too. Tall, weathered uprights, known locally as totems, recall the powerful timber architecture of indigenous Northwest Indian tribes with unpronounceable names. Influence is also claimed for the Japanese tradition of sensitive wood joinery, conveyed by immigrants from across the Pacific, like the Japan Current which keeps Hornby's climate mild. A Canadian frontier vernacular persists in stoutly framed barns and cabins clad in split cedar shingles.

Responses by Hornby's hand builders varied. Some, such as Dean Ellis, "didn't know anything about building," and began, characteristically, with the preconceived form of a *Domebook* geodesic (**425**). Windows were plexiglass, joints were waterproofed with silicon sealant, skin was shingled in aluminum

▶ **423** *Hawaiian Tree house*

▼ **424** DICK KEIGWIN
Renee's House, California, 1970, kitchen

▼ **425** DEAN ELLIS
Geodesic Dome, Hornby Island, British Columbia, Canada, 1973, exterior detail

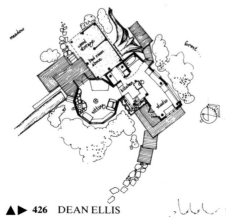

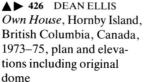

▲▶ **426** DEAN ELLIS
Own House, Hornby Island, British Columbia, Canada, 1973–75, plan and elevations including original dome

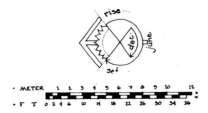

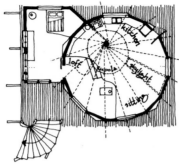

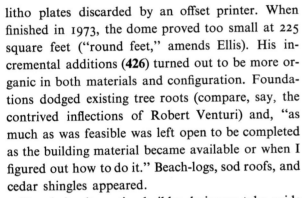

◀ 427 TIM BIGGIN
Log-Rhythmic Spiral House,
Hornby Island, British
Columbia, Canada, 1970–
75, structural elevation
and plan

▶ 428 TIM BIGGIN
Log-Rhythmic Spiral House,
Hornby Island, British
Columbia, Canada, 1970–
75, exterior

▼ 429 TIM BIGGIN
Log-Rhythmic Spiral House,
Hornby Island, British Columbia, Canada, 1970–75,
interior detail

litho plates discarded by an offset printer. When finished in 1973, the dome proved too small at 225 square feet ("round feet," amends Ellis). His incremental additions (426) turned out to be more organic in both materials and configuration. Foundations dodged existing tree roots (compare, say, the contrived inflections of Robert Venturi) and, "as much as was feasible was left open to be completed as the building material became available or when I figured out how to do it." Beach-logs, sod roofs, and cedar shingles appeared.

Hornby's alternative builder-designers take pride in working without blueprints, calculations, or even drawing-board dimensioning (unlike today's "gallery architecture" of schematized isometrics, rigid modular patterns, or tortured plans more impressive on paper than when experienced physically). They dwell instead on fitness for purpose (of rural living), flexibility, and improvisation. The houses often strive for energy conservation, yet construction itself is conditioned by the prodigal abundance of wood, discounting Fuller's design imperative: "Do more with less." Hornby floors and roofs are typically solid slabs of two-by-fours nailed edge-to-edge: simple and effective, but hardly minimal economy of means.

Even so, down-to-earth vernacularism need not conflict with wild structural experimentation. Tim Biggin's house (427–429) is a "log-rhythmic" spiral of logs whirling round a central post, upholding an ascending twist of roof (as in the Bavinger House of 1950–55 by Bruce Goff, himself an adept innovator and improviser). While such structural acrobatics have, since the exhibitionistic fifties, given way to low-profiled decorated sheds in modish architecture, Biggin's spatial circus is "sheer exuberance." Tom Burrows, for his Clifftop House (430–431) of 1972–

75, rediscovered the hyperbolic paraboloid once again, controlling its drama under a folksy sod roof. Triangular plays against rectangular in plan. Lloyd House roofed a ceramics studio (432) in undulating vaults (not unlike Gaudí's), and the compound curvature of his "falling leaf" roof (a choicer metaphor than Frank Lloyd Wright's Falling Water?) is at once lyrical and elegant in its structural grace (433–434).

If Dean Ellis learned from Hornby, others came prepared. Tim Biggin followed his father's trade as professional builder, and is also accomplished as a welder, blacksmith, mechanic, and general handyman. Lloyd House started out as a carpenter, yet became a builder-designer who helped other islanders

with their houses; both the ceramics studio and Leaf Retreat were for such clients, fee-paying or not. Tom Burrows, Boh Helliwell, and Michael McNamara were not, before Hornby, innocent of formal architectural schooling or even practice. Although they exorcized the profession through their craft alternatives, they also realized the architect's dream of building one's own house (436). Or someone else's: Helliwell, McNamara, and Ed Colin formed a partnership called Blue Sky Design in 1974 to build houses on commission. Even non-resident architects—Paul Merrick, for one—have designed Hornby houses, albeit in sympathy with the homegrown idiom.

Builder-designer collaboration and barn-raising cooperation among Hornby's five hundred or so families bridges the usual communications (or "taste") gap between architects and users. Island-wide social cohesion has also been promoted. The Round House, appended in 1974 to a community hall outgrown by the population influx, is small in scale, walled in native stone, and roofed in cedar shingles. "The building," it was reported, "was a unifier to the island," unimposing as civic architecture yet symbolic of a mutual meeting ground between conservative older inhabitants and the suspiciously young, citified, newer arrivals. Within the latter group, some semblance of physical community has developed since 1968 in the Shire, a loose cluster of year-round dwellings and summer retreats on shared land. (If the name Shire refers to Tolkien's novels, it is apposite enough to the Hobbit houses there.) Handmade houses may have replaced communes, but here collective alternative aspirations have been re-integrated through the same process of self-determination.

The movement as a whole has been called "the architecture of protest," but it is difficult to see how the anti-militarist convictions ascribed to Canadian hand

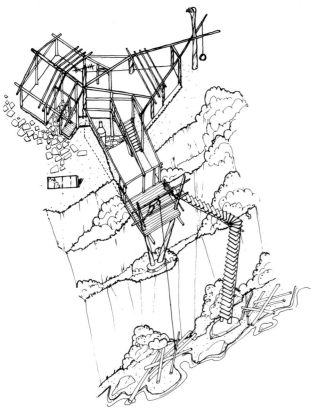

430 TOM BURROWS
Clifftop House, Hornby
Island, British Columbia,
Canada, 1972–75,
axonometric

431 TOM BURROWS
Clifftop House, Hornby
Island, British Columbia,
Canada, 1972–75, construc-
tion view

432 LLOYD HOUSE
*Ceramics Studio for Wayne
Ngan*, Hornby Island, British Columbia, Canada,
c. 1969–74, detail of door

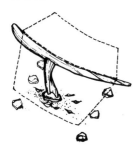

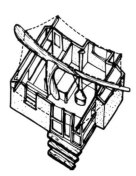

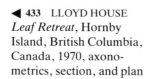

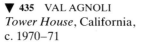

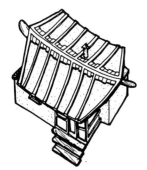

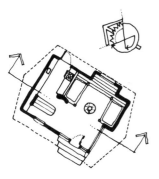

◀ **433** LLOYD HOUSE
Leaf Retreat, Hornby
Island, British Columbia,
Canada, 1970, axono-
metrics, section, and plan

▶ **434** LLOYD HOUSE
Leaf Retreat, Hornby Island,
British Columbia, Canada,
1970, exterior

▼ **435** VAL AGNOLI
Tower House, California,
c. 1970–71

builders, in an essay by Henry Elder,[11] manifest
themselves in the act of building, or the buildings' forms. Another essay, by Tony Ward, refutes
Elder by arguing that the phenomenon is not a protest, nor counter to mainstream culture, but "arises
from the very centre of West Coast consciousness
and ideology, and could more properly be considered
as a renaissance, a return to values and traditions
more Californian than anything."[12] Ward, however,
oversimplifies his case for cultural identity to the
other extreme. It is tempting to interpret socio-cultural values in architectural terms and vice versa.
But in a socio-cultural context, it is scarcely tenable
to speak of a movement motivated by personal freedom, material indulgence, and spiritual gratification
yet which can still be reconciled with the sub-com-
munes of the Shire, Canyon, or Woodstock.

Some self-built student facilities—neither true
communes nor single-family homesteads—have also
been consummated. At Franconia College, New
Hampshire, a finely detailed dormitory was constructed by a dozen of its future occupants under
the direction of Ed d'Andrea and Gary Dwyer in
1967. David Sellers, John Mallery, and students at
Goddard College, Vermont, built a design center
and sculpture studio in 1970 (**250**). Soon after, Sim

Labels on drawing:
laminated yellow cedar 2" x 4" roof
log structure
roof structure weaves & skylight.
windows slide into wall pockets...
laminated fir 2"x4" floor
cistern for rainwater collection.
wood storage
kitchen
fire
garden
cistern
compost toilet

▲ **436** MICHAEL MC-NAMARA, *Own House*, Hornby Island, British Columbia, Canada, 1972–76, axonometrics, plan, and sectional perspective

van der Ryn's students from Berkeley ad-libbed their own workshop at Inverness, California. Later, the Southcoast group, with Chip Lord and Tom Morey, supervised an arts building at Antioch College, Ohio. These were done as user-participation projects or architectural learning exercises, yet the private house remains the prime occasion for self-building, and with it the urge for cultural re-definition.

In the context of American architectural history, there has been recurrent vernacular revivalism ranging from Frank Lloyd Wright's midwestern Prairie Style to Charles Moore's Sea Ranch on the Pacific, while the celebrated late-nineteenth-century Shingle Style looked back to New England colonial cottages. And *these* searches for national roots[13] proceeded via designs by commercial practices for middle-class clients.

Hand builders hold many of the same design values as conventional architects when addressing the single-family residence: taking advantage of views and solar orientation, relating the house to its site in particular and to nature in general, tailoring it to the personalities as well as the needs of its intended occupants. Hand-built houses often accentuate integrity of materials and honesty of structure, which also coincides with the conventional architect's design morality. These tenets of Modernism may have been more often preached than practiced, due perhaps to remoteness from industrialized building techniques, but hand builders can and do observe them by virtue of dealing directly with construction. Robert Venturi has perceptively suggested that European Modernism arose in the twenties when subjective Expressionism was objectified into expression of function, structure, and materials; that is, the building's own programmatic, mechanical, and technological contingencies were to be expressed rather than the architect's creative soul. Woodbutchers compromise between personal and constructional expression, at times regaining a dy-

namic equilibrium, even a unity. It is this sophisticated, yet fundamentalist, approach which is alternative to most current trends, and which exercises their art and craft.

The "woodbutcher" in the subtitle of *Handmade Houses* is one of those self-deprecating semantic inversions, like freak or funk. Such carpentry—understated as if a casual skill—is at best neither ingenuous nor facile; the true woodbutcher is meticulously deliberate even in the use of the brutal chain saw. The log cabin has been refined to a pitch undreamt-of by Henry David Thoreau, and gone is the ineptitude of so much commune construction. When Val Agnoli describes his own house (437) as a "conservative building. It's just an A-frame turned around into an elliptical form," this hardly does justice to its sweeping curves or the almost obsessive finesse of its detailing. To build it took "not too long. Year and a half, maybe."[14] After this house of the late sixties, Agnoli did an equally striking tower (435) flared at the top, south of San Francisco. (Agnoli has a degree in architecture—he studied under Bruce Goff—but his father was a New England carpenter.) To these architectural artisans, craftsmanship must be personally fulfilling: Zen and the art of the well-turned doorpost; or firmness, commodity, and the delight of a beam end cut into a dragon's-head gargoyle. Nearly a century before, in 1880, William Morris prophesied "the victorious days when millions of those who now sit in darkness will be enlightened by an art made

by the people and for the people, a joy to the maker and the user."

In the early seventies (when the literature on handmades peaked), there was a vogue within the middleclass taste culture for ethnic chic and peasant dresses by Yves Saint-Laurent, candles and sandals, pine tables and earthenware—the earthier the better, and dearer. (This may not have been what William Morris had in mind, although his own Arts and Crafts Movement had a similar clientele.) Many who live in handmade houses are makers of crafts, as a vocation and livelihood, and not just users. Architecture itself was the craft followed by some master builders, but others hand built their houses as an extension of a "craft life-style." For instance, two jewelers, Bob De Buck and Jerry Thorman, wrought remarkable houses (438–441) for themselves in New Mexico. Without preamble, they simply nailed short lengths of scrap two-by-fours into laminated ribs or cellular membranes, working by a "visual sort of feel, there was no preplanning."[15] The undisciplined structure of highly irregular geometries grew to cover five thousand square feet. The wood was encased in flexible metal lath, then plastered inside and out. Burrowing into the desert, interiors became complex and cavernous, with polychromatic plexiglass skylights set like gemstones into the jumbled roof. The builders were not worried about leaks, in the desert climate. The resultant houses may be disorderly and owe nothing to the regional vernacular; and some perfectionist craftsmen might disapprove of their elaborate confusion, but Bob Easton (co-author of *Shelter*'s text) saw it and "was deconditioned in an instant. Bob and Jerry had sacrificed every sacred cow of architecture and building."[16] It is, as it were, an alternative to an alternative. It should be salutary for would-be self-builders to know that besides the standard do-it-yourself manuals, and the standards set by established woodbutchers, the possibilities are still as open as they were to Simon Rodia and Clarence Schmidt.

▲ **437** VAL AGNOLI *Own House*, California, c. 1968–69, exterior detail

▶ **438** BOB DE BUCK AND JERRY THORMAN, *Bob's House*, New Mexico, c. 1969–73, exterior of "roof"

◀ **439** BOB DE BUCK AND JERRY THORMAN, *Structure of scrap wood*, New Mexico, c. 1969–73, detail

◀ **440** BOB DE BUCK AND JERRY THORMAN, *Bob's House*, New Mexico, c. 1969–73, construction view

▲ **441** BOB DE BUCK AND JERRY THORMAN, *Bob's House*, New Mexico, c. 1969–73, interior

NOMADIC DESIGNS

IN THE LONG SHADOW OF HERMAN MELVILLE AND Joseph Conrad it would be presumptuous to cite the lure of escape by sea as a new alternative to land-bound immobility. Yet only in the sixties did boats—houseboats, actually, often self-built and in floating communities—join other vehicles of counterculture consciousness and personal freedom. Houseboat communities exist on the canals of Amsterdam, in London's upmarket Little Venice and the Thames, on California's Sacramento River delta, on the Hudson near Manhattan, and in Seattle, but the best known has been Waldo Point in San Francisco Bay, off Sausalito (**442**).[1]

Of the many hundreds of marine habitations anchored there, a few are, or were, shipshape vessels. Steve Siskind (significantly, an architect and planner keen to improve houseboating facilities through design and legislation) lives with his family aboard the *Isabel,* a former Danish cargo schooner, vintage 1913. It can, and does, frequently sail elsewhere, free as the wind. Not so the *Vallejo,* a wooden car ferry no longer seaworthy; however its considerable size makes for gracious living, complete with terraced gardens on the upper decks. Smaller conversions are more in the *African Queen* class.

It is more common for houseboats to be purpose built. Commercial models are, of course, available, to be used like recreational vehicle campers and similar in construction, but the alternative is to use any old hull, raft, or barge (ex-military landing craft are suitable) as a base for handmade superstructures which need not concede to traditional naval architecture. Mounted on these floating foundations are staid bungalows, fairy-tale cottages, A-frames, several geodesic and other domes, a large two-story building, a railway caboose gone to sea, tarpaper shacks, architect-designed "decorated sheds," and sculptural "ducks." The basic building material is wood—retrieved from flotsam, shingled in rustic cedar, worked into gingerbread gables (bargeboards, indeed)—with salvaged stained-glass windows and other homely touches taken from the lost architec-ture of the land. Most houseboats, lacking their own "grounds," have outdoor spaces like balconies, porches, and roofdecks, but they sometimes poignantly attempt to re-create backyards in miniature, with doghouses and Astroturf lawns. As in other handmades, much wit and ingenuity is lavished on painting and other decoration, for example, a clothes dummy used as a figurehead.

Sausalito's most ambitious arks were both built by Chris Roberts. One of them, not quite a Chinese junk, evinced Oriental overtones in its moon-gate windows and upturned eaves (**446**). The other, not so much a pagoda as a Gothic dream cathedral, called *The Madonna* (**443–445**), was artfully sculpted of timber (scrounged from wharves and docks) to a height of about one hundred feet, with only a small interior loft as living area. Unfortunately, late in 1974, this titanic houseboat burned to the waterline. (It must be a source of grim satisfaction to building inspectors that alternative architecture, rejecting restrictive regulations, does occasionally meet such a fate.)

Extolling their waterborne alternative, house-boaters have contributed their navel (or naval) contemplations to the counterculture's cosmic awareness. "When I lived on the bay I was studying astrology pretty heavy. I was impressed by my boat rising six feet with the tides. It helped me understand the gravity of the planets," testified "Patty," while "Bruce" observed: "When you live with all the elements, your space-time thing gets warped." These quotes come from *Water Squatters: The Houseboat Lifestyle.* The same book offers practical tips like the following, perhaps in answer to Bruce's warpage: "Everything should be put in waterproof containers to keep it dry . . . ," and advises, under General Maintenance: "Check the bottom every year or two."

There are the usual contradictions, too, in counterculture attitudes to the less-than-cosmic environment and not-so-natural ecology of San Francisco Bay. Much is made of the ideal boat's splendid isolation—"the simplicity of a Walden's pond"[2]—as a closed energy system, but alternative power sources remain elusive. A seven-foot-tall windmill, on a ferrocement sailboat, generated enough electricity to light a 100-watt bulb. In fact, most houseboats are tied umbilically to shoreside services, while discharging raw sewage into the sustaining water. For these and other reasons, officialdom has harassed the flotilla, which it regards as an offshore shantytown. Clumsy police tactics, such as towing boats away at gunpoint, only gained public sympathy for the houseboaters, but new regulations in 1975 promised to tidy this objectionable slum into a houseboat suburb, rising six feet with the tide. The community was still thriving in 1981, however.

As to Sausalito's cherished, threatened community identity: whereas one houseboater can say "I live on the water because I don't like being near other people. I moved onto the boat to get away," another finds, "To live on a houseboat in Sausalito is like moving into a floating trailer park."[3] Although resistance to forcible displacement did mobilize them against outside authority, the Sausalito population has always been transient. Yet the houseboats themselves are no more mobile than the mobile homes in that trailer park; few ever leave their moorings and fewer still are self-propelled. They are—without constituting a vernacular like Asian sampans[4]—handmade houses afloat, often of superlative personalized design. For a truly nomadic modern alternative, it is necessary to look to the paved highways of North America.

THE MYTH OF MOBILITY

NORTH AMERICAN SOCIETY HAS BEEN MOBILE, AND made a virtue of it. To be an American is to be an immigrant, or at least descended from immigrants. Horizontal mobility bore them westward from Europe, then across the continent by covered wagon and iron horse, choo-chooing up the thousands of exploitable miles. The frontier came to an end about when the nineteenth century did, but early in the twentieth Henry Ford acted on his dictum: "Where one car can go, all cars can go." Road-building paced automobile production in a self-perpetuating cycle with a growth rate many times that of the population itself. A seemingly unlimited supply of petroleum fueled horizontal mobility; the status gained in owning a car drove aspirations upward. Labor shortages during both World Wars drew internal migrations from agrarian to industrial areas, especially from South to North. The thirties knew continued flux as Woody Guthrie's jobless youths rode the rails to escape the Depression, while John Steinbeck's Oakies headed West once again from the dust bowls of the Plains. In the sixties, the South-to-North tide was reversed, yet the Sun Belt still beckoned seekers of the good life to the West Coast.

The national myth is not about whether Americans are still mobile—every year since 1948 one in five changed address—but about why this is a social and individual good. In Europe, the pattern has long been different; when the Huns, Vandals, Vikings, or Normans were on the move, it was not good news, and today a popular TV series called "Gypsy Caravan" equivalent to America's "Wagon Train" seems unlikely. But in the land of opportunity, horizontal movement is equated with vertical or social mobility. All those demographic shifts and flows meant expansion rather than dislocation, as individuals sought economic improvement *en masse* through gold rushes, free land in the next valley, factory work in the big cities, or a better position in the company's boomtown branch office. Many corporations follow policies of constantly transferring executives: IBM, as is well known, stands for "I've Been Moved."[5] Each horizontal move is also one up the ladder. One generation of rural blacks, poor whites, or ethnic immigrants would invest the inner city; the next, successful generation made it out to the suburbs as rising expectations led to another horizontal-vertical move.

Because this compulsive to-and-fro is more personally disruptive and socially destabilizing than most Americans are prepared to admit, it must be mythologized, idealized as the great American cultural dynamic. And when, in the early seventies, it seemed for the first time that future auto-mobility might be limited by energy shortages, the collective unconscious

▶ **442** *Houseboat Community*, Sausalito, California, photographed in 1980

443 CHRIS ROBERTS
The Madonna, Sausalito,
California, c. 1971–74,
photographed in 1971

444 CHRIS ROBERTS
The Madonna, Sausalito,
California, c. 1971–74,
interior

445 CHRIS ROBERTS
The Madonna, Sausalito,
California, c. 1971–74,
photographed in 1971

haps because a lower speed limit was imposed) on ritual journeys to nowhere, as if reclaiming that national character-determinant vested in mobility. Already popular was caravanning in trailers, including the legendary Airstream, plastered with souvenir travel stickers. These conveyances—now campers or recreational vehicles—proliferated, bearing brave names like Free Spirit, Happy Wanderer, or Keep on Truckin', never Dunroamin'. Another revealing mid-seventies fad was for the citizens' band car radios with which private drivers tuned in to the arcane and colorful argot of professional truck drivers, as if joining them in spirit. Recreational vehicle and trucker films joined the traditional American genre of road movies.[6]

The open road is no respecter of social distinctions such as mainstream or counterculture; it is all just Kar Kulture, with its own subcultures (its working yeomanry of truckers; its romanticized banditry of bikers like Hunter Thompson's mobile savages, the Hell's Angels; and its folk heroes). Yet mobility has been a driving force in counterculture lore. In its genesis, Jack Kerouac went *On the Road* between

446 CHRIS ROBERTS
Houseboat, Sausalito, California, c. 1970

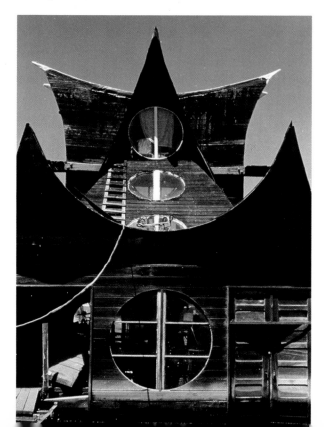

responded by affirming it all the more. Just as the myth of the Wild West (Buffalo Bill and the Prairie Houses) had been born out of the closure of the frontier, forestalling traumas deep in the national psyche, so the threatened extinction of the car—or the mobile American—began to off-breed desperate mutations. The critical dates would be 1890, when the U.S. Census reported no more free land, and 1973, the first oil crisis. Latterly, more Americans took to the roads without mileage actually increasing (per-

▼ **447** *Pickup truck with commercially manufactured camper*, early 1970s

▶ **448** *Homemade camper on pickup truck*, California, early 1970s

1947 and publication in 1955, blasting back and forth from coast to coast with "Dean Moriarty," whose real name was Neal Cassady, at the wheel. Kerouac was only Cassady's Boswell. His vehement creative energies had no other outlet but restless, rootless, experiential speed; to keep moving was to outrun the fate which befell a silent generation of non-conformists in Allen Ginsberg's poem "Howl": "I saw the best minds of my generation destroyed . . ." Moreover, Cassady is the missing link between fifties Beatnik prehistory and early sixties proto-hippies, for he was also the driver of "Furthur," the Day-Glo bus in which Ken Kesey's Merry Pranksters crossed the country in 1964, spreading psychedelic anarchy.[7] Their manic art-into-life-style as a flying squad of piratical, neo-Dada, holy fools was Cassady's own. He inspired Kesey as much as he had Kerouac, and became, posthumously, an underground cult figure.

Old World nomads had taken tribe and traditions with them; modern Americans require a measure of doublethink—or Jungian group-dream, or myth— to play an opportunistic mobility against its own attendant insecurities. Perhaps only within the counterculture has free movement been a positive alternative. The communes of the late sixties never sought permanence and so their transience was not failure; when one disbanded or members left, it was for other venues, other interests, or just to keep moving. Some communes were way stations on the road—as in the 1969 film *Easy Rider*—and some were peripatetic themselves: Hog Farm ran a fleet of buses captained by Hugh Romney, also a Prankster alumnus. A vehicle defines its fellow travelers, gives mutual direction to their trip—a placeless event and unstructured commitment. But one of the movement's most quoted aphorisms has been Kesey's: "You're either on the bus or off the bus."

◀ **449** *Homemade camper on pickup truck*, California, early 1970s, interior

▼ **450** *Bus with cartop cupola added*, early 1970s

▶ **451** *Converted schoolbus*, early 1970s

▼ **452** *Bus with second story and balcony added*, California, early 1970s

▼ **453** *Schoolbus with second story added, towing trailer*, Colorado, early 1970s

TRUCKITECTURE

THE SENTIENT, SELF-AWARE, "MATURE" COUNTERCULture of the late sixties and early seventies had no prior claim on all-American nomadism, but was in the van when it was given architectonic form. There is, obviously, an inherent disjunction between received concepts of permanent architecture and those of mobility. Perhaps only amateur designers could override this—by simply ignoring it, or turning the irony upon itself as a joke rather than a recrimination of logic. To describe individually designed homes on wheels, the term truckitecture was coined by photographers from Environmental Communications, who documented it in 1974 on the West Coast. Here, land of the freeways, nomadic truckitecture first thrived, and set the basic possibilities and technics for rendering vehicles habitable while retaining full mobility.

The type of vehicle chosen determines the modification. The small, open-backed, uniquely North American pickup is easily convertible, with commercial camper modules already manufactured to be mounted on it for vacations (**447**), then dismounted when the truck returns to hauling farm goods or whatever. Homemade accommodation, usually for one person, can be similarly built on (**448–449**). Size is limited,

but this playhouse scale is also its charm. Much larger is the standard country schoolbus (**451**), originally bright yellow, and well-wrought with heavy-duty working parts that mock the planned obsolescence of family cars. Schoolbuses, even if antiquated, are therefore good value; of such stock came the redoubtable, "Furthur." Serious remodeling often increases interior headroom, either by raising the roof over its full length, or by projecting cupolas. The bodies of smaller vehicles—cars or vans—can be cannibalized for this purpose (**450**). Skylights have been made from Airforce surplus turrets, nose cones, and canopies in bulbous perspex. Originally for sixty-six (smallish) passengers, schoolbuses provide up to three hundred square feet of living area, which is more than some domes or the *African Queen* class of houseboat.

Flatbed trucks come in various sizes, the longest surpassing even schoolbuses, and are as indefatigable. For example, a ten-wheel, 1948 International log truck, with fifteen gears to its powerful diesel, has been tamed into a comfortable family home still capable of cruising at speed up mountain grades. Living quarters in such trucks, unlike schoolbuses, are separate from driving cabs and must be built anew on the truckbed, but this can expedite more

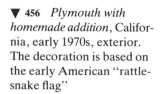

◀ **454** *International log truck converted for mobile living*, Oregon, 1975–76, section

▼ **455** *Volvo with rear end cut off, reversed, and remounted above*, early 1970s

▼ **456** *Plymouth with homemade addition*, California, early 1970s, exterior. The decoration is based on the early American "rattlesnake flag"

flexible planning. As the quest for elbow room is carried inside the housetrucks, second stories appear (sometimes with Juliet balconies; **452**), back porches cantilever outward, foreign body parts are grafted on. Trailers can be towed as outhouses (**453**), and many vehicles carry subsidiary bicycles or motorcycles as lighter transport—just as yachts carry dinghies —for short forays into still greater mobility. More like yachts themselves than most houseboats, these rolling homes can be gracious but must be compactly and efficiently organized (**454**). Besides the three types mentioned, almost any other will do, any design variation can be attempted, and many hybrid beasts have been engendered (**455–456**).

The technological base of any mass-produced

▼ **457** *Commercially manufactured Motor Home with custom painting*, California early 1970s

▼ **458** JITANOS PÈRE ET FILS, *Cadillac hearse with homemade addition*, California, early 1970s, exterior under construction. Wood craftsmanship by Jitanos père

motor vehicle is more advanced in construction and performance than that of residential architecture, quite apart from the power plant and control systems which are a vehicle's *raison d'être*. Modern designers of housing, from Le Corbusier to Buckminster Fuller, have envied the Citröen and Ford for this; these speak the language of neoprene gaskets and safety glass and monocoque metal shells —strong, light, and weathertight—rather than the "when all else fails use bloody great nails" attitude of the building trades. Truckitecture conversions accordingly call for a modicum of high-tech skills. These, as it happens, many North Americans do possess, endemically, gained as teenagers messing about with cars. Some graduated to customizing, that subcultural expression first celebrated by Tom Wolfe in *The Kandy-Kolored Tangerine-Flake Streamline*

▼ 459 JITANOS PÈRE ET FILS, *Cadillac hearse with homemade addition*, California, early 1970s, exterior completed. Resin finish by Jitanos fils

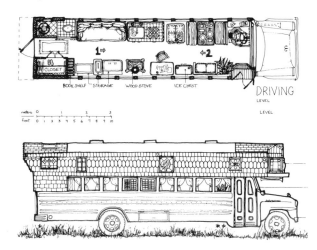

▼ 460 *Schoolbus converted into antiques showplace*, Oregon, 1975–77, driving-level plan and elevation

Baby of 1965. Personalizing and accentuating the stock industrialized product, the customizers matched their hot rods' ego-extending horsepower with flash-slick style. Vans, pickups, and campers were customized too, so—as long as minimally habitable—customizing overlaps with alternative truckitecture. Examples shown here include a commercial motor home individualized with racy supergraphics (**457**), and a 1959 Cadillac hearse with a rear addition in molded plywood, its resin finish borrowed from the sophisticated technology of surfboards (**458–459**).

A recent strain of truckitecture, however, seems to have turned away from the high-gloss look. Of about two dozen cases in *Rolling Homes*, 1979 (as attractive a book as *Handmade Houses* and similar in tone), only one could be called slick-tech: a flat-fronted

schoolbus glamorized externally with bright enamel, slanting windows, and speedlines, and internally with wall-to-wall carpeting, chromed spotlamps, and naugehyde padding. It was designed and built by a retired couple of an older generation, which may explain their choice of style: not unlike that of a Raymond Loewy Greyhound Scenicruiser. Other, much younger builders reveal nostalgia for design values they never knew personally; yet the cottage aesthetic seen in their truckitecture is consonant with many rustic handmade homes and houseboats (Ark-itecture?). Whereas in the thirties, many buildings had been streamlined like vehicles, in the seventies many housetrucks conversely took after American Gothic farmhouses right off the cover of *The Saturday Evening Post,* with shingles hung outside and rich woodwork within. Balustrades are back, and pot-bellied stoves—all trucking down the Interstates (**460–463**).[8]

The craft revival that makes this a nostalgia trip, however, goes beyond cozy domestication of the ten-wheel truck; it supplants the vehicle's own technological styling (**464**). Even so, quaintness is not purchased at the cost of immobility, nor blind funkiness. Truckitects will skillfully reinforce their stained-glass windows against the thousand natural shocks of road conditions. It may be that this atavism is not so much pre-industrial as anti-urban. Not only the architectural paradigms but the vehicles themselves originate in rural types: pickup, country schoolbus, long-haul truck. That would be consistent both with counterculture escapism and that American myth of mobility which has always avoided coming to terms with the city, promoting the frontier or suburbia as a safety valve for social discontent. If, as suggested, mobility now shows signs of failing, due to circumstances beyond technological control, then, rather than insisting reflexively upon its continuance as the mainstream has done, "rusticated" truckitecture compromises with the new reality of oil shortages—and the new craft mythos. The free-ranging vehicle, cultural artifact of modern nomadism, has been offered a stable architectural alternative, a chance to settle down.

Marshall McLuhan has posited that an obsolete technology or medium becomes an art form.[9] Since, "an American is a creature on four wheels,"[10] but since "the wheel itself is obsolescent,"[11] then it becomes the medium of the artist, in this case the alternative designer-craftsman. For, "The artist picks up the message of cultural and technological challenge decades before its transforming impact occurs. . . . The artist possesses the means of anticipating and avoiding the consequences of technological trauma."[12] Certainly much originality has been expended both in design (**465**) and expressive decoration

▼ 461 *Converted vehicles*, Oregon, 1971, 1972, 1975, 1977, elevations

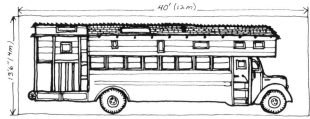

'37 INTERNATIONAL

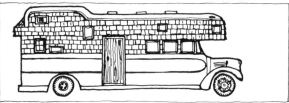

'48 INTERNATIONAL

'52 DODGE

'48 DODGE

'51 FEDERAL

'59 INTERNATIONAL

(**466**) of these house-cars, log cabins on wheels, and mobile family homes. However, the ideal of *self*-expression by owner-designers may be compromised by the common practice of trading converted vehicles at special markets convened for the purpose. Professionals in conversion will, like car customizers, offer their skills to clients. Even more depersonalized is the new breed of recreational vehicles which, borrowing the nomadic image of truckitecture and commercializing it, can be bought *pre*-customized. These not only come complete with stripes and air-brush effects direct from the factory, but often with murals painted on their sides. These usually depict the wide-open spaces of their symbolic mobility: Western landscapes of Marlboro Country, wild stallions and eagles flying free.

▶ **462** *Converted vehicle*, early 1970s

▼ **463** JOAQUIN DE LA LUZ, *Chevrolet flatbed truck with family accommodation added*, California, c. 1968

▲ 464 *Shingled van*, early 1970s

▲ 465 *Converted car with living quarters "upstairs,"* early 1970s. Note the retractable ladder

▶ 466 *Painted vehicle*, early 1970s

ALTERNATIVE TECHNOLOGIES

AFTER THE COMMUNES EXPENDED THEIR IMPETUS, alternative architecture forked in two distinct directions: one, as illustrated in the two previous chapters, led to craft-oriented handmade houses and nomadic designs; the other carried on the alternative technologies developed to build and service the communes themselves. So, for instance, after Lloyd Kahn and Jay Baldwin had collaborated on communal domes at Pacific High School, Kahn went on to edit *Shelter* for the hand builders while Baldwin gravitated to Integrated Life Support Systems Laboratories (ILSSL) in New Mexico (**467**). Research there, directed by Robert Reines, recalled the "whole-systems design strategy" of Baldwin's mentor Buckminster Fuller, but progressed empirically rather than by a simplistic faith in Fuller's formulae for operating Spaceship Earth—the ILSSL approach was rigorously scientific yet not on the scale of global engineering. By 1973 they could claim, for the first time, to have satisfied the energy needs of an experimental home (which happened to be a dome) solely with sun and wind.[1]

Steve Baer, erstwhile designer to the Southwestern communes, set up Zomeworks Humanufactory to capitalize on that experience, to make available technological skills thus acquired, and to keep on working for a new market. To keep on trucking, Zomeworks operated a converted schoolbus, based in Albuquerque, New Mexico. The house Baer built nearby for his own family (**468–471**) incorporated both his architectural and environmental alternatives, being so workable as to merit widespread publication in the counterculture media, yet so livable that it was featured also in *House and Garden* with a photograph of house-proud Baer, unbearded since his days at Drop City, Lama, Manera Nueva, and Libre.

Although the house does function for nuclear family living, its open plan has no corridors, nor even internal doors. Eleven zonahedra, on one level of two thousand square feet, cluster around a patio. Each zome is a rhombicuboctahedron, stretched and truncated to define spaces of various sizes and shapes

—no two the same. The constituent facets of the crystalline assemblage are, however, modular, with vertical, quadrilateral side walls, and they consist of aluminum panels with urethane-filled honeycombed cardboard sandwiched between inner and outer skins. This prefabricated construction contrasts with the slapdash methods of the communes, notwithstanding their similar zonahedral geometries (Baer's first cartop zome had employed the same rhombicuboctahedron). Likewise, early energy systems pioneered at Drop City have been reconsidered technically and made to work with ingeniously simple elegance.

Temperature control is provided by ninety fifty-five-gallon drums, filled with water and deployed in four banks on the sunny side of the house. In winter, massive styrofoam-insulated shutters (**469**) are opened every morning, exposing the outer faces of the drums, painted black for heat absorption, to the sun. The water-wall picks up solar radiation all day, then convects it into the house at night when the shutters are winched back to seal in the warmth accumulated (**470**). The opposite procedure is followed in summer: the shutters open at *night* to *cool* the water, which then cools the house during the day, when the shutters remain shut against the raw desert sun. The water's modulating effect is like that of a lake on the weather of its shores—cooling in daytime, warming at night—since water heats up more slowly and retains its heat longer than *terra firma*. This temperature differential also generates daily "sea breezes" and nightly "land breezes"; similarly the alternating diurnal cycle of the house's microclimate is regulated by ventilators atop each zome.[2]

The system is "passive," requiring five thousand gallons of water to be bottled up permanently as a heat-exchange medium, or solar storage battery. It is supplemented by the heat-retentive thermal mass of internal walls in local adobe and red-painted con-

Latitude   35°N   Heating degree days 4,400

▲ **467** ROBERT REINES *Integrated Life Support Systems Laboratories*, New Mexico, 1971–73, perspective

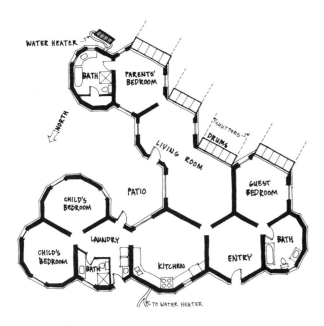

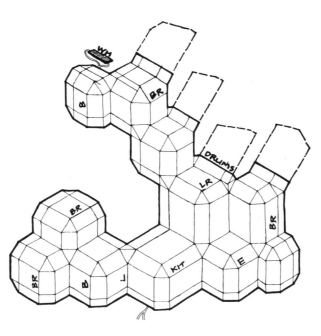

crete floors, and exploits the advantage of heating directly by sunshine. Baer's design affords a non-competitive accommodation using natural elements in deference to regional exigencies, not unlike the vernacular of New Mexico's Indians, who had been building their thick-walled, small-windowed adobe pueblos to be cool by day and warm by night since—if archaeological dating can be taken literally—the year I (A.D.). Certainly Baer's house looks more like a scientifically enlightened pueblo in reflective aluminum, with calculated thermodynamics, than mainstream American architecture. High stylists like Mies van der Rohe or Philip Johnson had only been able to ignore, with impunity, even rudimentary solar orientation through an energy-surplus technology: they had compensated by pumping in vast amounts of heating and air conditioning to make their glass high-rises physically habitable. Abstract architecture *caused* environmental problems;[3] Baer's house resolved existing natural forces *architecturally* and made them an asset.

Since New Mexico is also abundant in wind, a standard annular windmill draws well water. This is heated for domestic purposes by another type of solar collector: two black, glassed-in, absorption panels contain water circulating via copper tubing in a closed circuit fortified with antifreeze against frost. The panels act as radiators in reverse, gaining rather than dissipating heat, which is transferred to a reservoir filled from the well, and hot water tapped from it. This improves upon a solar water heater designed for the Manera Nueva commune which utilized rising hot air, trapped under dozens of castoff car windshields, ascending a hillside. This is an "active" general type of solar collector.[4]

Baer and his associates at Zomeworks, and Baldwin *et al.* at Integrated Life Support Systems Labora-

◀ 472 WOOD AND THOMASON, *Solar-heated house*, Colorado Springs, Colorado, 1974, exterior. Wood was owner-designer, using engineer Thomason's patented "trickle"-type collector

▼ 473 JAMES LAMBETH *Solar-heated swimming pool*, Springfield, Missouri, 1975. Architect Lambeth's lens-type collector, heating a pool for an apartment complex, won a citation from the American Iron and Steel Institute

tories, have particularized their designs for the reliable supply of New Mexico sun, and to offset the cool nights and hard winters of high altitudes, and both stress that no alternative energy solution will be universally applicable, or come easily—contrary to the impression given by magazines like *Mother Earth News* or *Lifestyle,* which publish a hopeful new windmill design every issue. Baer's house and the ILSSL dome are the results of years of investigation. Nor, they caution, are sun and wind entirely free: such systems will not compete economically with fossil fuels until the latter increase threefold or more in price. However, as this has in fact been happening, alternative sources have become attractive, even to those for whom the self-sufficiency of a commune or homestead is not a necessity, or to those who never believed in ideal planetary harmony as a credo. For, coincident with the energy crisis, middle-class Americans too acquired an ecological conscience. They professed concern about endangered species, pollution, and conservation; and, in commitment to these causes, those who could afford it solar heated their suburban split-levels (472–473). So, like Zomeworks, which undertakes design consultancy and sells alternative technology products, other manufacturers and mainstream architects now cater to the "eco-market." This pattern of co-option has been observed before, as in the popularization of geodesic domes;

yet alternative technology is especially ill-served by piecemeal implementation.

ENERGY, WASTE

ALTERNATIVE TECHNOLOGY IN BRITAIN TO AN EXTENT paralleled North American experiments without re-enacting the same historical cycle from communes to co-option. Roughly corresponding to Integrated Life Support Systems Laboratories or New Alchemy Institute[5] was BRAD, a small community in rural Wales dedicated to Biotechnic Research and Development, set up in 1972. Like *The Whole Earth Catalog* network, British underground press services kept abreast of research and development. It was the durable *Undercurrents* magazine which editorialized the shock of recognition that alternative technology —or AT, or Soft, Low Impact, Appropriate, Radical, People's, Liberatory, or Ecological Technology (pick your prefix)—was not so simple as "the willing megawatts that could be magicked from backyard windmills at the flick of a screwdriver . . . if we would only have faith . . . the first rays of the millennium would burst over the horizon before you could say 'self-sufficiency'!"[6] As in the U.S., there had been fond eco-dreams: a farmer in the West Country ran his car on chicken droppings—or at least the methane gas derived therefrom—*ergo* the energy crisis holds no peril for anyone. Yet the more re-

sponsible appreciated that environmental survival might well mean social and cultural changes in modes of consumption and standards of living, and that AT must be viewed, and pursued, within this wider frame of human reference.

Robin Clarke, a founder of BRAD, used the phrase Third Alternative to connote a realistic middle ground between high technology and the technophobia of organic neo-primitives. This Third Alternative, like the Third World, stands between the superpowers (both American corporate industry and Soviet state capitalism being technological heavies), like the Intermediate Technology of E.F. Schumacher. Schumacher's influential book *Small is Beautiful* points out that solar energy (or wind, or chicken droppings) cannot, by any "breakthrough," replace fossil fuels for industrial power. This is because the sun *diffuses* its yield over large areas and so works best for *decentralized* technologies—on a commune

▶ 475 GRAHAM CAINE
AND BRUCE HAGGART
Street Farm House, London,
England, 1972–73, interior
of greenhouse

▼ 474 GRAHAM CAINE
AND BRUCE HAGGART
Street Farm House, London,
England, 1972–73, elevation
and plan

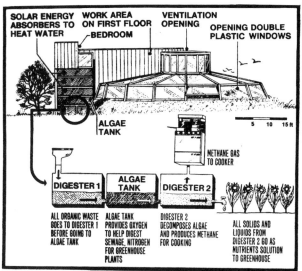

Ecological house: view of the sunny side. Enlarged detail shows three-stage sewage recycling plant which fits under the living quarters (left) and nourishes the garden (right).

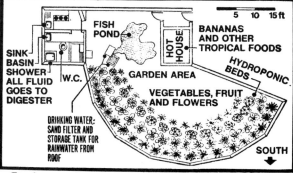

Eco-house plan view: flowers will grow among the vegetables for decoration.

▼ 476 *WOBO House*,
commissioned by Alfred
Heineken, The Netherlands,
1965

or village scale of social autonomy, with self-contained zero-growth local economies, rather than as central planning for unlimited material progress. Political implications follow. "Today, the main content of politics is economics, and the main content of economics is technology."[7] Whereas Schumacher, as economic advisor to Britain's National Coal Board (1950–70), ought to know, he departs decisively from Fuller's World Game plan and its apolitical technocracy.

But the major difference between American and British attitudes toward alternative technology has been the latter's political dimension and social perspective. In the lively manifestos of the British group

Street Farm (Graham Caine and Bruce Haggart), an ad-hoc post-industrial revolutionary dialectic is informed by horticultural similes—the decaying city as a compost heap for sprouting liberating tactics, a seed as a weapon, "weeding" existing technologies—and graphic images: anarchist cows invade the metropolis, eating the office buildings. "The reversal of the inorganic evolution . . . of hierarchical systems," they maintain, "will be signalled not with a dispersal of the city into the country but by a change in the quality of both"—that is, in the consumer-capitalist "illusions" or mythologies of city and country. This ideological intent, and its urban context, distinguished their Street Farm House (**474–475**) from other autonomous dwellings.[8] Here, self-sufficiency granted independence from present government-run energy monopolies and the socio-political control that goes with them. The house itself was a closed loop of energy and food production comprising a hydroponic greenhouse with a radially structured pneumatic roof, a methane generator supplied from the toilet, solar collectors, and a Savonius Rotor (vertical-axis windmill)—all serving a dwelling unit insulated by a sod roof and containing a fish pond. These interacting systems had not been perfected by

the time the house had to be dismantled, but the Street Farmers held "Process more important than Product."[9]

Hunting for alternative sources of building *material,* rather than energy, uncovered hidden treasures of *waste.* In Britain, even this was *theorized* according to the tenor of the times.[10] Martin Pawley's concept of Garbage Housing, first annunciated in magazine articles,[11] proceeded from a political, technological, and economic analysis of the availability of new accommodations, the shortage of which —from London boroughs to the Third World— seemed to be approaching some hopelessly Malthusian crisis of diminishing returns. After duly rejecting private enterprise, the Welfare State, and industrialized systems-design as inadequate providers, Pawley looked to "housing as a product of radical life styles." The new youth culture was not only prepared to share space collectively, without proprietary territoriality, but to short circuit linear industrial technology which "consumes raw materials in order to generate products which in turn become waste": thus communal housing at Drop City had been made of junked cars. Scavenging from the open end of Kleenex Culture expendability may have been done to save money rather than resources ("The only growing resource," they perceived, "is trash") but it now bore the force of eco-logical argument as well. So it seemed logical to Pawley that the surfeit of garbage could relieve the shortage of housing.

When the book *Garbage Housing* came out in 1975, its political prognosis differed markedly from the alternative technology movement's. Far from envisioning a future society of subdued technology at smaller scale, *Garbage Housing* accepted present levels of conspicuous consumption and proposed ways to reuse its plentiful mass of discarded packaging as housing materials. Since *recycling* manufactured goods back into raw materials is uneconomical, products should more directly be pre-designed for *secondary-use capability.* A specimen case had already been demonstrated: in 1960 the Dutch brewer Alfred Heineken had made the same propitious connection between garbage—discarded bottles of his exported beer—and housing. In underdeveloped countries too far away for bottle retrieval, housing was of low standard and insufficient volume. And even in the U.S., six bottles were produced for every brick. Heineken accordingly engaged N.J. Habraken, himself concerned with prefabricated housing,[12] to design a beer bottle with an afterlife as a glass brick —the WOBO, or WOrld BOttle. By 1963 tens of thousands had been made, yet only a prototype house (**476**) was ever constructed, and for marketing reasons beer-filled WOBOs were never sold.

Ironically, many houses had, since the nineteenth century, been built of bottles never intended for secondary use, especially in the mining fields of the American West and Australia, where "empties" constituted a readier building material than any other. Minimal housing in Third World barrios and bidonvilles has also been improvised from packing crates, flattened tins, and dead batteries (stacked as building blocks, like drystone masonry) for as long as those throwaways have been available. The survival needs of millions have therefore been met by garbage architecture—but without architects, or the intercession of those architectural students whose projects Pawley illustrates. Still, rationalization has continued beyond the publication of *Garbage Housing*; in 1976 Pawley's students at Rensselaer Polytechnic Institute, Troy, New York, built a house of six hundred square feet (**477–478**) for a professor there, using (or re-using) cardboard, bottles, tin cans, scrap rubber, and poly-

▲ **477** MARTIN PAWLEY AND STUDENTS, *Dora Crouch House*, Troy, New York, 1976. The central section of the long wall consists of translucent bottles which light the living room

◄ **478** MARTIN PAWLEY AND STUDENTS, *Dora Crouch House*, Troy, New York, 1976, interior

◄ **479** MICHAEL REY-
NOLDS, *Stephen Natelson
House*, Taos, New Mexico,
1974, exterior under
construction

▼ **480** MICHAEL REY-
NOLDS, *Stephen Natelson
House*, Taos, New Mexico,
1974, exterior completed
and stuccoed to prevent
rusting

ester cotton waste. The structural frame consisted of
columns and roof trusses made from the cardboard
cores of newsprint rolls, and non-bearing exterior
walls were of bottles and cans laid in mortar. Con-
nectors, sealants, insulation, roofing, and windows
were, as much as possible, secondhand as well.
Unfortunately the chief architectural interest of such
designs lies in having been built of cardboard, bottles,
tin cans, scrap rubber, or polyester cotton waste.
Less conventional in form, however, was the circular
house (**479–480**) which architect Michael Reynolds
built for a judge in Taos, New Mexico (1974). Seventy-five thousand tin cans—beer cans, mostly—
were baled into "tin bricks" of eight cans each, then
walls of them were plastered over to prevent rusting.
The house was completed at a cost of fifteen thousand
dollars.

◀ **481** EAT AND ENVIRO-
LAB, *Mirror Dome*, 1970,
exterior, shown during
development in a blimp
hangar, prior to installation
in the Pepsi Cola Pavilion
at Expo '70 in Osaka, Japan

TOWARD A SOFT ARCHITECTURE

PNEUMATIC STRUCTURES OFFER AN ALTERNATIVE
technology which uses air both as energy and as a
material resource. Strictly speaking, according to Dr.
Frei Otto's definition, pneumatics refer to envelopes
which become more stable, structurally rigid, when
filled with any gas or liquid—for example, a waterbed
—but for convenience pressurized air will be the
assumed filler unless otherwise specified. Pressurized
air has many advantages as a building material, being
lightweight, transparent, plentiful, more or less free,
ready to use in its natural state, and healthy to
breathe. The user of a pneumatic building can walk
right through its structural system without hindrance
or ill effects. This physical minimalism appealed to
Conceptual artists of the sixties, who created anti-
formalistic Happenings or non-objects in ephemeral
steam, smoke, ice, light, bubbles, and *air*. One of
them apostrophized it: "Air architecture is an art of
absence . . . Inflatable structures correspond to the
void in reality . . . an alternative to absoluteness,
inflexibility, and materiality."[13]

Air may be perfectly invisible but its virtual existence

should not be summarily discounted; it does have
substance and can exert force under pressure, as in,
for example, hurricanes. Long ago men learned to
take moving air as it came and harness its natural
mechanical energy for propelling sailboats and turn-

▲ **482** GRAHAM STEVENS
Inflatable cube

▶ **483** CHRYSALIS
*Single-membrane inflatable
of "no practical use"*

ing windmills. The ability to *contain* it, though, has
awaited fairly recent airtight technologies: rubber and
synthetics for pneumatic tires, life jackets and rafts,
balloons and inflatable females (or males, viz the
Michelin man). Most of these applications have been
straightforwardly functional, as are the radomes,
greenhouses, storage containers, pool covers, and
other "air buildings" in use today, and indeed in use
only because they perform in certain ways more efficiently than rigid structures. The simplest kind of
inflatable, with a skin upheld by slightly higher pres-

◀ **484** CHRYSALIS
Living-pod, exterior by day

▼ **485** CHRYSALIS
Living-pod, exterior
by night

sure inside than out, dispenses with internal supports, can be erected quickly and as easily deflated when no longer needed, and imposes negligible superincumbent loads of its own; it will rest lightly on rooftops or float on water. (So far from requiring supporting *foundations,* inflatables must be *anchored* to keep them from blowing away.) Since the enclosing skin, strongest in tension anyway, is very thin and light in proportion to the volume enclosed,[14] pneumatics are capable of almost unlimited span, unlike compression structures where, in a worsening inverse-square ratio, the material's strength is eventually overcome by its own dead load.

Among the largest inflatables to have been erected was the U.S. Pavilion at the Osaka World's Fair of 1970. The U.S. Pavilion at the previous fair, Montreal 1967, had been a Fuller dome, so not only had an inflatable succeeded a geodesic in the lightweight-engineering stakes, but the structure's official prestige now departed from previously utilitarian usages. Inflatables came out at Osaka in a full-blown debutante season. And although the U.S. Pavilion kept a diplomatically low profile, many others aired a free

range of innovative, even extravagant designs, especially those of Japanese industrial corporations. In Fuji's (**486**), parallel pneumatic tubes of equal length arched over a circular base. As their end points drew inward across increasingly smaller chords, the tubes bulged upward toward entrance and exit, through which visitors could move without airlocks, since only the tubes were pressurized. The saddle shape they delineated was a hyperbolic paraboloid. Another pavilion, sponsored by Pepsi Cola, conceived by EAT (Experiments in Art and Technology), and realized by Envirolab, centered on a ninety-foot-diameter dome (**481**), almost a sphere, of aluminized Mylar nylon. Inside, the mirror finish magnified reflections of visitors and colored balloons, with whispering-gallery acoustic distortions comparable to the visuals. The exacting technology had been adapted from orbital "Echo" satellites—for bouncing radio waves around the earth—yet here the reflecting surface was a concave rather than convex lens, and intended only as a spatial experience. The inflatable had come of age as architecture, even Architecture, admittedly if only for the temporary

facilitation of large spaces at relatively small cost, and for the fun-palace air of World's Fairs.

Historically, architecture has relied on static mass —the more the better—for stability, permanence, environmental control (at least keeping the weather out), and sometimes defensibility. Its resultant monumentality, as in public buildings, bore heavily upon the institutional authority structures it both housed and symbolized. In solid classical masonry or Corbusian concrete, it took its form language from the

necessity of transferring loads perpendicularly into the ground, giving a predominantly rectilinear geometry. This was worked into an aesthetic of related proportions and imbued with the moral order of the *right* angle. Modern architecture, if anything, re-emphasized the square grid and the post-and-lintel. Alternatively, inflatables obey strictures no less rational but of a very different three-dimensional geometry: in effect, cornerless, womb-like hollows embraced by continuous curved surfaces. Right angles, cubic volumes, or flat planes are hardly possible. Because gases expand omni-directionally, any air structure tends toward sphericality, its "final" form being a balance between that ideal sphere, the membrane configuration, and any other shaping agencies, such as restraining cables. Even geodesic and other domes, or space-frames and other non-rectangular structures, remain rigid, hard-shelled, or linear, while air architecture is yielding, evanescent, and soft.[15]

These qualities recommended inflatables for staging environmental events, often with audience participation and mixed media (projecting images onto the translucent skin from outside, etc.), as a self-justifying aesthetic or even sensual encounter, more perceptual than conceptual. Designers adept in pneumatic technology have been active throughout the Western art world. The American group Ant Farm has designed several spongy play spaces, designated Dreamcloud, Flagbag, and The World's Largest Snake. In 1970 Haus-Rucker-Co. of Düsseldorf installed a giant mattress at a New York museum. Graham Stevens of England found a lateral-thinking solution to walking on water: rolling an inflatable, with two-hour's-worth of air sealed

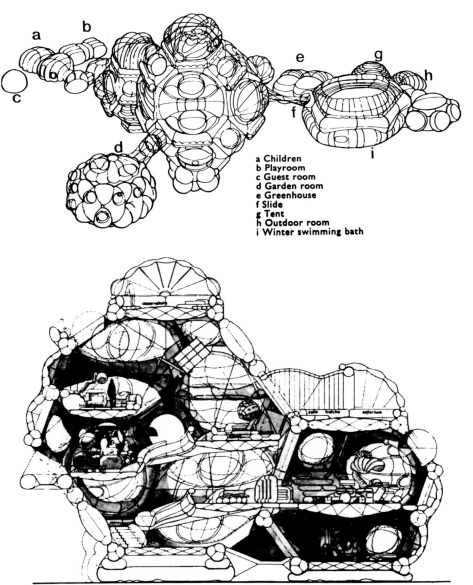

a Children
b Playroom
c Guest room
d Garden room
e Greenhouse
f Slide
g Tent
h Outdoor room
i Winter swimming bath

◀ **487** UTOPIE (J. AUBERT, A. STINCO, J.P. JUNGMAN) *Dyoden Project*, c. 1968, perspective and section

◀ **486** YUTAKA MURATA *Fuji Pavilion*, Expo '70, Osaka, Japan, 1970

▲ **488** CHRYSALIS *Dodecahedral inflatable*

▶ **489** *Great Pumpkin inflatable*, Antioch College, Ohio

inside, across the surface (**482**). Eventstructures of Amsterdam duplicated both giant mattress (32 1/2 feet square, first shown 1969) and waterwalk (in an inflated tetrahedron, 16 1/4 feet high, also 1969, and as a tube crossing a river, 1970). Both Haus-Rucker-Co. and Coöp Himmelblau, Vienna, have postulated intimate inner-space bubbles for sensory stimulation of one or two occupants, as well as overblown children's beachballs and suitcase environments you *can* take with you. The design team Chrysalis has authored modular inflatable "toys" (**483**), a hemispherical living-pod (**484–485**) ballasted by a ground-level collar filled with "heavy" water—drained upon deflation of the pod—and an "exploded" dodeca-hedron (**488**) made of opaque, translucent, and transparent plastic. The French student group Utopie proposed Dyoden (**487**), a design "in which *everything* is inflatable . . . to provide a complete experience

◀ **490** ANT FARM
Single-membrane inflatable, interior

▼ **491** SPACE STRUCTURES WORKSHOP, *Linked inflatables*, London, aerial view

◀ **492** POOR WILLIE PRO-
DUCTIONS, *Single-mem-
brane inflatable*, Whiz Bang
Quick City East, New York,
1972

▼ **493** POOR WILLIE PRO-
DUCTIONS, *Single-mem-
brane inflatable*, Whiz Bang
Quick City East, New York,
1972, deflated

of the pneumatic way of life."[16] This would seem a
longer-term habitation, if quite flexible (Blow up the
guest room, dear), in another polyhedral form which,
perhaps, looks obesely anthropomorphic. Since any
inflatable wants, and tries, to be a sphere, these geometries may be attempts to relieve sameness. (Besides,
spheres are difficult to fabricate; **489**.)

Inflatables found their transient uses in the counterculture too, and it was a poor love-in or rock festival
that lacked them. Yet this reversed the usual course
of counterculture alternatives being accepted by the
mainstream, for pneumatic technology had arisen
long before Aquarian consciousness, nor should
blow-up military shelters, Establishment exhibition
structures, or fashionable inflatable furniture have
been compatible. Moreover, practicable inflatables
depended on cheap *plastic,* and that very word had
become, as an adjectival epithet, accusative of a whole
culture, like the Marxist use of the term petit-bour-
geois. The inflatable alternative was, nonetheless, just
too much fun, too easy (**490**). Two sheets of inexpen-
sive polythene had only to be taped together round

their perimeters (not even heat-sealed, as with tougher
PVC) to make a voluminous pillow. A vacuum-
cleaner blower or window fan could maintain pressure, obviating the need for airlocks; the same orifices
that allowed access would also vent the air being continuously fed in. Pillows could be connected to each
other at their corners (**491**).

At Whiz Bang Quick City East, an alternative environmental design festival held in rural New York
State, such a structure was put up by some participants to camp in (**492**). It afforded instant, autonomous shelter from the great outdoors, and an incidental object lesson in alternative technology. Someone
chopping down a small tree for firewood misjudged
the fall and brought down the powerline. With its
blowers deprived of electricity, this inflatable—and
all the others—sighed limply to the ground (**493**).
The incident reminded the assembled alternative designers that AT is ultimately about where that "outside" energy comes from or, for that matter, the raw
materials to make the inflatable.

BEYOND THE FRINGE

ON A SAGEBRUSH-SPECKLED MESA, IN THE PURPLE shadows of the haunted mountains of the American Southwest, a number of youthful, denim-clad persons of both genders are seen handcrafting the outlandish architecture of an experimental community. The year is 1970, and to the casual observer these might seem to be of the same species as the Southwestern commune builders nearby. But there are differences not visible. This alternative was neither conceived nor designed by those building it, and they are paying for the privilege of doing so (having signed contracts promising both fees and labor). It is not a commune for a few dozen dropouts being built, but an "arcology" planned to house no less than three thousand inhabitants. Who these may be is unclear, but they will not be the builders, who will return to their colleges at summer's end. Meanwhile, they live in concrete boxes, cubes twelve feet on a side, with porthole windows. The project is, of course, Paolo Soleri's Arcosanti **(494)** in Arizona—an isolated megastructure to cover ten acres at a height of twenty stories. Although unconventional forms do not in themselves make for an alternative architecture, the underlying assumptions are, unlike other alternatives, intensely urbanistic.

Arcosanti is only a test model, full size but still minimal by Soleri's standards of scale. Thirty other arcologies—theoretical urban recipes compiled in his 1969 book *Arcology: The City in the Image of Man* —are all much more populous, ranging from Veladiga, a habitable dam for fifteen thousand people, to Babelnoah **(495)** of six million to be sited ideally in a coastal swamp. Each scheme is a single building integrating many human activities, labeled on plan, Promenade, Commercial, Public, Gardens, Cultural Center, Living, and so on. In drawings and models exhibited as "The Architectural Vision of Paolo Soleri" (1970) the standard comparative-size reference was a diminutive Empire State Building. Contrary to Marshall McLuhan's placeless, spaceless, global village of electronic media, Soleri's concentrated arcologies presuppose face-to-face contact, and can be traversed by foot or bicycle. Since cars are not allowed, vehicular circulation is not a form determinant as in other modern city planning.

Arcology, which combines the words architecture and ecology, is defined by Soleri as not only the result but the process—the "art and science"—of such design **(496)**. His art is subjective, a response to a lifetime's experience. His personal philosophy of civic culture at extreme density grew up with him in teeming industrial Turin. After graduating from architectural school in 1946, he came for the first time to Arizona as an apprentice to Frank Lloyd Wright at Taliesin West, and his own fee-paying apprentices, learning by working, are similar to Wright's. He returned in 1950 to Italy, where his design for a ceramics factory was built. (As an artistic outlet and for income in lieu of architectural commissions, Soleri has made ceramics himself, the forms of his "wind-bells" then being monumentalized into cities.) Back in Arizona by 1955, he built his own Earth House (1956–58) close to Taliesin. This half-buried house **(497)**, with ceramics studios **(498–500)** and apprentices' quarters added, grew into Cosanti **(501)**, an arcology, in effect, before the term was coined. It was the encroaching suburban sprawl of Phoenix that drove Soleri seventy miles north to the virgin site of Arcosanti. He nurses a deep distaste for cars and suburbs, and the flat, amorphous dispersal of community they produce: "The compact city . . . must be a solid, not a surface," and: "The three-dimensional city does not spread an inorganic crust . . . "

The *science* of arcology consists in arguments by analogy rather than application of the physical sciences, as in the planetary dynamics of Buckminster Fuller or the contingent ecologies of alternative technologists. Soleri's cardinal scientific analogy is the *compactness* he senses in nature and by which he justifies the critical mass of his urban societies. "Both vegetal and animal life are possible only within a condition of relative denseness. The degree of liveliness is proportional to the degree of compactness . . . Compactness is the 'structure' of efficiency . . . The city must then be predicated on compactness; lack of compactness is lack of efficiency."[1] He narrowly but carefully refrains from adducing the anthill or beehive, by qualifying compactness with *complexity*. "Miniaturization," furthermore, "is the *deus ex machina* of complexity."[2] The human brain or computer, this analogy runs, works faster when the circuitry is condensed, so that synapses are shorter. Cities should be similar. Confronted with the ethologists' dreaded "behavioral sink," he answers: "It might well be that we as humans need exactly the sort of conditions the rat cannot stand. In other words, as cultural creatures we have to crowd."[3] That may be true, but it is hardly sociological evidence.

Other analogies are implicit in the design imagery: the city as an organic cell with central nucleus, the preconceived urban structure as "bare bones" which life-styles will "flesh out." But whatever the applicability of such reasoning, Soleri's highly saturated super-urbanism is a drastic rejoinder to counterculture trends away from the city. Soleri is an artist-architect of strong individual style. If his oeuvre is judged purely artistically, then in his early studies for bridges the muscular metaphor does work for the structural tendons and sinews, while his more geometrical, monolithic cities unavoidably suggest environments boring at best, oppressive at worst. Yet other artist-architects have speculated on environments which exist only when "switched on" by users, unlike Soleri's skeletal forms in search of human functions.

They are less interested than Soleri in the metropolis as collective house, and more in magical new technologies:[4] the metamorphic, sensuous inflatables touched upon in the previous chapter; software media; instant space-making lasers and holography. Their designs reify physical fantasies to be shared, rather than monuments to their own undoubted talents.

ROGUE DESIGNERS
WHATEVER AND HOWEVER THEY DESIGN, ALTERNATIVE designers operate on society's fringes: like rogue elephants they do not follow the herd. This apartness need not imply heroic individualism, lone wolves like Soleri or the romanticized (alienated) artist. Indeed, more often than not, they work as collaborative groups, with group names subsuming members'.

▼ **494** PAOLO SOLERI *Arcosanti*, Arizona, 1969–, exterior of north apse and foundry apse. This represents less than one-fifth of the projected total

They can be bands of alternative technologists, like Zomeworks, roving among wilderness outposts, or urban guerrillas infiltrating the thick of cosmopolitan culture, like Coöp Himmelblau and Missing Link in Vienna. American design communes included Southcoast, Onyx, Truth Commandos, Elm City Electric Light Sculpture Company. The Grocery Store, Kamakazi Design Group, Mind Huns, Space Cowboys, All Electric Medicine Show, Crystal Springs Celery Gardens, and Crash City. Experimental Happenings were held at architecture schools: Time Slice, Electronic Oasis, Sonic Mirage, Infinity Feedback, Astro Daze, and Globe City.

Their productions negate longstanding boundaries of professional classification, and crosscut between disciplines, perhaps introducing elements of theater,

or gaming simulation. If not within recognized professional practice, design is still their avocation. Avant-garde architects, even with credentials, may exhibit conceptual alternatives before the profession rather than build, but as stipulated in the Introduction to this section, such groups as the prototypical Archigram of sixties London, or Florence's Archizoom, Superstudio, and 9999, must be excluded here in favor of those whose majority output has been realized or performed as experiential environment, however transitory.

Even rogue designers have design conferences, although not much akin to the annual conventions of professional bodies. Limited space permits recounting only two or three. "Alloy" took place at the vernal equinox, 1969, in dramatically bleak mountains near La Luz, New Mexico, appropriately halfway between the site of the first atomic bomb detonation and an Apache reservation. Conceived and organized by Steve Baer and Stewart Brand, it was an historic gathering of the tribes—the Southwestern communes being well represented—and of alternative designers of diverse persuasions, about one hundred and fifty in all. They met in a large polyhedral dome, courtesy of Zomeworks, to discuss the right uses of technology, relations between communes and the profit economy of the outside world, and ecological responsibilities within. Steve Durkee from Lama, Peter Rabbit of Drop City/Libre, and

▶ **498** PAOLO SOLERI
Cosanti, Arizona, 1956–70,
exterior detail of ceramics
studios, built 1959, photographed in 1969

▼ **499** PAOLO SOLERI
Cosanti, Arizona, 1956–70,
interior of ceramics studios

Lloyd Kahn and Jay Baldwin came. So broad was
the variance of views, from technophobic fundamen-
talists to computer buffs advocating a cybernetic
"group mind," that no absolute consensus was reached
or sought. Yet "Alloy" still demarcated a common
ground of concern among those who could, perhaps,
have come together only outside established auspices;
Stewart Brand's romantic notion of an Outlaw Area
for environmental freebooters was taken from Fuller:
". . . the whole development of technology has
been in the outlaw area," especially on the sea.[5] In
any event, free spirits have not often been able, conversely, to spark together within the design professions or at their conferences. An alloy is a composite
metal stronger than the sum of its constituents.[6]

Whiz Bang Quick City was held in the spring of
1972 at two locations simultaneously: WBQC West,
near Pasadena, California (**502**), and East (**503–504**)
in the Catskills of New York State (not far geo-
graphically or in spirit from the Woodstock Festival
two years earlier). East and West kept in touch by air-
mailed videotapes and wirephotos transmitted across
the country. Global village media notwithstanding,
each site evolved its own character, yet together presented a visual index to the repertoire of alternatives

◀ **500** PAOLO SOLERI
Cosanti, Arizona, 1956–70,
exterior view into north
studio apse, built 1964,
photographed in 1965

▼ **501** PAOLO SOLERI
Cosanti, Arizona, 1956–70,
aerial view, photographed
in 1972

through the camping shelters brought by participants: inflatables, tensile structures, space-frames,
domes, zomes and polyhedra, tipis, converted vehicles, and habitable amoeboids of urethane foam.
While those attending were more likely to be architecture students than veteran communards, plus a
variety of experimental design groups, both "instant
cities" fostered a festival atmosphere, if not the serious forum of "Alloy."

Jim Burns had characterized these rogue designers
as figurative "arthropods," in his 1972 book of that
title. Like that zoological phylum, which includes
insects, they are articulate, divided into segments, and
capable of regeneration. The metaphor is over-
strained, nor do all Burns's arthropods fit the present
context of alternatives, but one such design group did
take its name from social insects. Ant Farm was inspired by an educational toy seen in 1968: a cross-
section of ant burrows encased between two panes of
clear plastic, whereby the ants were revealed to be
enviably cooperative and effective builders of "underground" architecture. With co-founders Chip Lord
and Doug Michels at core, and a number of sometime
associates, Ant Farm can be singled out because their

work since 1968 neatly encapsulates most of the themes considered here. The Ant Farm office at Sausalito, for example, was connected with the houseboat community. They flirted with geodesics and, more intensively, pneumatics, publishing an *Inflatacookbook* in 1970. Their own largest inflatable measured one hundred feet square. Ant Farm lent another inflatable, fifty feet square (505), to shelter production staff compiling *The Last Whole Earth Catalog* in the inhospitable desert of Death Valley in 1971. They inflated smaller ones for camping while on the road as pneumads (506). For nomadic roadworks they hypothesized a nationwide Truckstop Network, and equipped a Media Van for themselves with video recorders (507), a solar collector, and inflatable shower. In this, Ant Farm's traveling circus made its rounds, demonstrating inflatables and putting on public rituals.

"Media Burn" may be interpreted as, perhaps, symbolizing or celebrating the collision of hardware and software technologies. On the Fourth of July, 1975, at San Francisco's famous Cow Palace, their Phantom Dream Car—a snow-white Cadillac customized with an enormous dorsal fin—was driven at the national speed limit of fifty-five m.p.h. through a flaming wall of television sets (508). In 1974 they presided over the public burial of a "Time Capsule" (509–511), in the form of an Oldsmobile Vista Cruiser. Consumer durables from the shops of a typical

American small town filled suitcases in the luggage compartment. The interment is to be exhumed in the year 2000. Yet obviously Ant Farm regards the automobile itself as the prime cultural artifact of the twentieth century. Also in 1974 they engineered an updated megalithic monument (512–513) consisting of ten Cadillacs set upright into the ground near Route 66, Amarillo, Texas, in an alignment reminiscent of ancient processions of stone slabs at Avebury in England or Carnac (Car–nac?) in France.

The principals of Ant Farm are, however, trained architects. Their House of the Century (HOC), designed in 1972 and built in 1973, seems a professional commission, for a wealthy couple on their private lake in Texas (514–524), just as Soleri's Cosanti Foundation or Arcosanti could be mistaken for youth communes. And, just as the zonahedral family pueblo of Steve Baer was homey enough to make the glossy pages of *House and Garden*, Ant Farm's HOC was so sybaritic a pleasure dome that it appeared as a weekend "Playboy Pad" in that magazine, December 1973. (Nor should there be

▲ **502** *Whiz Bang Quick City West*, California, 1972, interior of inflatable with one of the conference organizers, David Lieberman

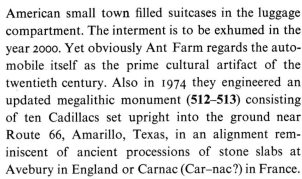

◄ **503** *Whiz Bang Quick City East*, New York, 1972, view showing icosahedron and two geodesic domes

▲ **504** *Whiz Bang Quick City East*, New York, 1972, exterior of tensile structures

▶ **505** ANT FARM *Inflatable Pillow*, Freestone, California, 1970

▶ **506** ANT FARM
Portable Inflatable and Media Van, c. 1971

▲ 509 ANT FARM
"Time Capsule," Lewiston, New York, 1974, view of capsule and cases to be buried

◄ 507 ANT FARM
Media Van, c. 1971, interior showing mobile video equipment

▼ 508 ANT FARM
"Media Burn," San Francisco, California, 1975, photographed at the climax of the event

any undue coyness regarding the house's phallic shape, although never preconceived as a Freudian symbol.) Patrons of the arts, the clients gave their designers a free hand to create a sculpture for living in, yet the result received a citation in house design from the American professional journal *Progressive Architecture*.

► 510 ANT FARM
"Time Capsule," Lewiston, New York, 1974, detail of articles to be buried

◄ 511 ANT FARM
"Time Capsule," Lewiston, New York, 1974, capsule, sealed with tar, being buried

Even so, the volumetric morphology clearly derives from Ant Farm's inflatables with their seamless surfaces and lack of corners, only now made rigid enough to withstand Texas hurricanes. The structure is in fact ferrocement, as applied to alternative home-domes. Construction blends esoteric technology with biomorphic forms, evident in the space-age "tongue" entrance and the plastic "eyeball" windows whose red and yellow blobs approximate optical phosgenes (the illusory dancing spots perceived on the insides of the eyelids). Automotive technology in particular —not unexpectedly from Ant Farm, but atypical in residential building—furnished the upholstery which pads the interior like the ceiling of a car, or like the soft lining of a bodily organ. Despite the science-fiction argot of "mobile nutrient servoid" or "media control panel," this is a handmade house, from the labor-intensive ferrocement shell to the craftsmanship within, for which "there were no working drawings or details,"[7] and which the architects executed themselves. The floor, solid laminated two-by-fours, was hollowed out *in situ* around the fireplace (a stuffed iguana now resides there), and for seating around the low dining table. In the kitchen, the woodblock was built up into a pedestal, out of which a sink was carved, and all wood sealed with surfboard resin. Between the twin bowls of the sink is placed a miniature, spherical TV set which juxtaposes a media picture just below the oval "picture window" displaying its panorama of the lake and landscape beyond. Thus one may—while washing dishes—select alternate pictorial realities: the framed natural view or the TV screen. Again, nature and (electronic) art are seen literally to be complements of each other. And at the topmost point of the house, where a cross would be on a church or a flag on a public building, is a heraldic but functional TV antenna. (Ants, too, have antennae.) Furthermore, from across the lake the house itself can be viewed above and behind the blind screens of one hundred defunct TV sets arrayed on the foreshore. Altar-shrines of the household gods, these recall their earlier use by Ant Farm as sacrificial objects in the "Media Burn" rite, or as architectonic blocks like the ten Cadillac menhirs buried upright (and commissioned by the same clients).

The main living space flows between the two "lobes" and slants up the tower, on the vertical side of which are superimposed sleeping lofts for parents and children, reached by a circular ladder. Also rising through the tower, penetrating the lofts, is a chimney duct from the fireplace and furnace behind. These heating appliances separate the conversation pit from the bathroom, tucked into the base of the tower but still on the main living level. The bathroom floor is excavated to form a sunken wooden tub, waterproofed, like the kitchen sink, with clear surfboard varnish. The bathroom boasts a standard toilet; however, this is connected by a transparent plastic tube to a custom-made overhead water tank, glass-fronted like an aquarium. The toilet reservoir is adjacent to a bulbous fiber-glass growth, rearing out of the floor and containing a shower head for the tub, two lighting globes "budded" out of the top, and a round mirror over a hand-basin cavity. The basin's spigot could be an epiglottis or clitoris, yet if anatom-

◀ **512** ANT FARM
Cadillac Ranch, Amarillo, Texas, 1974, detail. Each Cadillac is set in concrete

◀ **513** ANT FARM
Cadillac Ranch, Amarillo, Texas, 1974, overall view. Cadillac models are, from left to right: 1949, 1951, 1954, 1956, 1957, 1958, 1959, 1960, 1962, 1963

▶ **514** ANT FARM
House of the Century, near Houston, Texas, 1972–73, interior of entrance

ical metaphors are sought they can be found in the overall house shape—the tower being a nose or a penis, with the flanking lobes as breasts or eggs—and found to be, at best, teasingly ambivalent.

Such symbolism may be construed as a private architectural conversation between Ant Farm and their clients, who had some "interest in science." Biomorphic imagery—painted graphics of organic cells—is also used decoratively (**523**). The organic metaphors of Paolo Soleri are related, but handled with deadpan high seriousness compared to the anthropomorphic puns intimated by the House of the Century. The disparities in formalistic means are more forceful than the similarities in underlying organic meanings. Unlike Ant Farm, Soleri does not enlist software, either media or inflatables, yet HOC's closed forms are not so much soft as swelling, taut almost to the point of bursting, full of hedonistic,

◄ **515** ANT FARM
House of the Century, near Houston, Texas, 1972–73, aerial view

▼ **516** ANT FARM
House of the Century, near Houston, Texas, 1972–73, exterior showing entrance

immanent life. What vitiates Soleri's biomorphism is its lack of sensuality, humorlessly befitting those occult metaphors of his; his art is at some philosophical remove, or aesthetic distance, from life. In contrast, Chip Lord of Ant Farm believes: "Architecture is not something outside the head trying to push its way in; it is more like a layer of fantasy-reality between you and life."[8] For Ant Farm, architecture itself mediates.

Biomorphism, however, bears a larger if problematic relevance to the House of the Century. HOC was designed the year after Charles Jencks predicted, in his *Architecture 2000* of 1971, "the most significant architectural movement of this century—the Biomorphic School." Jencks based this forecast on the anticipated "influence of major biological inventions in the 1980s and '90s."[9] Did Ant Farm, having read *Architecture 2000,* mean to stake an early

▶ **517** ANT FARM
House of the Century, near Houston, Texas, 1972–73, kitchen area

▼ **518** ANT FARM
House of the Century, near Houston, Texas, 1972–73, interior detail showing kitchen sink

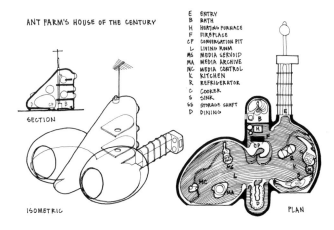

claim to biomorphism with their house of 1972–73? In this connection their name for it, House of the Century, is rather suggestive, in lieu of any other explanation.[10] To thereby align themselves with that "most significant architectural movement of this century" may be another Ant Farm in-joke, but there is more to HOC's biomorphism than its name.

Jencks had, advisedly, hedged his history of the future in that he *expected* biomorphic technology to be available by the eighties or nineties, yet *projected* the stylistic school from trends already present in a minor, subdominant way. Therefore the coming biomorphic movement need not await the biological engineering which would enable houses to be "grown," since some architects had, by 1971, invoked the *imagery* of that technology in the speculative spirit of science fiction. However, these few architects were not aware (until *Architecture 2000*?) of each other, nor of contributing to a tradition which might someday coalesce into a movement or school. Jencks mentioned Soleri, among others.[11] Yet Ant Farm, regardless of their self-conscious gesture in

naming the house, also worked in that intuitive tradition, and recapitulated it in their design process. From the earlier models for a more convoluted form, reminiscent of an Antoni Gaudí structure, HOC was tightened up. Its compact symmetry now looks like that of Erich Mendelsohn's Einstein Tower (1921)—called organic by Einstein himself—and its plan like Frederick Kiesler's unbuilt Endless House (1923), which Hans Arp likened to eggs and wombs. (HOC partakes of much the same fusion of the biomorphic and the surreal.) Ant Farm's inclusion of "mobile servoids" gave their space capsule the technological props of the Living Pod project by David Green of Archigram (1966).

What the House of the Century does not invoke is the mainstream tradition of European Modernism. Ant Farm's references—automobile construction and nomadism, biomorphic imagery, craft building—are to anything but the Bauhaus. HOC is white enough, but its ferrocement shell and voluptuous interior have nothing to do with an International Style geometry of right angles and Euclidian planes, and its media software is more up-to-date than the nuts and bolts of the first machine age. Neither is HOC's immaculate slickness of finish and detail in the same high-tech taste as postwar Late-Modernism, even when that factory aesthetic is applied to residences. Yet there has been an in-house alternative, within the profession, to the Modernist tradition: the Post-Modern

style, which rapidly became a new orthodoxy in the seventies. As European Modernism had dictated a language of building technology, so a certain strain of Post-Modernism manipulated that language itself, once removed from its technological roots. The old purist language may be parodied into postclassical Mannerism, or traduced by deliberate solecisms, but it is still used. (Language can even remain grammatical, the semiologists tell us, while making nonsense or lying, communicating false messages.) Alternative designers, having broken with Modernism and its burden of European aesthetics, seek elsewhere: sometimes in a return to American cultural values, or vernaculars both traditional and popular, sometimes in the newness of geodesics or inflatables.

HOC's assured, professional standard of design puts it tangent to mainstream office products, but in an important regard it has more affinity with alternative practice. Commissions are usually designed by *architects* and constructed by *builders,* separately paid by the *client.* Ant Farm both designed and built the House of the Century, yet were engaged and remunerated as *artists* by a *patron.* The economics of their "labor charge" cannot be calculated, as with craftsmen-designers, let alone contractors who (according to architects) exist only to execute architects' designs which are otherwise complete on paper. Most of Ant Farm's manual effort went into sculpting that

◀ **522** ANT FARM
House of the Century, near
Houston, Texas, 1972–73,
dining area

▼ **523** ANT FARM
House of the Century, near
Houston, Texas, 1972–73,
detail of interior, looking
toward entry

laminated floor, handcarving an integral living environment from it. There is also an echo of alternative self-building in the way the floor effected a secondary use for the wooden scaffolding which had supported the ferrocement armature. Direct involvement in the visceral process of shaping architecture—improvising design with power tools rather than pencils and tracing paper—is what finally divides Ant Farm from office-bound architects, and what makes a performing art of this alternative architecture, or of counterculture Funkitecture generally.

If the House of the Century, having been programmed as an art object, is not of or for a socially radical counterculture, that is a matter of circumstantial context: it is surely a Funk object stylistically. It answers all the criteria of that alternative aesthetic: not just pluralistic in imagery but in free choice of materials and participatory means of construction. Funk affects and reflects its design even though Ant Farm's "clean" Funk is more fluent in craftsmanship than the junk-and-funk of the commune builders. HOC is, as it were, High Funk, to make the distinction Peter Selz (already quoted in the Introduction to this section) made in charting the contemporaneous course of Funk sculpture. He saw it too developing away from Early Funk's earthy, expendable assemblages: "Although neatness or sloppiness is not the issue here, there is a general trend toward greater care in execution . . . But the imagery, the attitude,

the feeling remains funk just the same . . . In fact, this precision of finish only enhances the ironic quality of the work."[12] This is equivalent in Funk architecture to the progression from Drop City to the House of the Century, to the dextrous carpentry of Hornby Island, or to Steve Baer's aluminum solar house.

Architectural ideas cannot be so contingent upon circumstance, nor as casually categorized as alternative or mainstream. HOC's designers can be imagined as architecture students of the early sixties ingesting the then-current avant-garde of Archigram or Hans Hollein, but their funky metaphors have become more mixed. (Is HOC really no more—or less— biomorphic and erotic than American car styling: two eyeball headlights athwart a nasal or phallic tailfin?)[13] The broader context of what amounts to Funk Style has been described, or defined by example, in all the foregoing chapters. Paradoxically, however, an interpretive attempt such as this—to isolate the working aesthetics of an alternative architecture—might seem to mitigate against a healthy cross-pollination with the profession. But fortunately this does not hinder their mixing in the real world of building, as in the House of the Century. Rogue designers need not remain outsiders.

▶ **524** ANT FARM
House of the Century, near
Houston, Texas, 1972–73,
exterior detail

525 RICARDO BOFILL AND TALLER DE ARQUITECTURA, *La Fabrica*, San Just Desvern, Spain, 1970–75, exterior

Appendices

BIOGRAPHIES
OF THE ARCHITECTS

A

Aalto, Alvar

ALVAR AALTO WAS BORN IN KUORTANE, NEAR JYVÄSKYLÄ, Finland, in 1898, and studied at the Helsinki Technical University, where he received his Dip. Arch. in 1921. A recognized master of the Modern Movement, Aalto maintained his own practice in Finland from 1923 until his death in 1976, and gained an international reputation as the most human architect of the International Style. Aalto's many commissions were mainly confined to public buildings, and include educational facilities for the Massachusetts Institute of Technology—Seniors' Dormitory (Baker House), Cambridge, Massachusetts (1947–48)—for the Finnish Technical Institute at Otaniemi, Finland (competition 1949, several buildings constructed between 1960 and 1975), and a master plan for the Reykjavik university area, Iceland (project 1976); religious buildings including Muurame Church, Finland (1926–29), Vuoksenniska Church, Imatra, Finland (designed 1956, constructed 1957–59), and the Parish Center at Riola, Bologna, Italy (1966–78); libraries including Viipuri Municipal Library, Finland (competition 1927, constructed 1930–35, destroyed 1943), and Mount Angel Benedictine College Library, Oregon (1965–70); government and civic buildings including Säynätsalo Town Hall, Finland (competition 1949, constructed 1950–52), and the Finnish Public Pensions Institute, Helsinki 1952–56); medical facilities such as the Paimio Tuberculosis Sanatorium, Finland (competition 1928, constructed 1929–35); cultural facilities including the "House of Culture," Helsinki (1955–58), and the Cultural Center, Wolfsburg, West Germany (competition 1958, constructed 1959–62); commercial and industrial buildings including the Cellulose Factory and Housing, Sunila, Finland (1935–39, extended 1951–54), and the Rautatalo Office and Commercial Building, Helsinki (competition 1952, constructed 1953–55). His private houses included the Villa Mairea, Noormarkku, Finland (1937–39), and the Villa Louis Carré, Bazoches-sur-Guyonne, France (1956–59). He won many awards for his buildings and projects, and there have been several exhibitions of his work which has been published internationally in numerous books and periodicals. Aalto was also a pioneer of wood technology for furniture design, and in 1935 established Artek furniture design company with Aino Aalto and Maire Gullichsen. He was professor of architecture at the Massachusetts Institute of Technology from 1946 to 1948, and president of the Academy of Finland from 1963 to 1968. He was awarded honorary doctorates from many universities throughout the world, and was an honorary member of many institutions including the American Institute of Architects, the American Academy of Arts and Letters, the Association of Finnish Architects, and the Akademie der Bildenden Künste, Vienna. During his lifetime Aalto wrote several books and contributed articles to many international magazines.

Ahrends, Burton and Koralek

THIS PRACTICE, BASED IN LONDON, ENGLAND, WAS SET UP in 1961 by Peter Ahrends, Richard Burton, and Paul Koralek, who had studied together at the Architectural Association in London from 1951 to 1956. Since 1961 the practice work in England has included housing, both private and Government financed such as Chalvedon Housing, Basildon New Town, Essex (1975–77); schools; libraries such as the Maidenhead Library, Berkshire (1972); university and other higher education buildings such as a residential building at Keble College, Oxford (Phase I 1972, Phase II 1976) and Arts Faculty Building, at Trinity College, Dublin, Ireland (1975–); and commercial and industrial buildings such as a warehouse, showrooms, and offices for Habitat in Wallingford, Berkshire (1974). They are currently working on several projects including the Mary Rose Ship Museum in Portsmouth and a department store for the John Lewis Partnership in Kingston, Surrey. Their work has been published internationally in many periodicals and books.

Aida, Takefumi

TAKEFUMI AIDA WAS BORN IN TOKYO, JAPAN, IN 1937, AND studied at Waseda University, Tokyo, gaining his B. Arch. in 1960 and his M. Arch. in 1966. His current practice, established in 1970, is Takefumi Aida Architect and Associates, based in Tokyo. Since 1968 he has designed several houses in Japan including Nirvana House, Kanagawa (1972), Annihilation House, Kanagawa (1972), House like a Die, Shizuoka (1974), and Stepped-Platform House, Kanagawa (1976), as well as the PL Institute Kindergarten, Osaka (1974), and Toy Blocks House I ("Tomo" Dental Office), Yamaguchi, and Toy Blocks House II (Matsuda Building), Kanagawa (both 1979). He is currently working on two houses, Toy Blocks House III and House UMB. Aida won second prize in the Shinkenchiku Residential Design Competition in 1966, and his work has been exhibited and published in Europe, the U.S., and Japan. Since 1971 he has been a member of the Japanese group ArchiteXt, and since 1977 professor at the Shibaura Institute of Technology in Tokyo.

Andrews, John

JOHN ANDREWS WAS BORN IN SYDNEY, AUSTRALIA, IN 1933, and studied at the University of Sydney (B. Arch. 1956) and, under José Lluis Sert (*q.v.*), at Harvard University (M. Arch. 1958). He worked for Edwards Madigan Torzillo in Sydney (1957) and for B. Parkin, Don Mills in Toronto, Canada (1958–62), before becoming a principal of John Andrews Architects in Toronto (since 1962) and of John Andrews International Pty., Ltd. based in Sydney (since 1972). His completed buildings include many university buildings such as a master plan for Scarborough College, University of Toronto (Phase I 1964–66, Phase II 1969–72), Student Housing Complex B, University of Guelph, Ontario (1965–68), Weldon Library, University of Western Ontario (1967–

71), Gund Hall, Graduate School of Design, Harvard University, Cambridge, Massachusetts, (1968–70), School of Art, Kent State University, Ohio (1970–72), student residence for Canberra College of Advanced Education, Australia (1973–75), master plan for Kelvin Grove College of Teacher Education, Brisbane, Australia (1973), and Library and Union Facilities for the Royal Melbourne Institute of Technology, Melbourne, Australia (1979); commercial, industrial, and government buildings in Australia including Cameron Offices, Belconnen Town Centre, Canberra (1968–75), Woden East Area Development, Canberra (project 1973), and Hooker Tower, Sydney (1971–74). His other buildings include African Place—"Man and his World"—for Expo '67 in Montreal (1965–67), plan for Metro Centre Stage I, Toronto (1967–74), Passenger Terminal, Port of Miami, Florida (1967–70), David Mirvish Gallery, Toronto (1971–72), plan for Belconnen Town Centre Mall, Canberra (1972), development study of Sydney Central Station (1977), and site location study of the Museum of Australia (1977). He has won many awards for his work which has been published internationally in books and periodicals. Andrews was a member of the staff (1962–69) and then chairman (1967–69) of the School of Architecture at the University of Toronto.

Ant Farm

ANT FARM WAS FOUNDED IN 1968 BY ARCHITECTS CHIP Lord and Doug Michels. Lord studied at Tulane University, New Orleans, and executed supergraphics in his own flat in New Orleans (1968). Michels studied at Yale School of Architecture and executed supergraphics for the offices of Charles Moore (1965) and his own flat in New Haven, Connecticut (1966). As Ant Farm, Lord and Michels undertook professional commissions, such as their House of the Century in Texas (1972–73). Their work in the field of geodesics, pneumatics, and inflatables, often in conjunction with other designers or groups, includes projects such as Truckstop Network; their own Media Van; "Time Capsule" (1974); their Cadillac Ranch, a megalithic monument consisting of ten Cadillacs set upright in the ground near Route 66, Amarillo, Texas (1974); and "Media Burn," San Francisco (1975). They have written *Inflatacookbook* (1970) and *Automerica* (1977).

Archigram

ARCHIGRAM FIRST APPEARED IN 1961 IN THE FORM OF A magazine edited by Peter Cook and David Greene and featuring the work of Michael Webb. The group became more identifiable in 1963–64 when the original three were joined by Warren Chalk, Dennis Crompton, and Ron Herron to design the "Living City" exhibition at the Institute of Contemporary Arts, London, England, and publish *Archigram 4*—the "Zoom" issue which, through the enthusiasm of the critics Reyner Banham and Peter Blake, rapidly won them international recognition. Their main concern has always been with experimental projects such as Computer City (1964, Dennis Crompton), Plug-In City (1964–66, Peter Cook), Walking City (1964, Ron Herron), Living Pod (1965, David Greene), and Instant City (1968, sponsored by the Graham Foundation, Chicago). The group established an architectural office in 1970 after having won a major invited international competition for the design and construction of an entertainment center in Monte Carlo (Peter Cook, Dennis Crompton, and Ron Herron). The office continued for five years, completing projects such as the "Malaysia" exhibition at the Commonwealth Institute, London (1973), Children's Playground at Milton Keynes (1973, Ron Herron and Dennis Crompton), and Rod Stewart's Pool, Ascot (1973, Ron Herron and Dennis Crompton with Diana Jowsey). Their work has been published internationally in many periodicals including *Architecture d'Aujourd'hui, Architectural Design, Bauen und Wohnen, Hogar y Arquitectura, Domus, Japan Architect* and *A + U.*

Archizoom

ARCHIZOOM, FOUNDED IN FLORENCE, ITALY, IN 1966, IS A group of designers consisting of Andrea Branzi, Gilberto Corretti, Paolo Deganello, Massimo Morozzi, and Dano and Lucia Bartolini. They have designed dream beds including Naufragio di Rose (1968) and Rosa d'Arabia (1968); dream wardrobe; chairs such as the "Mies" chair (1968); a community center in Prato (within the old castle, 1967); a homogeneous residential structure; a homogeneous living diagram; Gazebo-Meditation Center (1968); No-Stop City—a Climatic Universal System (1970); and No-Stop Interior Landscape. They have exhibited widely. Archizoom, together with Superstudio, edited the Milanese magazine *IN.*

Arquitectonica

THE THREE PRINCIPALS OF ARQUITECTONICA, WHICH WAS set up in 1976 in Coral Gables, Florida, are Bernardo Fort-Brescia, Hervin Romney, and Laurinda Spear.

Bernardo Fort-Brescia was born in Lima, Peru, in 1951, and studied in the U.S. at Princeton University (B.A. in Architecture and Urban Planning 1973) and at Harvard University (M. Arch. 1975). In 1976 he was a co-founder of Arquitectonica and has been a principal since that time. Fort-Brescia was also a co-founder in 1977 of the Architectural Club of Miami and has been president since 1977.

Hervin Romney was born in 1941, and studied at Cooper Union, New York City (1962–65) and at Yale School of Architecture, where he received his Master of Environmental Design in 1975. He worked for the architectural office of Harrison & Abramovitz in New York from 1961 to 1965, and for various architectural firms in the Washington, D.C. area between 1965 and 1969, and 1971 and 1973. In 1977 he became president of Arquitectonica International Corporation. Romney was assistant editor of *Perspecta 15* and teaching assistant to Vincent Scully and Charles Moore.

Laurinda Spear was born in Rochester, Minnesota, in 1950, and studied at Columbia University (M. Arch. 1975) and at the Massachusetts Institute of Technology (Master in City Planning). Since March 1976 she has been a member of Arquitectonica. Spear was a founding member of the Architectural Club of Miami in 1977.

The work of Arquitectonica includes Il Gattopardo Apartment Building, Quito, Ecuador (1976); house for Dr. and Mrs. H.C. Spear in Miami, Florida (1977); Brickell Biscayne Corporation Condominium for Helmsley Enterprises, Inc. ("The Palace"), Miami (1978); and "The Atlantis" Condominium, Miami (1978). They have won several citations in the Progressive Architecture Design Awards for their work, which has been exhibited in museums in the U.S. and reviewed internationally in periodicals.

Aulenti, Gaetana

GAE AULENTI WAS BORN IN PALAZZOLO DELLO STELLA, Italy, in 1927, and studied at Milan Polytechnic, where she received her Dip. Arch. in 1954. She has been in private practice in Milan since 1954. Her completed buildings include houses, schools, and commercial and industrial buildings such as the Knoll Showrooms in Boston, Massachusetts (1971), and the Fiat Showrooms in Turin, Italy (1972 and 1973). Her other works include "New Design for Italian Furniture" exhibition interiors, Milan (1960); a Theatrical Space project, Naples, Italy, and Paris, France (1975, with Luca Ronconi); Meda Elementary School competition project, Italy (1967, awarded first prize); and sets for the play *The Wild Duck* at the Teatro di Genova, Genoa, Italy (1977), and for the play *Wozzeck* at the Teatro alla Scala, Milan (1977). Aulenti was visiting lecturer at the College of Architecture, Barcelona, Spain, and at the Cultural Center, Stockholm, Sweden, from 1969 to 1975; and a member of the editorial staff of *Casabella* in Milan from 1954 to 1962. She has been a member of the board of directors of *Lotus* in Milan since 1974 and a member of the Association for Industrial Design in Milan since 1960 (vice-president in 1966).

Aymonino, Carlo

CARLO AYMONINO WAS BORN IN ROME, ITALY, IN 1926, and studied at the University of Rome, where he received his Dip. Arch. in 1950. He has been in private practice in Rome since 1951. Together with Maurizio Aymonino, Baldo de Rossi, and Alessandro de Rossi, Aymonino founded Studio AYDE, of which he has been a director since 1960. His completed buildings in Italy include housing developments such as the INA-Casa Housing Developments at Tiburtino, Rome (1950), and at Brindisi ("Commenda Ovest," 1957–59), and the Monte Amiata Housing Development, Gallaratese, Milan (1967–74 with Aldo Rossi and others); university and school buildings such as the G. Marconi School of Science and the High School Campus at Pesaro (1970–76); and commercial buildings such as the apartment-office complexes in Savona (1963–67). Other buildings in Italy include the Piazza XX Settembre redevelopment, Fano (1973), and the Civic Center in Pesaro (1979). His competition projects include a covered market in Pescara (1954); National Library, Rome (1959); Paganini Theater reconstruction, Parma (1966); and a Psychiatric Hospital in Mirano (1966). Aymonino co-edited *Casabella* from 1959 to 1964 and lectured at the University of Rome from 1951 to 1974. He has written several books and many articles for periodicals including *Casabella, Controspazio,* and *A + U.* Since 1974 Aymonino has been dean of the Graduate School of Architecture at the University of Venice.

B

Baer, Steve

STEVE BAER WAS BORN IN LOS ANGELES, CALIFORNIA, IN 1938, and studied for a year at Amherst College, Massachusetts (1956), and then dropped out and went to work in the California oilfields and subsequently joined the army. He has designed structures for communes in the U.S. at Drop City, Colorado (1966); Lama Commune, New Mexico (the Center, 1967); Libre, Colorado, and Manera Nueva, New Mexico (1968); and his own house at Corrales, New Mexico (1971–72). He founded Zomeworks in 1969 and since then has been designing and building solar houses and energy systems. In 1969 he organized the "Alloy" conference. Baer has written two books, *Dome Cookbook* (1968) and *Zome Primer* (1970).

Barnes, Edward Larrabee

EDWARD LARRABEE BARNES WAS BORN IN CHICAGO, ILlinois, in 1915, and studied under Marcel Breuer at Harvard University, where he received his B. Arch. in 1942. Since 1949 he has worked in his own practice based in New York City. His completed buildings in the U.S. include master plan and major buildings for the State University of New York at Potsdam (1965–74) and Purchase (1968–78); Rochester Institute of Technology Dormitory Complex, New York (1964–67/70); Christian Theological Seminary, Indianapolis, Indiana (1969); Crown Center, Kansas City, Missouri (1973); Sarah M. Scaife Gallery, Carnegie Institute, Pittsburgh, Pennsylvania (1975); IBM World Trade/Americas Far East Headquarters, Mount Pleasant, New York (1971–75); and Visual Arts Center, Bowdoin College, Brunswick, Maine (1978). He has won several awards for his work, and became Fellow of the American Institute of Architects (1966), Associate (1969), and Academician (1974) of the National Academy of Design, and Fellow (1978) of the American Academy of Arts and Sciences. An exhibition of his work—"Edward Larrabee Barnes"— was held in the Scaife Gallery in 1974. Barnes was architectural design critic and lecturer at Pratt Institute, New York City (1953–59) and at Yale University (1957– 59). He is currently a member of the Urban Design Council in New York, and a trustee of The Museum of Modern Art in New York.

Becket, Welton

WELTON BECKET WAS BORN IN SEATTLE, WASHINGTON, IN 1902, and studied at the University of Washington, graduating in 1927 with a degree in architecture. He worked as a designer-draftsman for a small architectural office in Los Angeles (1929), and then in private practice in Seattle (1929–33). From 1933 he worked in partnership with Walter Wurdeman and Charles Plummer (died 1939), and after Wurdeman's death in 1949 continued the firm as Welton Becket and Associates, serving as president from 1949 until his death in 1969. Offices were established in San Francisco (1949), New York City (1950), and Houston (1960). The firm's completed buildings, mainly in the U.S., include many department stores such as the Bullock's stores in Pasadena, California (1947), in Westwood, California (1950), and in La Habra, California (1969), the Stonestown Shopping Center in San Francisco, California (1951), and Center Plaza, Boston, Massachusetts (1966); hotels including the Nile Hilton Hotel in Cairo, Egypt (1959), the Manila Hilton in the Philippines (1968), and the Hyatt Regency Hotel and Reunion Tower, Dallas, Texas (1973–78); commercial and industrial buildings including the Ford Motor Company General Office Building, Dearborn, Michigan (1956), Phillips Petroleum Building, Bartlesville, Oklahoma (1964), and Equitable Life Building, Los Angeles, California (1969); government buildings such as the U.S. Embassy in Warsaw, Poland (1963); Los Angeles International Airport (1962); and the Ford Motor Company Pavilion, World's Fair, New York (1964). Becket was master planner and supervising architect at the University of California in Los Angeles from 1949 to 1969. Since his death the practice has continued under the direction of his son, Welton Becket, Jr., maintaining the same business principles and dedication to total design envisaged by its founder.

Behnisch & Partner

BEHNISCH & PARTNER WAS FOUNDED BY GÜNTER BEHNisch, Fritz Auer, Winfried Büxel, Manfred Sabatke, Erhard Tränkner, and Karlheinz Weber in Stuttgart, West Germany, in 1966, although some members of the team had worked together since the late fifties. The practice's work encompasses school and university buildings, shopping centers, residences, cultural facilities, commercial and industrial buildings, and town planning. Buildings to date in West Germany include Bremen University (1967); roof of the Olympic Stadia, Munich (1972, with Günther Grzimek); Königstrasse/Schlossplatz pedestrian precinct, Stuttgart (1973); buildings for the Federal Government, Bonn (competition project 1973); District Hospital, Waldkraiburg (1973); School and Sports Center in Rothenburg (1975 and 1977); Hostel and Nursing Home for elderly people, Reutlingen (1976); and Study and Education Center for the Evangelist Church in Württemberg (1979). The practice is currently working on a project for an Industrial Training Center in Bruchsal and is planning several more projects including a school, government and administrative buildings, a health center, and a sports hall. They have won many awards for their work, which has been published internationally in many books and periodicals.

Birkerts, Gunnar

GUNNAR BIRKERTS WAS BORN IN RIGA, U.S.S.R., IN 1925 and subsequently emigrated to West Germany, where he studied at the Technische Hochschule in Stuttgart, graduating in 1949 with a Dip. Arch. In 1949 he emigrated to the U.S. and worked in the offices of Eero Saarinen and Minoru Yamasaki before setting up his own practice, Birkerts and Straub, in 1959 and then Gunnar Birkerts and Associates in 1962, both based in Birmingham, Michigan. His major projects to date include university buildings, schools, and office buildings in the U.S. such as the Federal Reserve Bank of Minneapolis, Minnesota (1967–74), and the IBM Office Building in Southfield. Michigan (1974). He is currently working on designs for several buildings including the U.S. Embassy building in Helsinki, Finland, the University of Michigan Law School Library, Ann Arbor, and the Museum of Glass, Corning Glass Works, New York. Since 1954 he has received many awards for his designs, and there have been several exhibitions of his work. He has published numerous articles in leading architectural magazines in the U.S., Europe, and Japan, and has also written a book, *Subterranean Urban Systems* (1974). Birkerts is at present professor of architecture at the University of Michigan.

Blom, Piet

PIET BLOM WAS BORN IN AMSTERDAM, THE NETHERLANDS, in 1934, and studied at the Architecture Academy in Amsterdam under Aldo van Eyck (*q.v.*), graduating in 1962 with a Dip. Arch. He has been in private practice in Monnikendam, The Netherlands, since 1967. His completed buildings in The Netherlands include Boerdirij Students' Building (1963) and Bastille Students' Building/ Community Center (1967–69), both at Twente Technical University, Enschede; Kasbah Housing Development, Hengelo (1972–73); and Speelhuis Leisure Center, Helmond (1975–78). His projects include Subterranean Development under the Rozengracht, Amsterdam (1975); Jordaan District Redevelopment Plan, Amsterdam (1975); and two apartment buildings in Rotterdam (1978– 79). His work has been published internationally in periodicals including *Architecture d'Aujourd'hui, Lotus,* and *Bauen und Wohnen.*

Bofill, Ricardo

RICARDO BOFILL WAS BORN IN BARCELONA, SPAIN, IN 1939, and studied at the Escuela Tecnica Superior de Arquitectura in Barcelona (1955–56) and at the Architecture University of Geneva, Switzerland (1957–60). He founded Taller de Arquitectura, based in Barcelona, in 1960. His completed buildings include many residential and holiday apartments such as the Barrio Gaudí Residential Complex, Reus, Spain (1964–70), El Castell Apartment Building, Sitges, Spain (1964–66), La Manzanera (Xanadu) Apartment House, Calpe, Spain (1966), La Muralla Roja Holiday Apartments, Calpe (1968), the Walden 7 Residential Complex, San Just Desvern, Barcelona (1970–75), and Les Arcades du Lac, Saint-Quentin-en-Yvelines, France (1975–81); other buildings include the Meritxell Religious Center, Andorra (1973–78) and Le Parc de la Marca Hispanica Monument, Le Boulou-Le Perthus, France (1974–76). Bofill has taken part in various exhibitions held recently in Venice, Paris, Berlin, and New York.

Böhm, Gottfried

GOTTFRIED BÖHM WAS BORN IN OFFENBACH AM MAIN, WEST Germany, in 1920, and studied at the Technische Hochschule in Munich, where he received his B. Eng. in 1946, and at the Akademie der Bildenden Künste in Munich for one year (1947). He worked in the office of his father,

Dominikus Böhm, from 1947 until his father's death in 1955, when he set up in private practice in Cologne, West Germany. His completed buildings in West Germany include a Town Hall in Bensberg (1963–66); Children's Village, Bensberg-Refrath (1964); Pilgrimage Church at Neviges (1972); housing for the elderly, Düsseldorf-Garath (1972); Pilgrimage Church at Hergatz (near Wangen, 1972); housing complex, Cologne-Chorweiler (1973); Diocesan Museum, Paderborn (1975); State Bureau for Data Processing and Statistics, Düsseldorf (1979); and Neckermann Store facade and renovation, Braunschweig (1979). He is currently working on designs for a Town Hall in Rheinberg, an apartment building and garage in Saarbrücken, and on the old town center in Bonn-Bad Godesberg. His projects include new buildings for the Wallraf-Richartz Museum in Cologne (1975), housing for the German Embassy in Moscow, Russia (1975), and Karlsberg High School in Bremerhaven, West Germany (1979). In 1980 he won first prizes for his designs in West Germany for a High School in Bremerhaven; a Parishioners' Center in Essen-Kettwig; and an auditorium and music school in Essen-Werden. Böhm is a member of the Akademie der Künste and the German Academy for Urban and Regional Planning. Since 1963 he has been professor of architecture at the Institute of Technology in Aachen.

Botta, Mario

MARIO BOTTA WAS BORN IN 1943 IN MENDRISIO, SWITZERland, and studied at the Art College in Milan, Italy (1961–64), and at the Istituto Universitario di Architettura in Venice, Italy (1964–69). In 1969 he started work as a professional architect with a studio in Lugano,

Switzerland. His completed buildings in Switzerland and northern Italy include several one-family houses such as those at Riva San Vitale (1972–73) and at Ligornetto (1975–76); a Secondary School at Morbio Inferiore (1972–77); a Library in the Capuchin Convent at Lugano (1976–79); and a Craft Center at Balerna (1977–79). His other works include projects for a master plan for the new Lausanne Polytechnic, Switzerland (1970), and for terrace houses at Riva San Vitale (1979) and several competition entries for administrative buildings such as the new administrative center at Perugia, Italy (1971), schools, a library, housing estates, and the enlargement of Zürich station, Switzerland (1978). Botta has taken part in several exhibitions, and has lectured at universities throughout Europe. His work and projects have been published internationally in many periodicals.

Brown, Neave

NEAVE BROWN WAS BORN IN UTICA, NEW YORK, IN 1929, and studied at the Architectural Association in London, England, from 1950 to 1956. He worked as assistant architect with Lyons Israel & Ellis in London (1958–61), with the Middlesex County Council Architects Department (1961–63), and with the London Borough of Camden from 1965 to 1978, during which time he designed Fleet Road housing and the Alexandra Road development. He has also worked independently in Dar es Salaam, Tanzania (1956–58), and in London (1963–78) when he designed the Piccadilly Galleries in Cork Street. Brown also designed the "Léger and Purist Paris" exhibition at the Tate Gallery, London (1970–71) and the "Thirties, British Art and Design" exhibition at the Hayward Gallery, London (1979).

Colquhoun + Miller

COLQUHOUN + MILLER WAS ESTABLISHED IN 1961 BY ALAN Colquhoun and John H. Miller, who were joined by Richard J. Brearley in 1973 and John Hunter in 1977. The completed buildings of the practice in England include the Chemistry Buildings at the Royal Holloway College, London (1970); an Activity Centre in Bletchley, Buckinghamshire (1974); two Community Centres in London (1977); and a Home for the Elderly in Haringey, London (1977). They are currently working on housing at Haringey; 152 houses for central Milton Keynes, and additions to and conversion of the Whitechapel Art Gallery in London. Their projects include the U.K. Canning Plant for Coca Cola Export Corporation in conjunction with the Milton Keynes Development Corporation (1975) and Two Mile Ash, Milton Keynes (250 houses, 1977). They have also designed exhibitions, the most recent of which is a traveling exhibition—"Ten Great 20th Century Houses"—for the Arts Council of Great Britain.

Cullinan, Edward

EDWARD CULLINAN WAS BORN IN LONDON, ENGLAND, IN 1931. After graduating from Cambridge University in 1954 he studied at the Architectural Association in London for two years. He currently shares a practice with M.A. Chassay, A.H. Peake, S. Prasad, M.N. Beedle, C.E.M. Herniman, R. Nicholson, and G. Oliver. Since 1958 he has designed, in England, private residences including his own house in London (1965) and housing complexes such as the one at Highgrove in Ruislip, Middlesex (1977), as well as several offices and workshops for Olivetti throughout the United Kingdom (1971–72). He is currently working on sixteen flats at Leighton Crescent for the London Borough of Camden, 160 houses at Milton Keynes, and office reorganization and conversion for Wolff Olins, Ltd. in London. Cullinan was winner of the Civic Trust European Architectural Heritage Year Award in 1975. He has written articles for *Architectural Design* and the *RIBA Journal*.

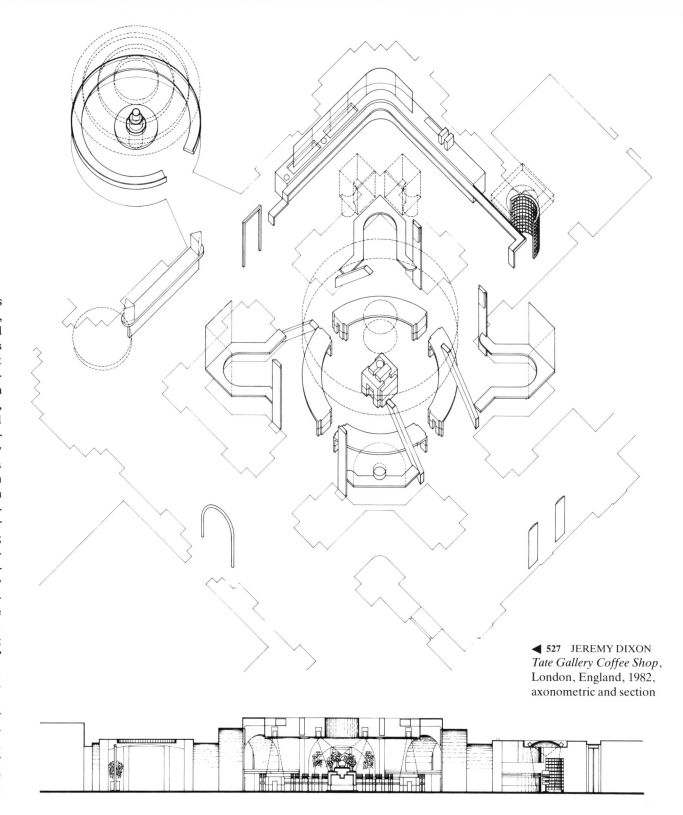

527 JEREMY DIXON
Tate Gallery Coffee Shop,
London, England, 1982,
axonometric and section

Darbourne & Darke

THE PRACTICE OF DARBOURNE & DARKE, WHICH WAS established in 1961, has five partners: John Darbourne, Geoffrey Darke, Bernard Grimes, Jeremy Lever, and Michael Burgess. The large majority of the practice's work in England is public housing including housing at Lillington Street, Pimlico, London (1961–68), at Marquess Road, Canonbury, London (1966), at Camden Road, Holloway, London (1969), at Brookvale, Runcorn, Cheshire (1969), at Pershore, Worcestershire (1970), and at Ham Lands, Richmond, Surrey (1973); other buildings include Pimlico Library, London (1970), a new stand for Chelsea Football Club, London (1971), a children's day center, Islington, London (1972), and an urban area study, Stuttgart, West Germany (competition project 1976). Several of their projects in England are presently under construction: housing at Powis Square for the Royal Borough of Kensington & Chelsea, London; a Day Centre for the Physically Handicapped for the London Borough of Haringey; Second Computer Laboratory and Offices for IBM United Kingdom, Ltd. at Hursley Park, Hampshire; and housing at Colne Road, Twickenham, for the London Borough of Richmond. They are currently working on designs for Phase II housing at Queens Road Estate, Richmond; housing redevelopment and rehabilitation at Haverstock Hill, London; doctors' surgeries in Kent; housing redevelopment in Tadcaster, Yorkshire; and new living accommodation and rehabilitation at Stanford Open Prison, Isle of Sheppey, London. Darbourne & Darke have won many awards for their work including first prize in two limited competitions for housing in Hannover, West Germany (1978), and for housing, shops, and schools in Bolzano, Italy (1980). An exhibition of the architecture of Darbourne & Darke was held at the RIBA Heinz Gallery in London in 1977.

De Feo, Vittorio

VITTORIO DE FEO WAS BORN IN 1928 IN NAPLES, ITALY, AND studied at Rome University. He currently shares a practice with Enrico Ascione, Fabrizio Aggarbati, and Carla Saggioro. His completed buildings in Italy include Psychiatric Hospital, Frosinone (1960); Tribunal and Court of Appeal, Rome (1964); Recreation Center Building for Italian Broadcasting Corporation (RAI), Rome (1965); High School, Rome (1967); Special Education Center, Terni (1967); Institute for Draftsmen, Terni (1968–72); and two libraries and cultural centers at Torre del Greco (1970) and at Nocera Inferiore (1970). De Feo is currently working on a design for low-cost public housing in Rome. His competition entries include government buildings such as the new Office Building for the Chamber of Deputies of the Italian Parliament, Rome (1967), and Regional Administration Center at Trieste (1974); hospitals; housing; theaters such as Performing Arts Centers in Udine (1975) and Forli (1976); school and university buildings such as the Technical Agrarian Institute in Rome (1980); Service Station Prototype for Esso (1971); and National Assembly Offices of TANU at Dar es Salaam, Tanzania (1971). He has written three books and many articles for Italian periodicals and newspapers. He is currently professor of architecture at Rome University.

Derbyshire, Andrew

ANDREW DERBYSHIRE WAS BORN IN 1923 IN SHEFFIELD, England, and studied at Cambridge University and at the Architectural Association in London. His current partnership is Robert Matthew, Johnson-Marshall and Partners based in London. His completed buildings in England include Marchwood Power Station; Castle Market in Sheffield; Hillingdon Civic Centre, London; Preston Guild Hall, Lancashire; University of York; and the Central Lancashire New Town Outline Plan; and he is currently working on a design for the Castle Peak Power Station in Hong Kong. He has both published articles and delivered broadcasts on auditorium acoustics, building economics, the planning and construction of universities and new towns, and new forms of public transport.

Deslaugiers, Francois
FRANCOIS DESLAUGIERS WAS BORN IN ALGERIA IN 1934, and studied at the Ecole Nationale Supérieure des Beaux-Arts in Paris, France, graduating in 1966 with a Dip. Arch. Between 1954 and 1973 he worked in various architectural offices in Paris including the office of P.C. Jullien (1961–65) and of L. Arretche from 1965 to 1971, during which time his work in France included the Law Faculty at Nantes (1969–70), the Lycée Polyvalent Experimental in Paimpol, and five information centers for the Ministry of Finance (1969–70). In 1973 he set up in private practice and received commissions from the Department of Income Tax for a regional information center for the Parisian district (1975–79) and for the extension of the regional information center in Lille (1974); he also designed four information centers for the Ministry of Finance as well as designing extensions to two existing centers. Since 1972 he has taught in the Environmental Studies Department at the University of Paris.

Dixon, Jeremy
JEREMY DIXON WAS BORN IN 1939, AND STUDIED AT THE Architectural Association in London, England, receiving his diploma in 1964. He worked for Alison and Peter Smithson (1965–66), Frederick Macmanus and Partners (1966–71), and for the Milton Keynes Development Corporation (1971–73), before setting up in private practice. From 1973 to 1977 he was in partnership with Cross Gold Jones Sansom, and since 1977 has had his own practice based in London. His projects in England include housing at Plough Way, Rotherhithe (1966–71); exhibition at the Hayward Gallery, London (1971, with Chris Cross, Chris Woodward, and Sven Rindl); housing at Milton Keynes (1971–73, with Ed Jones); Weiss House in Buckinghamshire (1974, with Fenella Dixon); houses and flats in St. Mark's Road, London (1975–80); and Sim House in Essex (1979–, with Fenella Dixon). Since 1972 Dixon has taught at the Architectural Association, London.

Durkee, Steve
STEVE DURKEE WAS BORN IN 1938 AND GREW UP IN NEW York City. He began to exhibit Pop paintings in 1962, and in 1963 formed the Us company with the poet Gerd Stern and the electronics expert Michael Callahan, based in an abandoned church in Bamerville, New York. The Us company performed multimedia works of collective authorship, with the occasional live participation of Marshall McLuhan, at Rochester, New York (1963), and at the University of British Columbia, Canada (1964). During a West Coast lecture tour with Richard Alpert in 1965–66, Durkee met Buckminster Fuller (q.v.). In June 1967 Durkee was one of the founders of the commune Lama, based in San Cristóbal, New Mexico; and he collaborated with Steve Baer (q.v.) on designs for the Lama Center and kitchen domes. It was Durkee who coined the term zome.

Eisenman, Peter
PETER EISENMAN WAS BORN IN 1932 IN NEWARK, NEW Jersey, and studied at Cornell University (B. Arch. 1955) and at Columbia University (M.S.Arch. 1960); he then went to Cambridge University, England, where he received his M.A. (1962) and Ph.D. (1963) in the theory of design. His completed buildings in the U.S. include House I in Princeton, New Jersey (1967–68); House II in Hardwick, Vermont (1969–70); House III in Lakeville, Connecticut (1969–70); and House VI in Cornwall, Connecticut (1972–76). His projects include House X, Bloomfield Hills, Michigan (1975–77), and House IIa, Palo Alto, California (1978), as well as several competition projects such as Liverpool Cathedral, England (1960), and Boston City Hall, Massachusetts (1961). Eisenman has taken part in many exhibitions including "40 under 40" (Architectural League of New York 1966) and "Five Architects" (Princeton University 1974). He has taught at Cambridge University (1960–63), and Princeton University (1965–66), and has been professor at Cooper Union, New York City, since 1975. Eisenman has been director of the Institute for Architecture and Urban Studies in New York City since 1967, and editor of the journal *Oppositions* since 1973. In 1970 he was vice-president of the Architectural League of New York. He has contributed articles to international magazines, and has written several books including *House of Cards* (1978).

Ellwood, Craig
CRAIG ELLWOOD WAS BORN IN CLARENDON, TEXAS, IN 1922, and studied structural engineering at night classes at the University of California at Los Angeles Extension Division (1949–54). He worked for a construction company in Los Angeles (1946–48) before becoming the principal of Craig Ellwood Associates, based in Los Angeles (1948–76). Since 1976 he has devoted himself to painting and sculpture, and lives part of the time in Italy. His completed buildings in the U.S. include many private residences such as Hale House, Beverly Hills, California (1949–50), Courtyard Apartments, Hollywood, California (1952), Case Study House 18 for the magazine *Arts and Architecture*, Los Angeles (1955), Daphne House, Hillsborough, California (1960), Rosen House, Brentwood, California (1961), and Chamorro House, Los Angeles (project 1962–63); other buildings include Scientific Data Systems Building, El Segundo, California (1966 and 1967), Arts Center College of Design in Pasadena, California (1970–75), Security Pacific National Bank, East Hollywood, California

(1972–73), and fifteenth-century farmhouse restoration in Tuscany, Italy (1979). He has won several awards for his work, and taken part in several exhibitions. Ellwood has lectured at Yale University (1959 and 1960), Cornell University (1960), and Syracuse University (1961).

Erskine, Ralph
RALPH ERSKINE WAS BORN IN LONDON, ENGLAND, IN 1914 and moved to Sweden in 1939. He studied at Regent Street Polytechnic, London, receiving his Dip. Arch. in 1937, and at the Royal Academy of Arts in Stockholm, Sweden (1944–45). Since 1946 he has been in private practice in Drottningholm, Sweden, and is now in partnership with Aage Rosenvold. In 1955 Erskine bought a Thames barge, *Verona*, sailed it to Drottningholm, and there converted it into offices. He established a branch office on the Byker Estate at Newcastle-upon-Tyne, England, in 1968. Erskine has designed some eighty projects, most of which have been built in collaboration with his partner Rosenvold. Principal among these many varied buildings are the housing for factory workers at Storvik-Hammarby, Sweden (1946–47); houses in Sweden such as Villa Molin (1947) and Villa Gadelius (1961), both at Lidingö, near Stockholm, Villa in Steel (dome house), Sorunda on Lisön (1955–56), Villa Nordmark, near Södertälje (1962), and his own house and office at Drottningholm (1963); factories in Sweden such as the Cardboard Factory at Fors (1950–53) and Paper-pulp Factory at Storvik-Hammarby (1953); housing schemes in Sweden and England such as Ortdrivaren Housing Development, Kiruna (1961–62), Barberaren Housing Estate, Sandviken (1962–64 and 1968–70), housing for a mining village at Svappavaara (1963–64), Byker Housing Estate, Newcastle-upon-Tyne (1969–80), Studland Park Housing Estate, Newmarket (1970–76), and Eaglestone Housing Estate, Milton Keynes (1973–77); a primary school at Gyttorp, Sweden (1961); a post-graduate college for Clare Hall, Cambridge, England (1967–69); a housing township in North Canada at Resolute Bay (1973); a skiing hotel/center at Borgafjäll (1948–50), as well as an enclosed shopping center at Luleå (1955), both in north Sweden. Erskine has taken part in a number of exhibitions. He has been a member of Team Ten since 1959.

Fathy, Hassan

HASSAN FATHY WAS BORN IN EGYPT IN 1899 AND HAS HIS own practice in Cairo. His completed buildings include the Royal Society of Agriculture Building, Bathim, Egypt (1937); Prototype House, near Cairo (1938); New Town of Gourna, Egypt (1945–48); Village of Mit-el-Nasara rebuilding, Egypt (1954); Prototype Houses in El Dareeya, Saudi Arabia, (1966); and two projects in Jedda, Saudi Arabia, for a V.I.P. Mansion (1974) and Middle-Class House (1974). Fathy's books include *Architecture for the Poor* (1973) and *The Arab House in the Urban Setting: Past, Present and Future* (1972). He is currently professor of fine arts and head of the Architectural School at the University of Cairo.

Feilden, Bernard

BERNARD FEILDEN WAS BORN IN LONDON, ENGLAND, IN 1919, and studied at the Bartlett School of Architecture (1938) and at the Architectural Association in London, where he received his Dip. A.A. in 1949. He worked as an assistant in the office of J. Douglas Matthews in London (1949–50) and E. Boardman and Son in Norwich, Norfolk (1950–54), before setting up in private practice in Norwich in 1954. From 1956 to 1977 he was in partnership with David Mawson in Norwich. Feilden was architect for Norwich Cathedral from 1963 to 1977, surveyor to the fabric for York Minster (1965–77), surveyor to St. Paul's Cathedral in London (1969–77), and consultant architect to the University of East Anglia (1969–77). His work in England has included conservation and restoration work on Norwich Cathedral (since 1955), York Minster (1973), and St. Paul's Cathedral (1977); several buildings and master plan and landscaping for the University of East Anglia (1970); Watney Mann Brewery in Norwich (1972); Hyde Park Estate, London (1977, as consultant); and kitchens for Buckingham Palace, London (1977, with Graham Keith). Since 1977 Feilden has been director of the International Center for Conservation in Rome, Italy.

Foster, Norman

NORMAN FOSTER WAS BORN IN MANCHESTER, ENGLAND, IN 1935, and studied at the University of Manchester School of Architecture and Department of Town and Country Planning (1956–61) and at Yale University, where he received his M. Arch. in 1962. From 1963 to 1967 he was a partner with Wendy Foster and Richard Rogers (*q.v.*) in Team 4, London, and since 1967 he has been a partner in Foster Associates, also based in London. His completed buildings in England include residences such as the Norman and Wendy Foster House in Hampstead, London

(1979); commercial and industrial buildings such as the Reliance Controls Factory, Swindon (1966), Fred Olsen Passenger Terminal and Operations Centre, Millwall, London (1970), and a showroom in Regent Street, London (1974), IBM Advance Head Office, near Portsmouth, Hampshire (1971), and Technical Park, Greenford, Middlesex (1978 and Phase II 1979), the Willis Faber Dumas, Ltd. Head Office, Ipswich (1972–75), and Orange Hand Shops for Burtons, Ltd. in London, Nottingham, Brighton, and Reading (1972); and cultural facilities such as the Sainsbury Centre for the Visual Arts at the University of East Anglia (1975–78). He is currently working on designs for the new headquarters of the Hong Kong and Shanghai Banking Corporation. Foster has won several awards for his work, which has been published internationally in books and periodicals.

Friday Architects/Planners

THE PARTNERS OF FRIDAY ARCHITECTS/PLANNERS, WHICH was established in 1970 in Philadelphia, Pennsylvania, are Frank Mallas, Donald Matzkin, and David Slovic. Their completed buildings, mainly in Philadelphia, include the Planned Parenthood Association (1974–75, 1978–79, 1979–); the Old Pine Community Center (1974–77); Barrier-Free Access to Public Buildings (1975–79); and Grays Ferry Citizens Center (1976–79). They are currently working on Temple University Student Activities Center and Improvements and Market Street Family Housing, both in Philadelphia, and are now beginning schematic designs for the R.W. Brown Community Center and Burlington Mall. The competition designs of this practice include Thousand Oaks Civic Center, California (1970), and the Minnesota State Capitol Annex (1977); and there have been several exhibitions of their work in the U.S. Individuals from Friday have lectured at universities in New York, Philadelphia, and Texas; and David Slovic is currently Philadelphia correspondent for *Skyline* and has written three books—*The Aesthetics of the Ugly* (1977), *The Beaux-Arts Redux* (1978), and *American Diner* (1979).

Fujii, Hiromi

HIROMI FUJII WAS BORN IN TOKYO, JAPAN, IN 1935, AND studied and worked in Professor Take's studio at Waseda University, Tokyo (1958–64). He then worked for Angelo Mangiarotti in Milan, Italy (1964–66), with Alison and Peter Smithson in London, England (1966), and for Yorke, Rosenberg, and Mardall, also in London (1967). Since 1968 he has been principal of Hiromi Fujii Architects and Associates, based in Tokyo. His buildings and projects in Japan consist mainly of houses such as the Suzuki House and Apartment in Tokyo (1971), Miyajima House in Tokyo (1973), and Todoroki House, Tokyo (1975); but he has also designed Snack 7, a restaurant in Tokyo (1972), and Marutake Office Building, Saitama (1976). Fujii has written many articles for Japanese periodicals including $A + U$ and *The Japan Architect*.

Fuller, R. Buckminster

BUCKMINSTER FULLER WAS BORN IN MILTON, MASSAchusetts, in 1895, and studied at Harvard University from 1913 to 1915. Although not an architect in the usual sense of the word, Fuller has influenced architecture through his numerous inventions, lectures, and theoretical

writing. His concern with ways of employing the world's resources so efficiently as to be able to provide a higher standard of living for humanity has led him to unique solutions to these problems such as the World Game (1969). According to Fuller, his "inventions, realizations, and discoveries" include the discovery of energetic/synergetic geometry (1917), the invention of the Dymaxion House (1927), Bathroom (1930), and Car (1932), the 4D House (1928), Tensegrity structures (1945), Geodesic structures (1947), and Floating Tetrahedronal City (1968). One of his best-known and most successful structural innovations is the geodesic dome, examples of which include the United States Early Defense Warning System in the Arctic (1954), Palais des Sports, Paris (1959), Cinerama Theater, Hollywood, California (1963), U.S. Pavilion at the Canadian Universal and International Exhibition, Expo '67, Montreal, Canada (1967), United States Research Station, Antarctica (1972), and Weather Radome, Mount Fuji, Japan (1973). There have been many exhibitions, in both the U.S. and Europe, of his work, for which he has won innumerable awards over the years. Fuller was editor of *Shelter* (1930–32) and of *World Magazine* (1972–75), and has disseminated his ideas through numerous articles and books including *Operating Manual for Spaceship Earth* (1968), *World Resources Inventory* (1968), *I seem to be a Verb* (1970), and *Synergetics: Explorations in the Geometry of Thinking* (1975).

G

Gehry, Frank O.

FRANK GEHRY WAS BORN IN TORONTO, CANADA, IN 1929, and studied in the U.S. at the University of Southern California, Los Angeles (1949–51), and at the Harvard Graduate School of Design (1956–57). Between 1953 and 1961 he worked as architectural designer and planner for various offices in the U.S. including Victor Gruen Associates (1953–54, 1958–61) and Pereira and Luckman (1957–58), and since 1962 has been a principal in Frank O. Gehry and Associates, Inc., based in Los Angeles. His completed buildings in the U.S. include private residences such as Bixby Garden Townhouses, Garden Grove, California (1968, with Walsh and O'Malley), Ron Davis Studio/House, Malibu, California (1976), and his own house in Santa Monica, California (1978–79); commercial and industrial buildings such as the Gemini G.E.L. Lithography Shop and Gallery remodeling, Hollywood, California (1976), Berger, Berger, Kahn,

and Shafton Law Offices, Los Angeles (1977), and Mid-Atlantic Toyota Distributorship (warehouse and offices), Glen Burnie, Maryland (1978); and cultural facilities such as a temporary acoustical shell for the Hollywood Bowl, Los Angeles (1970), and the Los Angeles Children's Museum (1979). He has designed exhibitions including "Art Treasures from Japan" (1965) and "King Tut" (1977), both at the Los Angeles County Museum of Art, as well as taking part in several exhibitions. Gehry is a member of the Los Angeles 12.

Goff, Bruce

BRUCE GOFF WAS BORN IN ALTON, KANSAS, IN 1904. In 1916, at the early age of twelve, he was apprenticed to the firm of Rush, Endacott, and Rush in Tulsa, Oklahoma, where he worked until 1933. Goff was in private practice in Chicago, Illinois (1935–42), Berkeley, California (1945–46), Bartlesville, Oklahoma (1956–64), Kansas City, Missouri (1964–71) and, since 1971, in Tyler, Texas. His work is in the organic tradition and consists mainly of private houses built in collaboration with his clients such as Unseth House, Park Ridge, Illinois (1940–41); Triaero Vacation House, Fern Creek, Kentucky (1940–41); Ford House, Aurora, Illinois (1949); Wilson House, Perdido Bay, Pensacola, Florida (1950); Bavinger House, Norman, Oklahoma (1950–55); Comer House, Dewey, Oklahoma (1956); Joe D. Price House, Bartlesville, Oklahoma (1956, 1966, 1970); Gutman House, Gulfport, Mississippi (1958); Gryder House, Ocean Springs, Mississippi (1960); Dace House, Beaver, Oklahoma (1964); Nicol House, Kansas City, Missouri (1964); Hyde House, Kansas City, Kansas (1965);

◀ **528** TERRY FARRELL *Clifton Nurseries*, Covent Garden, London, England, 1981, night view

▶ **529** MICHAEL GRAVES *Public Library*, San Juan Capistrano, California, 1981, model

Plunkett House, Lake Village, Tyler, Texas (1970); and Glen Harder House, Mountain Lake, Minnesota (1970). His other buildings include Riverside Music Studio, Tulsa, Oklahoma (1928), and a Chapel for the U.S. Navy Seabee Aleutian Base Facilities, Adak, Aleutian Islands (1944). His work has been published internationally in books and periodicals. Besides his work in architecture and education as head of the School of Architecture at Oklahoma University (1948–55), Goff has continued painting since 1920.

Graham, Bruce

BRUCE GRAHAM WAS BORN IN BOGOTA, COLOMBIA, OF American parents in 1925. He studied in the U.S. at the University of Dayton (1942–43), at the Case School of Applied Sciences in Cleveland (1943–44 and 1946), and at the University of Pennsylvania (B. Arch. 1948). After graduating he moved to Chicago, Illinois, where he has lived and worked ever since. From 1949 to 1951 he worked in the office of Holabird, Roche, and Burgee, and then became chief of design in the Chicago office of Skidmore, Owings, and Merrill, and nine years later, in 1960, he became a partner. His completed buildings, mainly in the U.S., include Inland Steel Company Headquarters in Chicago (1958); Brunswick Office Building, Chicago (1965); Civic Center, Chicago (1965); Equitable Life Assurance Society of the United States Office Building, Chicago (1965); John Hancock Center, Chicago (1965–70); One Shell Plaza Office Building, Houston, Texas (1971); First Wisconsin Center Bank and Office Buildings, Milwaukee and Madison, Wisconsin (1974); Sears Tower, Chicago (1974); W.D. and H.O. Wills Corporate Headquarters and Tobacco Processing Facility in Bristol, England (1974); New World Center Multi-Use Complex, Hong Kong (1978); and Arab International Bank Multi-Use Complex, Cairo, Egypt (1980). His latest projects are two Hyatt International Hotels in Cairo (1980) and in Kuwait City (1981).

Graves, Michael

MICHAEL GRAVES WAS BORN IN INDIANAPOLIS, INDIANA, in 1934, and studied at the University of Cincinnati (B. Arch. 1958) and at Harvard University (M. Arch. 1959). Since 1964 he has been principal of Michael Graves, Architect, based in Princeton, New Jersey. His completed buildings in the U.S. include many private houses such as Hanselmann House (1967), Snyderman House (1972), and Crooks House (1976), all at Fort Wayne, Indiana; Benacerraf House (1969), Alexander House (1971 and 1973), Claghorn House (1974), and Schulman House (1976), all at Princeton; Plocek House ("Keystone House"), Warren Township, New Jersey (1977); and Kalko House, Green Brook, New Jersey (1978). Other buildings in the U.S. include Union County Nature and Science Museum, Mountainside, New Jersey (1967); Ear, Nose, and Throat Associates Medical Office, Fort Wayne (1971); Gunwyn Ventures Investment Office, Princeton (1972); Abrahams Dance Studio, Princeton (1977); Fargo-Moorhead Cultural Center between Fargo, North Dakota, and Moorhead, Minnesota (1977–78); and Sunar Furniture Showroom, New York City (1979). In addition to his built work, Graves has been influential through his projects and drawings and has designed murals both for his own buildings and for Transam-

monia, Inc., New York City (1974), the School of Architecture at the University of Texas (1974), John Witherspoon School, Princeton (1978), and the A.M.M.C. offices, New York City (1980). He recently submitted the winning design for the Portland Public Service Building in Portland, Oregon (1980). He has taken part in many exhibitions in the U.S. and Europe, including "40 under 40" (New York, 1966), "Five Architects" (Princeton University, 1974), and "Michael Graves: Projects 1967–1976" (New York, 1976). Graves has been a lecturer and professor at Princeton University since 1962.

Gwathmey, Charles

CHARLES GWATHMEY WAS BORN IN CHARLOTTE, NORTH Carolina, in 1938, and studied at the University of Pennsylvania (1956–59) and at Yale University (1959–62), gaining his M. Arch. in 1962. His current practice, formed in 1968, is Gwathmey, Siegel & Associates, which is based in New York City. The firm has designed a wide variety of buildings in the U.S., including institutional and commercial buildings such as Whig Hall Student Center, Princeton University, New Jersey (1972), and Knoll International Showroom and Office Building, Boston, Massachusetts (1978); public housing; and private residences such as Steel and Grey Residences in Bridgehampton, New York (1971), Cogan Residence in East Hampton, New York (1972), and Friday Residence in Greenwich, Connecticut (1973); as well as a broad range of projects for interiors such as Pearl's Restaurant in New York City. The practice is currently working on East Campus Student Housing for Columbia University, New York City; a science building for Westover School, Middlebury, Connecticut; a building for Greenhill School in Dallas, Texas; Eastern Long Island Regional Art Center in Brookhaven, New York; and Peace Street Housing Project, Columbus, Indiana. The work of Gwathmey, Siegel & Associates is known internationally, and has been recognized through numerous publications, exhibitions, and awards. Gwathmey has been professor of architectural design at Pratt Institute, New York City (1964–66), Princeton University (1966–68), Cooper Union, New York City (1969–70), Harvard University (1970–72), University of California at Los Angeles (1974–76), Yale University (1976–77), and at the Institute of Architecture and Urban Studies in New York City (1978–80). His work was included in the exhibition "Five Architects" (Princeton University, 1974).

Hara, Hiroshi

HIROSHI HARA WAS BORN IN KAWASAKI, JAPAN, IN 1936, and studied architecture at the University of Tokyo (1955–59), receiving his doctorate in 1964. His current practice is Atelier Φ, based in Tokyo. His completed buildings in Japan include several houses such as Awazu House, Kawasaki (1972), Hara House, Machida (1974), and Niramu House, Tokyo (1978); the Shyokydo print gallery; Keishyo Kindergarten, Machida City (1968); and Toba Maritime Museum, Tokyo (1972). He is currently working on several buildings including a nursery school, the Spanish Embassy Building in Tokyo, and Hotel Sakuragaokakaikan. Hara was a founder/director of the Research Studio for Architecture and Space (RAS), and since 1969 has been associate professor at the Institute of Industrial Science, University of Tokyo.

Hardy Holzman Pfeiffer Associates

THIS PRACTICE, BASED IN NEW YORK CITY, WAS SET UP IN 1967 by Hugh Hardy, Malcolm Holzman, and Norman Pfeiffer. Their work in the U.S. includes restoration and extensions of cultural facilities such as the Cincinnati Playhouse in the Park, Ohio (1963–65), Newark Community Center of Arts, New Jersey (1969), the Cooper-Hewitt Museum, New York City (1976), and the St. Louis Art Museum, Missouri (1977); the design of new cultural facilities such as the Orchestra Hall, Minneapolis (1974), the Brooklyn Children's Museum, New York City (1977), and the Boettcher Concert Hall at the Denver Center for the Performing Arts, Colorado (1978); houses including Hadley House, Martha's Vineyard, Massachusetts (1967), Schaefer House (project 1972), and von Bernuth House, Dobbs Ferry, New York (1974); other buildings include Mount Healthy School, Columbus, Indiana (1972), Occupational Health Center, Columbus (1973), and Firemen's Training Center, New York City (1975).

Hejduk, John

JOHN HEJDUK WAS BORN IN 1929 IN NEW YORK CITY AND studied at Cooper Union (1947–50). He worked in the office of I.M. Pei (*q.v.*) and Partners from 1956 to 1958 and set up in private practice in 1965 in New York City. His work consists mainly of projects such as the Diamond Series Houses (1962–66), One-Half House (1966), Bernstein House, Mamaroneck, New York (1968), and Bye House, Ridgefield, Connecticut (1972–74); as well as the renovation and restoration of the foundation building of Cooper Union in New York City (1975) and the installation design of several exhibitions. Since 1966 he has participated in many exhibitions in Europe and the U.S. including "Five Architects" (Princeton University, 1974) and "Cemetery for the Ashes of Thought" at the Venice Biennale, 1975, and his work has been published internationally in periodicals and books. Hejduk has taught at the University of Texas (1954–56), Cornell University (1958–60), and Yale Graduate School of Design (1961–64), as well as at universities in Europe. Since 1964 he has been professor of architecture and, since 1975, dean of the School of Architecture at Cooper Union.

Helliwell, Boh

BOH HELLIWELL WAS BORN IN 1944 AT THUNDER BAY, northwest Ontario, Canada, and studied architecture and environmental studies at the University of Manitoba from 1963 to 1969, and architecture at the Architectural Association, London, England, from 1972 to 1974. Since 1974 he has worked on Hornby Island, Canada, with Blue Sky Design, a design/build group which also includes Ed Colin and Michael McNamara (q.v.). Helliwell has been involved in the design of many buildings and houses including Rothstein Chalet; and in environmental schemes such as the Banff National Park (with Jack Long) and Lincoln Park Development, Calgary (1976, awarded first prize with Jack Long and Gary Andrishak). He is currently working on designs for Graham House on Hornby Island, Rothstein guest house, and Wyndam-Helliwell barn conversion. He has contributed articles on handbuilt houses to magazines including *Architectural Design* and *The Canadian Architect*; and co-authored an article with Jack Long entitled "Architectural and Environmental Guidelines—Banff National Park."

Hertzberger, Herman

HERMAN HERTZBERGER WAS BORN IN AMSTERDAM, THE Netherlands, in 1932, and studied at the Delft Technical University. After graduating in 1958, he set up his own office in Amsterdam. His completed buildings in The Netherlands include a student hostel in Amsterdam (1959–66); the Lin Mij factory extension in Amsterdam-Sloterdijk (1964); the Montessori Primary School in Delft (1966); eight experimental houses (Diagoon) in Delft (1971); Centraal Beheer Office Building in Apeldoorn (1972, with Lucas & Niemeyer); De Drie Hoven Old People's Home in Amsterdam (1974); and the Vredenburg Music Center in Utrecht (1979). He is currently working on designs for housing in Westbroek (near Utrecht) and in Kassel, West Germany; city renewal in Amsterdam; extensions to the Sint Joost Academy of Arts in Breda and to the Montessori School in Delft; and a building for the State Department of Social Security in The Hague. His work has been published internationally in many periodicals and books. Hertzberger was editor of the Dutch magazine *Forum*, together with Aldo van Eyck (q.v.), Jacob Bakema, and others from 1959 to 1963. He has been visiting professor at universities in the U.S. and Canada, and since 1970 has been professor at the University of Delft.

Higueras, Fernando

FERNANDO HIGUERAS'S BUILDINGS AND MANY PROJECTS include private residences, collective housing, hotels, school and university buildings, offices, hospitals, religious buildings, industrial buildings, and urban projects. Among his completed buildings are the Central Institute for Restoration of the Ministry of Education and Science in Madrid, Spain (1965, awarded first prize in a national competition); a new major theater in Burgos, Spain (1967, awarded first prize in a national competition); a new Town Hall in Amsterdam, The Netherlands (1967); and a new Town Hall in Ciudad Real, Spain (1970). In 1980 he was the only Spanish architect invited to take part in a restricted international competition in Cologne to design a building to commemorate the twenty-fifth anniversary of the firm DOM. His projects and completed buildings have won many awards since 1953, and have been reviewed in magazines and books. Higueras has contributed articles to many Spanish periodicals.

Hollein, Hans

HANS HOLLEIN WAS BORN IN VIENNA, AUSTRIA, IN 1934 and studied at the Akademie der Bildenden Künste in Vienna, and in the U.S. at the Illinois Institute of Technology (1958–59), and at the University of California, Berkeley, where he received his M.Arch. in 1960. Between 1960 and 1964 he worked in various architectural offices in Australia, South America, Sweden, and Germany, and then set up in private practice in Vienna. His completed buildings include the Retti Candle Shop, Vienna (1965); Richard Feigen Gallery, New York City (1970); Olivetti Building, Amsterdam, The Netherlands (1970); Guest Rooms at the Siemens Headquarters, Munich, West Germany (1972); Schullin Jewelry Shop, Vienna (1974); Perchtoldsdorf Town Hall interior renovation, Austria (1976); Museum of Glass and Ceramics, Tehran, Iran (1977); Austrian Travel Bureau, Vienna (1978); and Israel Tourist Information and Travel Agency, Vienna (1979). He has taken part in several exhibitions including "Hans Hollein: Work and Behaviour, Life and Death, Everyday Situations" at the Venice Biennale (1972). Hollein has been editor of *Bau* since 1965, and professor at the Academy of Art, Düsseldorf, West Germany, since 1970.

Hopkins, Michael John

MICHAEL HOPKINS WAS BORN IN 1935 IN DORSET, ENGLAND, and studied at the Architectural Association in London, where he received his A.A. Dip. His current practice is Michael Hopkins Architects based in London. His completed buildings in England include a house in Hampstead, London (1978), which won the RIBA Architecture Award (1977) and the Civic Trust Award (1979), and a draught beer department for Greene King in Bury St. Edmunds, Suffolk (1978). Hopkins is currently working on office buildings for Tube Investments in London, for IBM in Birmingham, and for Dataflow in The Netherlands; a warehouse for Greene King in Bury St. Edmunds and a building system, SSSALU (Short Span Structure in Aluminium), which won the Award of Merit in the 1980 International Aluminium Extrusion Design Competition.

▲ 530 HANS HOLLEIN
Haus Molag, Vienna, Austria, 1977, 1980–81, model

I

Ishii, Kazuhiro

KAZUHIRO ISHII WAS BORN IN 1944 IN TOKYO, JAPAN, AND studied at the University of Tokyo under Arata Isozaki (*q.v.*) and at Yale University School of Architecture under Charles Moore (*q.v.*), James Stirling (*q.v.*), and Louis I. Kahn (*q.v.*), where he received his M.Ed. in 1974. He worked for Isozaki in Tokyo in 1969, and since 1970 has been in private practice there. His completed buildings in Japan include "54 Windows" (Soya Clinic and Residence) in Kanagawa (1975); schools such as "54 Roofs" (Takebe Nursery School), Okayama (1979), and Naoshima Junior High School, Kanagawa (1979); and private houses such as Ishii Residence in Tokyo (1972) and the Honda Residence in Aoyama, Tokyo (1978). He is currently working on houses in Okayama, and on the Akiyama Building. Ishii has lectured at Waseda University in Tokyo and at the University of California at Los Angeles, and has written many articles and a book, *Yale, Architecture, Commuting* (1977).

Ishiyama, Osamu

OSAMU ISHIYAMA WAS BORN IN OKAYAMA, JAPAN, IN 1944, and studied at the Waseda University School of Architecture, Tokyo, completing the graduate course in 1968. In that same year he organized a group of architects and craftsmen named DAM-DAN. His completed buildings include the Fantasy Villa. Ishiyama became a lecturer at Waseda University School of Architecture in 1972.

Isozaki, Arata

ARATA ISOZAKI WAS BORN IN 1931 IN OITA CITY, JAPAN. HE graduated from the University of Tokyo in 1954, and worked with Kenzo Tange (*q.v.*) until 1963, when he set up his own practice, Arata Isozaki Atelier, based in Tokyo. His work in Japan includes several private houses such as the Nakayama House in Oita (1964) and Yano and Aoki Houses in Tokyo (1964 and 1979); the head office and six branch offices of the Fukuoka Mutual Bank (between 1967 and 1973); the Iwata Girls' High School in Oita (1963–64); libraries in Oita (1962–66) and Kitakyushu (1972–74); museums such as the Gunma Prefectural Museum of Fine Arts in Takasaki (1971–74) and the Kitakyushu City Museum of Art (1972–74); public buildings such as the Fujimi Country Club, Oita (1973–74), Kamioka Town Hall (1975–78) and West Japan General Exhibition Center, Kitakyushu (1975–78); and the site planning, layout of urban trunk facilities and mechanics and electronics for the Festival Plaza at Expo '70, Osaka. Works in progress include the Town Center of Tsukuba Academic New Town, Tsuchiura, for the

Japan Housing Corporation and the Audio Visual Center of Oita City. Isozaki contributed several projects to the Japanese "Metabolism" exhibition of 1962, and has also participated in the XIV Triennale (Milan, 1968); the 1976 Venice Biennale, at which he was responsible for the layout of the Japanese section; "Arata Isozaki Retrospective" (London, 1976); "A New Wave of Japanese Architecture" (U.S., 1978); and "Space-Time in Japan MA" (New York, 1979). His work has been published internationally, and his collected writings are available in two volumes—*Kukan-e* (1971) and *Shuho-ga* (1979). Isozaki has lectured at universities throughout the world, and has been a visiting professor at American schools including the University of California at Los Angeles, Columbia University, and the Rhode Island School of Design.

Ito, Toyo

TOYO ITO WAS BORN IN 1941 IN SEOUL, KOREA, AND STUDIED at the University of Tokyo, Japan. From 1965 to 1969 he worked in the office of Kiyonori Kikutake (*q.v.*) and in 1971 founded URBOT in Tokyo. His work in Japan includes private houses in Tsujido (1970), in Sengataki, in Nakano (1975–76), in Kamiwada (1976), and in Chuo-Kinkan (1979); Hotel D Sugadaira (1977); and two PMT Buildings (1978 and 1979, one at Nagoya). He is currently translating into Japanese *The Mathematics of the Ideal Villa and Other Essays* by Colin Rowe.

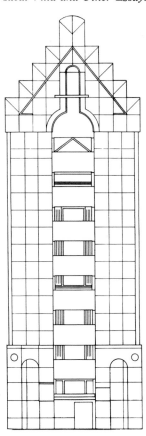

◀ 531 KAZUHIRO ISHII
Gable Building, Tokyo,
Japan, 1978–80, elevation

▶ 532 PHILIP JOHNSON
Office Building, Houston,
Texas, 1981–, model

J

Jahn, Helmut

HELMUT JAHN WAS BORN IN 1940 IN NUREMBERG, WEST Germany, and studied at the Technische Hochschule in Munich (1960–65) and in the U.S. at the Illinois Institute of Technology (1966–67). Since 1967 he has worked for C.F. Murphy Associates in Chicago, and became a partner and the director in charge of planning and design in 1973. His completed buildings in the U.S. include sports facilities such as the Kemper Memorial Arena in Kansas City, Missouri (1974), the St. Mary's College Athletic Facility at South Bend, Indiana (1977), and La Lumière Gymnasium, La Porte, Indiana (1978); garages; libraries such as the Michigan City Public Library, Indiana (1977); courts buildings in Maywood, Illinois, and Richmond, Virginia (1976); and public buildings such as the Kansas City Convention Center, Missouri (1976). He is currently working on designs for a police headquarters in Chicago; offices; a library; a post office; a bank; and two convention centers, one in Atlantic City, New Jersey, and the other in Des Moines, Iowa. He has won many awards for his work, which has been published in several international publications. Jahn has lectured at various universities and professional societies, and has contributed articles to magazines including *Bauen und Wohnen* and *Architectural Record*.

Johansen, John

JOHN JOHANSEN WAS BORN IN 1916 IN NEW YORK CITY, and studied at Harvard University, where he received his B.S. in 1939 and M.Arch. in 1942. He worked for Marcel Breuer (1942) and for Skidmore, Owings, and Merrill (1945–48) before setting up his own practice in New Canaan, Connecticut. Since 1970 he has been in partnership with Ashok M. Bhavnani based in New York City. His completed buildings, mainly in the U.S., include the Museum of Art, Science, and Industry, Bridgeport, Connecticut (1961); the U.S. Embassy in Dublin (1964); the Indianapolis Opera House, Indiana (1963); Goddard Library for Clark University, Worcester, Massachusetts (1968); Mummers' Theater, Oklahoma City (1970); as well as schools and several private residences and housing schemes. He is currently working on a design for Staten Island College, New York City. Johansen's work has won several awards and been exhibited and published in several international architectural magazines. He has lectured extensively in the U.S. and Europe, and in addition to being an architect he is also a painter and printmaker, and has written a book entitled *The New Urban Aesthetic* (1972).

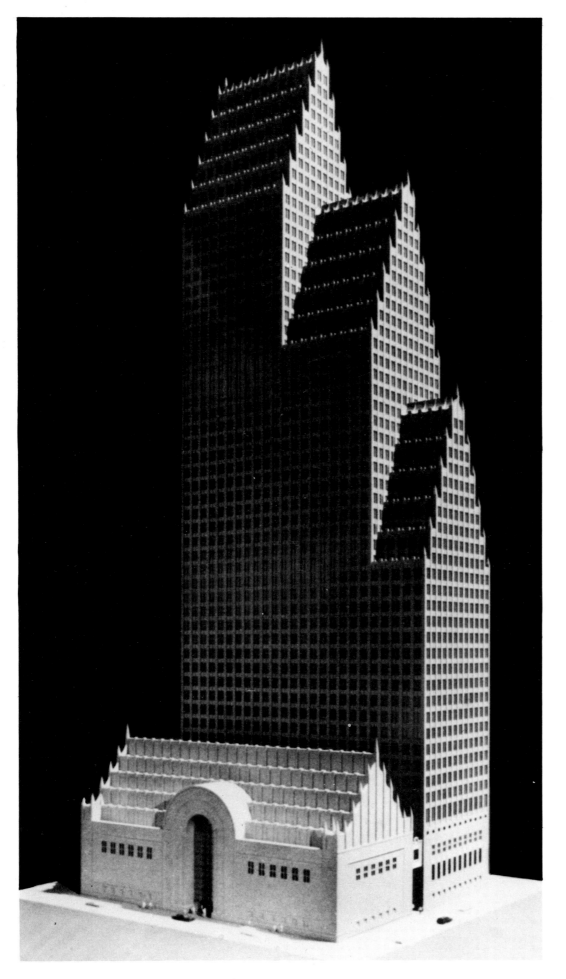

Johnson, Martin

MARTIN JOHNSON WAS BORN IN SALE, CHESHIRE, ENGLAND, in 1946, and studied at the Manchester College of Art (1964–67) and at the Architectural Association in London (1967–71), receiving his A.A. Dip. in 1971. He worked with Michael Brown, landscape architect, in London (1971–72) before setting up in private practice based in Dorking, Surrey, in 1972. His architectural works in England are mainly small scale and include a private house and group practice for three doctors in Ealing, London (1975); a house for Graham Ovenden, Cornwall (1975–); the interior design and furniture for a private library (designed 1978, pending): a large decorative "Victorian" conservatory in Somerset (1979); rebuilding of a house in Holland Street, London (designed 1978, pending); and he is currently working on the restoration of a thirteenth-century Peel Tower and Hall in Northumberland. Johnson has taken part in three exhibitions including one at the Royal Academy of his design for the Ovenden House (1978).

Johnson, Philip

PHILIP JOHNSON WAS BORN IN CLEVELAND, OHIO, IN 1906, and studied at Harvard University (1923–30) and at the Harvard Graduate School of Design, where he received his B.Arch. in 1943. He was director of the Department of Architecture at The Museum of Modern Art in New York from 1930 to 1936, and again from 1946 to 1954. Johnson first practiced as an architect in Cambridge, Massachusetts (1942–46), and then in 1954 set up in private practice in New York City. Since 1967 he has been in partnership with John Burgee in Johnson/Burgee Architects based in New York City. His completed buildings in the U.S. include houses such as the controversial Glass House (Philip Johnson House, 1949) and Hodgson House (1951) both in New Canaan, Connecticut, Oneto House, Irvington, New York (1951), and Boissonnas House, New Canaan (1956); religious buildings including Kneses Tifereth Israel Synagogue, Port Chester, New York (1956), and Garden Grove Community Church, California (1976–80); cultural facilities such as the New York State Theater, Lincoln Center, New York City (1964); museums including the Amon Carter Museum of Western Art, Fort Worth, Texas (1961), Sheldon Memorial Art Gallery, University of Nebraska, Lincoln (1963), the East and Garden Wing additions to The Museum of Modern Art, New York City (1964), and the Art Museum of South Texas, Corpus Christi (1972); libraries including the Boston Public Library addition, Massachusetts (1974); commercial and industrial buildings including the Seagram Building, New York City (with Mies van der Rohe and Kahn and Jacobs, 1958), I.D.S. Center, Minneapolis, Minnesota (1973), Pennzoil Place, Houston, Texas (1976), and the AT&T Building, New York City (1978–); university buildings such as the Kline Science Center, Yale University, New Haven, Connecticut (1965); and other work including Asia House, New York City (1959), New York State Pavilion at the World's Fair, New York (1964), John F. Kennedy Memorial (1966) and Thanksgiving Square (1977), both in Dallas, Texas. Johnson has won many awards and prizes for his work, and both his work and writings have been extensively published.

Kahn, Louis I.

LOUIS I. KAHN WAS BORN ON THE ISLAND OF SAARAMA, Estonia (now U.S.S.R.), in 1901, and emigrated to the U.S. in 1905. He studied at the University of Pennsylvania, graduating in 1924 with a degree in architecture. After working in various architects' offices as a draftsman and designer, he was in private practice in Philadelphia from 1937 until his death in 1974. His many completed buildings in the U.S. include housing commissions such as the Morton Weiss House, Norristown, Pennsylvania (1948–49), Mill Creek Public Housing, Philadelphia (1952–62), and Esherick House, Chestnut Hill, Pennsylvania (1959–61); cultural facilities including the Theater of the Performing Arts, Fine Arts Center, Fort Wayne, Indiana (1965–74); museums including the Yale Art Gallery, New Haven, Connecticut (1951–53), and the Kimbell Art Museum, Fort Worth, Texas (1966–72); university buildings including the Richards Medical Research Building, University of Pennsylvania, Philadelphia (1957–64), Library and Dining Hall for the Phillips Exeter Academy, New Hampshire (1967–72), and the Center for British Art and Studies, Yale University (1969–74). His other buildings include Laboratory Buildings, Housing and Community Center for the Salk Institute, La Jolla, California (1959–65); Unitarian Church and School Building, Rochester, New York (1959–67); Sher-E-Banglanagar, new capital complex, including Ayub Hospital, for Dacca, Bangladesh (1962–74); Institute of Management, Ahmedabad, India (1962–74); and a Family Planning Center in Khatmandu, Nepal (1970–74). There have been exhibitions in the U.S. and Europe of Kahn's work, which has won many awards and prizes and been published internationally in books and periodicals. Kahn was consultant architect to the Philadelphia City Planning Commission from 1946 to 1952 and from 1961 to 1962; chief critic in architectural design (1947–52) and professor of architecture (1948–57) at Yale University; and professor of architecture at the University of Pennsylvania from 1957 to 1974. He was a member of Team Ten.

Kallmann and McKinnell

THIS PARTNERSHIP WAS SET UP IN BOSTON, MASSACHUSETTS, in 1962 by Gerhard Kallmann and Noel McKinnell. Their completed buildings in the U.S. include City Hall, Boston (1968, with Edward Knowles); Phillips Exeter Academy Athletic Facilities, New Hampshire (1970); Boston Five Cents Savings Bank (1972); master plan for Harvard University athletic facilities, Cambridge, Massachusetts (1972); Dudley Street Library, Boston (1976); Woodhull Medical and Mental Health Center, New

York City (1977); and Cardinal Cushing Park, Boston (1977). They have won several awards for their work, which has been published internationally in magazines including *Architects' Journal, Newsweek,* and *Architecture d'Aujourd'hui.*

Kijima, Yasufumi

YASUFUMI KIJIMA WAS BORN IN HAEJU, KOREA, IN 1937, and studied at Waseda University, Tokyo, Japan, graduating in 1962. He worked in the studios of Kenzo Tange (*q.v.*) and Ichiro Kawahara, and since 1970 has been head of the Yasufumi Kijima + YAS and Urbanists studio in Tokyo. His work in Japan includes Matsuo Shrine, Kumamoto (1975–76); Good Russet House; Small Feudal House; Villa on a Hillside, Atami; La Mancha's House (Somegoro's House); Shobu-Kan; the Julian House; the White House, Minami Azabu (1977); and a structure in Shirakawa Park, Kumamoto. His projects include one for the Prime Minister's House in Dublin, Ireland (1979). He is currently working on a design for the Yaesu Tennis Club House. Kijima has contributed articles to *A + U* and *The Japan Architect,* and written a book entitled *Mediterranean Architecture* (1979). Since 1971 he has taught at the School of Architecture at Kumamoto University, Japan.

Kikutake, Kiyonori

KIYONORI KIKUTAKE WAS BORN IN KURUME CITY, JAPAN, in 1928, and studied at Waseda University, Tokyo (1946–50). Since 1953 he has been principal of Kiyonori Kikutake and Associates based in Tokyo. His completed buildings in Japan include Sky House (Kikutake House), Tokyo (1958); Izumo Shrine Administration Building, Izumo (1963); Tokoen Hotel, Yonago (1964); Pacific Hotel, Chigasaki (1966); Tower for Expo '70, Osaka (1970); Pasadena Heights Housing, Mishima (1974); and "Aquapolis," International Ocean Exposition, Okinawa (1975). His competition projects include the International Conference Hall at Kyoto, Japan (1963), and United Nations Low-Cost Housing, Lima, Peru (1969, awarded first prize). Kikutake has won many awards and prizes for his work, taken part in exhibitions, and written several books. Since 1965 he has been director of the Urban Industry Company in Tokyo, and, since 1974, director of the Japan Architects Association, of the Association of Tokyo Architectural Design Supervision, and of the Japan Society of Future Research. He has been a lecturer at Waseda University since 1959, and is currently executive director of the Tokyo Y.M.C.A. Institute of Design.

Kleihues, Josef Paul

JOSEF PAUL KLEIHUES WAS BORN IN RHEINE, WEST GERMANY, in 1933, and studied at the Technical University in Stuttgart (1955–57) and in Berlin, where he received his Dip. Ing. in 1959. Since 1962 he has been in private practice in Berlin as an architect and town planner. His completed buildings in Germany include private residences and public housing such as the Block 270 Housing Development, Vineta Platz, Berlin (1972–76, with M. Schonlau), and Town Center Housing and Commercial Development, Wulfen New Town (1975–80, with U. Falke); medical facilities such as the Neukölln Hospital, Berlin (1973–81, with J. König); cultural facilities such as the Museum

in Blankenheim (1976–81, with R. Hauser); and commercial and industrial buildings such as the Main Workshops for the Municipal Refuse Collection Depot, Berlin (Phase I 1969–73, Phase II 1975–79, with W. Stepp). He is currently working on the German Steel Museum at Solingen (with M. Baum) and the Gerleve Monastery extensions, Coesfeld (with Eggers and U. Falke). Kleihues was initiator and director of "Life and Work on the Ruhr," an Industrial Environmental Study Project (1975–78); has been initiator and director of Dortmund Architecture Days since 1975 and of Dortmund Architectural Exhibitions since 1976; and he is currently director of the Internationale Bauausstellung Berlin 1984. He has been professor of design and architectural theory at the University of Dortmund since 1973, and editor and publisher of *Dortmunder Architekturhefte* since 1975.

Koolhaas, Rem

REM KOOLHAAS WAS BORN IN AMSTERDAM, THE NETHERLANDS, in 1944. He was first a filmscript writer and then studied architecture at the Architectural Association in London, England. He moved to New York in 1972 and started incidental collaboration with O.M. Ungers at Cornell University. A year later he became Visiting Fellow at the Institute for Architecture and Urban Studies in New York City. He is currently a partner in the Office for Metropolitan Architecture (*q.v.*), and is working on a major commission for the extension of the Dutch Parliament in The Hague. Koolhaas has written a book entitled *Delirious New York: A Retroactive Manifesto for Manhattan,* which was published in 1978.

Krier, Leon

LEON KRIER, YOUNGER BROTHER OF ROB KRIER (*q.v.*), WAS born in Luxembourg in 1946 and moved to England in 1968. He attended the University of Stuttgart, West Germany, for six months (1967–68), and then was assistant to James Stirling (*q.v.*) in London (1968–70 and 1973–74) and project partner with J.P. Kleihues (*q.v.*) in Berlin (1971–72). He set up his own practice in 1974. Among his projects are social centers for the Piazza Navona, Piazza San Pietro, and Via Corso in Rome, Italy (1977); urban schemes for the La Villette Quarter, Paris, France (1976), and the city center of West Berlin, West Germany (1977); and educational complexes such as the Lycée Classique, Echternach, Luxembourg (1970), and a school for five hundred children at Saint-Quentin-en-Yvelines, France (1977–79). His most recent projects are designs for a facade for the Venice Biennale (1980) and for a recreational and urban area at Tegel, West Berlin (1980). Krier is author of *The Reconstruction of the European City* (1978) and editor of *James Stirling: Buildings and Projects 1950–74* (1974) and *Rational Architecture* (1978). Krier has lectured at the Architectural Association, at the Royal College of Art in London, England, and at Princeton University.

▶ 533 ROB KRIER
Ritterstrasse Housing,
Berlin, West Germany,
1978–80

Krier, Robert

ROB KRIER WAS BORN IN LUXEMBOURG IN 1938 AND subsequently emigrated to Austria. He studied at the Technical University in Munich, West Germany, receiving his Dip. Ing. Arch. in 1964, and then worked in the offices of O.M. Ungers (*q.v.*) in Cologne (1965–66) and of Frei Otto (*q.v.*) in Berlin and Stuttgart (1967–70) before setting up in private architectural and urban studies practice in Vienna, Austria, in 1976. Although his completed buildings comprise only the Siemer House, Warmbronn, West Germany (1968–73), Dickes House, Bridel, Luxembourg (1974), and Social Housing, Ritterstrasse, Berlin, West Germany (1978–80), Krier has been influential through his theories on urban space and has produced urban schemes for cities such as Stuttgart, Vienna, and Berlin. Krier has written several articles and books including *Stadtraum in Theorie und Praxis* (1975; Eng. trans. *Urban Space*, 1979), and is currently completing a sequel volume, *Architectural Composition*. He has been professor at the Technical University in Vienna since 1975.

Kroll, Lucien

LUCIEN KROLL WAS BORN IN BRUSSELS, BELGIUM, IN 1927, and studied architecture at the Ecole Nationale Supérieure de la Cambre and city planning at the Institut Supérieur de la Cambre and the Institut Supérieur International d'Urbanisme in Brussels. He was in partnership with the architect Charles Vandenhove in Brussels from 1951 to 1957, and in private practice in Brussels since 1957, when he established Atelier Kroll. His completed buildings include large-scale housing complexes such as that at 20 avenue Louis Berlaimont, Auderghem, Brussels (1961–65), the Dominican House, Froidmont, Belgium (1975), and the housing development for Cergy-Pontoise New Town, near Paris, France (1978–79); schools; religious buildings such as the Benedictine Monastery in Gihindamuyaga, Rwanda (1969), and the Convent for the Dominican Sisters, Ottignies, Belgium (1974–75); and university buildings such as the Para-

medical Faculty Buildings Complex for the Catholic University of Louvain, Woluwe, Belgium (1970–77, partially built). Kroll has organized numerous art and architecture exhibitions in Belgium since the fifties and designed several exhibitions including "Exposition Esthétique Industrielle," Liège, Belgium (1956), and "Belgian Architecture," Colegio di Arquitectos, Barcelona, Spain (1965). He was a founder member of Institut d'Esthétique Industrielle, Brussels, in 1956; and since 1970 has been professor of architecture at the Ecole St.-Luc de St.-Gilles in Brussels.

Kurokawa, Kisho

KISHO KUROKAWA WAS BORN IN AICHI PREFECTURE, JAPAN, in 1934, and studied at Kyoto University (B. Arch. 1957) and, under Kenzo Tange (*q.v.*), at the University of Tokyo (M. Arch. 1959; Dip. Arch. 1964). In 1962 he established Kisho Kurokawa Architect and Associates, of which he has been president since 1968, based in Tokyo. His completed buildings in Japan include "Otome Toge" Drive-in Restaurant, Hakone (1969); Capsule House at the Celestial Theme Pavilion, Expo '70, Osaka (1970); Takara Group Pavilion, Expo '70, Osaka (1970); Leisure Capsule LC-30X (1972); Nakagin Capsule Tower Building, Tokyo (1970–72); City Hall, Waki Cho (1975); Fukuoka Bank Head Office, Fukuoka (1971–75); Sony Tower, Osaka (1976); and the National Ethnology Museum, Osaka (1977). He has won several awards for his work, and taken part in a number of exhibitions including "Metabolism," Tokyo (1962), "Team Ten," Urbino, Italy (1964), and "Capsule Architecture," Rome, Italy (1973). Kurokawa is president of Urban Design Consultants, Inc. in Tokyo, principal of the Institute for Social Engineering, Inc. in Tokyo, adviser to the Japanese National Railways, and analyst for the Japan Broadcasting Corporation. Since 1960 he has been a member of the Metabolist Group. Kurokawa has written many articles and books including *Metabolism in Architecture* (1977) and *Concept of Space* (1977).

Lasdun, Sir Denys

DENYS LASDUN WAS BORN IN LONDON, ENGLAND, IN 1914, and studied at the Architectural Association in London (1931–34). He worked in association with Wells Coates in London (1935–37), and then joined Tecton in 1937, acting as partner from 1946 until the firm was dissolved in 1948. From 1949 to 1959 he was in partnership with Lindsey Drake in London. Since 1960 he has been a principal in Denys Lasdun and Partners, which was renamed Denys Lasdun Redhouse and Softley in 1978. His completed buildings in England include several housing schemes in London during the fifties; schools and university buildings including Hallfield Primary School, London (1951), Fitzwilliam College, Cambridge (1959), University of East Anglia, Norwich, Norfolk (1962–69), Charles Wilson Social Centre, University of Leicester (1963), the School of Oriental and African Studies and the Institute of Education and Advanced Legal Studies for the University of London (1965, 1973–78); medical facilities such as the Royal College of Physicians, London (1960–64); cultural facilities including the National Theatre on the South Bank, London (1967–76); and two feasibility studies—for the Courtauld Institute, University of London precinct (1977), and for IBM U.K., Ltd. Headquarters Buildings, South Bank, London (1978). Lasdun has won many awards for his work which has been published internationally in books and periodicals, and he has taken part in several exhibitions including "Ten Years of British Architecture 1945–1955" (London, 1956) and "The Architecture of Denys Lasdun and Partners" (London, 1976). He has lectured at universities in Britain and the U.S. including Massachusetts Institute of Technology and Harvard University.

Le Corbusier

LE CORBUSIER WAS BORN CHARLES-EDOUARD JEANNERET IN La Chaux-de-Fonds, Switzerland, in 1887. He emigrated to France in 1917, and adopted the pseudonym Le Corbusier in 1920. He studied engraving at the School of Applied Arts, La Chaux-de-Fonds (1900–05), and then worked in the offices of the architects Josef Hoffmann in Vienna (1907), Auguste Perret in Paris, and Peter Behrens in Berlin (1910). He worked in private practice as an architect, based in Paris, from 1917 until his death in 1965. Le Corbusier was one of the most prolific and important architects of the twentieth century, and a recognized pioneer of the Modern Movement. His many buildings and projects include private residences such as the Domino Houses (project 1914), Citrohan Houses (first project 1920), La Roche-Jeanneret Houses, Auteuil, France (first project 1923), Villa Savoye, Poissy, France

(1929–31), Charles de Bestegui Apartment, Paris, France (1930–31), and Week-End House at La Celle-Saint-Cloud, Paris (1935); large-scale housing projects such as the apartment block at 24 rue Nungesser-et-Coli, Paris (1933), Durand Housing, Oued-Ouchaia, Algeria (project 1933–34), and the Unité d'Habitation buildings at, for example, Marseilles, France (1946–52); government buildings such as those at Chandigarh, India (1950–65), namely, High Court, Governor's Palace, Secretariat Building, and Legislative Assembly Building; religious buildings including Notre-Dame-du-Haut, Ronchamp, France (1950–55), and Couvent de la Saint-Marie-de-la-Tourette, Eveux-sur-l'Arbresle, near Lyons, France (1957–60); university buildings including the Carpenter Center for the Visual Arts, Harvard University, Cambridge, Massachusetts (1961–64, under the supervision of J.L. Sert); office buildings including the United Nations Headquarters in New York City (1947, as one of a team of international architects); and the Pavillon de l'Esprit Nouveau, Exposition des Arts Décoratifs, Paris, France (1925). There have been many exhibitions of his work at galleries and museums throughout the world, and his work has been reviewed internationally in countless books and magazine articles. Le Corbusier was architectural adviser at Chandigarh, India, from 1951 to 1959; and founder editor, with Amédée Ozenfant and Paul Dermée, of the magazine *L'Esprit Nouveau* (1919–25). He was a founder member in 1928 of C.I.A.M. and of A.S.C.O.R.A.L. in Paris in 1942. Between 1921 and 1956 Le Corbusier lectured extensively at universities in Europe and the U.S., as well as writing many books including *Vers une Architecture* (1923), *La Ville Radieuse* (1935), *La Maison des Hommes* (1942, with François de Pierrefeu), and *Les Trois Etablissements Humains* (1945). He died at Cap Martin, France, in 1965.

Lumsden, Anthony

ANTHONY LUMSDEN WAS BORN IN BOURNEMOUTH, ENGLAND, in 1928, and emigrated to the U.S. in 1954. He studied at the University of Sydney School of Architecture in Australia, receiving his B. Arch in 1951. He was project designer with Eero Saarinen and Associates in Bloomfield Hills, Michigan, from 1954 to 1960, then senior designer with Kevin Roche/John Dinkeloo in Hamden, Connecticut (1962–64). Since 1964 he has been vice-president and principal in charge of design at Daniel, Mann, Johnson, and Mendenhall (DMJM) in Los Angeles, California. His completed buildings in the U.S. include Beverly Hills Jewelry Store, Los Angeles (1966, with Cesar Pelli); One Park Plaza, Los Angeles (1970–72); Century Bank Building, Los Angeles (1971–72); Naval Air Reworks Facility, San Diego, California (1972); Marina City, Los Angeles (1972–73); Sepulveda Bridge, Los Angeles; (1973); El Monte Bus Station, Los Angeles (1974); Portland Plaza Building, Portland, Oregon (1974); Roxbury Plaza Building, Beverly Hills, California (1974); University Station, Los Angeles (1975); Los Angeles College, Van Nuys, California (1978); and East Los Angeles Medical Center (1979–80). His projects include Convention Center, Lugano, Switzerland (1972), Sepulveda Water Reclamation Plant, Los Angeles (1972), and Bumi Daya Bank, Jakarta. Indonesia (1972–76). Lumsden has won many awards for his work, and has taken part in several exhibitions in the U.S. and Europe.

McNamara, Michael

MICHAEL MCNAMARA WAS BORN IN 1944 IN IOWA, AND studied art and sociology at De Pauw University, Indiana, from 1963 to 1965, and then, from 1965 to 1968, sociology and architecture at the University of Oregon. He served his architectural apprenticeship in Portland, Oregon (1968), and in Vancouver, Canada (1969–71), and also studied for a year at the Architectural Association in London, England. He moved to Hornby Island in 1971, and set up Blue Sky Design in 1974 with Ed Colin and Boh Helliwell (*q.v.*). He has designed various houses in Canada, both in mainland British Columbia and on Hornby Island, and also a houseboat in Vancouver. McNamara is presently working on designs for the Graham House, Goold House, and renovations to the Usher House, all on Hornby Island; as well as being involved with several projects including Whistler White Water recreational development on Whistler Mountain, British Columbia, two houses, and the continuing development and redevelopment of his own house. He is at present design chairman for Hornby Island new school.

Meier, Richard

RICHARD MEIER WAS BORN IN 1934 IN NEWARK, NEW JERSEY, and studied at Cornell University, where he received his B. Arch. in 1957. Before setting up his own practice, Richard Meier and Associates, Architects in New York City in 1963, he worked in several offices on the East Coast of America including Skidmore, Owings, and Merrill (1959–60) and Marcel Breuer and Associates (1960–63). His completed buildings in the U.S. include residences such as Smith House, Darien, Connecticut (1965–67), and Douglas House, Harbor Springs, Michigan (1971–73); multifamily housing such as Twin Parks Northeast Housing, New York City (1969–72), and Westbeth Artists' Housing, Greenwich Village, New York City (1967–70); medical facilities; museums; cultural facilities; school and university buildings including Elementary School, Columbus, Indiana (1978–), and Hartford Seminary Foundation, Hartford, Connecticut (1978–); commercial and industrial buildings; and town planning. Other buildings include the Monroe Developmental Center, Rochester, New York (1969–74); the Bronx Developmental Center, New York City (1970–76); and The Atheneum (1975–79), the Theatrum (1975), and Pottery Shed for the Robert Lee Blaffer Trust (1975–78), all at New Harmony, Indiana. An adjunct professor of architecture at Cooper Union, New York City, from 1964 to 1973, Meier has also served as visiting professor at Yale University (1975 and 1977) and at Harvard University (1977); as well as lecturing extensively throughout the U.S., Europe, and Japan. His work has been published internationally in many periodicals and books; and he has taken part in several exhibitions including "40 under 40" (New York, 1966) and "Five Architects" (Princeton University, 1974).

Miyawaki, Mayumi

MAYUMI MIYAWAKI WAS BORN IN NAGOYA, JAPAN, IN 1936, and studied at the University of Tokyo, graduating in 1959 and gaining his master's degree in architecture in 1961. In 1964 he established Mayumi Miyawaki, Architect and Associates. His completed buildings in Japan include Blue Box House, Tokyo (1971); Green Box House No.2; White Triangle Restaurant; and branches of the Akita Sogo Bank at Honjō (1973), Morioka, Futatsui, and Kakunodate. In 1971 he participated in the formation of ArchiteXt. Miyawaki was chairman of the Education and Public Relations Committee of the Japan Architects Association in 1972, and in 1976 he became director of that association. He has lectured in Japan

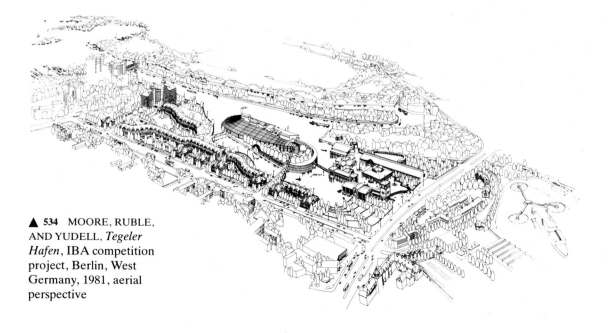

▲ **534** MOORE, RUBLE, AND YUDELL, *Tegeler Hafen*, IBA competition project, Berlin, West Germany, 1981, aerial perspective

at the Sapporo Design Institute (1968), the Kyoritsu Women's College (1971), the Y.M.C.A. Design School (1973), Hiroshima University (1975), and in the architecture department of the Tokyo University School of Engineering (1975).

Moore, Charles

CHARLES MOORE WAS BORN IN BENTON HARBOR, MICHIGAN, in 1925, and studied at the University of Michigan (B. Arch. 1947) and at Princeton University, where he received his M.F.A. (1956) and Ph.D. (1957). He was a partner in Moore Lyndon Turnbull Whitaker in Berkeley, California, from 1962 to 1965, and later (1965–70) of MLTW/Moore Turnbull also in Berkeley; and from 1970 to 1975 he was a principal in Charles W. Moore Associates. Since 1975 he has been a partner in Moore Grover Harper. His numerous completed buildings and projects in the U.S. include many private residences such as Moore House, Orinda, California (1962), Klotz House, Westerly, Rhode Island (1967–70), Tempchin House, Bethesda, Maryland (1968–69), Koizim House, Westport, Connecticut (1969–71), and Burns House, Santa Monica Canyon, California (1972–74); housing schemes such as Xanadune at St. Simon Island, Georgia (1972); university buildings including the Faculty Club for the University of California at Santa Barbara (1966–68) and Kresge College for the University of California at Santa Cruz (1965–74); designs for houses, athletic clubs, and condominiums at Sea Ranch, a recreational community north of San Francisco (from 1964 onward); and the Piazza d'Italia in New Orleans, Louisiana (1975–80) in collaboration with Ron Filson, the Urban Innovations Group (U.I.G.), and Perez Associates, Inc. of New Orleans. Moore has recently received his first European commission—as winner of the Berlin Internationale Bauausstellung 1984 competition for sports, cultural, and residential facilities on Berlin's Tegel Harbor. Moore has won several other awards for his work which has been published internationally in books and periodicals including *Architectural Design, A + U,* and *Architecture d'Aujourd'hui.* Moore has taught at several American universities including Yale University (1962–75). Since 1975 he has been professor of architecture at the University of California at Los Angeles.

Mozuna, Monta Kikoh

MONTA KIKOH MOZUNA WAS BORN IN KUSHIRO CITY, JAPAN, in 1941, and studied at Kōbe University (1961–65). From 1969 to 1974 he was principal of Monta Mozuna Mobile Molgue based in Kōbe, and since 1977 he has been principal of Mozuna Monta Atelier based in Tokyo. His completed buildings in Japan include Anti-Dwelling Box, Hokkaido (1971); Heaven Phase, Wakayama (1976); Yin-Yang House, Hokkaido (1977); a museum in Hokkaido (1977); and Zen Temple, Tokyo (1978). His projects include Cosmic Heritage Projects I, II, III (1975). He is currently working on Mirror House (Yosue House) and the Kushiro Museum. Mozuna has taken part in a number of exhibitions, including "A New Wave of Japanese Architecture," which toured the U.S. in 1978. He lectured at Kōbe University from 1965 to 1976. Mozuna is at present researching a book on Japanese traditional architecture and preparing a catalogue for the "Basara" exhibition.

OMA

THE OFFICE FOR METROPOLITAN ARCHITECTURE WAS OFficially founded in 1975 in New York City, but its principals have been active since the early seventies. These are Rem Koolhaas (*q.v*), and Elia Zenghelis (with Zaha Hadid from 1977 to 1979) in association with Madelon Vriesendorp, Zoe Zenghelis, and O.M. Ungers (*q.v.*).

Elia Zenghelis was born in Greece in 1937. He studied at the Architectural Association in London, England, and then joined Douglas Stephen & Partners. Zenghelis has taught at the Architectural Association in London, and at Columbia, Princeton, and the University of California at Los Angeles in the U.S.

Since its inception OMA has worked on the premise that only a specialized architecture can vindicate the potential of the metropolis as a basis for modern culture. OMA began by considering the problems of London— the "Sleepwalking Metropolis"—in their project Exodus, or the Voluntary Prisoners of Architecture (1972), but shifted their attention to New York in the mid-seventies with a series of theoretical projects which investigated the architectural phenomena that have established themselves within the grid of Manhattan in order to develop a definition of the Culture of Congestion. These consisted of conceptual-metaphorical projects that reconstructed an "ideal" Manhattan, e.g., the City of the Captive Globe (1972) and the Story of the Pool (1976); idealized projects which were in some way extreme but realizable, e.g., the Hotel Sphinx (1975) and the Welfare Palace Hotel (1976–77); and realistic projects that could be realized within existing financial and political structures but incorporating the principle of "Manhattanism," e.g., Roosevelt Island Housing Competition (1975). Alarmed by the proliferation of architectural theories, ideologies, and models during the seventies, OMA has subsequently concentrated on projects that could test and implement its intentions, such as the competition entry for the extension of the Dutch Parliament in The Hague (1978).

From 1980 the office concentrated on Europe. The London office was expanded with Stefano de Martino and Ron Steiner becoming its London partners, and work from Holland and Greece led to the opening of offices in Rotterdam and Athens. The OMA team in Rotterdam includes Jan Voorberg, Stefano de Martino, Kees Christiaanse, Willem Jan Newtelings, Gerard Comello, and Ruurd Roorda, and the office in Athens consists of Katerina Galani and Ilias Veneris. The office has just been joined by Alex Wall to work in conjunction with both the Rotterdam and London offices.

Recent work by OMA includes the Aarnheim Prison

Rehabilitation in Rotterdam, The Hague Dance Theater in Scheveningen, and a planning study for Amsterdam Noord in which OMA is building one street and supervising the whole project. In Greece, two projects are currently under development—the Antiparos Houses and Therma Hotel—with a central Athens complex under investigation. OMA has also contributed two premiated schemes for Koch-Friedrichstrasse and Lützowstrasse to the Internationale Bauausstellung, Berlin (1984).

Otto, Frei

FREI OTTO WAS BORN IN 1925 IN SIEGMAR, SAXONY, EAST Germany, and studied at the Technical University of Berlin, where he received his Dip. Ing. in 1952. He set up his own office in Berlin in 1952, and has worked as a consultant since 1972. He was a founder in 1958 of the Development Center for Lightweight Construction, Berlin, and since 1964 has been a director of the Institut für leichte Flächentragwerke (Institute of Lightweight Structures) at Stuttgart Technical University. Although he is known primarily for his tensile architecture, he also contributed substantially to pneumatic theory in the late fifties, and pioneered prefabricated grid shell systems and the development of convertible roofs. Since 1955 he has designed many exhibition pavilions, for example, for the Cologne Garden and Berlin Interbau Exhibitions in 1957, and for the Swiss National Exhibition at Lausanne in 1963; he also worked on the German Pavilion at Expo '67 in Montreal, Canada, and the roofing for other sports facilities and for several open-air theaters, such as that in Wunsiedel, West Germany (1967). He has also designed a hotel and conference center in Mecca, Saudi Arabia (1968–72). His projects include a sports center in Kuwait (1968, with Kenzo Tange); the City in the Arctic (1970–71); Shadow in the Desert (1972); and a government center in Riyadh, Saudi Arabia (from 1978). From 1958 to 1970 he lectured at universities in the U.S., as well as at several schools and universities in Germany, including the Hochschule für Gestaltung in Ulm. He has won many awards for his work. The Museum of Modern Art in New York held an exhibition of his work in 1971, which was subsequently revived in 1975 and 1977 and traveled through Europe, America, and Asia. Otto has written many articles and books.

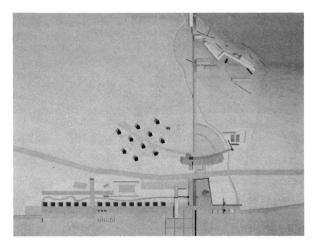

▲ 535 OMA
Therma Hotel. Lesvos, Greece, 1982–,
concept plan painting by Zoe Zenghelis

P

Pei, Ieoh Ming

I.M. PEI WAS BORN IN CANTON, CHINA, IN 1917, AND emigrated to the U.S. in 1935. He studied at the Massachusetts Institute of Technology and at the Harvard Graduate School of Design, where he received his M. Arch. in 1946. He was director of architecture with Webb and Knapp, Inc., in New York City from 1948 to 1955, and since 1955 has been a partner in I.M. Pei and Partners, also based in New York City. His completed buildings in the U.S. include commercial and industrial buildings such as the U.S. National Bank of Denver (Mile High Center), Colorado (1955), and National Airlines Terminal, Kennedy International Airport, New York City (1970); government buildings including the National Center for Atmospheric Research, Boulder, Colorado (1967), and Dallas City Hall, Texas (1977); university buildings such as University Plaza, New York University, New York City (1967), and Dreyfus Chemistry Building, Massachusetts Institute of Technology,

Cambridge, Massachusetts (1970); and cultural facilities such as the Everson Museum of Art, Syracuse, New York (1968), the Des Moines Art Center addition, Iowa (1968), the Mellon Art Center/The Choate School, Wallingford, Connecticut (1972), East Building, National Gallery of Art, Washington, D.C. (1978), John Fitzgerald Kennedy Library Complex (1979) and the Museum of Fine Arts, both in Boston, Massachusetts (1980). His buildings that are currently in progress are the Texas Commerce Tower, Houston; Nestlé Corporate Headquarters, Purchase, New York; Art and Media Center for the Massachusetts Institute of Technology; Raffles City, Singapore; and New York City Convention Center. Pei has won many awards for his work, which has been published internationally in books and periodicals.

Peichl, Gustav

GUSTAV PEICHL WAS BORN IN 1928 IN VIENNA, AUSTRIA, and studied at the Akademie der Bildenden Künste in Vienna (1949–53), receiving his Dip. Arch. in 1953. He has been in private practice in Vienna since 1953. His completed buildings include public housing in Vienna (1960); interior design for Caravelle Aircraft, Austrian Airlines (1961); the Austrian Pavilion at New York's World's Fair (1962–64); branch office for Austrian Airlines, Sofia, Bulgaria (1963); two schools—an elementary school at Krim, Vienna (1961), and Konvent der Dominikanerinnen: High School, Dormitories, Gymnasium, and Cafeteria, Vienna (1963–65); RZ-Meidling Rehabilitation Center, Vienna (1965–67); and broadcasting stations for the Austrian Broadcasting Company (ORF) throughout Austria built between 1970 and 1980. Peichl was editor of the architectural magazine *BAU* from 1964

to 1969, and has worked as a political cartoonist under the pseudonym Ironimus for newspapers in Munich and Vienna since 1955. Since 1973 Peichl has been professor in the School of Architecture at the Akademie der Bildenden Künste, Vienna. He has written a book entitled *Technic and Architecture* (1979).

Pelli, Cesar

CESAR PELLI WAS BORN IN 1926 IN TUCUMAN, ARGENTINA, and studied at Tucuman University, receiving his Dip. Arch. in 1949. In 1952 he emigrated to the U.S. and attended the University of Illinois, receiving his M. S. Arch. in 1954. Pelli spent the following ten years working in the office of Eero Saarinen and Associates, in Bloomfield Hills, Michigan, and New Haven, Connecticut, during which time he acted as project designer for both the TWA Terminal at Kennedy International Airport, New York City, and the Vivian Beaumont Theater at Lincoln Center for the Performing Arts, New York City. In 1964 he joined Daniel, Mann, Johnson, and Mendenhall (DMJM) in Los Angeles, California, as director (1964–66), then vice-president (1966–68), of design. From 1968 to 1977, Pelli was partner in charge of design at Gruen Associates in Los Angeles, where he and a team of designers won first prize in an international competition for the U.S. Organization Headquarters and Conference Center in Vienna, Austria (1969). Notable buildings completed by Gruen Associates under Pelli's direction include the Pacific Design Center in Los Angeles (1975) and the U.S. Embassy in Tokyo, Japan (1976). After becoming Dean of the School of Architecture at Yale University in 1977, Pelli opened his own architectural office, Cesar Pelli and Associates, in

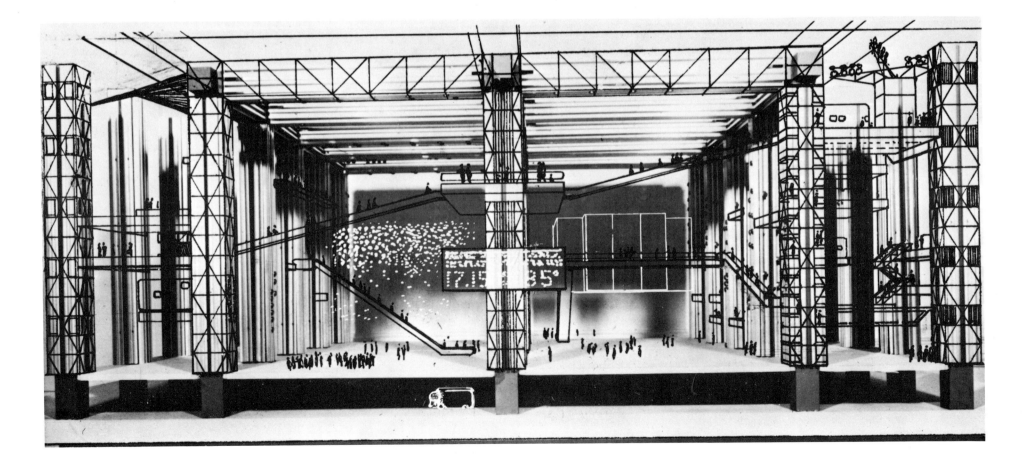

New Haven, Connecticut. His work has received several awards. He is currently working on a residential tower and gallery expansion for The Museum of Modern Art in New York City.

Piano, Renzo

RENZO PIANO WAS BORN IN GENOA, ITALY, IN 1937, AND studied at Milan Polytechnic, Italy, receiving his Dip. Arch. in 1964. Since 1970 he has been in partnership with Richard Rogers, based in London, and since 1977 with Peter Rice (the leading structural engineer on the Pompidou Center's superstructure), based in Genoa, Paris, and London. His completed buildings include commercial and industrial buildings such as Roof Light System for Olivetti, Ivrea, Italy (1968, with M. Zanuso), Fitzroy Street Commercial Centre, Cambridge, England (1970, with Richard Rogers and Fitzroy Robinson), B & B Italia Offices, Como, Italy (1971, with Richard Rogers), Universal Oil Products U.K. Head Office and U.O.P. Fragrances, Ltd. Laboratory, Tadworth, Surrey, England (1973–74, with Richard Rogers), Aston Martin Lagonda, Ltd. Offices, Showroom, Restaurant, Squash Court, and Housing, London, England (1973, with Richard Rogers), and Research Laboratories for P.A. Management Consultants, Cambridge, England (1974–75, with Richard Rogers); housing such as a residential district in Genoa, Italy (1969); cultural and leisure centers such as the Italian Industry Pavilion for Expo '70, Osaka, Japan (1970), and the Pompidou Center in Paris, France (1971–77, with Richard Rogers). Piano has lectured at universities in the U.S. and Europe, and written a book (with Richard Rogers and others) entitled *The Building of Beaubourg* (1978).

Portman, John

JOHN PORTMAN WAS BORN IN 1924 IN WALHALLA, SOUTH Carolina, and studied at the Georgia Institute of Technology, where he received his B. Arch. in 1950. He then worked with two Atlanta firms prior to opening his own office in 1953. Portman now heads the Atlanta firm of John Portman and Associates, architects and engineers; is the principal executive of Portman Properties, a real estate development firm; and is chairman of the Atlanta Merchandise Mart, the cornerstone of his first major project—Atlanta's Peachtree Center (1961–). His completed buildings in the U.S. include the Hyatt Regency O'Hare Hotel in Chicago, Illinois (1967–71); the Embarcadero Center in San Francisco, California, which includes the Hyatt Regency Hotel (1972–74); the Fort Worth National Bank Building in Fort Worth, Texas (1974); the Bonaventure Hotel in Los Angeles, California (1974–77); the Brussels International Trade Mart, Belgium (1975); and the Renaissance Center in Detroit, Michigan (1977); as well as many other hotels and shopping centers, and several schools. He is currently designing the Pavilion, a deluxe hotel in Singapore. Among

his numerous honors and awards is the American Institute of Architects Medal for Innovations in Hotel Design, which he received in 1978. He has written a book with Jonathan Barnett, *The Architect as Developer* (1976).

Portoghesi, Paolo

PAOLO PORTOGHESI WAS BORN IN ROME, ITALY, IN 1931, and studied at the University of Rome, where he received his Dip. Arch. in 1957. He set up in private practice in 1958, and has been in partnership with Vittorio Gigliotti since 1964. His completed buildings in Italy include private residences such as Casa Baldi, Rome (1959–61), Casa Andreis, Scandriglia (1964–67), Casa Bevilacqua, Gaeta (1966–71), and the Casa Papanice, Rome (1969–70); office buildings such as Monte dei Paschi Agency in Rome (1974–78); cultural facilities; schools; the Sacra Famiglia Church at Salerno (1969–73); and a Mosque and Islamic Center in Rome (1976–77). His projects include on Old People's Home in Montecatini, Italy (1963), and the Italian Chamber of Deputies Office Building in Rome (1967). He is currently professor of history at Milan Polytechnic (since 1967); art director of Officina Edizione in Rome (since 1964); director of *Controspazio* in Bari (since 1969); and editor of *ITACA* in Rome (since 1977). Portoghesi has written several books on Gothic, Baroque, and Art Nouveau architecture. He was director of "The Presence of the Past"—the first international exhibition of architecture at the Venice Biennale, 1980.

Price, Cedric

CEDRIC PRICE WAS BORN IN STONE, STAFFORDSHIRE, England, in 1934, and studied at Cambridge University (M.A. 1955) and at the Architectural Association in London, where he received his Dip. A.A. in 1957. In 1960 he founded his present practice, Cedric Price Architects, based in London. His works in England include leisure and cultural facilities such as the Fun Palace Project for Joan Littlewood, London (1961), the Aviary at London Zoo, Regents Park (1961, with Frank Newby and Lord Snowdon), and a Community Centre for Inter-Action Trust, London (1972–77); and industrial and commercial development for private companies and for the government such as Potteries Thinkbelt, Staffordshire (project 1964), and Two Tree Island Development, Southend, Essex (1972, with Yorke, Rosenberg, and Mardall). Price was co-founder with Frank Newby in 1969 of the Lightweight Enclosures Unit in London, and in 1971 of Polyark: Architectural Schools Network. He has written numerous articles for *A.A. Journal, Architectural Design, New Society*, and other international magazines, as well as giving radio and television broadcasts in the U.K., Europe, and the U.S. on architectural planning and design subjects.

R

Ranalli, George

GEORGE RANALLI WAS BORN IN 1946 IN NEW YORK, AND studied at Pratt Institute in New York City (1968–72) and at Harvard University Graduate School of Design, from which he received his M. Arch. in 1973. He has designed in the U.S. a clothes shop, called First of August, in New York City (1976–77), and his projects include Frehley House in Stratford, Connecticut (1979), and a garden for the Fashion Institute of Technology in New York City (1979). Ranalli is currently working on Callender School renovation (converting an old school house into six dwelling units) in Newport, Rhode Island. Since 1977 he has taken part in exhibitions both in the U.S. and Europe. Ranalli has lectured at universities in the U.S. and, since 1976, has been assistant professor of architectural design at Yale University.

Kevin Roche, John Dinkeloo and Associates

KEVIN ROCHE AND JOHN DINKELOO WERE FOUNDER PARTNERS in 1966 of this practice, based in Hamden, Connecticut.

Kevin Roche was born in Dublin, Ireland, in 1922, and studied at the National University of Ireland (1940–45) before emigrating to the U.S. and studying at the Illinois Institute of Technology (1948–49). After working for Eero Saarinen and Associates in Hamden, Connecticut, from 1950 to 1966, he became a partner in Kevin Roche, John Dinkeloo and Associates.

John Dinkeloo was born in 1918 in Holland, Michigan, and studied at the University of Michigan, where he received his B. Arch. in architectural engineering in 1942. He was a partner with Eero Saarinen and Associates from 1959 to 1966, and then became a partner in Kevin Roche, John Dinkeloo and Associates.

Since 1961 the practice work in the U.S. has included museums, cultural facilities, and commercial and industrial buildings such as the Oakland Museum, California (1961); the Ford Foundation Headquarters in New York City (1963); the Knights of Columbus Headquarters in New Haven, Connecticut (1965); the College Life Insurance Company of America Headquarters in Indianapolis, Indiana (1967); the Federal Reserve Bank of New York, New York City (1969); One U.N. Plaza, New York City (1969, 1974–76); the Worcester County National Bank in Worcester, Massachusetts (1970); the Fort Wayne Complex in Fort Wayne, Indiana (1972); and most recently the Conoco Headquarters in Houston, Texas (1979).

Rodia, Simon

SIMON RODIA WAS BORN IN ROME, ITALY, IN 1879, AND moved to the United States before he was twelve years old. Not much is known of his early years: he worked in logging and mining camps, held jobs as a night watchman and construction worker, and was employed in Los Angeles, California, as a tile setter and telephone repairman. He bought a house and lot in Watts, Los Angeles, and in 1921 started building the Watts Towers, which took thirty-three years to complete. When the work was finished, he deeded his lot and his Towers to a neighbor and moved away from the area. Although the Towers were in danger of demolition in the late fifties, their preservation was ensured after a court hearing and a pull test of the tallest spire. They are now in the care of the Committee for Simon Rodia's Towers in Watts. Rodia died in 1965.

Rogers, Richard

RICHARD ROGERS WAS BORN OF BRITISH PARENTS IN 1933 in Florence, Italy, and studied at the Architectural Association in London, England (1953–59), and at Yale University School of Architecture (1961–62). He worked with Norman (*q.v.*) and Wendy Foster and Su Rogers in Team 4 (1963–68), and with Renzo Piano (*q.v.*) from 1970. His current practice is Richard Rogers + Partners, based in London. Rogers's completed buildings include commercial and industrial buildings such as Fitzroy Street Commercial Centre, Cambridge, England (1970, with Renzo Piano), B & B Italia Offices, Como, Italy (1971, with Renzo Piano), Universal Oil Products U.K. Head Office and U.O.P. Fragrances, Ltd. Laboratory, Tadworth, Surrey, England (1973–74, with Renzo Piano), Aston Martin Lagonda, Ltd. Offices, Showroom, Restaurant, Squash Court, and Housing, London, England (1973, with Renzo Piano), and Research Laboratories for P.A. Management Consultants, Cambridge, England (1974–75, with Renzo Piano); and cultural centers including the Pompidou Center in Paris, France (1971–77, with Renzo Piano). Rogers is currently working on designs for Lloyds' Redevelopment in the City of London; Cummins/Fleetguard factory in France; Inmos semiconductor manufacturing facility; and Patscentre Laboratories Phase II, Cambridge. His projects include office systems for Knoll International, New York, and Autonomous House. Rogers has won many awards and competitions, and his work has been published internationally in periodicals. He has lectured at universities in the U.S. and England, and has written a book (with Renzo Piano and others) entitled *The Building of Beaubourg* (1978).

Rose, Peter

PETER ROSE WAS BORN IN MONTREAL, CANADA, IN 1943, and studied at Yale University (1961–70), where he received his M. Arch. in 1970. He was in partnership with F. Andrus Burr and J.V. Righter in Montreal from 1970 to 1974, when he set up in private practice in Montreal. His completed buildings in Canada include his own house in Magog, Quebec (1970); Marosi House (1976) and Bradley House (1977), both in North Hatley, Quebec; Pavillon Soixante-Dix (ski pavilion) at St. Sauveur, Quebec (1976–78, with Peter Lankin and J.V. Righter); and a Clubhouse for the Redbird Ski Club, Mont Tremblant, Quebec (1978–). Rose was a designer

▶ 537   ALDO ROSSI
*Block 10 Kochstrasse/
Friedrichstrasse*, IBA
competition project, Berlin,
West Germany, 1981,
massing model

with Arcop Associates in Montreal in 1972, and since 1970 has been president of the Endless Construction Company in Montreal. He has acted as visiting critic at Canadian and American universities, including Yale University (1974–78).

Rossi, Aldo

ALDO ROSSI WAS BORN IN MILAN, ITALY, IN 1931, AND studied at Milan Polytechnic, receiving his Dip. Arch. in 1959. He is currently in private practice in Milan. His completed buildings in Italy include Town Hall Square and Monumental Fountain, Segrate, Milan (1965, partially realized); Gallaratese 2 Apartment Complex, Milan (1969–70); De Amicis School restoration and additions, Broni (1969–70); single-family housing, Broni (1973, with G. Braghieri); and the Teatro del Mondo, Venice (1979). His many projects and competition projects in Italy include Monument to the Resistance, Cuneo (1962, with L. Meda and G.U. Polesello); Monumental Fountain, City Hall, Milan (1962, with L. Meda); Paganini Theater and Piazza della Pilotta, Parma (1964); School at Trieste (1968–69, with R. Agosto, G. Grassi, and F. Tentori); Municipal Cemetery, Modena (projects 1971, 1973, 1976, for which he received first prize with G. Braghieri; construction 1980–); Villa at Borgo Ticino (1973, with G. Braghieri); general building code and plan for Fagnano Olona (1973); Local Government Office Building, Trieste (1974, with G. Braghieri and M. Bosshard); Student Building, University of Trieste (1974, with G. Braghieri, M. Bosshard, and A. Cantafora); and plan for the city center of Florence (1977, with Carlo Aymonino and others). Rossi has written a number of books, including *L'Architettura della Città* (1966), a study in the typology and morphology of cities; his work has been published internationally in exhibition catalogues and periodicals. Rossi has taken part in many exhibitions throughout Europe, and was in part responsible for the architectural section of the XV Triennale in Milan (1973). He was professor of architectural composition at Milan Polytechnic from 1970 to 1971; director of the International Seminar of Architecture held in Spain in 1976; and is currently editor of *Casabella*.

Rudolph, Paul (Marvin)

PAUL RUDOLPH WAS BORN IN ELKTON, KENTUCKY, IN 1918, and studied at the Alabama Polytechnic Institute (B. Arch. 1940) and at Harvard Graduate School of Design

(M. Arch. 1947) under Walter Gropius. From the establishment of his own office in 1952 (after a four-year partnership with Ralph Twitchell in Florida) to the present, Rudolph has worked on approximately one hundred and sixty commissions, built and unbuilt, fifty-eight of which were houses, apartment interiors, or additions and remodelings, such as the Healy Guest House ("Cocoon House"), Sarasota, Florida (1948), and his own apartment in New York City (1973). The remaining commissions, mainly in the U.S., comprise almost every conceivable building type or urban design problem: for example, the U.S. Embassy in Amman, Jordan (1954, project); educational buildings such as the Jewett Arts Center, Wellesley College, Massachusetts (1955), the Art and Architecture Building, Yale University, New Haven, Connecticut (1958–64), and the Creative Arts Center, Colgate University, Hamilton, New York (1963); campus plans such as that for the Southeastern Massachusetts Technological Institute, North Dartmouth (1963); master plans including buildings for major housing or civic projects; Sarasota-Bradenton Airport, Florida (1955, project); a parking garage in New Haven (1959); a stadium in Saudi Arabia (1968, project); Lake Region Yacht and Country Club in Winter Haven, Florida (1959); office buildings including the Blue Cross/Blue Shield Headquarters in Boston, Massachusetts (1957), the IBM Corporation Complex, East Fishkill, New York (1962), and the Burroughs Wellcome and Company Corporate Headquarters, Durham, North Carolina (1969); libraries including the restoration of the Pitts Theology Library, Emory University, Atlanta, Georgia (1974); government and civic buildings including the Government Service Center in Boston (1963); two important exhibitions including the "Building Arts" exhibition at the Jewett Arts Center in 1960; various plans for parks and other recreational facilities; and innumerable other projects such as the unbuilt Graphic Arts Center and Apartments in New York City (1967). Rudolph has won many awards for his work, which has been published internationally in books and periodicals. He was chairman of the School of Architecture at Yale University from 1958 to 1965, and has contributed articles to many international magazines.

S

Schmidt, Clarence

CLARENCE SCHMIDT WAS BORN IN NEW YORK CITY IN 1897. By 1940 he had established residency in Woodstock, New York, and was employed building drystone walls. He built his own house and terraced garden on the slopes of Ohayo Mountain, New York, and from about 1948 expanded and transformed the five-acre site into what is now known as the House of Mirrors. By 1967 the Ohayo Mountain complex had reached saturation point, and when the House of Mirrors burned down in 1968 he moved into his car, which became the basis for a new house, the Mark II. At the end of 1971, Mark II also caught fire, and in 1972, at the age of seventy-five, Schmidt was confined to a nursing home.

Sert, José Lluis

JOSÉ LLUIS SERT WAS BORN IN BARCELONA, SPAIN, IN 1902. He studied at the Escuela Tecnica Superior de Arquitectura in Barcelona, where he received his Dip. Arch. in 1929. He worked in Paris, France, from 1929 to 1931 as assistant to Le Corbusier and Pierre Jeanneret, and had his own practice in Barcelona from 1929 to 1937, during which time he helped to organize the G.A.T.C.P.A.C. group of architects, affiliated with C.I.A.M. In 1939 he emigrated to the U.S. and has been in practice there since, his current partnership being Sert, Jackson and Associates, established in 1963 and based in Cambridge, Massachusetts. His completed buildings, mainly in the U.S., include housing, most notably the Peabody Terrace Married Students' Housing, Harvard University, Cambridge, Massachusetts (1963–64), "Eastwood" Housing, Roosevelt Island, New York (1971–75), and "Riverview" Housing, Yonkers, New York (1971–75); campus work at Harvard University, including the Center for the Study of World Religions (1958–60), Holyoke Center (1958–65), Carpenter Center for the Visual Arts (1961–63, as supervisory architect for Le Corbusier), and Undergraduate Science Center (1970–73); Central Campus of Boston University on the Charles River, Boston, Massachusetts (1960–66); museums including the Museum of Contemporary Art for the Maeght Foundation, Saint-Paul-de-Vence, France (1959–64), and the Miró Foundation Center for the Study of Contemporary Art, Barcelona

(1972–75). There was an exhibition of his work in Madrid, Spain, in 1978, and his buildings have been recognized and published internationally in periodicals and books. Sert was professor of architecture and Dean of the Graduate School of Design at Harvard University from 1953 to 1969, and also consultant to the Harvard Planning Office (1956–69). He was president of C.I.A.M. from 1947 to 1956. He is co-author of several books, including *The Heart of the City* (1952), *Antoni Gaudí* (1960), and *The Shape of Our Cities* (1961).

SITE

SITE (SCULPTURE IN THE ENVIRONMENT) IS A MULTIdisciplinary architecture and environmental art organization chartered in New York City in 1970 for the purpose of exploring new concepts for the urban/suburban visual environment. Through a process or perspective which the group terms De-architecture, the projects of SITE shift the traditional emphasis of building from formal concerns to information and commentary, from architecture as design to architecture as art. The principals of the current SITE group are Alison Sky, Emilio Sousa, Michelle Stone, and James Wines. Their completed buildings in the U.S. include showrooms for Best Products Co., such as Peeling Project, Richmond, Virginia (1971–72), Indeterminate Facade, Houston, Texas (1974–75), Notch Project, Sacramento, California (1976–77), Tilt Showroom, Towson, Maryland (1976–78), Hialeah Showroom, Florida (1978–79), and Cutler Ridge Showroom, Florida (1978–79); as well as unbuilt proj-

ects such as Interstate 80 Rest Stop, Nebraska (1974), Molino Stucky (project entry for the Venice Biennale, Italy, 1975), Terrarium Showroom in California (1978, pending), Madison Avenue project in New York City (1978, pending), and Water Gallery (1978, pending). In addition to built objects, SITE have produced a series of books on environmental arts and architecture under the collective title *ON SITE:* the most recent survey of their work is *SITE: Architecture as Art* (1980). Since its inception there have been over six hundred articles dealing with the projects and ideas of SITE in the architecture, art, and popular press of twenty-five countries.

Smith, Thomas Gordon

THOMAS GORDON SMITH WAS BORN IN 1948 IN OAKLAND, California, and studied at the University of California, Berkeley, where he received his B.A. in painting and sculpture in 1970 and his M.Arch. in 1975. His completed buildings include Laurentian House and Tuscan House, Livermore, California (1979–80); he is currently working on an altar, tabernacle, and rood screen for the Church of St. Joseph of Arimathea in Berkeley. Since 1976 his project work has consisted mainly of private houses such as the Doric House (1976), Ionic House, and Paulownia House (1977), Matthews Street House (1978), and Richard Long House (three projects, 1978–80), and there have been several exhibitions of his work in American museums. Smith has lectured at American universities and contributed articles to various magazines and catalogues.

▶ **538** JAMES STIRLING, MICHAEL WILFORD AND ASSOCIATES, *The Clore Gallery for the Turner Collection*, Tate Gallery, London, England, 1980–84, detail of the model

Soleri, Paolo

PAOLO SOLERI WAS BORN IN TURIN, ITALY, IN 1919 AND emigrated to the U.S. in 1955. He studied at Turin Polytechnic, graduating with a doctorate in architecture in 1946. Awarded a scholarship, he went to the U.S., where he took up an apprenticeship with Frank Lloyd Wright in Arizona from January 1947 to September 1948. In 1950 he returned to Italy and worked in private practice in Turin and southern Italy until 1955. Since 1956 he has been president of the Cosanti Foundation in Scottsdale, Arizona. His built work, mainly in the U.S., includes the House in the Desert, Cave Creek, Arizona (1951–52, with Mark Mills); Artistica Ceramica Solimene Ceramics Factory, Vietri-sul-Mare, near Salerno, Italy (1953); Earth House, Scottsdale (1956); the Cosanti Foundation, Scottsdale (1956–70); Outdoor Theater, Institute of American Indian Arts, Santa Fe, New Mexico (1966); and Arcosanti (community for five thousand people), near Cordes Junction, Arizona (1969–). His work has been published internationally in periodicals and in a book entitled *The Architecture of Bridges* (1948). Soleri has taken part in several exhibitions including "The Architectural Vision of Paolo Soleri" at the Corcoran Gallery, Washington, D.C. (1970). Soleri's writings include the books *Arcology: The City in the Image of Man* (1970) and *The Bridge Between Matter and Spirit is Matter Becoming Spirit* (1973). His involvement with the Arcosanti projects has been time consuming, and the need to raise sufficient capital to complete the project (which will possibly take between fifteen and twenty years) has taken Soleri from Los Angeles, California, to Delhi, India, as well as to most of the European capitals over the past decade on lectures, broadcasts, and promotional tours.

Stern, Robert A.M.

ROBERT STERN WAS BORN IN NEW YORK CITY IN 1939, AND studied at Columbia University (B.A. 1960) and at Yale University (M.Arch. 1965). He was designer in the office of Richard Meier (*q.v.*) in New York (1966), and in partnership with John S. Hagmann from 1969 to 1977. Since 1977 he has been principal of Robert A.M. Stern Architects, based in New York City. His completed buildings in the U.S. include many private residences such as Wiseman House, Montauk, Long Island, New York (1966–68), Poolhouse for the Danziger House, Purchase, New York (1970–71), Beebe House, Montauk (1971–72), Poolhouse for the Bourke House, Greenwich, Connecticut (1974), Lang House, Washington, Connecticut (1974), Westchester House, Armonk, New York (1975), Leonard Stern Townhouse, New York City (1975), McGarry/Appignani Bedroom, East Hampton, Long Island (1979), and Cohn Houses, Chilmark, Massachusetts (1980), and Llewellyn Park, New Jersey (1980); other buildings include the Jerome Greene Building, Columbia University School of Law, New York City (1975–77). His most recent projects are the Chicago Tribune Tower (1980), Venice Biennale exhibit (1980), and "Modern Architecture after Modernism," a pavilion in the "Forum Design Exhibition" at Linz, Austria (1980). He has received numerous awards for design including first prize in a national competition for one thousand units of housing for Roosevelt Island, New York (1975); and his work has been published internationally in books and periodicals. Stern has organized many symposia and ex-

hibitions including "40 under 40" (a traveling exhibition, 1966), a continuing series of exhibits for the Architectural League of New York in 1965–66, an exhibition called "Some Younger New York Architects" (Columbia University and Boston Architectural Center, 1971–72), and "The Presence of the Past" (Southern California Institute of Architecture, 1980). Stern has been lecturer and professor at Columbia University since 1970; in addition, he has lectured at universities throughout the U.S. and has written books and articles on contemporary architecture for many periodicals.

Stirling, James

JAMES STIRLING WAS BORN IN 1926 IN GLASGOW, SCOTLAND, and studied at Liverpool University (1945–50), where he received his Dip. Arch. and then, until 1952, at the School of Town Planning and Regional Research in London. He was senior assistant with Lyons, Israel, and Ellis from 1953 to 1956, and during this period was also involved with the I.C.A. Independent Group. Stirling set up in private practice in 1956 with James Gowan (until 1963), and then with Michael Wilford (from 1971). Since 1956 his practice work, mainly in England, has included housing such as Runcorn New Town Housing, Cheshire (1967–76), and low-cost housing in Lima, Peru (1969–76); school and university buildings such as the Leicester University Engineering Building (1959–63), Cambridge University History Building (1964–67), Andrew Melville Hall, University of St. Andrews, Fife, Scotland (1964–68), Queens College, Oxford (1966–71), and Rice University School of Architecture, Houston, Texas (1979–); museums such as the Tate Gallery Extension in London (1980–); commercial and industrial buildings including the Olivetti Training School in Haslemere, Surrey (1969–72); and several projects in West Germany such as the headquarters of Siemens AG, near Munich (1969), Meineke Strasse, Berlin (1976), Staatsgalerie New Building and Chamber Theater, Stuttgart (1977–82), and Bayer A.G. PF Zentrum, Monheim (1978). There have been several exhibitions of his work; and he has given lectures in the U.S. and throughout Europe on his partnerships' buildings and design philosophy. Stirling was awarded the RIBA Gold Medal in 1980.

Superstudio

SUPERSTUDIO, FOUNDED IN 1966, IS A GROUP OF DESIGNERS based in Florence, Italy. There are six members: Adolfo Nataline and Cristiano Toraldo di Francia, co-founders of Superstudio, Roberto Magris (joined 1967), Piero Frassinelli (joined 1968), and Alessandro Magris and Alessandro Poli (both joined 1970). Their projects include Continuous Monument (1967); Istogrammi d'Architettura (1969); Memorial Park and Monument to the Partisans of the Resistance, Modena, Italy (1970); and designs for interior furnishings. Superstudio, together with Archizoom, edited the Milanese magazine *IN*.

Taft Architects

TAFT ARCHITECTS WAS FOUNDED IN 1972 IN HOUSTON, Texas, by John J. Casbarian, Danny Samuels, and Robert H. Timme. Their completed buildings—all in Texas—include Peaceable Kingdom Barn, Navasota (1973); M. Penner Men's Store, Houston (1974); Rosenberg Building, Galveston (1975); 213–215 Tremont Street, Galveston (1975); Galveston Historical Foundation Exhibition Modules, Galveston (1975); Estes House, Houston (1976); Purnell Stables, Waller (1978); Municipal Control Building addition, Quail Valley, Houston (1979); Rockefeller's Night Club, Houston (1979); Hendley Building, Galveston (1979); and Grove Court Townhouses, Houston (1980). They are currently working on four buildings: three in Houston—Y.W.C.A. Downtown Branch and Metropolitan Office Building, Catholic Student Center, and Brown Townhouse; and one in Beaumont, Texas—Adaptive Re-use and Restoration of Jefferson Theater. The firm has received national design recognition including four awards from the Texas Society of Architects, three from the Houston chapter American Institute of Architects, two from the national American Institute of Architects Homes for Better Living Program, and a design citation from *Progressive Architecture*. The partners in Taft Architects are also on the faculty at the School of Architecture at Rice University and the University of Houston.

Takeyama, Minoru

MINORU TAKEYAMA WAS BORN IN SAPPORO, JAPAN, IN 1934, and studied at Waseda University, Tokyo (1956–58), receiving his M.Arch in 1958, and at Harvard University on a Fulbright scholarship (1959–60). Between 1960 and 1964 he worked for several architects in the U.S. and Denmark including José Lluis Sert, Hideo Sasaki, Isamu Noguchi, Jørn Utzon, Arne Jacobson, Finn Juhl, and Henning Larsen. Since 1965 he has been president of Minoru Takeyama and the United Actions, based in Tokyo and Sapporo (from 1975). His completed buildings in Japan include private residences such as Atelier Indigo (his own studio), Sapporo (1976), and public housing; hotels such as the Hotel Beverly Tom in Hokkaido (1973); hospitals such as the Nakamura Brain Surgery Hospital in Sapporo (1978); commercial and industrial buildings such as Ichi Ban Kahn and Ni Ban Kahn Omni-Rental Stores in Tokyo (1970) and the Pepsi Cola Canning Plant in Hokkaido (1972). He has taken part in several exhibitions including "Body Furniture" (1970) and "Body Lighting" (1974), both in Tokyo. Takeyama has written several books and many articles for Japanese periodicals, and has served as visiting lecturer, critic, and professor at universities in Japan and the U.S. He has been a member of ArchiteXt since 1971, and a member of the board of the Japan Architects Association since 1975.

Tange, Kenzo

KENZO TANGE WAS BORN IN IMABARI, JAPAN, IN 1913, AND studied at the University of Tokyo (1935–38 and 1942–45), receiving his D.Eng. in 1959. Since 1961 he has been principal of Kenzo Tange & Urtec, urbanists and architects, based in Tokyo. His completed buildings, mainly in Japan, include Hiroshima Peace Center (1949–56); Prefectural Government Office, Kagawa (1955–58); National Gymnasia for the Tokyo Olympics (1961–64); St. Mary's Cathedral, Tokyo (1961–65); Press and Broadcasting Center, Yamanashi (1961–67); Kagawa Prefectural Gymnasium (1962–64); Dentsu Office Building, Tokyo (1965–67); University of the Sacred Heart, Taipei, Taiwan (1965–67); Yukari Nursery School, Tokyo (1966–67); Shizuoka Press and Broadcasting Center, Tokyo (1966–67); Kuwait Embassy and Chancery, Tokyo (1966–70); and master plan, trunk facilities, and Festival Plaza for Expo '70, Osaka (1966–70, as head of a group of architects). Since 1970 Tange's work has been increasingly —though not exclusively—outside Japan and includes such buildings as the Turkish Embassy and Chancery, Tokyo (1973–77); Headquarters Building, University of Tokyo (1973–77); Farah Park Hotel, Tehran, Iran (1974); Sogetsu Hall and Office, Tokyo (1974–77); Imperial Iranian Embassy, Tokyo (1975–); three buildings comprising the new Presidential Palace, a public garden, and Sports City in Damascus, Syria (1975–); Japanese Embassy in Mexico City, Mexico (1975–76); and King's Palace and the Crown Prince's Palace in Jidda, Saudi Arabia (1977–). Tange has won many awards and prizes for his work which has been published internationally in books and periodicals. He has been professor at the University of Tokyo since 1946, as well as visiting professor at the Massachusetts Institute of Technology (1959–60) and at Harvard University (1972). Tange, who has honorary doctorates from American and European universities, has written several books including *Japan in the 21st Century* (1971, with Kenzo Tange Team).

Terry, Quinlan

QUINLAN TERRY WAS BORN IN 1937 IN LONDON, ENGLAND, and studied at the Architectural Association in London (1955–61), receiving his diploma in 1961. He worked with Raymond Erith from 1962 until Erith's death in 1973 on designs in England such as Kingswalden Bury, Hertfordshire (1970), new Common Room building at Gray's Inn, London (1971), and the restoration of St. Mary's, Paddington Green, London (1972). Work in England undertaken after Erith's death includes seven houses at Frog Meadow, Dedham, Essex (1969–80); ten garden buildings at West Green (1974–79); Waverton House, Gloucestershire, for Jocelyn Hambro (1979–80); Church Hall for St. Mary's, Paddington Green (1980): and Newfield Park, Ripon, Yorkshire, for Michael Abrahams (1980–81). Terry has lectured in London, Oxford, Cambridge, Edinburgh, Stockholm, and Barcelona.

Tigerman, Stanley

STANLEY TIGERMAN WAS BORN IN 1930 IN CHICAGO, IL-linois, and studied at the Massachusetts Institute of Technology (1948–49) and at Yale University School of Architecture (1959–61), receiving his M.Arch. in 1961. He served his architectural apprenticeship in the fifties and early sixties with several practices including George F. Keck, Skidmore, Owings, and Merrill, Paul Rudolph, and Harry Weese. Since 1964 he has been principal of Stanley Tigerman and Associates based in Chicago, and is at present architect-in-residence at the American Academy in Rome, Italy. His completed buildings include five polytechnics in Bangladesh (1966–76); Illinois Regional Library for the Blind and Physically Handicapped, Chicago (1974–78); and several private houses such as Hot Dog House in Harvard, Illinois (1972–73), Daisy House, Porter, Indiana (1975–77), and Animal Crackers (Blender House), Highland Park, Illinois (1976–78). Tigerman is currently working on designs for Pensacola Place; House with a Pompidour; Anti-Cruelty Society Building; Villa Proeh; Bahai Archives; and the Gold Apartment. His projects include The Little House in the Clouds; Instant City; and Floating City. He has won thirty-two awards for his work, which has been published internationally in eighty books and over six hundred magazine and newspaper articles. Tigerman has taught at many universities, and is currently preparing three books for publication. He has been American correspondent for *Architecture d'Aujourd'hui* since 1966; and has represented the U.S. at the Venice Biennales of 1976 and 1980.

Turnbull, William

WILLIAM TURNBULL WAS BORN IN 1935 IN NEW YORK CITY and studied at Princeton University (1952–59). He worked in the office of Skidmore, Owings, and Merrill in San Francisco, California, from 1960 to 1963, when he became a partner in Moore Lyndon Turnbull Whitaker (later MLTW/Moore Turnbull) based in San Francisco. He became a director of this practice as MLTW/Turnbull Associates in 1970. Buildings in the U.S. designed by Turnbull after his independence from Charles Moore (*q.v.*) include numerous private houses such as the Zimmermann House, Fairfax County, Virginia (1975), and Allewelt House, Modesto, California (1975); university buildings such as the Pembroke Dormitories for Brown University, Providence, Rhode Island (1970); Research Building remodeling, San Francisco (1973); and a Library and Cultural Center in Biloxi, Mississippi (1977). At present he is working on San Francisco Port Promenade; State Office Building, Sacramento, California; Hines House in Aspen, Colorado; and Cakebread Winery. Turnbull has taken part in several exhibitions and has won many awards for his work, which has been reviewed internationally in many periodicals and books. He is author of *Global Architecture: MLTW/The Sea Ranch* (1971) and *Global Architecture: Sea Ranch Details* (1976), and has lectured at universities throughout the U.S.

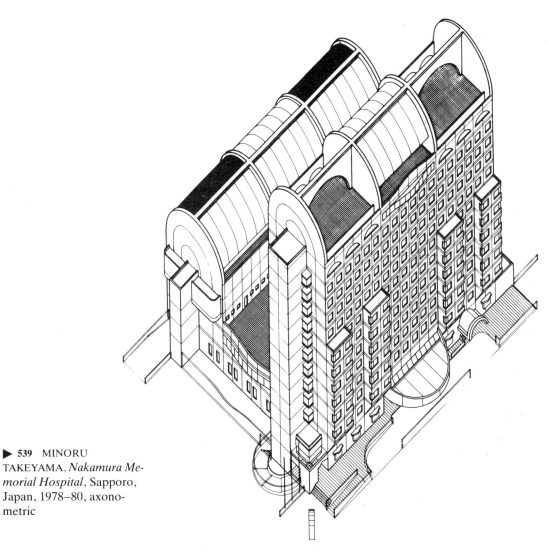

▶ **539** MINORU TAKEYAMA, *Nakamura Memorial Hospital*, Sapporo, Japan, 1978–80, axonometric

Ungers, Oswald Mathias

O.M. UNGERS WAS BORN IN 1926 IN KAISERSESCH, WEST Germany, and studied architecture at the Technical University in Karlsruhe (1947–50). In 1950 he commenced private architectural practice in Cologne, moved to Berlin in 1964, and to Ithaca, New York, in 1970. His completed buildings in West Germany, most of which were built in the fifties, consist mainly of private residences such as his own house in Cologne (1959); and public housing such as the apartment blocks in Dellbrück, Cologne (1958), and Wuppertal (1959). Since 1960, Ungers has produced several influential projects and competition entries for housing schemes such as Student Housing in Enschede, The Netherlands (1964), Ruhwald Housing Estate, Berlin (1966, 1967–68), and housing in Marburg (1976), as well as a scheme for Bremen University (1976), museum complexes including that at Tiergarten (1965), and courts such as the design for the Supreme Court in West Berlin (1979) and a new Courthouse complex (Kammergericht, 1978–79). He has acted as professor of architecture at Cornell University, Harvard University, and the University of California in Los Angeles, and has written numeous articles and books on architecture.

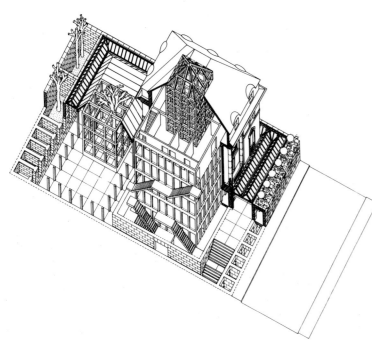

▲ **540** O.M. UNGERS
Architectural Museum,
Frankfurt, West Germany,
1981, cutaway axonometric

Van Eyck, Aldo

ALDO VAN EYCK WAS BORN IN DRIEBERGEN, THE NETHER-lands, in 1918, and studied at the Eidgenössische Technische Hochschule in Zürich, Switzerland (1939–43). He worked as an architect in the Public Works Department in Amsterdam (1946–50) before setting up in private practice in The Hague and Amsterdam in 1952. Since 1971 he has been in partnership with Theo Bosch. His completed buildings, mainly in The Netherlands, include sixty-four houses for the elderly in Amsterdam (1954); a Children's Home in Amsterdam (1957–60); low-income housing in Lima, Peru (1968–70); housing at Zwolle, The Netherlands (1975–77); and Housing for Single-Parent Families in Amsterdam (1976–80). He has won many awards for his work including first prizes for two competition projects: Protestant Church, Driebergen (1965), and master plan for Nieuw Markt area, Amsterdam (1970). Van Eyck was editor of the Dutch magazine *Forum* from 1959 to 1967. Since 1951 he has been visiting lecturer and professor at universities in the U.S. and Europe, as well as writing articles for many magazines. Van Eyck has been a member of Team Ten since 1953.

Van Klingeren, Frank

FRANK VAN KLINGEREN WAS BORN IN AMSTERDAM, THE Netherlands in 1919, and studied civil engineering at Amsterdam Technical College. His completed buildings include the Dronten and Eindhoven agoras in The Netherlands, as well as shops, houses, industrial buildings, community halls, cultural facilities, and the Niarchos shipyard in Athens, Greece. Since giving up his practice in 1972 due to ill health, he has given lectures and seminars at technical colleges in various European countries, and has sat on the jury in twenty competitions in Belgium, France, The Netherlands, Germany, and Austria. He has contributed articles about Hellenic shipyards, the Dronten and Eindhoven agoras, and the philosophy behind their design to leading European architectural magazines.

Venturi and Rauch

THE PARTNERSHIP OF VENTURI AND RAUCH WAS FORMED IN Philadelphia, Pennsylvania, in 1964 by Robert Venturi and John Rauch, and now includes Venturi's wife Denise Scott Brown (joined 1967) and associates Steven Izenour and David Vaughan.

Robert Venturi was born in Philadelphia in 1925, and studied at Princeton University (1943–50), receiving his B.A. in 1947 and M.E.A. in 1950. Between 1950 and 1958 he worked as a designer for the firms of Oscar Stonorov in Philadelphia, Eero Saarinen in Bloomfield Hills, Michigan, and Louis I. Kahn in Philadelphia. He was professor of architecture at the University of Pennsylvania from 1957 to 1965 and at Yale University from 1966 to 1970. Venturi has written articles for many international periodicals and several books including *Complexity and Contradiction in Architecture* (1966) and *Learning from Las Vegas* (1972, with Denise Scott Brown and Steven Izenour).

John Rauch was born in Philadelphia in 1930, and studied at the University of Pennsylvania, graduating in 1957 with a degree in architecture.

Denise Scott Brown was born Denise Lakofski in 'Nkana, Zambia, in 1931, and emigrated to the U.S. in 1958. She studied at the University of Witwatersrand, Johannesburg, South Africa (1948–51), at the Architectural Association in London, England (1952–55), and at the University of Pennsylvania (1958–60), receiving her Master in City Planning in 1960 and her M.Arch. in 1965. Scott Brown has lectured at many American Universities and has written several books and numerous articles for international periodicals.

The completed buildings in the U.S. of Venturi and his partners include both private houses such as the Vanna Venturi House, Chestnut Hill, Pennsylvania (1962), Trubek and Wislocki Houses, Nantucket Island, Massachusetts (1970), Brant House, Greenwich, Connecticut (1971–73), Carl Tucker III House, Katonah, New York (1974–75), Brant House, Tuckers Town, Bermuda (1975–78), and Brant-Johnson House, Vail, Colorado (1976–77); and public buildings including North Penn Visiting Nurses Association Headquarters Building, North Pennsylvania (1960, Venturi and Short), Guild House, Philadelphia (1960–63), Humanities Building (1968) and Social Sciences Building (1970–78) at the State University of New York in Purchase, Dixwell Fire Station, New Haven, Connecticut (1970), Franklin Court, Philadelphia (1972–76), Allen Art Museum extension, Oberlin College, Ohio (1974–77), and Pennsylvania State Faculty Club, Pennsylvania State University (1974–77). Their projects in the U.S. include National Football Hall of Fame (1967), Thousand Oaks Civic Center, California (1969), California City Planning Study (1970), Yale Mathematics Building, New Haven, Connecticut (1970), City Edges Planning Study, Philadelphia (1973), Galveston Development Project, Texas (1975), Pennsylvania Avenue Project, Washington, D.C. (1978–79), and Basco Showroom, Bristol Township, Pennsylvania (1979). Their work has been published internationally in many books and periodicals, and they have taken part in several exhibitions in the U.S. and Europe including "The Work of Venturi and Rauch" (which toured the U.S. in 1965), "40 under 40" (New York, 1965), and "Palaces for People" (New York, 1977).

Walker, Derek

DEREK WALKER WAS BORN IN RIBCHESTER, LANCASHIRE, England, in 1931, and studied architecture, town planning and landscape architecture at Leeds University and at the University of Pennsylvania. He became a chartered architect and planner in 1957 and set up his own office, Derek Walker and Partners, based in Leeds and London, in 1958. Walker worked for the Milton Keynes Development Corporation from 1970 to 1976 as chief architect and planner, and then returned to private practice (Derek Walker Associates based in London, Milton Keynes, Leeds, and Rome). He is also a partner in an interior design, furniture design, and graphics business (Walker Wright Botschi). His buildings in England include the Sacred Heart Church in Leeds (1967) and St. Benedict's, Garforth (1967); three houses that each won the Architectural Design Project Award—Gould House in Leeds (1966), Serenson House in Liverpool (1967), and Ingledew Housing in Leeds (1968); and several buildings in Milton Keynes between 1970 and 1977 such as Sewage Works, System Building for Industry (which won the Office of the Year Award), and Central Area Housing. His current

designs include housing and showrooms in Milton Keynes; an office complex in London; Mizda village in Libya; and Dahran shopping center in Saudi Arabia. Since 1960 he has won many awards for his work. Walker has lectured widely in the U.K. and abroad, has written articles for magazines, and has four books in preparation, including one on the architecture and planning of Milton Keynes.

Walker, Roger

ROGER WALKER WAS BORN IN 1942 IN HAMILTON, NEW Zealand, and studied at the University of Auckland. His completed buildings include houses, commercial buildings, apartment schemes, various tourist buildings, and an airport building; he is currently working on designs for a shopping arcade in Wellington, New Zealand, a workingmen's club, several houses, and Te Awamutu Export Houses. Walker placed second in the competition for the Palmerston North Civic Centre, New Zealand. He has written a book entitled *Architecture 1820–1970*.

Watanabe, Toyokazu

TOYOKAZU WATANABE WAS BORN IN 1938 IN AKITA PREfecture, Japan, and studied at Fukui University, from which he graduated in 1961. From 1964 to 1970 he studied at the Research Institute of Architecture, and then spent two years at the Urban Consultant's Office. His completed buildings in Japan include Doctor's House and Surgery, Ibaraki City (1974); Nakauchi House, Nara (1974–75); Kimura House, Osaka (1975); Romanesque Momoyamadi housing, Osaka (1977); Hō House, Kyoto (1978); and Nakano House, Hyōgo (1979). His projects include Yoshino Artists' Village, Japan, and housing in Jidda, Saudi Arabia. He is currently working on a town house at Izumi, Japan, and a house for a painter.

Yamashita, Kazumasa

KAZUMASA YAMASHITA WAS BORN IN AICHI, JAPAN, IN 1937, and studied at the School of Architecture at the Tokyo Institute of Technology, graduating in 1959. Between 1959 and 1969 he worked in various architects' offices: Nikken Sekkei (1959–64 and 1966–69), Professor Paul Schneider-Esleben in Düsseldorf, West Germany (1964–65), and Colin St. John Wilson in 1966, when he also traveled in the Middle East and Asia. In 1969 he established Kazumasa Yamashita, Architect and Associates. His completed buildings in Japan include Hirano Dental Clinic, Hiratsuka (1973); Kitamura House; Face House, Kyoto (1974); and Office Building, Tokyo (1979). He has lectured in Japan at the Tokyo Institute of Arts and Design (1969), at the Residential School of the Department of Domestic Science of the Japan Women's College (1976), and at the Schools of Architecture at the Nagoya Institute of Technology (1976) and at the Tokyo Institute of Technology (1977).

▶ **541** DEREK WALKER/ MKDC, *Central Milton Keynes*, Buckinghamshire, England, 1974–77, aerial perspective drawing by Helmut Jacoby

is better for him than sharpness of definition: like romantic or democratic, or indeed Modern, it is a good banner under which to gather everything. This generalizing tendency does explain part of its success and one of its attractions for Davis. It also explains why those such as E. H. Gombrich are suspicious of the label. As he told me in conversation, it has the same "historicizing" sound as Modernism, suggesting that history is on its side and that it is marching inexorably "post" the Modern period. *This* kind of historicism—the belief in the *Zeitgeist,* progress, the new rendering the old obsolete—was precisely the devil which I claimed Post-Modernism was exorcising from its predecessor. See Charles Jencks, *The Language of Post-Modern Architecture,* Academy Editions, London, 1977, and Rizzoli, New York, 1978; rev. ed., 1981.

7.

See Paul Goldberger, "Architecture: After Post-Modernism" in *The New York Times Book Review,* September 7, 1980, pp. 9, 33–34. For his article on Hardy Holzman Pfeiffer see "Brash, Young and Post-Modern" in *The Sunday Times Magazine,* February 20, 1977.

8.

The title of Hubbard's book, *Complicity and Convention: Steps Towards an Architecture of Convention* (MIT Press, Cambridge, Massachusetts, 1980), is an obvious play on Robert Venturi's title, *Complexity and Contradiction in Architecture.* The book is a partially convincing argument for convention, an argument which, of course, Post-Modernists have made continuously. Hubbard is confusing them with Late-Modernists.

9.

In *The Language of Post-Modern Architecture,* pp. 121–122, I distinguish Modernist aspects in Eisenman's work. I should have used "Late-Modern" for "Supremely Modernist," but my point was to distinguish Eisenman's complex space from his other concerns, which he claimed at the time were ultra-Modern.

10.

A typically early argument on the subject is that of Christian Norberg-Schulz in *Intentions in Architecture* (1964); but the subject never stopped being debated even during the height of the Modernist taboo.

11.

Supposing we were to argue that Peter Eisenman and Richard Meier were Post-Modernists and believed in applied ornament (variable 16), representation (17), metaphor (18), and symbolism (21). They would, of course, deny this, as they have done, but a too-clever historian could disregard their intentions and systematically misread their buildings on each one of these scores. The applied ornament is balcony rails and useless columns, the representation is of the space-time continuum, the metaphor is a ship in both cases, and the symbolism alludes to the Puritan revolution and Cistercianism. This kind of misreading may reveal interesting, suppressed meanings, but it dislocates the architects from the tradition they work in and which they continue.

12.

Charles Jencks, "History as Myth" in Jencks and Baird (eds.), *Meaning in Architecture,* Barrie and Jenkins, London, and George Braziller, New York, 1969.

13.

Alison and Peter Smithson, *Without Rhetoric,* Latimer Publications, London, 1973, and MIT Press, Cambridge,

NOTES

Introduction

1.

See "Post-Modern Classicism—the New Synthesis," *Architectural Design,* Nos. 5/6, 1980, pp. 15–18, an issue I edited. The argument is that Post-Modern Classicism does not have a shared metaphysics, cosmic symbolism, or homogeneous set of norms and forms as did previous classical revivals, in particular eighteenth- and nineteenth-century neoclassicism. Also, it is still Modernist in part, and so must be termed Post-Modern and not neoclassical.

2.

See Arnold Toynbee, *A Study of History,* Vol. 8, Oxford University Press, New York, 1954–59, p. 388; *The Present Day Experiment in Western Civilization,* Oxford University Press, London, 1962, pp. 26–37; and Geoffrey Barraclough, *An Introduction to Contemporary History,* Basic Books, New York, 1965.

3.

Daniel Bell, *The Cultural Contradictions of Capitalism,* Basic Books, New York, 1976, p. 104, quoted from Robert Stern's "The Doubles of Post Modern" in "Beyond the Modern Movement," *The Harvard Architectural Review,* Vol. 1, Spring 1980, pp. 81–82, note 24. Stern's double distinctions between traditional and schismatic Post-Modernism are helpful, if cumbersome, and they might have been clarified had he developed a theory of Late-Modernism in place of his "schismatic post-modernism." Stern's essay is also helpful in assembling some quotations on the subject from sources outside architecture.

4.

Ihab Hassan, "Joyce, Beckett, and the Post-Modern Imagination" in *Tri Quarterly,* Vol. XXXIV, Fall 1975, p. 200. Hassan's usage was pointed out to me by Peter Eisenman.

5.

Arthur Drexler, *Transformations in Modern Architecture,* The Museum of Modern Art, New York, 1979, p. 15.

6.

Douglas Davis, the art and architecture critic for *Newsweek,* initially applied the term Post-Modern to typically Late-Modern buildings—those of Cesar Pelli and Kevin Roche. More recently, however, he seems to have adopted the usage proffered here—seems because he argues in favor of a vagueness (Douglas Davis, "Post-Everything" in *Art in America,* February 1980, pp. 11–13—an interesting compilation of views). An encompassing word

Massachusetts, 1974. This position is complicated by the fact that it implicitly advocates "Rhetoric without rhetoric," that is, neutral objectivity like the *Neue Sachlichkeit*, which itself is a form of rhetoric. However, the position can degenerate quickly into one which promotes unselfconscious building which does not know what it is representing.

14.

Maggie Keswick has illustrated several of these pavilions in her book *The Chinese Garden*, Academy Editions, London, and Rizzoli, New York, 1978, pp. 83, 85, 120, 200.

CHAPTER I
LATE-MODERN DEPARTURES

1.

See George Kubler, *The Shape of Time*, Yale University Press, New Haven, Connecticut, 1962, pp. 80–81. The concept was put forward in 1888 by Adolf Göller.

2.

In his Gallaratese apartment complex, Milan, and elsewhere. Rossi, a Marxist, might not admit to "aesthetic fatigue," disliking its consumerist overtones. However, Socialists, as others, are subject to boredom and its attendant consumption cycles.

3.

See Arthur Drexler, *Transformations in Modern Architecture*, pp. 2, 18–90, 112–156. The classification even mixes in "structure," "People" (e.g., Louis Kahn), and "concepts" (e.g., Fragments). Drexler has an erroneous notion of Post-Modernism, as can be seen by his false attributions to Hamlin, etc. (pp. 14–15).

4.

Ibid., "Organic Form," pp. 54–57. Besides the architects mentioned here (David Jacob, Daniel Grataloup, TAO Design, Vittorio Giorgini, Günther Domenig) there is the work of John Johansen, Fritz Frusher (Wisconsin House), Pierre Szekely (holiday village in Brittany), Ron Kessinger (Golden, Colorado), Winslow Wedin (Maple Plain, Minnesota), and Valerie Batorewicz (with Uniroyal in Connecticut). Also, the self-builders mentioned by William Chaitkin below. Spraying foam on various armatures has yet to result in a sophisticated aesthetic, or one to be combined with the right-angled world of production.

5.

Some of Peichl's sketches of these horizontal "ships" resemble Erich Mendelsohn's drawings: they accentuate the horizontal and dynamic lines with a thick stroke, and the countervolumes and TV aerials with opposite strokes.

6.

See "Rikyu Gray" in *The Japan Architect*, January 1978, and "Architecture of Grays" in *The Japan Architect*, June 1979. Kurokawa has probably been influenced in this latest move by Arata Isozaki's gray work (see Chapter 9).

7.

The writings on Johnson are by now extensive. See John Jacobus, *Philip Johnson*, New York, 1962; Henry-Russell Hitchcock, *Philip Johnson: Architecture 1949–65*, New York, 1966; *A + U*, 1979 6; *Philip Johnson Writings* (ed. Robert A.M. Stern), New York, 1978.

8.

For information on I.M. Pei's earlier work, see *A + U*, 1976 1.

9.

For Kahn, see Heinz Ronner, Shared Jhaveri, and Alessandro Vasella, *Louis I. Kahn Complete Works 1935–1979*, Westview Press, Inc., Boulder, Colorado, 1977, and a review of the literature by William Jordy in *JSAH*, Vol. XXXIX, No. 1, March 1980, pp. 85–89.

10.

See Reyner Banham, *The New Brutalism, Ethic or Aesthetic?*, The Architectural Press, London, 1966. Brutalism as a movement may be considered as a Late-Modern critique of Modernism, although obviously it has many Modernist elements and ideological strands as well.

11.

For J.L. Sert's two housing schemes, see "Design Alternatives for Low-to-Moderate-Income Urban Housing" in the *Architectural Record*, August 1976, pp. 101–109.

12.

See, for instance, Oriol Bohigas, "Aldo van Eyck or a New Amsterdam School" in *Oppositions 9*, 1977, pp. 21–36.

13.

See Chapter 7 for a further discussion. The Serliana is derived from Serlio's illustration of a temple window (1537) which has a large central arch and smaller side openings creating an ABA rhythm, often called the Palladian motif.

14.

See John M. McKean, "Rainbow House" in *Building Design*, June 13, 1980, p. 25.

15.

See Peter Eisenman, "Commentary" in *Oppositions 9*, 1977, p. 21; Arnulf Lüchinger, "Structuralismus" in *Bauen und Wohnen*, Ar. 5, 1974, pp. 209–212 on Hertzberger's Centraal Beheer.

16.

Centraal Beheer has been widely published. See, for instance, "A Dutch Landscape" by Graham Moss in *Building Design*, September 26, 1975; the issue of *A + U* devoted to Hertzberger (77:03); articles by Oriol Bohigas, Alan Colquhoun, and others in the American architectural press; my own *Late-Modern Architecture*, Academy Editions, London, and Rizzoli, New York, 1980, pp. 10–11. For the Music Centre, see *A + U*, 80:04, pp. 57–74.

17.

See Herman Hertzberger, "Architecture for People" in *A + U*, 77:03, pp. 124–146.

18.

Oxymoron is a condensed paradox—for instance, the hard softness of the slick-tech look.

19.

See Peter Collins, *Changing Ideals in Modern Architecture*, Faber and Faber, London, 1965, p. 125.

20.

See my *Late-Modern Architecture*, pp. 11, 46–49 for extreme examples of ornament swallowing the building.

21.

See Reyner Banham, *Megastructures, Urban Futures of the Recent Past*, Thames and Hudson, London, 1976, and Harper & Row, New York, 1977.

22.

See Chapter 8. Apparently Behnisch, who placed second in the Stuttgart competition of 1977, attacked Stirling's circles for being historicist and reminiscent of the thirties.

23.

Joan Kron and Suzanne Slesin, *High-Tech,* Potter, New York, 1978, and Allen Lane, London, 1979. The word is a compilation of high-style and technology and clearly relates to several trends of Late-Modernism discussed here.

24.

I have compared it to Bernini's Palazzo Chigi-Odescalchi (1664) in *Late-Modern Architecture,* p. 11.

25.

Richard Rogers told me that he became aware of these parallels during design, but that they were not consciously sought.

CHAPTER 2
SLICK-TECH
THE RHETORIC OF CORPORATE
PROFICIENCY

1.

Slick-tech is an alternative label to high-tech, and one which I first started using in 1977 to distinguish the sleek, polished, and slippery surfaces of mirror-plate buildings from the more normal curtain walls. It obviously subsumes the Supersensualist attitudes toward plastic and other high-gloss artifacts which I wrote about in 1971. See my *Late-Modern Architecture,* chapters 1.3 and 2.3.

2.

Italy: The New Domestic Landscape, Achievements and Problems of Italian Design (ed. Emilio Ambasz), The Museum of Modern Art, New York, 1972. The subtitle of the exhibition catalogue accurately reflects the dual attitude of the critics.

3.

See "Private Residence, Chicago Suburb" in *Progressive Architecture,* August 1976.

4.

Stirling's Olivetti Training School has been published extensively. See *James Stirling, Buildings and Projects, 1950–74,* Thames and Hudson, London, 1975 and references in my *Late-Modern Architecture.*

5.

See John Portman and Jonathan Barnett, *The Architect as Developer,* McGraw-Hill, New York, 1976.

6.

For I.M. Pei's work, see *A + U,* 1976 1. For an interview with Henry Cobb concerning the John Hancock Tower, see *The International Herald Tribune,* May 23, 1977, p. 12.

7.

A discussion of rhetoric and the membrane can be found in my *Late-Modern Architecture,* chapter 1.3. See also *Philip Johnson and John Burgee* (ed. Nora Miller), New York, 1979.

8.

See *The Architectural Review,* November 1978, pp. 302–303.

9.

For the connections between Mannerism and Post-Modernism, see C. Ray Smith, *Supermannerism: New Attitudes in Post-Modern Architecture,* Dutton, New York, 1977, pp. 78–99. For my argument that Late-Modernism is also Mannerist, see *Late-Modern Architecture,* chapters 1.2 and 1.3, and the beginning of the next chapter in this book.

10.

For Norman Foster's work, see *A + U,* 75:09 and various issues of *Architectural Design* (for example, Vol. 49, No. 2, 1979, devoted to the Sainsbury Centre).

CHAPTER 3
TWENTIES REVIVALISM
THE WHITE, IDEAL PAVILIONS
OF PRIVATE LIFE

1.

The Five architects were named in a book of that title first published in 1972. Sometimes called The New York Five or The Whites, they are Richard Meier, John Hejduk, Charles Gwathmey, Michael Graves, and Peter Eisenman.

2.

See *Five Architects; Eisenman, Graves, Gwathmey, Hejduk, Meier,* Oxford University Press, New York, 1972, pp. 111–121; also *A + U,* 1976 4 devoted to Meier, and *Richard Meier Architect,* Oxford University Press, New York, 1975, with essays by Kenneth Frampton, Arthur Drexler, Philip Johnson, and Colin Rowe.

3.

Colin Rowe, *The Mathematics of the Ideal Villa and Other Essays,* MIT Press, Cambridge, Massachusetts, 1976. The title essay was first published in *The Architectural Review* in 1947.

4.

Peter Papademetriou, "Le Corbusier à la mode . . . ," in *Architectural Design,* January 1971, p. 24. See also the reply by Eisenman in the August issue, p. 520.

5.

"My Statement" in *A + U,* 1976 4, pp. 76–77.

6.

See Kenneth Frampton, "Frontality vs. Rotation" in *Five Architects,* pp. 9–13.

7.

See "Out of Time and Into Space" in *A + U,* 1975 5, pp. 3–4.

8.

See Kenneth Frampton, "John Hejduk and the Cult of Humanism" in *Five Architects,* pp. 135–142.

9.

See *A + U,* 1978 2, " 'Monte Amiata' Housing Complex, Gallaratese, Milan." Lena Wertmuller used the spin and twirl of this scheme in her film *All Screwed Up.*

10.

See Peter Eisenman, "Cardboard Architecture: House I" and "Cardboard Architecture: House II" in *Five Architects,* pp. 15–17, 25–27. "Cardboard is used to question the nature of our perception: . . . is this a building or is it a model? Cardboard is used . . . as a marking or notational system . . . meant to signify the virtual or implied layering . . . "

11.

It took me some years to understand Eisenman's review of our book *Meaning in Architecture (Architectural Forum,* July/August 1970), since it concentrated on an article I wrote elsewhere and not on the book. But later I saw that *his* preoccupation with elitism had led him to concentrate on my article as it was more relevant to this issue (and to the time he spent in England).

12.

See "I guess you win, Peter," the clients' comments on

House III in *Progressive Architecture,* May 5, 1974, pp. 94–96.

13.

See my discussion of Eisenman and Graves in "Irrational Rationalism—The Rats Since 1960," reprinted in *Late-Modern Architecture,* pp. 130–145.

14.

Colin Rowe and Robert Slutzky, "Transparency: Literal and Phenomenal" in *Perspecta 8,* 1963, and "Part 11" in *Perspecta 13/14,* 1971. The first is reprinted in Colin Rowe, *The Mathematics of the Ideal Villa.* For a critical review, see Rosemarie Haag Bletter, "Opaque Transparency" in *Oppositions 13,* 1978, pp. 121–126.

15.

See *Architectural Monographs 5: Michael Graves,* Academy Editions, London, and Rizzoli, New York, 1979, p. 36.

CHAPTER 4
LATE-MODERN SPACE
A SIGN OF AGNOSTICISM

1.

For some of Cedric Price's ideas and projects, see "Potteries Thinkbelt" in *New Society,* June 2, 1966; Royston Landau, *British Architecture,* London, 1968, pp. 74–87; Reyner Banham, *The New Brutalism*; Charles Jencks, *Modern Movements in Architecture,* Harmondsworth and New York, 1973, pp. 284–288. For the Inter-Action Centre there are many articles in magazines (for example, *Building Design,* April 22, 1977).

2.

For the kind of techno-logic expressed here, see Reyner Banham, "Flatscape with Containers" (1966) in *Meaning in Architecture,* pp. 103–108. Banham is discussing the logic of containers and fork-lift trucks and their effect on the environment—the production of "flatscapes"—but the logic extends to the supermarket and shed.

3.

See my "The Supersensualists" (1971–72), reprinted in *Late-Modern Architecture,* pp. 88–97, and my *Modern Movements in Architecture,* pp. 56–57 for quotes from unpublished manuscripts. See also *Italy: The New Domestic Landscape,* pp. 240–251.

4.

See "The Supersensualists."

5.

For Helmut Jahn's work, see, for instance, articles in *Progressive Architecture,* No. 7, 1978, pp. 58–68; *A + U,* 78:07, pp. 3–30; and "Way-out Ahead" by Jim Chapman and Richard Saxon, an interview with Jahn in *Building Design,* June 15, 1979, pp. 26–27. The authors use my typology, including even the notion of "Late-Modern fetish," quite without acknowledgment, thankfully.

6.

The literature on the Pompidou Center is inflationary, but for an early discussion, see *Architectural Design,* Vol. 47, No. 2, 1977, devoted to it.

7.

For Norman Foster, see *A + U,* 75:09, an issue devoted to his work, and *Architectural Design,* Vol. 49, No. 2, 1979, devoted to the Sainsbury Centre, mistakenly hailed as a victory of Modern rather than Late-Modern design by several critics.

8.

Ibid., and also the Introduction to my *Late-Modern Architecture,* pp. 6–9.

9.

For gridism, see my "The Rhetoric of Late-Modern Architecture" in *Late Modern Architecture,* pp. 54–57. Gridism, the irrational grid, is the opposite of the Modernist grid in that the emphasis is placed on the aesthetic and signifying, even emblematic, planes of expression, often *to the detriment of actual function.* Many people misunderstand this, even Late-Modernists themselves, but certainly not Hiromi Fujii or Peter Eisenman.

10.

See Kenneth Frampton, *A New Wave of Japanese Architecture,* Catalogue 10, IAUS, New York, 1978, introduction pp. 7–8 and pp. 28–37. Also Chris Fawcett, "Ideas which operate in the space between floor and ceiling: Fujii Hiromi's Projects" in *Architectural Association Quarterly 6,* No. 2, 1974, pp. 22–30.

11.

For Ranalli's "New York Brownstone," see *Architectural Design,* Vol. 47, Nos. 7/8, 1977, pp. 553–557.

12.

For Anthony Lumsden, see *A + U,* 76:10, pp. 13–16, and subsequent issues of *A + U* and *Domus.*

13.

For Richard Meier, see Chapter 3, Twenties Revivalism, notes 1 and 2.

14.

Arata Isozaki has been extensively published in *The Japan Architect* with several issues devoted to his work. See especially "An Architect in Ambivalence," January 1972; August 1972; and for the Gunma Museum, March 1976.

15.

Arata Isozaki, "Nine Metaphors" in *The Japan Architect,* October/November 1977, p. 21.

16.

Ibid.

Post-Modernism

CHAPTER 5
FROM HISTORICISM
TO RADICAL ECLECTICISM

1.

There were attacks on the International Style when it was conceived in the twenties, by, among others, Lewis Mumford, Goodhart-Rendel, and the Nazis. In the fifties and early sixties, Herbert Gans's *The Urban Villages* and Jane Jacobs's *The Death and Life of Great American Cities* attacked the urban results of Modernism. Norman Mailer, again Mumford, and soon a battalion of critics followed, and these attacks were summarized in Oscar Newman's *Defensible Space* (1972), Malcolm MacEwen's *Crisis in Architecture* (1974), Peter Black's *Form Follows Fiasco* (1976), Brent Brolin's *The Failure of Modern Architecture* (1976), my own *The Language of Post-Modern Architecture* (1977), David Watkin's *Morality and Architecture* (1977), and Gerald R. Blomeyer's *In Oppositions Zur Moderne* (1980). This is only a small, Anglo-Saxon part of the literature (the Blomeyer has many English translations) but the Dutch, Spanish, and Italians were not slower to fault aspects of Modernism.

2.

See Harold Rosenberg, *The Tradition of the New,* New York, 1959, McGraw–Hill paperback, New York, 1965, p. 11. "The famous 'modern break with tradition' has lasted long enough to have produced its own tradition. Exactly one hundred years have passed since Baudelaire . . . " Sigfried Giedion's view of the Modern tradition in architecture is slightly less dedicated to constant revolution and a case could be made that mainstream Modern architecture had become fairly stable by the fifties in spite of its ideology of change.

3.

Bruno Zevi started to attack the formalism of Saarinen and others in the fifties; Reyner Banham attacked neo-Liberty (*The Architectural Review,* April 1959); Nikolaus Pevsner followed with an attack on historicism (1961); Banham's article "On Trial" was published in *The Architectural Review* in 1962; Robin Middleton and *Architectural Design* had attacked Israeli and Dutch designers, Philip Johnson, etc., by 1967.

4.

See *Philip Johnson Writings,* a selection of his essays and occasional pieces. See p. 122 for the quote: "we cannot today *not* know history," 1961, presented to the Architectural League Forum as the opening salvo to the "European" Reyner Banham, who did not "rise to" the oc-

casion (p. 118). Banham, in a review of my *The Language of Post-Modern Architecture* (*TLS,* November 17, 1978), cites an early use of the term Post-Modern in an article on the Dumbarton Oaks Museum (*Architectural Forum,* March 1964), but again it is only in the title, and inconsequential. (See also my answer in *TLS,* December 1, 1978.)

5.

See Robin Boyd, *New Directions in Japanese Architecture,* New York and London, 1968, p. 102.

6.

See Paolo Portoghesi, *Borromini, architettura come linguaggio,* Rome, Cambridge, Massachusetts, and London, 1967, last chapter. See also *Paolo Portoghesi Projects and Drawings 1949–1979,* Centro Di, Florence, and Academy Editions, London, 1979, especially for a list of Portoghesi's writings on Borromini.

7.

Paolo Portoghesi; also Christian Norberg-Schulz, *Alla ricerca dell' architettura perduta, le opere di Paolo Portoghesi e Vittorio Gigliotti,* Officina Edizione, Rome, 1975, pp. 18–28, and my own *Late-Modern Architecture,* pp. 15–18.

8.

See *Late-Modern Architecture,* pp. 15–18.

9.

Norberg-Schulz, *op. cit.*

10.

Paolo Portoghesi, pp. 81–152.

11.

See "Post-Modern Mosque" in *Architectural Design,* Nos. 1/2, 1980, pp. 24–29.

12.

See Robert Venturi, *Complexity and Contradiction in Architecture,* The Museum of Modern Art, New York, 1966; with Denise Scott Brown and Steven Izenour, *Learning from Las Vegas,* MIT Press, Cambridge, Massachusetts, 1972; re-edited with a bibliography, 1977; *Architectural Monographs 1: Venturi and Rauch,* Academy Editions, London, and Rizzoli, New York, 1978 (also with a bibliography). Also see various issues of *A + U* (74:11, 78:01, etc.); an exhibition catalogue edited by Stan von Moos, Zürich, 1979; *Robert Charles Venturi: A Bibliography* by Lamia Donmato, Vance Bibliographies, Monticello, Illinois, 1978. Venturi, like Charles Moore, has "raids" on the past for its lessons and for specific ideas. Portoghesi also uses the past this way, but then treats it in a disinterested fashion in scholarly investigations which reveal rhetorical types.

13.

See Vincent Scully, *The Shingle Style Today or The Historian's Revenge,* George Braziller, New York, 1974, especially p. 1 for the previous sources from the fifties, including Scully's own *The Shingle Style,* New Haven, Connecticut, 1955.

14.

See *Meaning in Architecture;* Geoffrey Broadbent, Richard Bunt, and Charles Jencks, *Signs, Symbols and Architecture,* John Wiley & Sons, Chichester, New York, Brisbane, Toronto, 1980, summarizes some international work in this field.

15.

See Charles Moore and Gerald Allen, *Dimensions, Space, Shape & Scale in Architecture,* New York, 1976; Charles

Moore, Gerald Allen, and Donlyn Lyndon, *The Place of Houses*, Holt, Rinehart & Winston, New York, Chicago, San Francisco, 1974; Kent C. Bloomer and Charles W. Moore, *Body, Memory and Architecture*, New Haven, Connecticut, and London, 1977; "The Works of Charles W. Moore," *A + U*, 78:05, with a selected bibliography.

16.

Moore has taken part in several participatory exercises, and has also designed a church with Ruble and Yudell using participatory methods (1979). For the importance of participation and its relation to taste cultures, see *The Language of Post-Modern Architecture*, pp. 88, 104–107.

17.

See *ibid.* (third edition), postscript.

18.

Ibid., and *Progressive Architecture*, March 1979, which contains an excellent article by Martin Fuller.

19.

See *Buildings for Best Products*, The Museum of Modern Art, New York, 1979. See also Stanley Tigerman's entry, illustration 289.

20.

See Robert A.M. Stern, *New Directions in American Architecture*, expanded edition, New York, 1977; *A + U*, 75:10, issue devoted to Stern and Hagmann, with essays by Stern on "Bow-fronted Houses" and "Influences"; *GA Houses 7*, Tokyo, 1976 for five houses and an article; *Architectural Design*, Vol. 47, No. 4, 1977 for his thoughts on Post-Modernism; and *The Harvard Architectural Review*, 1980, for his most detailed thoughts on this subject.

21.

See also Harold Bloom, *The Anxiety of Influence: A Theory of Poetry*, New York, 1973.

22.

The literature on nineteenth- and early twentieth-century architecture of San Francisco and the Bay Area is now extensive, but see in particular: Thomas Aidala, *The Great Homes of San Francisco*, San Francisco and London, 1974; Sally Woodbridge (ed.) *Bay Area Houses*, Oxford University Press, New York, 1976; David Gebhard *et al.*, *Samuel and Joseph Cather Newsom: Victorian Architectural Imagery in California 1878–1908*, catalogue, UCSB, Santa Barbara, 1979; *Bernard Ralph Maybeck (1862–1957): The Extraordinary Californian Architect, A Bibliography* by James Carlton Starbuck, Vance Bibliographies, Monticello, Illinois, 1978.

23.

Geoffrey Broadbent, "The Road to Xanadu and Beyond" in *Progressive Architecture*, September 1975, p. 79.

24.

See *Late-Modern Architecture*, pp. 93–97; "Post-Modern Classicism," *Architectural Design*, Nos. 5/6, 1980.

25.

See *Architectural Monographs 5*, p. 64. Michael Graves and I had many discussions in 1975 about the importance of explicit versus implicit metaphor and historical references; see my critique that his Benacerraf House is too implicit in its coding in *The Language of Post-Modern Architecture*, p. 67.

26.

See below, in Chapter 10, "Positive/Negative Reversals" and "Demi-Forms and Structured Surprise."

27.

Le Corbusier and the Tragic View of Architecture, London, and Cambridge, Massachusetts, 1973, pp. 150–152; *The Language of Post-Modern Architecture*, pp. 48–49.

28.

See below, in Chapter 10, "The Shifted Axis."

29.

See *Architectural Monographs 5*, p. 86.

CHAPTER 6
FROM STRAIGHT REVIVALISM TO DISTORTED ORNAMENT

1.

Henry-Russell Hitchcock, *Architecture: Nineteenth and Twentieth Centuries*, Penguin Books, Harmondsworth, 1971, p. 533.

2.

See Conrad Jameson, "Architects' Error" in *New Society*, May 8, 1975; "Enter Pattern Books, Exit Public Housing Architects: A Friendly Sermon" in *The Architects Journal*, February 11, 1976; "Radical Traditionalism: A Definition of Territories and Methods" in *Architecture: Opportunities, Achievements* (ed. Barbara Goldstein), RIBA Publications, London, 1977.

3.

Hassan Fathy has not built very much, and Gourna has been ill-used because ancient relics were found on the site—it was pillaged, etc. See his *Architecture for the Poor*, New York, 1973.

4.

For Maurice Culot and his group *ARAU*, see his journal *Archives d'Architecture Moderne*, published in Brussels since October 1975; particularly numbers 9, 10, 12, 14. Also see *Wonen-TA/BK*, August 1975, Nos. 15/16.

5.

Quinlan Terry worked with Raymond Erith, whose practice he continues. See *Classical America IV* (ed. William A. Coles), W.W. Norton & Co., New York, 1977, pp. 125–152; *Architectural Design*, Vol. 49, Nos. 3/4, 1979, pp. 107–116, which illustrates his work to date; and *Quinlan Terry*, Academy Editions, London, and St. Martin's Press, New York, 1980.

6.

See, especially, *Classical America IV*, with articles on Terry, the Getty Museum, and Philip T. Shutze, among others.

7.

An early discussion by Allan Greenberg on Lutyens was his "Lutyens' Architecture Restudied" in *Perspecta 12*, 1969, pp. 129–152.

8.

Ornament became an important topic of debate in the late seventies. A symposium was held at the Architectural Association in London on the subject by myself and Nikolaus Taylor in December 1978—"The Question of Ornament" (unpublished). See Stephen Kieran, "On Ornament" in *VIA*, III, 1977; Boyd Anger, "A Return to Ornament" in *The Architectural Review*, 1976, which generated a controversy that ran for several issues. An exhibition at the Cooper-Hewitt Museum, New York, was organized by Richard Oliver in 1978, and most recently E.H. Gombrich published his wide-ranging *The Sense of Order, a Study in the Psychology of Decorative Art* (Phaidon, Oxford, 1979).

9.

See my "The Free Orders, the Semantic Use of Form" in *Architectural Design*, Nos. 5/6, 1980, pp. 6–10.

10.

Yasufumi Kijima, "Making an Image Sketch After the Building is Finished," in *The Japan Architect*, October/November 1977, p. 48. The issue is on Post-Metabolism.

CHAPTER 7
NEO-VERNACULAR
THE SIGN OF AN INSTANT COMMUNITY

1.

Neo-Vernacular and its related developments, often called Realism or the New Realism in Europe and the shed aesthetic or neo-Shingle Style in America, have not received the detailed scholarly discussions they deserve. Fragments of such a synthesis can be found in my own *The Language of Post-Modern Architecture*, pp. 96–103; Arthur Drexler, *Transformations in Modern Architecture*, pp. 134–154; Sutherland Lyall, *The State of British Architecture*, The Architectural Press, London, 1980.

2.

See Colin Amery and Lance Wright, "Lifting the Witches Curse" in *The Architecture of Darbourne and Darke*, RIBA Publications, London, 1977.

3.

Jane Jacobs, *The Death and Life of Great American Cities*, Penguin Books, Harmondsworth, 1961.

4.

See Robert Maguire, "Something out of the Ordinary" in *Architecture: Opportunities, Achievements*, pp. 69–73.

5.

For Moore on "place," see Robert A.M. Stern, *New Directions in American Architecture*, p. 70; for a European discussion, see my *Modern Movements in Architecture*, pp. 301–327. A comprehensive discussion of the subject can be found in Christian Norberg-Schulz, *Genius Loci: Towards a Phenomenology of Architecture*, Academy Editions, London, 1980 (first published as *Genius loci*, Milan, 1979).

6.

Genius loci.

7.

For a discussion of Van Eyck, see Chapter 1. Van Eyck has told me personally that he does not like brick, nor is he fond of its overuse, and thus the Zwolle Housing should probably be seen as responding more to Theo Bosch's interests than to his own.

8.

Andrew Derbyshire, "Building the Welfare State" in *Architecture: Opportunities, Achievements*, p. 29.

9.

Linda Groat and David Canter, "Does Post-Modernism Communicate?" in an issue of *Progressive Architecture* partly devoted to Post-Modernism, December 1979, called "After Modernism" and edited by Suzanne Stephens.

10.

See "Post-Modern Classicism," *Architectural Design*, Nos. 5/6, 1980, for a fuller discussion by Jeremy Dixon of this scheme and its classification in yet another tradition.

CHAPTER 8
AD HOC AND URBANIST
TOWARD A CITY WITH MEMORY

1.

C.I.A.M. VIII was held at Hoddesdon, England, in 1951 on the subject of "The Urban Core," something people were to be attracted to by "spontaneity." Slabs in the park continued to be built, however, in Brasilia, Chandigarh, or at the Inter-Bau exhibition, Berlin, 1956–57—even by the younger generation. Team Ten modified this approach somewhat during the sixties.

2.

See Alison Smithson, *Team 10 Primer*, Cambridge, Massachusetts, and London, 1968, and Alison and Peter Smithson, *Ordinariness and Light: Urban Theories 1952–60*, Cambridge, Massachusetts, and London, 1970.

3.

For Bruce Goff, see *Architectural Design*, No. 10, 1978, an issue devoted to his work; Jeffrey Cook, *The Architecture of Bruce Goff*, Crosby Lockwood Staples, Ltd., London, and Harper & Row, New York, 1978; David G. De Long, *The Architecture of Bruce Goff: Buildings and Projects 1916–1974*, Garland Publishing, New York, 1977.

4.

See my "Bruce Goff, The Michelangelo of Kitsch" in *Late-Modern Architecture*, p. 164.

5.

Geometric themes are often the starting point for Goff; see Robert Kostka, "Bruce Goff and the New Tradition" in *The Prairie School Review*, second quarter, 1970, p. 11.

6.

See Charles Jencks and Nathan Silver, *Adhocism, The Case for Improvisation*, London and New York, 1972.

7.

See C. Ray Smith, *Supermannerism*, pp. 26–27.

8.

For Roger Walker, see *The Architects Journal*, November 8, 1978, pp. 883–891.

9.

See Russell Walden, "Walker's double code," letter to *The Architects Journal*, February 21, 1979, p. 56.

10.

See John M. Johansen, "The Mummers Theater: A Fragment not a Building" in *Architectural Forum*, May 1968, pp. 65–66.

11.

See Mats Egelius, "Ralph Erskine, the Humane Architect" in *AD Profile 9*, or *Architectural Design*, Nos. 11/12, 1977, an issue devoted to Erskine's work.

12.

See *A + U*, 79:11, pp. 5–56, devoted to Lucien Kroll's work.

13.

See my *The Language of Post-Modern Architecture*, p. 111. Kahn, Giedion, Scully, Rowe, Bacon, Ungers, Moore, and Venturi became interested in Hadrian's Villa in the late fifties and early sixties.

14.

Colin Rowe and Fred Koetter, *Collage City*, MIT Press, Cambridge, Massachusetts, 1978, and London, 1979.

15.

Ibid., p. 7.

16.

See O.M. Ungers, "A Vocabulary" in *Lotus International 15*, 1977, pp. 88–97.

17.

See Geoffrey Broadbent, "The Road to Xanadu and Beyond" in *Progressive Architecture*, September 1975.

18.

See "Post-Modern Classicism" *Architectural Design*, Nos. 5/6, 1980.

19.

See my "Irrational Rationalism—The Rats Since 1960" in *Late-Modern Architecture*, pp. 130–145. Also see Aldo Rossi et al., *Architettura Razionale, XV Triennale di Milano*, Milan, 1973; *Lotus International 11*, 1976; *Architecture d'Aujourd'hui*, April 1977, an issue devoted to "Formalisme—Réalisme"; *Rational Architecture: Reconstruction of the European City 1978*, Editions Archives d'Architecture Moderne, Brussels, 1978.

20.

See Rem Koolhaas, *Delirious New York: A Retroactive Manifesto for Manhattan*, Oxford University Press, New York, and Thames and Hudson, London, 1978, pp. 242–256.

21.

Ibid.

22.

For J.P. Kleihues, see *2c Construccion de la Ciudad*, No. 9, June–September 1977, and *Lotus International 15*, 1977.

23.

Leon Krier has been published extensively in *Architectural Design* since 1977; see, for instance, Vol. 48, No. 4 and Vol. 49, No. 1.

24.

See *Architectural Design*, Vol. 49, Nos. 3/4, pp. 98–104.

25.

Ibid., p. 103.

26.

Rob Krier, *Urban Space*, Academy Editions, London, and Rizzoli, New York, 1979, with foreword by Colin Rowe (first published in German in 1973 as *Stadtraum*).

27.

See *Aldo Rossi* (ed. Francesco Moschini), Centro Di, Florence, and Academy Editions, London, 1979.

28.

See "James Stirling and Partner" in *Architectural Design*, Vol. 47, Nos. 9/10, pp. 596–613 for a discussion of the German projects. Also see "Stirling Gold," *Architectural Design*, Nos. 7/8, 1980, an issue devoted to his work on the occasion of his being awarded the RIBA Gold Medal.

CHAPTER 9
METAPHOR AND METAPHYSICS
THE QUANDARY OF CONTENT

1.

The codes of architecture most specific to architecture are not necessarily the most important, a point argued by many semiologists within other fields. Clearly architecture, like opera, is based on about twenty codes—it is impure and mixed in its essence.

2.

See Le Corbusier, *Oeuvre Complète*, Vols. VI, VII, VIII, Thames and Hudson, London, 1970.

3.

See *Roland Coate Architect Directions*, privately printed, Los Angeles, 1975; and Thomas S. Hines, "Alexander House" in *Progressive Architecture*, August 1976, pp. 58–61.

4.

See *SITE Architecture as Art*, Academy Editions, London, 1980, with contributions by Pierre Restany, Bruno Zevi, and SITE.

5.

For some of Stanley Tigerman's later work, see *A + U*, 79:11, pp. 89–124, with an essay by Ross Miller.

6.

See *Buildings for Best Products*.

7.

See my *The Language of Post-Modern Architecture*, pp. 113–117 and references, and *Bizarre Architecture*, Academy Editions, London, and Rizzoli, New York, 1979, pp. 14–15, 60–76.

8.

See Osamu Ishiyama, "Tokyo, 2001" in *The Japan Architect*, October/November 1977, pp. 36–38, and *A New Wave of Japanese Architecture*, pp. 42–47.

9.

See Mario Botta, *A + U*, 78:06, pp. 98–102, and *Mario Botta*, Electa Editrice, Milan, 1979, and Academy Editions, London, 1981, exhibition catalogue and book with introduction by Kenneth Frampton.

10.

See "Post-Modern Classicism," *Architectural Design*, Nos. 5/6, 1980.

11.

For Mayumi Miyawaki, see "The Pluralism of Japanese Architecture" in *Late-Modern Architecture*, pp. 123–125 and references.

12.

"Hiroshi Hara, an Interview with David Stewart" in *Architectural Association Quarterly 10*, No. 4, 1978, pp. 8, 10.

13.

See *Late-Modern Architecture*, pp. 119–121.

14.

See *The Japan Architect*, October/November 1977, an issue on "Post-Metabolism" edited by Ishii, and especially pp. 39–42 for his own work.

15.

See *ibid.*, pp. 55–57; *A New Wave of Japanese Architecture*; and for the houses discussed here, *The Japan Architect*, June 1978, pp. 17–72.

16.

Quoted from Chris Fawcett, "An Anarchist's Guide to Modern Architecture" in *Architectural Association Quarterly 727*, No. 3, 1975, p. 41.

CHAPTER 10
POST-MODERN SPACE
LAYERING, ELISION, AND SURPRISE

1.

Sigfried Giedion, *Space, Time and Architecture*, Harvard University Press, Cambridge, Massachusetts, 1941, fifth edition, 1967, pp. 30, 110–133, 430–448. His student, Christian Norberg-Schulz, has continued to explore these spatial ideas, especially "interpenetration" (Mansart), "pulsating juxtaposition" (Guarini), and "syncopated interpenetration" (Neumann, etc.). See his *Baroque Architecture,* History of World Architecture, Harry N. Abrams, Inc., New York, and Academy Editions, London, 1974, and *Late-Baroque Architecture* in the same series. Cornelis van den Ven mentions Albert E. Brinckmann (1908) as starting this line of research. See his *Space in Architecture,* Van Gorcum Assen, Amsterdam, 1978, p. 113.

2.
See Colin Rowe, "The Chicago Frame," 1956, reprinted in *The Mathematics of the Ideal Villa.*

3.
See Colin Rowe and Robert Slutzky, "Transparency: Literal and Phenomenal" in *Perspecta 8*, 1963, and "Part II" in *Perspecta 13/14*, 1971. For a critical review, see Rosemarie Haag Bletter, "Opaque Transparency" in *Oppositions 13*, 1978, pp. 121–126. Layered, shallow space relates to Rowe's "phenomenal transparency" as it is set up by implied or actual gridded space tightly layered.

4.
Asymmetrical symmetry is common to many periods of architecture, but it is most emphasized in the Queen Anne Revival and in Post-Modernism.

5.
Demi-forms are most notable in Late-Baroque, ad hocist, and Post-Modern work.

6.
Graves studied the plans of the Villa Madama for its positive/negative reversals, and the Hôtel Matignon for its shifted axis, and was influenced by these plans before he had seen the realities.

7.
See Edmund Leach, *Culture and Communication: The Logic by which Symbols are Connected,* Cambridge University Press, 1976, pp. 71–79; my discussion in "Meanings of Chinese Gardens" in *The Chinese Garden,* pp. 197–199; and "Post-Modern Space" in *The Language of Post-Modern Architecture,* pp. 118–126. The distinctive features of Post-Modern space are the shifted axis, asymmetrical symmetry, elision, ambiguity, liminal space, screens, aedicules, tight layering, skews and diagonals, reverse perspectives, positive/negative reversals, demiforms, and structured surprise or mystery.

8.
See the discussions by Moore and others in *The Place of Houses,* pp. 50–64.

9.
Discussed by Moore, *ibid.,* p. 60.

10.
Ibid., pp. 62–63, and "The Work of Charles Moore," *A + U,* 1978 5, p. 306.

11.
See *GA Houses 1* (ed. Yukio Futagawa), Tokyo, 1976, pp. 98–103.

12.
Robert Venturi discusses the diagonal in *Complexity and Contradiction in Architecture,* pp. 56–58, and C. Ray Smith in *Supermannerism,* pp. 100–111.

13.
See the discussions by Vincent Scully in *The Shingle Style Today or The Historian's Revenge,* p. 19, and Rosemarie Haag Bletter, "Rite of Passage and Place" in *A + U,* 1978 5, pp. 64–67.

14.
Coy Howard, from a written description of the house, 1979, not published.

15.
Piazza S. Ignazio can be read as having five oval spaces with a double focus and double meaning, either implying that the housing is center stage, with entrances (streets) to either side, or, more correctly, that S. Ignazio occupies the focus. This ambiguity backs up the positive/negative reversals.

16.
Architectural Monographs 5, pp. 64–67.

17.
Charles Moore, "Hadrian's Villa: A Whole World in a Circle and a Square," first published in *Perspecta 6*, 1958, and later in *Dimensions,* pp. 79–94. Moore stresses that the eclectic memories of Hadrian (like our subway advertisements) were not reproduced: "He transformed them" (p. 82). Part of the transformations are in a Roman Baroque style.

18.
Colin Rowe, *Collage City,* p. 78.

19.
See my *Late-Modern Architecture,* pp. 26–29, with a letter from Smith contrasting his implicit phallic shape with Tigerman's explicitness.

20.
See my *The Language of Post-Modern Architecture,* pp. 124–126.

21.
The self-referential nature of the aesthetic sign is not widely understood, and is too involved for full discussion here. Briefly, it depends on rhetorical cues which switch perception from primary use to the sign itself. See *Signs, Symbols and Architecture.* In spite of carefully pointing out that Eisenman is basically a Late-Modernist using Post-Modern space, some think that I have termed him a Post-Modernist—which he emphatically is not.

22.
See "Frank Gehry: The Search for a 'No Rules' Architecture" in *Architectural Record,* June 1976; "Parts, Arts and Architecture" by Edward Gunts in *The News American,* Baltimore, Maryland, July 22, 1979; and *Progressive Architecture,* July 1979 and March 1980 for articles devoted to his work.

Alternatives

INTRODUCTION

1.
"What is lyrical and believable in an imaginary form might be banal and unnecessary in fact"(Claes Oldenburg, *Proposals for Monuments and Buildings 1965–69,* Big Table Publishing Co., Chicago, 1969). Since that statement was made, some of his monuments have in fact been built.

2.
Theodore Roszak, *The Making of a Counter Culture: Reflections on the Technocratic Society and Its Youthful Opposition,* Faber and Faber, London, 1970.

3.
Charles Dickens, *A Tale of Two Cities,* Book I, Chapter 1: "It was the best of times, it was the worst of times, it was the age of wisdom, it was the age of foolishness, it was the epoch of belief, it was the epoch of incredulity, it was the season of Light, it was the season of Darkness, it was the spring of hope, it was the winter of despair."

4.
Quoted in *Shelter* (ed. Lloyd Kahn), Random House, New York, 1973, p. 107.

5.
Oscar Newman, *New Frontiers in Architecture: CIAM '59 in Otterlo,* Universe Books, New York, 1961.

6.
Charles Jencks and George Baird (eds.), *Meaning in Architecture.*

7.
Charles Jencks, *Architecture 2000: Predictions and Methods,* Praeger, New York, 1971, p. 79. See William P. Mangin and John C. Turner, "The Barriada Movement" in *Shelter and Society* (ed. Paul Oliver), Barrie and Rockliffe/The Cresset Press, London, 1969.

8.
Anatole Kopp, "Architecture of the Left," International Institute of Design Summer Session, London, 1971, printed in *Architectural Design,* Vol. 43, April 1972, pp. 222–223.

9.
Ibid., p. 223.

10.
Quoted in William Hedgepeth, *The Alternative: Communal Life in New America,* Macmillan, New York, 1970.

11.
Quoted in *ibid.,* p. 159.

12.
Peter Rabbit, *Drop City,* Olympia Press, New York, 1971, p. 29.

13.

Peter Selz, *Funk,* University of California, Berkeley, 1967, p.5.

14.

Quoted in *ibid.,* p.3. Eight statements by the artists about Funk, in the catalogue's appendix, leave us little wiser.

15.

Tom Wolfe, *The Electric Kool-Aid Acid Test,* Bantam, New York, 1968, pp. 113–114: "They made a point of not putting it into words. That in itself was one of the unspoken rules . . . to define it, was to limit it."

16.

Communard, quoted in Robert Houriet, *Getting Back Together,* Abacus/Sphere, London, 1973, p.124.

CHAPTER 11
THE COMMUNE BUILDERS

1.

Peter Rabbit, *Drop City,* Olympia Press, New York, 1971, p. 20. Peter Rabbit is an assumed name but, as he points out, so are all names. His book is essential reading on the subject, and very engaging.

2.

Baer, born 1938 in California, had settled in Albuquerque by 1959 after dropping out of Amherst College. The contact in London, 1965, occurred during service with the U.S. Army in Germany, before he returned to New Mexico.

3.

Graphically explained in Steve Baer, *Dome Cookbook,* Lama Foundation, New Mexico, 1968, with mathematical proofs, personal design philosophy, biographical details, and practical experience. See Baer's later *Zome Primer,* Zomeworks Corporation, New Mexico, 1970.

4.

Caption and title from articles in, respectively, *Architecture d'Aujourd'hui,* No. 141, 1968–69, pp. 82–84, and *Abitare,* No. 79, October 1969, pp. 24–31.

5.

Quoted in "Communes of the Southwest USA" in *Architectural Design,* No. 12, 1971, p. 736, and *Shelter* (ed. Lloyd Kahn), Random House, New York, 1973, p. 107.

6.

Robert Houriet, *Getting Back Together,* p. 221.

7.

Bill Voyd, "Funk Architecture" in *Shelter and Society,* p. 156. This is a shorter history of Drop City than Peter Rabbit's, but takes much of its text verbatim from Steve Baer's earlier *Dome Cookbook,* uncredited.

8.

Houriet (*op. cit.,* p. 179) believes this is too high, and gives the actual number of communes as "about twenty." William Hedgepeth, *The Alternative: Communal Life in New America,* p. 69, guessed "upwards of a dozen."

9.

Durkee, born 1938, exhibited Pop paintings around 1962, but in 1963 joined a poet and an electronics wizard to form Us Company. The group lived and worked together in an abandoned church (whose altar they replaced with a "kinetic tabernacle"). Multimedia works of collective authorship were performed with the occasional live participation of Marshall McLuhan, then little known, who influenced Durkee and vice versa. On a tour in 1965–66,

Durkee met Buckminster Fuller, yet he had already begun to mingle technocultural messages of McLuhan and Fuller with insights into selfhood from Meyer Baba and Baba Ram Dass, etc.

10.

The lower figure comes from *The New York Times* survey of thirty-four states, published December 17, 1970. The higher is from Dr. B.D. Zablocki, a University of California sociologist, published in *The San Francisco Chronicle,* February 17, 1970.

11.

Keith Melville, *Communes in the Counter-Culture: Origins, Theories, Styles of Life,* Morrow and Co., New York, 1972, p. 201.

12.

Houriet, *op. cit.,* pp. 267, 271, 274.

13.

Quoted in Odell Shepard, "Utopia in America" in *The American Story* (ed. Earl Schenk Miers), Channel Press, Great Neck, New York, 1956, p. 162.

14.

Subtitle of Morton and Lucia White's classic, *The Intellectual versus the City,* 1962.

15.

Promotional material quoted in Jerry Hopkins, *Festival: American Music Celebrations,* Macmillan, New York, 1970, p. 110. *Time* magazine said of Woodstock: "History's biggest happening . . . may well rank as one of the most significant political and sociological events of the age."

16.

Marshall McLuhan, *Understanding Media,* McGraw-Hill, New York, 1964, p.94: ". . . thus ends space as the main factor in social arrangements," etc.

17.

Quoted in Houriet, *op. cit.,* p. 217.

18.

Quoted in Richard Fairfield, *Communes USA,* Penguin Books, Harmondsworth, 1972, p. 165.

19.

Quoted in Michael Goodwin, "The Ken Kesey Movie" in *Rolling Stone,* March 7, 1970.

20.

See Rabbit, *op. cit.,* p. 148. "The hardest time in a commune, particularly Drop City, is the time after the building gets done . . . a time of dissolution."

21.

"Red Rockers" in *Domebook Two* (ed. Lloyd Kahn), Mountain Books, Santa Barbara, 1971, p.61. Compare the report on Red Rockers revisited in Kahn's later *Shelter,* pp. 138–139.

22.

This is to qualify certain opinions of Richard Reid in "Rooms" in *Architectural Design,* Vol. 48, Nos. 2/3, 1978, pp. 80–85. Reid has it that Mies's Farnsworth House is a Modern "single cell" equivalent to the medieval Great Hall; that Le Corbusier thought a "new kind of plan" could regenerate "modern living"; and that in Wright's 1902 Willitts House such "freedom in the communal heart of domestic living had not been seen since the open hall houses of medieval Europe." However, the spaces provided by these architects did not induce their clients to come full circle to medieval extended family living, which the open communes did approximate.

23.

For a fuller discussion see my "I Sometimes Dream of a Larger and More Populous House" in *Journal of the London Architecture Club,* No. 1, 1976. The quotation comes from Thoreau, musing wistfully in his cabin by the pond: "My dwelling was small, and I could hardly entertain an echo in it; but it seemed larger for being a single apartment and remote from neighbours. All the attractions of a house were concentrated in one room; it was kitchen, chamber, parlour . . . I sometimes dream of a larger and more populous house, standing in a golden age . . . which shall consist of only one room, a vast, rude, substantial primitive hall . . . whose inside is as open and manifest as a bird's nest, and you cannot go in at the front door and out at the back without seeing some of its inhabitants . . . "

24.

According to Dave Noble, "Survival of Squatters' City," *The Observer Colour Supplement,* December 16, 1979, p. 47.

25.

A member in communication with me confirmed their awareness of "the way in which the built environment and the interior design of buildings influences patterns of social interaction . . . we should plan our design rather carefully so as to, hopefully, facilitate the sort of social relationships that we want here." Since their layout in fact allows more privacy than "living in a heap," perhaps they have taken heed of American open communes, or are observing Edward T. Hall's "proxemics" for Northern Europeans.

CHAPTER 12
GREAT CIRCLES

1.

"Communes of the Southwest USA" in *Architectural Design,* No. 12, 1971.

2.

Since geodesics were protected by patent, the cost of the *Popular Science* plans was inclusive of royalty fee. However, the mysteries of the dome were revealed along with other do-it-yourself offerings like "Little Red Barn for Backyard Storage," "Basic Rooms You Can Add to Any House," "You Can Fly a Ski Kite," and "Build a Redwood Canoe."

3.

"It was the best idea, because everything we were trying to do to give the students a sense of independence and autonomy was contradicted by their life at home" (*Domebook Two,* p. 32).

4.

Ibid., pp. 13, 33. As to making no drawings, this means no architects' blueprints; they did make models and mathematical calculations.

5.

Large-scale structures had, of course, been engineered by Nervi, Maillart, Candela, and others. See my "Ferrocement" in *Domebook Two,* pp. 68–69.

6.

R. Buckminster Fuller, *Ideas and Integrities,* Collier-Macmillan, Toronto, 1963, p. 32.

7.

R. Buckminster Fuller and Robert Marks, *The Dymaxion World of Buckminster Fuller,* Anchor Press/Doubleday, New York, 1973, p. 20.

8.

Reyner Banham, *Theory and Design in the First Machine Age,* Praeger, New York, 1960, p. 326. Banham's concluding chapter "Functionalism and Technology" is a critique of functionalist style as incompatible with Fuller's technological discipline.

9.

Drop City quote from Bill Voyd, "Funk Architecture" in *Shelter and Society,* pp. 158–159; Libre quote from "Communes of the Southwest USA" in *Architectural Design,* No. 12, 1971. Neither of these communes gathered food in the agricultural way (Droppers regularly scrounged day-old bread and bruised fruit from supermarkets), but McLuhan had said that whereas man had once been a food gatherer, he was now an information gatherer, thus anticipating *The Whole Earth Catalog.*

10.

John G. Neihardt, *Black Elk Speaks,* Bison Books, University of Nebraska Press, Lincoln, 1932.

11.

According to *The Penguin English Dictionary:* "(sl.) old-fashioned person." But more traditional colloquial (and architectural) associations had been with fairness, honesty, uprightness, equality, etc.

12.

Letters quoted on pp. 100, 94, 50 respectively. The last is interesting in view of McLuhan: ". . . tribal man had freely extended his body to include the cosmos. Acting as an organ of the cosmos, tribal man accepted his bodily functions as modes of participation in the divine energies . . . Housing was an image of both the body and the universe for tribal and non-literate societies," but is disproportionate to the eight-foot-diameter dome which, before collapsing, brought on the correspondent's vision.

13.

Quoted in William Hedgepeth, *The Alternative: Communal Life in New America,* pp. 153, 118 respectively.

14.

Steve Baer, *Dome Cookbook,* p. 40. Baer also says rude things about cubes.

15.

The dome was illustrated in the exhibition catalogue, *Twentieth Century Engineering,* The Museum of Modern Art, New York, 1964, fig. 61. In his *Dome Cookbook* Steve Baer mentions seeing it there. *Shelter* did its own primary-source research; historically valuable in itself, its effect was to preempt and discredit Fuller, as intended.

16.

"I don't even consider how any structure is going to look until after it is finished . . . To me 'beautiful' apparently emerges as an ejaculation, spontaneously released by my total set of subconscious control coordinates . . . when my entire chromosomic neuron bank is momentarily in 'happy' correspondence with my entire experience (memory) neuron bank. I speak of my brain as if it were a computer. It is" (Buckminster Fuller, "Prospect for Humanity" in *Saturday Review,* August 1964).

CHAPTER 13
HANDMADES

1.

According to the 1968 census, whose further statistics—to the effect that forty percent of self-built houses had no mortgages—suggest financial economy as a major do-it-yourself motivation.

2.

Quoted in Jean Dethier and David Elalouf, *Architectures Marginales aux Etats-Unis,* Centre Pompidou, Paris, 1975, p. 33.

3.

Quoted in *Shelter,* p. 55.

4.

Dethier and Elalouf, *op. cit.,* p. 32.

5.

Quoted in brochure of Committee for Simon Rodia's Towers in Watts, 1961.

6.

Local rumor intimated it was when Rodia's wife (not mother) died that he began the endeavor to fill an emotional vacuum; this might further characterize it as a memorial "shrine." As for specific references to religious architecture: Antoni Gaudí's towers for the Sagrada Familia had been raised by 1906, so it is not impossible that he could have gleaned the idea, perhaps through his predominantly Spanish-speaking Chicano neighbors (who knew him well as Señor Rodilla). All it would have needed was a postcard from Barcelona, about 1921. However, this must remain unsupported speculation. Rodia himself died in 1965.

7.

Quoted in William C. Lipke and Gregg Blasdel, *Schmidt,* University of Vermont, Burlington, 1975.

8.

Tony Dugdale, "The Romantic Renegades" in *Architectural Design,* Vol. 48, No. 7, 1978, p. 446.

9.

These are the sort of people Melville, in the quote above, presumed were "playing around" with handmades as a "craze." Yet the credentials of Boedicke, for example, included study under Buckminster Fuller as well as twenty years' experience in the building trades before handcrafting his own house.

10.

As criticized in Deanna Petherbridge's review, "Speculation or Documentation?" in *Architectural Design,* Vol. 48, No. 7, 1978, pp. 439–441.

11.

Henry Elder, "The Woodbutchers' Art and the Architecture of Protest," *ibid.,* pp. 447–449.

12.

Tony Ward, "Handmade Houses: A Search for Identity," *ibid.,* pp. 480–488.

13.

Shingle Style, especially, was spurred to this quest by the 1876 Centennial of American Independence. See Vincent Scully's *The Shingle Style and the Stick Style.* Scully's later *The Shingle Style Today or The Historian's Revenge* (1974) takes credit for making contemporary architects aware enough of late-nineteenth-century precedent to revive it, but the currency of this Neo-Neo-Vernacular only illustrates that the search for cultural identity continues, in mainstream design as in self-built.

14.

Interview with Val Agnoli in *Shelter,* pp. 154–155.

15.

Interview with Bob De Buck and Jerry Thorman, *ibid.,* pp. 144–147.

16.

Ibid., p. 145.

CHAPTER 14
NOMADIC DESIGNS

1.

For history, see Ben Dennis and Betsy Case, *Houseboat,* Smuggler's Cove Publishing, Seattle, 1977.

2.

Quoted in Beverly Dubin, *Water Squatters,* Capra Press, Santa Barbara, California, 1975, p. 58.

3.

Ibid., pp. 18 and 35 respectively.

4.

Houseboat populations in Hong Kong harbor, Canton, Bangkok, Kashmir, and Benares are hailed in *Water Squatters* as if kindred spirits, but the sampan really has no Western counterpart. (It is as native vernacular that it is included in *Shelter.*) Moreover, the Asian houseboaters are, illegally, water squatters, while American ones have been suburbanized into marinas, sometimes harboring pretensions to yacht clubs.

5.

Alvin Toffler, *Future Shock,* Bantam/Random House, New York, 1970, p. 80. One of Toffler's major themes is transience and its psycho-social consequences, "The Economics of Impermanence," "The New Nomads," "Migration to the Future," and many more. The point is well made and statistically verified that "the professional and technical populations are among the most mobile of all Americans," i.e., not lower-income fortune seekers or dispossessed migrants but "corporate gypsies," long-range commuters, college students studying away from home, brain-drain jet-setters.

6.

E.g., *Slither* (1973) and *Smokey and the Bandit* (1977) respectively.

7.

See Tom Wolfe, *The Electric Kool-Aid Acid Test.*

8.

Some of these countrified housetrucks do travel in convoy and meet for craft fairs. The Northwest Touring Company is such "a community of craftspeople," and one of its members has "transformed an ordinary bus into a showplace for his collection of antiques and kitsch known as The American Institute of Obnoxious Art." Jane Lidz, *Rolling Homes; Handmade Houses on Wheels,* A. & W. Visual Library, New York, 1979, p. 12.

9.

Marshall McLuhan, *Understanding Media,* Introduction, p. viii.

10.

Ibid., p. 217.

11.

Ibid., p. 220. McLuhan prefaces this with "in the electric age," of course, "the wheel itself is obsolescent," not because of any energy crisis.

12.

Ibid., pp. 65–66. The ideas quoted have been used axiomatically: the argument follows its own logic by linking them, and is not an argument presented by McLuhan who, writing when he did, could not draw upon phenomena such as truckitecture or even customizing, counterculture, or craft revival, nor—as mentioned—the energy crisis of the seventies.

CHAPTER 15
ALTERNATIVE TECHNOLOGIES

1.

Disallowing prior claims by, say, Steve Baer's house on the grounds that it included back-up systems: fireplaces for heating, propane gas for cooking, and mains electricity for lighting.

2.

In three north-facing rooms, another Baer invention called Skylid supplements the water-wall. Aluminum louvers, fitted beneath transparent skylights, respond automatically to temperature changes by opening or closing as necessary. With them open, the house's interior surfaces soak up and later release solar energy. Like the shutters of the water-wall, the Skylid louvers close either to keep in the house's heat or keep out the sun's.

3.

Sun control is the most glaring deficiency. When Mies van der Rohe's all-glass Farnsworth House proved uninhabitable, the client brought suit. Philip Johnson has admitted his buildings cannot work without air conditioning. Typically, when all elevations are glazed, the sunward side must be cooled even in winter, to counter solar gain, while the north side, losing heat through the glass, is overheated mechanically. The air-handling equipment required may account for sixty percent of the building's cost, with similarly disproportionate running expenses throughout its life.

4.

Technical literature on domestic solar energy is extensive and growing daily. For a brief survey of American types, including more by Steve Baer, see Ian Hogan and Costis Stambolis, "Solar Boom" in *Architectural Design*, April 1976, pp. 242–247.

5.

Established in 1969, NAI has built scientific testing stations on Cape Cod and Prince Edward Island, in California, and in Costa Rica. See statement by Canadian spokesman Dr. John Todd, and eyewitness report by Jay Baldwin in *Soft-Tech, Co-Evolution Quarterly*, Penguin edition, 1978, pp. 148–167.

6.

Undercurrents, No.5, London, 1973.

7.

E.F. Schumacher, *Small is Beautiful; A Study of Economics as if People Mattered*, Abacus/Sphere, London, 1974, pp. 131–132.

8.

See *Architectural Design*, January 1976, pp. 19–51. It has been objected that while such designs disregard social relations in their isolation, they cannot be truly "autonomous" either, insofar as they are dependent on high-technology components, the politics of whose production they cannot affect.

9.

See interview by Peter Harper and Godfrey Boyle (of *Undercurrents*) in *Radical Technology*, Wildwood House, 1976, pp. 170–171.

10.

In the early sixties, British avant-garde architecture had entertained notions of throwaway buildings and "plug-in" components of limited life-span; without having been actualized, this profligacy was no longer conceptually tenable by the pollution-conscious late sixties and the anticipated scarcities of the early seventies.

11.

Architectural Design, February 1971, pp. 86–94; *Harpers and Queen*, September 1973, p. 88.

12.

His *De Dragers en de Mensen* (Support Structures and People) was published in Holland in 1961, and in English as *Supports: An Alternative to Mass Housing*, Architectural Press, London, 1972, and Praeger, New York, 1973.

13.

Willoughby Sharp, *Air Art*, Kineticism Press, New York, 1968, p. 7. Conceptual preoccupations can be traced back to Duchamp's "50 c.c. of Paris Air," 1919.

14.

Frei Otto, *Tensile Structures*, Vol. 1: *Pneumatic Structures*, MIT Press, Cambridge, Massachusetts, 1967. Soap bubbles, used by Otto and others to "model" inflatables, have ultra-thin membranes of liquid film cohering only by surface tension. At the other, macrocosmic end of the scale, the earth's atmosphere is an air envelope constrained by gravity.

15.

Of course, inflatables can and have been combined with geodesics: domes made with inflated panels, inflated "pillows" between the struts as in Jay Baldwin's Bubble Dome, or the struts themselves pneumatic tubes.

16.

"Pneu World," *Architectural Design*, June 1968, p. 276. See *Structures Gonflables*, Musée d'Art Moderne, Paris, 1967.

CHAPTER 16
BEYOND THE FRINGE

1.

Quoted in Annette del Zoppo, *The Work of Paolo Soleri*, Environmental Communications, Venice, California, 1973.

2.

Paolo Soleri, "The Two Suns Arcology" in *Architectural Association Quarterly*, Vol.7, No.2, 1975, p. 38. This article addresses the physical and metaphysical parameters behind his design for the Teilhard de Chardin Cloister at Arcosanti, incorporating his theology: "The city of the two suns, the sun father of mass-energy and the sun son of the spirit, is the complex, miniaturized city." Soleri's prose, like his cities, can be rather dense. He was raised a Roman Catholic, calls himself a sun-worshiper, and invokes the sun in his name, Soleri.

3.

Quoted in David Butler, "In the Image of Man" in *Playboy*, Vol.19, No.6, June 1972, p. 168.

4.

Although Soleri's master plans often call for "automated industries" buried beneath his arcologies, Arcosanti itself is being built by amateurs, by hand, and by traditional concrete-vaulting methods. Asteromo, his artificial-satellite arcology, takes a molded ceramic form unlikely to meet weight limits of orbital payloads.

5.

The Fuller quote is from Calvin Tomkin's profile, "In the Outlaw Area" in *The New Yorker*, January 8, 1966. Brand's gloss on it is in *The Last Whole Earth Catalog*, Portola Institute, Menlo Park, California, 1971, p. 223.

6.

See *Supplement to the Whole Earth Catalog*, March 1969, pp.18–27, partly reprinted in *The Last Whole Earth Catalog*, pp. 111–117.

7.

Jim Murphy, "House of the Century" in *Progressive Architecture*, May 1973, p. 128.

8.

Quoted in Jim Burns, *Arthropods: New Design Futures*, Academy Editions, London, 1972, p. 10.

9.

Charles Jencks, *Architecture 2000: Predictions and Methods*, p. 7.

10.

The Latin *hoc* is relevant here, but Ant Farm have also used an alternative acronym selected from the initials THOTC: THC (terahydrocannabinol), known in the underground as the active ingredient in marijuana. Thus, as in their architecture, technology abets fantasy.

11.

Charles Jencks, *op. cit.*, p. 99.

12.

Peter Selz, *Funk*, p. 6.

13.

Presentation drawings for HOC acknowledged, with a visual footnote, the inspiration of a streamlined Cord automobile. See also Ant Farm, *Automerica*, Dutton, New York, 1977.

JENCKS, CHARLES. *Late-Modern Architecture*. Academy Editions, London, and Rizzoli, New York, 1980.

KRON, JOAN AND SLESIN, SUZANNE. *High-Tech: The Industrial Style and Source Book for the Home* with foreword by Emilio Ambasz. Potter, New York, 1978, and Allen Lane, London, 1979.

ROSS, MICHAEL. *Beyond Metabolism: The New Japanese Architecture*. McGraw-Hill, New York, 1978.

ROWE, COLIN. *The Mathematics of the Ideal Villa and Other Essays*. MIT Press, Cambridge, Massachusetts, 1976.

SELECTED BIBLIOGRAPHY

The body of writings on contemporary architecture is vast and is constantly being added to, especially by periodicals. It is to these that the reader is first directed for information on the continuing development of current theory and practice. The majority of magazines are probably already familiar to most readers. They include *A + U*, *The Architects' Journal*, *Architectural Association Quarterly*, *Architectural Design*, *Architectural Forum*, *Architectural Record*, *The Architectural Review*, *Architecture d'Aujourd'hui*, *Archives d'Architecture Moderne* (quarterly), *Bauen und Wohnen*, *Baumeister*, *Bauwelt*, *Building Design*, *Casabella*, *Domus*, *The Harvard Architectural Review*, *International Architect*, *The Japan Architect*, *Lotus International*, *Oppositions*, *Perspecta*, *Progressive Architecture*, *Undercurrents*, *Werk*, and *Zodiac*. For the work of individual architects and practices see *Architectural Design Profiles*, *A + U*, *Architectural Monographs*, *GA*, and other special issues. For specific work also consult magazine references contained in the notes to each chapter. The following selection of book titles, exhibition catalogues, and magazines is intended as a guide to the most important works to have appeared to date on Late-Modern and Post-Modern architecture and alternatives.

Late-Modernism

AMBASZ, EMILIO (ed.). *Italy: The New Domestic Landscape, Achievements and Problems of Italian Design*. The Museum of Modern Art, New York, 1972.

BANHAM, REYNER. *The New Brutalism, Ethic or Aesthetic?* The Architectural Press, London, 1966.

——. *Megastructures, Urban Futures of the Recent Past*. Thames and Hudson, London, 1976, and Harper & Row, New York, 1977.

DREXLER, ARTHUR. *Transformations in Modern Architecture*. The Museum of Modern Art, New York, 1979.

FAWCETT, CHRIS. *The New Japanese House: Ritual and Anti-Ritual Patterns of Dwelling*. Granada, London, Toronto, Sydney, and New York, 1980.

Five Architects: Eisenman, Graves, Gwathmey, Hejduk, Meier with contributions by Arthur Drexler, Colin Rowe, Philip Johnson, and Kenneth Frampton. Oxford University Press, New York, 1972; rev. ed. 1975.

FRAMPTON, KENNETH. *A New Wave of Japanese Architecture*. Catalogue 10. IAUS, New York, 1978.

Post-Modernism

BLOOMER, KENT C. AND MOORE, CHARLES W. *Body, Memory and Architecture*. Yale University Press, New Haven, Connecticut, and London, 1977.

BROADBENT, GEOFFREY; BUNT, RICHARD; AND JENCKS, CHARLES. *Signs, Symbols and Architecture*. John Wiley & Sons, Chichester, New York, Brisbane, and Toronto, 1980.

HEWITT, M.; KRACAUER, V.; MASSENGALE, J.; AND MCDONOUGH, M. (eds.). "Culture and the Social Vision." In *Via*, No. 4, MIT Press, Cambridge, Massachusetts, 1980.

ISHII, K. AND SUZUKI, A. (eds.). "Post-Metabolism." *The Japan Architect*, No. 247. October/November 1977.

JENCKS, CHARLES. *The Language of Post-Modern Architecture*. Academy Editions, London, 1977, and Rizzoli, New York, 1978; rev. and enl. ed. 1981.

—— (ed.). "Post-Modernism." *Architectural Design*, No.4, 1977.

—— (ed.). "Post-Modern History." *Architectural Design*, No. 1, 1978.

—— (ed.). "Post-Modern Classicism." *Architectural Design*, Nos. 5/6, 1980.

—— (ed.). "Free-Style Classicism." *Architectural Design*, Nos. 1/2, 1982.

JENCKS, CHARLES AND BAIRD, GEORGE (eds.). *Meaning in Architecture*. George Braziller, New York, and Barrie and Jenkins, London, 1969.

KOOLHAAS, REM. *Delirious New York: A Retroactive Manifesto for Manhattan*. Oxford University Press, New York, and Academy Editions, London, 1978.

KRIER, ROB. *Urban Space* with foreword by Colin Rowe. Academy Editions, London, and Rizzoli, New York, 1979.

MOORE, CHARLES; ALLEN, GERALD; AND LYNDON, DONLYN. *The Place of Houses*. Holt, Rinehart & Winston, New York, Chicago, and San Francisco, 1974.

PORTOGHESI, PAOLO *et al. The Presence of the Past: First International Exhibition of Architecture—Venice Biennale 1980*. Edizione "La Biennale di Venezia," Venice, and Academy Editions, London, 1980.

ROWE, COLIN AND KOETTER, FRED. *Collage City*. MIT Press, Cambridge, Massachusetts, 1978, and London, 1979.

SCULLY, VINCENT. *The Shingle Style Today or The Historian's Revenge*. George Braziller, New York, 1974.

SMITH, C. RAY. *Supermannerism: New Attitudes in Post-Modern Architecture*. Dutton, New York, 1977.

STERN, ROBERT A. M. *New Directions in American Architecture.* George Braziller, New York, 1969; rev. ed. 1977.

STEVENS, SUZANNE (ed.). "Beyond Modernism." *Progressive Architecture,* December 1979.

VENTURI, ROBERT. *Complexity and Contradiction in Architecture.* The Museum of Modern Art, New York, 1966.

VENTURI, ROBERT; SCOTT BROWN, DENISE; AND IZENOUR, STEVEN. *Learning from Las Vegas.* MIT Press, Cambridge, Massachusetts, 1972; re-edited with a biblio. 1977.

Alternatives

ANT FARM. *Inflatacookbook.* Sausalito, California, 1970.

BAER, STEVE. *Dome Cookbook.* Lama Foundation, New Mexico, 1968.

———. *Zome Primer.* Zomeworks Corporation, New Mexico, 1970.

BALDWIN, J. AND BRAND, STEWART (eds.). *Soft-Tech.* Penguin Books, Harmondsworth, 1978.

BALLANTINE, DAVID AND HANEY, ROBERT. *Woodstock Handmade Houses.* Ballantine Books, New York, 1974.

BOEDICKE, ART AND SHAPIRO, BARRY. *Handmade Houses.* Scrimshaw Press, San Francisco, California, 1973.

———. *The Craftsman Builder.* Simon & Schuster, New York, 1977.

BOYLE, GODFREY AND HARPER, PETER (eds.). *Radical Technology.* Wildwood House, London, 1976.

BRAND, STEWART (ed.). *The Last Whole Earth Catalog.* Portola Institute, Menlo Park, California, 1971.

BURNS, JIM. *Arthropods: New Design Futures.* Academy Editions, London, 1972.

DENNIS, BEN AND CASE, BETSY. *Houseboat.* Smuggler's Cove Publishing, Seattle, 1977.

DICKSON, DAVID. *Alternative Technology and the Politics of Technical Change.* Fontana, London, 1974.

DUBIN, BEVERLY. *Water Squatters.* Capra Press, Santa Barbara, California, 1975.

FULLER, R. BUCKMINSTER. *Ideas and Integrities.* Collier-Macmillan, Toronto, 1963.

——— AND MARKS, ROBERT. *The Dymaxion World of Buckminster Fuller.* Anchor Press/Doubleday, New York, 1973.

HEDGEPETH, WILLIAM. *The Alternative: Communal Life in New America.* Macmillan, New York, 1970.

HOURIET, ROBERT. *Getting Back Together.* Abacus/Sphere, London, 1973.

JENCKS CHARLES. *Architecture 2000: Predictions and Methods.* Praeger, New York, and Studio Vista, London, 1971.

KAHN, LLOYD (ed.). *Domebook Two.* Mountain Books, Santa Barbara, California, 1971.

——— (ed.). *Shelter.* Random House, New York, 1973.

LIDZ, JANE. *Rolling Homes: Handmade Houses on Wheels.* A. & W. Visual Library, New York, 1979.

LIPKE, WILLIAM C. AND BLASDEL, GREGG. *Schmidt.* University of Vermont, Burlington, 1975.

MCLUHAN, MARSHALL. *Understanding Media.* McGraw-Hill, New York, 1964, and Abacus/Sphere, London, 1974.

MELVILLE, KEITH. *Communes in the Counter-Culture.* Morrow and Co., New York, 1972.

OLIVER, PAUL (ed.). *Shelter and Society.* Barrie and Rockliffe/The Cresset Press, London, 1969.

OTTO, FREI. *Tensile Structures,* Vol. 1: *Pneumatic Structures.* MIT Press, Cambridge, Massachusetts, 1967.

PAWLEY, MARTIN. *Garbage Housing.* The Architectural Press, London, 1975.

PRENIS, JOHN (ed.). *The Dome Builder's Handbook.* Running Press, Philadelphia, 1973.

RABBIT, PETER. *Drop City.* Olympia Press, New York, 1971.

ROSZAK, THEODORE. *The Making of a Counter Culture.* Faber and Faber, London, 1970.

RUDOFSKY, BERNARD. *Architecture without Architects.* The Museum of Modern Art, New York, 1964, and Academy Editions, London, 1973.

SCHUMACHER, E.F. *Small is Beautiful.* Abacus/Sphere, London, 1974.

SCHUYT, MICHAEL AND ELFFERS, JOOST. *Fantastic Architecture.* Thames and Hudson, London, 1980.

SELZ, PETER. *Funk.* University of California, Berkeley, 1967.

SHARP, WILLOUGHBY. *Air Art.* Kineticism Press, New York, 1968.

WAMPLER, JAN. *All Their Own: People and the Places They Build.* Oxford University Press, New York, 1978.

PHOTOGRAPHIC CREDITS

We wish to thank the following for making illustrative material available for publication: Aerophoto–Schiphol B.V. 47; Afdeling Voorlichting 43; Takefumi Aida 313; Jesse Alexander 285; Gil Amiaga 194; *Architectural Design* 467, 475; *The Architectural Review* 399; Arquitectonica 242, 302; Art Center of Design, Pasadena 36; Carlo Aymonino 126; Morley Baer 235, 330; Behnisch & Partner/Christian Kandzia 53, 55; Biennale di Venezia 281; Piet Blom 42; Blomeyer 533; B. Bognar 304; Gottfried Böhm 9; Mario Botta 305; Brecht-Einzig Limited (photos Richard Einzig) 10–11, 86–88, 150; Peter Carl 134; Centre Pompidou, Paris 365, 383, 409, 412, 417, 419, 421–422, 444, 446, 479–480; William Chaitkin 364, 367, 379, 383, 393, 395, 405–407, 411, 418, 442–443, 445, 468, 492–493, 502–504, 520; Martin Charles 35; Louis Checkman 20; Dennis Crompton 46, 538; Edward Cullinan 241; George Cserna 161–162; Richard Davis p. 2, 243, 246; Vittorio de Feo 127–128; *Design* magazine/Tim Street-Porter 234; Cathy de Witt 386; Jeremy Dixon 244–245, 527; John Donat 57, 115–117, 282, 541; *Eastern Daily Press* 238; Peter Eisenman 129–133; Environmental Communications 368, 372–373, 376, 390–391, 397, 400, 413, 415, 419, 438, 440–441, 447–449, 451, 455, 457, 463, 469, 481, 484–486, 489, 494, 499–501, 506, 508, 510, 513, 516, 519, 521–524; Hassan Fathy 220; James Fesler 215–216; Fischer Fine Art 89, 113; Frederick Fischer 343; Foster Associates 114, 154–155; Chai French 188; Hiromi Fujii 159; M. Fujitsuka 319; Frank O. Gehry 357–360; Alexandre Georges 23–24, 94; Ross Giblin 252–253; Keith Gibson 239; Bruce Goff 247–248, 251; Marian Goodman Gallery 104; P. Goulet 62; Michael Graves 1, 135–138, 189, 214, 217–219, 301, 329, 342, 347–348; Allan Greenberg 224–225; Yves Guillemaut 526; Gwathmey Siegel and Associates 123; Hiroshi Hara 311; Hardy Holzman Pfeiffer Associates 56; John Hejduk 124–125; Heinrich Helfenstein 203–204; Boh Helliwell 425, 428–429, 431–432, 434; Boh Helliwell, Michael MacNamara, and Ron Ellis 426–427, 430, 432–433, 436; Herman Hertzberger 46, 48–52; Fernando Higueras 228; Jürgen Hilmer 286; Hans Hollein 71–73, 80, 205–213, 530; Michael Hopkins 61; Coy Howard 345; Franz Hubmann 79; Kazuhiro Ishii 240, 316, 531; Osamu Ishiyama 295–296; Arata Isozaki 166, 168, 307; Toyo Ito 160; Helmut Jahn 152, 156; *The Japan Architect* (photos Masao Arai) 308–309, 312; *The Japan Architect* (photos Mitsuo Matsuoka) 314, 318; *The Japan Architect* (photo Taisuke Ogawa) 299; Charles Jencks 3–6, 21, 25, 33–34, 37–39, 59, 63, 70, 74–75, 96–97, 103, 105–107, 112, 167, 173, 179–180, 182, 184, 233, 236, 254, 258–260, 297, 352–353, 355–356, 361–363; J. M. Johansen 255, 257; Martin Johnson 229; Philip Johnson 101–102, 532; Dalu Jones 220; Howard N. Kaplan 293–294; Alan Karchmer 185; Rhomi Khosla 284; Yasufumi Kijima 231–232; Ken Kirkwood 60, 153; Paul S. Kivett 151; J. P. Kleihues 269; Rem Koolhaas 267; Charlene Koonce 374; Balthazar Korab 90; Leon Krier 270–272; Robert Krier 273, 275–276; Lucien Kroll 261; Eugene Kupper 354; Kisho Kurokawa, architect & associates 16, 58; Kisho Kurokawa, architect and associates (photos Tomio Ohashi) 15, 17–18; Rollin R. La France 174; Ian Latham 44–45, 237; Jane Lidz 454, 460–461; David Lieberman 502; Nathaniel Lieberman 28, 100; Anthony Lumsden and DMJM 22, 108–109, 163; Norman McGrath 183; Richard Meier 2, 120, 122, 139–143, 165; Ryuji Miyamoto 298; Milton Keynes Development Corporation (photo Pineham Photo) 149; MLTW/Moore Turnbull 331, 351; MLTW/Turnbull Associates 336; Joseph W. Molitor 7; Charles W. Moore Associates 178, 332–333, 341; Moore Grover Harper 334, 340; Moore, Ruble, and Yudell 534; André Morain 158; Morphosis 303; Monta Mozuna 320–323; Ugo Mulas 76; Osamu Murai 170, 230, 310; Christian Norberg-Schulz 30–31; S. Okamoto 317; OMA 535; Martin Pawley 476; I. M. Pei 98; Gustav Peichl 12–14; Cesar Pelli 111; Perez Associates, Inc. 181; John Portman and Associates 91–93; Paolo Portoghesi 171–172; Cedric Price 144–145, 536; Joe Price 249; Proto Acme 529; Luftbild Max Prugger 54; Marvin Rand 110; Jo Reid 148; Jo Reid and John Peck 528; Giada Ricci 265; Righter, Rose, and Lankin 187; Cervin Robinson 335; Kevin Roche, John Dinkeloo and Associates 95, 99; Richard Rogers 64–69, 147; Steve Rosenthal 40; Aldo Rossi 277–278, 537; Kuniharu Sakumoto 169; S.A.U.P., UCLA 354; Deidi Von Schaewen p. 4, 200, 525; David Sellers 250; Sert, Jackson and Associates 41; SITE (Ronald Feldman Fine Arts) 287–288; Thomas Gordon Smith 195–196, 328, 350; François Spoerry 221; Robert A. M. Stern 190–193, 227, 327; James Stirling 32, 85, 279–280, 283; Ed Stoecklein 226, 326; Ezra Stoller/Esto, Inc. 19, 26–27, 118, 121, 164; Tim Street-Porter 344; Superstudio 157; Jerzy Surwillo 77–78; Douglas Symes 197; Taft Architects 199; Minoru Takeyama 306, 539; Quinlan Terry 222–223; Peter Thaler 198; Stanley Tigerman 289–292; Jean-Luc Touillon 266; Philip Turner 81–83; O. M. Ungers 262–263, 540; United Arts Corporation 84; U.I.G. 186; Frank van Klingeren 146; John Veltri, Picture Concepts, Inc. 256; Venturi and Rauch 175–177, 324, 339; Venturi and Short 346; Serena Vergano 200–202, 264; Inge + Arved von der Ropp 8; Tohru Waki 315; Gilles Walusinski 274; Clare Wheldon 477–478; Kazumasa Yamashita 300; Mona Zamdmer 29; Elia Zenghelis 268.

For Academy Editions only: Dennis Crompton (dust jacket, front); Princeton Photographics (dust jacket, back).

ACKNOWLEDGMENTS

WE ARE INDEBTED TO MICHAEL GRAVES, PETER EISEN-man, Norman Foster, Charles Moore, Robert Stern, and Hans Hollein for the discussions which have sharpened the categories used in this book and made us appreciate the effort of architects in upholding distinctions—especially between Late- and Post-Modern architecture—and to Christian Norberg-Schulz, Vincent Scully, and Paolo Portoghesi, who have offered much useful comment in our joint discussions on these subjects. A book of this scope is inevitably a team effort, and we express our gratitude to all who have at some time worked on its production, including the staff of Academy Editions in London and of Harry N. Abrams, Inc. in New York. We would especially like to acknowledge Andreas Papadakis for originally conceiving the idea for the project, Frank Russell for his editorial work, and Maggie Keswick for reading manuscripts and offering suggestions for their improvement. As information has been based wherever possible on primary sources, our especial thanks go to all the architects who have willingly contributed information and material, and without whose help this book would not have been possible.

INDEX

Numbers in italics refer to the illustrations

B

F

G

Gable Building, Tokyo (Ishii), elevation, *531*

Gallaratese neighborhood, Milan (Rossi), 173

Gans, Herbert, 112

"Garagia Rotunda," Truro, Massachusetts (Jencks), 17, 183; *4, 297*; interior, *6*; rotunda, *5*

Garbage Housing (Pawley), 275, 276

Gardella, Ignazio, 112

Garden Grove Community Church, Garden Grove, California (Johnson/Burgee), 25; exterior under construction, *21*; model, *20*

"Garden of Eden," Kansas (Dinsmoor), 246

Garnet-Crystal Dome, Manera Nueva, New Mexico (Baer), 225; *370*

Gaudí, Antoni, 25, 124, 127, 159, 249, 252, 256, 297

Gehry, Frank O., 118, 203, 204, 207, 214–16, 309; Gehry House, 204, 215–16; *360–63*; Mid-Atlantic Toyota Distributorship Offices, 214–15; *357–59*

Gehry, Frank O., and Associates, 214, 215, 216, 217

Gehry House, Santa Monica, California (Gehry and Associates), 204, 215–16; axonometric, *360*; exterior, *363*; interior, *361*; kitchen, *362*

Geodesic Dome, Drop City, Colorado, 226; exterior after abandonment, *375*

Geodesic Dome (Fuller), 236; elevation and roof plan, *398*

Geodesic Dome, Hornby Island, British Columbia (Ellis), 255–56; exterior detail, *425*; plan, including original dome, *426*

Geodesic Dome, Pacific High School, Santa Cruz Mountains, California (Kahn, Lloyd), 234; *389*

geodesic domes, *see* domes, geodesic

Geodesic Domes, Libre, Colorado, 225, 234; *371, 387*

Geometric Expressionism, 25, 26

Georgian architecture, 142

Giedion, Sigfried, 16, 17, 163, 200

Gigliotti, Vittorio, 112, 113

Gilbert, Cass, 29

Ginsberg, Allen, 266

Goff, Bruce, 25, 77, 158–60, 162, 256, 260, 309–10; Bavinger House, 159, 256; Price House, 25, 159–60; *247–49, 251*

Goldberger, Paul, 15, 111

Goldenberg House, Rydal, Pennsylvania (Kahn, Louis), 203

Gothic architecture, 179, 203, 239

Gottlieb, Lou, 230

Gourna New Town, Egypt (Fathy), 142–43; *220*

government buildings, 130, 134, 145, 153–54, 179; *205, 206, 225, 239, 284*; *see also* city halls

Gradidge, Roderick, 145

Graham, Bruce, 29, 310; Hancock Center, 29; *37*

Graham, Bruce, and SOM, 35

GRAU, *see* Roman Group of Urban Architects

Graves, Michael, 15, 83–86, 88, 137–41, 160, 208, 212; anthropomorphism and, 140–41, 182; Benacerraf House, 83; Best Products Showroom, 120, 122; *189*; biography of, 310; Claghorn House additions, 137; Crooks House Project, 137, 209, 211; *347*; Fargo-Moorhead Cultural Center, 13, 140–41; *217–19*; French & Co., 185; *301*; Hanselmann House, 83–84; *134, 135*; influence of: Le Corbusier, 77; Lutyens, 145; Kalko House, 201; *329*; Mezzo House Project, 205; Newark Museum Carriage House, 205, 207; *342*; Plocek ("Keystone") House, 211; Portland Public Service Building, 12, 13; *1*; Public Library, *529*; Schulman House, 137–38; *214*; Snyderman House, 83, 84–86; *136–38*; Sunar Furniture Showroom, 138–40; *215, 216*; Warehouse Conversion: Private Residence, 211; *348*

Grays Ferry Citizens Center, Philadelphia (Friday Architects), 126–27; *198*

Great Mosque, Cordoba, 113

Great Pumpkin inflatable, Antioch College, Ohio, 283; *489*

Greek architecture, 77, 100, 157, 159, 178, 239

Green, David, 297

Greenberg, Allan, 124, 144–45; Manchester Courthouse, 145; *225*; Mid-Town Manhattan Park Project, 145; *224*

Greene Hall, Columbia University School of Law, New York City (Stern), 145; interior, *226*

Greenwich, Connecticut: Bourke House, poolhouse for (Stern and Hagmann), 122; *191, 192*; Brant House (Venturi and Rauch), 115, 205; *175, 339*

Grey Walls (Lutyens), 209

Groat, Linda, 154

Gropius, Walter, 17, 117

Grzimek, Günter, 41

Guarini, Guarino, 113, 206

Guimard, Hector, 122

Gully, Boyce Luther, 246; house of, Phoenix, Arizona, *412*

Gund Hall, Graduate School of Design, Harvard University, Cambridge (Andrews), 29–30; *38*; interior, *39*

Gunma Prefectural Museum of Fine Arts, Takasaki, Japan (Isozaki), 105, 187; *167*; deep and supplemental structure, *168*; interior entrance space, *169*

Gwathmey, Charles, 25, 77, 78, 310; residence and studio of, Amagansett, New York, 78; *123*

H

I

Hyatt Regency Hotel, Atlanta (Portman and Associates), 60–61, 63; *92*

Hyatt Regency Hotel, Dallas (Becket and Associates), 68–69; *105*; interior, *107*; rear view, *106*

Hyatt Regency Hotel, San Francisco (Portman and Associates), 60–61, 63; interior, *93*

Hyatt Regency O'Hare Hotel, Chicago (Portman and Associates), 60–61, 63; *91*

Iceberg Palace (Bell, L.), 67; *104*

Ideas and Integrities (Fuller), 237

I.D.S. Center, Minneapolis (Johnson/Burgee), 66; *100*

Illinois Institute of Technology (Mies van der Rohe), 213

Imatra, Italy, church at (Aalto), 24, 204

Indian architecture, *see* American Indian architecture

inflatable cube (Stevens), 281–82; *482*

Inflatable Pillow, Frestone, California (Ant Farm), 288–89; *505*

inflatable structures, 17, 278–83, 287, 288–89, 291; *481–93, 502, 505, 506*

Inflatacookbook (Ant Farm), 288

"Influences" (Stern), 122

Institute for Draftsmen, Terni, Italy (de Feo, with Ascione), 80; *128*

Institute of Education and Advanced Legal Studies Building, University of London (Lasdun and Partners), 29; *34*

Integrated Life Support Systems Laboratories (ILSSL), New Mexico (Reines), 272, 273, 274; perspective, *467*

International Style, 12, 13, 15, 74, 112, 239, 297; *see also* Modern architecture

Ishii, Kazuhiro, 156, 192–93, 312; "54 Roofs" Nursery School, 156; *240*; "54 Windows" (Soya Clinic), 192–93; *315, 316*; Gable Building, *531*

Ishiyama, Osamu, 160, 182, 312; Pipe No. 7: Fantasy Villa, 182; *295, 296*

Islamic architecture, 113

Isozaki, Arata, 13, 25, 74, 105, 107, 187, 312; Fujimi Country Club, 13, 187; *307–9*; Gunma Prefectural Museum of Fine Arts, 105, 187; *167–69*; Nagazumi Branch of the Fukuoka Mutual Bank, 105; *166*

Istogrammi d'Architettura Project (Superstudio), 100; *157*

Italy, 112, 115, 150

"Italy: The New Domestic Landscape," exhibition, Museum of Modern Art, New York City, 52

Ito, Toyo, 101, 103, 312; PMT Building, 103; *160*

Izenour, Steven, 115

J

Jacobs, Jane, 150

Jacoby, Helmut, perspective drawing by, *541*

Jahn, Helmut, 93, 96, 312; Bartle Exhibition Hall, 93, 96; *148, 152*; St. Mary's College Athletic Facility, 96; *151*

Jameson, Conrad, 124, 142, 143, 144, 149

Japan, 112, 179, 187

Japanese architectural motifs, 112, 159, 160, 255

Jeanneret, Pierre, 148

Jefferson, Thomas, 116

Jefferson Starship Dome (Buckman), 241; *404*

Jencks, Charles, 15, 16, 111, 115, 117, 140, 182, 185, 295, 297; "Garagia Rotunda," 17, 183; *4–6, 297*

Jitanos Père et Fils, 268, 269; Cadillac hearse, 269; exterior, *458, 459*

Joass, J. J., 124

Johansen, John, 160, 162, 312; Johansen House II, 160; *256, 257*; Mummers Theater, 160; *254, 255*

Johansen House II, Stanfordville, New York (Johansen), 160; *257*; interior, *256*

Johnson, Ben, 58, 70, 72; *Dark Reflections*, 70, 72; *113*; *Domed Roof Lights*, 58; *89*

Johnson, Martin, 146, 313; Ovendun House, 146; *229*

Johnson, Philip, 42, 58, 77, 122, 145, 273, 313; Art Museum of South Texas, 25; *19*; AT&T Building, 13, 124–25; *194*; Garden Grove Community Church, 25; *20, 21*; I.D.S. Center, 66; *100*; Museum for Pre-Columbian Art, 112; Office Building, *532*; Pennzoil Place, 66–67, 207; *101–3*

Johnson/Burgee Architects, 29, 30, 66, 67, 126

Jones, Inigo, 116

Journal of the Society of Architectural Historians, The, 77

Jung, Carl, 160, 178

Jungman, J. P., 281

Juvarra, Filippo, 134, 205

M

Morningstar West commune, California, 230

Morphosis, 185; Flores House, *303*

Morris, William, 260

Mosque and Islamic Center, Rome (Portoghesi and Gigliotti), 113; interior perspective, *172*

Mother Earth News magazine, 274

Motor Home, with custom painting, 269; *457*

Mozuna, Monta, 101, 194, 196–98, 317; Anti-Dwelling Box, 194; *317*; Heaven Phase House, 196; *318*; Mirror House, 197; *321*; Okawa House, 197; Yin-Yang House, 196; *319, 320*; Zen Temple, 197–98; *322, 323*

Mummers Theater, Oklahoma City (Johansen), 160; *254*; stage-level plan, *255*

Murata, Yutaka, 281; Fuji Pavilion, Expo '70, 279; *486*

Murphy, C.F., Associates, 96, 98

Murray, Keith, 150; Student Housing Court, 3, *234*

Museum for Pre-Columbian Art, Dumbarton Oaks, Washington, D.C. (Johnson, P.), 112

Museum of Glass and Ceramics, Tehran, Iran (Hollein), 134–35; first-floor showroom, *207, 208*; second-floor showroom, *209, 210*

Museum of Modern Art, New York City, exhibitions at, 52, 120, 145, 179

museums, 25, 26, 41, 44, 46, 49, 96, 98, 100, 105, 134–35, 140–41, 163, 168, 175; *18, 19, 26, 27, 30, 31, 57, 64–69, 147, 153–55, 167–69, 207–10, 217–19, 269, 282, 283*

music centers, 22, 35; *50–52*

Musician's House, The, photograph by Shapiro from *Handmade Houses*, 254; *419*

Myers, Barton, 118

"My Statement" (Meier), 75

Nagazumi Branch of the Fukuoka Mutual Bank, Fukuoka, Japan (Isozaki), 105; interior, *166*

Nakamura Memorial Hospital, Sapporo, Japan (Takeyama), axonometric, *539*

Nash, John, 135, 145

Natelson House, Taos, New Mexico (Reynolds), 277; exterior completed, *480*; exterior under construction, *479*

National Ethnology Museum, Osaka, Japan (Kurokawa), 25; *18*

National Gallery of Art—East Building, Washington, D.C. (Pei and Partners), 26; *26*; interior, *27*

National Theatre, London (Lasdun), 22

Nation House, Wellington, New Zealand (Walker, R.), 160; *252*

Negroponte, Nicholas, 243

neo-Liberty movement, 146

Nervi, Pier Luigi, 113

Netsch, Walter, 205

Neumann, Balthasar, 200

Neutra, Richard, 77

New Alchemy Institute, 274

Newark Museum Carriage House, Newark, New Jersey (Graves), 205, 207; ground-floor plan, *342*

New Buffalo commune, New Mexico, 222, 226, 227, 228, 229, 230–31; *377, 378*

New England, 228

Newfield, Mickley, Ripon, Yorkshire, England (Terry), 143–44; forecourt elevation of first design, *223*

New Harmony, Indiana: Atheneum, The (Meier), 12, 18, 26, 78, 86, 88–89; *2, 139–43*; city planning for (Owen), 229

"New Japan Style," 112

Newman, Oscar, 232

New Mexico, 220, 221, 226, 228, 273, 274

Newsom brothers, 126, 201

New York City, 166, 223, 262; AT&T Building (Johnson/Burgee), 13, 124–25; *194*; Bronx Developmental Center (Meier), 103, 105; *164, 165*; CBS Building (Saarinen), 35; Convention Center (Pei), 25; "Eastwood" Housing, Roosevelt Island (Sert, Jackson and Associates), 30; *40, 41*; First of August Store (Ranalli), 103; *161, 162*; Ford Foundation Headquarters (Roche, Dinkeloo and Associates), 63; French & Co. (Graves), 185; *301*; Greene Hall, Columbia University School of Law

(Stern), 145; *226*; Metropolitan Museum of Art (Roche, Dinkeloo and Associates), 63; One U.N. Plaza (Roche, Dinkeloo and Associates), 63–64; *99*; "Riverview" Housing (Sert, Jackson and Associates), 30; Seagram Building (Mies van der Rohe), 33, 237; Sunar Furniture Showroom (Graves), 138–40; *215, 216*; TWA Terminal (Saarinen), 22

New York University Lecture Hall (Breuer), 22

New York Times, 15

Niemeyer, Oscar, 168

Nilsson House, Bel Air, California (Kupper), 213–14; axonometric, *354*; exterior, *356*; interior, *355*

9999, Florence, Italy, 286

Nirvana House, Kanragawa, Japan (Aida), 183

Nolli, Giambattista, 163, 168

Norberg-Schulz, Christian, 152

North Penn Visiting Nurses Association Headquarters Building, North Pennsylvania (Venturi and Short), 209; ground-floor plan, *346*

No-Stop City (Archizoom), 91

Notch Project, Best Products' catalogue showroom, Sacramento, California (SITE), 179; *287*

Notre-Dame-du-Haut, Ronchamp, France (Le Corbusier), 21, 25, 140, 178

S

Saarinen, Eero, 22, 35, 69, 112

Saggioro, Carla, 80

Sainsbury Centre for the Visual Arts, University of East Anglia, Norwich, Norfolk, England (Foster Associates), 41, 98, 100; axonometric, *155*; exterior, *153*; exterior detail showing ready-made panels, *57*; interior, *154*

St. Mark's Road Housing, London (Dixon), 6, 8, 156–57; axonometrics of front and rear, *244*; facade, *243*; lower ground-floor plan and section, *245*; oblique street view, *246*

St. Mary's College Athletic Facility, South Bend, Indiana (Jahn), 96; interior, *151*

St. Paul's School, New Hampshire (Barnes), 151

SS. Sindone, Turin, Italy (Guarini), 113

San Francisco, 17, 125, 126, 223; Hyatt Regency Hotel (Portman and Associates), 60–61, 63; *93*; Matthews Street House Project (Smith, T.G.), 126, 201; *195, 328*

Sanwa Building, Kikuchi, Japan (Toki), 185; *304*

Sausalito, California, Waldo Point houseboat community at, 262–63; *442–46*

Sauvage, Henri, 122, 124

Sawade, J., 163; Student Hostel Competition Project, *262*

Scarpa, Carlo, 112

Scharoun, Hans, 22

Schinkel, Karl Friedrich, 118, 175

Schmidt, Clarence, 160, 246–47, 249, 251–52, 254, 260, 321; House of Mirrors, 249, 251–52; *417, 418*

schoolbuses, 267, 268, 269, 272; *451, 453, 460*

schools, 103, 105, 151, 156–57, 173; *164, 165*, 240, 243–46, 277; *see also* universities and colleges

Schulitz, Helmut, 41–42; Architect's Home, *59*

Schullin Jewelry Shop, Vienna (Hollein), 52, 54–55; *77*; exterior detail, *78*; interior, *79*; plan and section, *80*

Schulman House, Princeton, New Jersey (Graves), addition, 137–38; street elevation, *214*

Schumacher, E. F., 274, 275

Schwitters, Kurt, 252

Scolari, Massimo, 15; Venice Biennale, facades, *3*

Scott, Geoffrey, 182

Scully, Vincent, 16, 25, 122, 182

Seagram Building, New York City (Mies van der Rohe), 33, 237

Sea Ranch, California, *see* Condominium I

Seattle, Washington, 262

Seinäjoki Theater project (Aalto), 205

Sellers, David, 160, 259; Design Center, 259; *250*

Selz, Peter, 223, 298

Semi-circular Civic Building Project, Piazza Navona, Rome (Krier, L.), 168; perspective, *272*

Serlio, Sebastiano, 135

Sert, José Lluis, 17, 30, 321; "Eastwood" Housing, 30; *40, 41*

Sert, Jackson and Associates, 36

Shapiro, Barry, 254; photographs by, *419, 422*

Shelter (Kahn, Lloyd), 243, 254, 260, 272

Shelter and Society (Oliver), 225

Shingle Style, 115, 122, 151, 259

Shingle Style Today, The (Scully), 122

shopping centers, 90, 91–92, 98, 160; *149*

showroom, 138–40; *215, 216*

"Signs of Life: Symbols in the American City," Venturi exhibition, 115

single-membrane inflatable (Ant Farm), 283; interior, *490*

single-membrane inflatable, at Whiz Bang Quick City East, New York (Poor Willie Productions), 283; *492*; deflated, *493*

single-membrane inflatable of "no practical use" (Chrysalis), 282; *483*

Siskind, Steve, 262

SITE, 179, 321; Notch Project, 179; *287*; Tilt Showroom, 179; *288*

Slick, Grace, 241

Slutzky, Robert, 84

Small is Beautiful (Schumacher), 274

Smith, Barry, 254–55

Smith, C. Ray, 111, 205

Smith, Thomas Gordon, 124, 125, 126, 200, 201, 212–13, 321; Long House Project, 212–13; *350*; Matthews Street House Project, 126, 201; *195, 328*; Tuscan and Laurentian Houses, 126; *196, 197*

Smith House, Darien, Connecticut (Meier), 74–75, 77; entrance facade, *120*; site and lower-level plans, *119*; southeast facade, *118*

Smithson, Alison, 17, 29

Smithson, Peter, 17, 29, 143

Snyderman House, Fort Wayne, Indiana (Graves), 83, 84–86; east facade, *136*; first-floor plan, *138*; south

facade, *137*

Soane, Sir John, 203, 204

solar energy, *see* alternative energy, solar

solar-heated house, Colorado Springs (Wood and Thomason), 274; exterior, *472*

solar-heated swimming pool, Springfield, Missouri (Lambeth), 274; *473*

Soleri, Paolo, 178, 284–85, 289, 294, 297, 322; Arcosanti, 284, 289; *494, 496*; Babel II Project (Babelnoah), 284; *495*; Cosanti, 284, 289; *497–501*; Veladiga, 284

Sony Tower, Osaka, Japan (Kurokawa), 25; *15*; axonometric, *16*; exterior detail of lifts and toilet capsules, *17*

Sottsass, Ettore, 52

Southern Illinois University, Carbondale, 236, 239

Space Structures Workshop, 282; linked inflatables, *283*; *491*

Space, Time and Architecture (Giedion), 200

Spear House, Miami (Arquitectonica, with Koolhaas), 156; aerial view, *242*

Speelhuis Leisure Center, Helmond, The Netherlands (Blom), 30–31, 156; *43*; cutaway perspective, *42*

Spherical Dome, Lake Havasu City, Arizona (Woods, Bill), 239; *401*

Spoerry, François, 143; Port Grimaud, *221*

Staatsgalerie New Building and Chamber Theater, Stuttgart (Stirling), 13, 36, 175, 177; elevation and cross section, *283*; model, *282*

stadia, 21, 22, 36; *53–55*

Stalinist Baroque revival style, 142

Stamp, Gavin, 145

Star Trek, film, 57

Star Wars, film, 57

Steiner, Rudolf, 22

Stella, Frank, 77

Stepped-Platform House, Kanagawa, Japan (Aida), 190; elevation, *313*; exterior, *314*

Stern, Robert A.M., 13, 14, 111, 120, 122, 145, 200–201, 322; Best Products Showroom, 120, 122; *190*; Bourke House, poolhouse, 122; *191, 192*; Cohn Poolhouse, 145; *227*; Greene Hall, 145; *226*; Lang House, 200; McGarry/Appignani Bedroom, 122; *193*; Westchester House, 200–201; *326, 327*

Stern House, Woodbridge, Connecticut (Moore Associates), 205; ground-floor plan, *341*; interior, *340*

Stevens, Graham, 281–82; inflatable cube, *482*

Stick Style, 77

Stinco, A., 281

Stirling, James, 13, 29, 36, 57–58, 138, 174–75, 177, 322; Clore Gallery for the Turner Collection, *538*; Meineke Strasse Project, 174–75; *279, 280*; Melville Hall, 29; *32*; Olivetti Training School, 57–58; *85–88* (painting of, *89*); Staatsgalerie New Building and Chamber Theater, 13, 36, 175, 177; *282, 283*

Stone, Ed, 112

stores, 50, 52, 54–55, 91, 103, 135, 137, 179, 239; *71–75, 77–80, 161, 162, 211–13, 287, 288, 401*

straight revivalism, *see* revivalism

Street Farm House, London (Caine and Haggart), 275; elevation and plan, *474*; interior of greenhouse, *475*

Structuralism (Structuralists), 32, 35; Dutch, 33, 35, 37

Student Hostel Competition Project, Berlin (Ungers and Sawade), 163; plan, *262*

Student Housing Court 3, University of Surrey, Guildford, England (Maguire and Murray), 150; *234*

Stupinigi palace (Juvarra), 205

Stuttgart, West Germany: Reconstruction Project (Krier, R.), 168; *273*; Staatsgalerie New Building and Chamber Theater (Stirling), 13, 36, 175, 177; *282, 283*

Sullivan, Louis, 124, 182

Summerson, Sir John, 116, 203

Sunar Furniture Showroom, New York City (Graves), 139–40; "Easel Mural" for, 138–39; *215*; textile room, *216*

Supermannerism: New Attitudes in Post-Modern Architecture (Smith, C.), 111, 205

supermarkets, 90, 91

Superstudio, Florence, Italy, 91, 100, 286; Istogrammi d'Architettura Project, 100; *157*

Surrationalism, 166–68, 185, 188

Sydney Opera House (Utzon), 22

Synthetic Cubism, 138

Taft Architects, Houston, 127, 322; Quail Valley Municipal Control Building Addition, 127; *199*

Tafuri, Manfredo, 170

Takara Group Pavilion, Expo '70, Osaka, Japan (Kurokawa), 37; *58*

Takeyama, Minoru, 25, 187, 322–23; Hotel Beverly Tom, 187; *306*; Nakamura Memorial Hospital, *539*

Taliesin West, 284

Taller de Arquitectura, 13, 127–28, 166; Arcades du Lac, 13, 166; *265, 266*; Barrio Gaudí, 166; *264*; Fabrica, La, 525; Meritxell Religious Center, 128; *201, 202*; Parc de la Marca Hispanica Monument, 127; *200*; Viaduct Housing, 4, 6

Tange, Kenzo, 22, 60, 112, 148, 323

Taos, New Mexico: Hopi pueblo, 226, 228; *376*; Natelson House (Reynolds), 277; *479, 480*

Tate Gallery Coffee Shop, London (Dixon), *527*

Tatlin, Vladimir, 205

Taut, Bruno, 22

Tawapa commune, New Mexico, 228

Taylor, Nikolaus, 145

Team Ten, 30, 158, 222

Teatro del Mondo, Venice (Rossi), 174; *281*

Tegeler Hafen, IBA competition project, Berlin (Moore, Ruble, and Yudell), aerial perspective, *534*

Tempchin House (Moore), 204

Temple Dome, Ananda Meditation Retreat and Spiritual Community, California, 234; interior, *388*

tents, Munich Olympics of 1972 (Behnisch & Partner, with Grzimek), 36; *53–55*

Terragni, Giuseppe, 80

Terry, Quinlan, 124, 143–44, 145, 149, 323; Bahai Temple, 143; Newfield, 143–44; *223*; Waverton House, 143–44; *222*

Tetra Design Services, Ltd., 6

Theater Dome, Drop City, Colorado, 224; *368*

theaters, 22, 160, 174, 175; *254, 255, 281–83*

Therma Hotel, Lesvos, Greece (OMA), concept plan, painting of (Zenghelis, Z.), *535*

Thomas, John Hudson, 125–26

Thompson, Hunter, 265

Thoreau, Henry David, 230

Thorman, Jerry, 260; Bob's House, *438–41*

Tiergarten Museum, West Berlin (Ungers), 163

Tigerman, Stanley, 55, 68, 179, 182, 183, 323; Animal

Crackers House, 179, 182; *292–94*; "Best Home of All," 179; *289*; Daisy House, 179, 182; *291*; Hot Dog House, 179; Pensacola Place, 179, 182; *290*; Private Residence, 55, 68; *81–83*

Tilt Showroom, Towson, Maryland (SITE), 179; *288*

"Time Capsule" event, Lewiston, New York (Ant Farm), 289; *509–11*

Time magazine, 239

Tinguely, Jean, 252

tipis, 226–27, 238, 239; *379*

Todoroki House (Fujii), 103

Toki Shin, 185; Sanwa Building, *304*

Tokoen Hotel, Yonago, Japan (Kikutake), 112; *170*

Tokyo: Blue Box House (Miyawaki), 188; *310*; Miyajima House (Fujii), 103; *159*; Office Building (Yamashita), 183, 185; *299, 300*; Olympic Stadia (Tange), 22; Zen Temple (Mozuna), 197–98; *322, 323*

Tolmers Village, London, 233

Tower House, California (Agnoli), 260; *435*

Toynbee, Arnold, 14, 111

Transformations in Modern Architecture (Drexler), 21

Treasury of Atreus, Mycenae, 209

Trevi Fountain, Rome, 118

Triangular Civic Building Project, Piazza San Pietro, Rome, Italy (Krier, L.), 168; perspective, *271*

Trubek and Wislocki Houses, Nantucket Island, Massachusetts (Venturi and Rauch), 115; *176*

truckitecture, 267–70; *447–66*

trucks, converted: flatbed, 267–68, 269; *454, 463*; pickup, 267, 269; *447–49*

Tube-Frame-and-Pillow-Dome, Pacific High School, Santa Cruz Mountains, California (Baldwin), 235; *395*; interior, *396*

Turnbull, William, 15, 116, 202, 204, 213, 323; Faculty Club, 202; *330, 331*; Kresge College, 15, 116, 213; *179, 351–53*; Zimmerman House, 204; *335, 336*

Tuscan and Laurentian Houses, Livermore, California (Smith, T.G.), 126; *197*; perspective, *196*

TWA Terminal, New York City (Saarinen), 22

Twin Oaks commune, Virginia, 228, 229, 230

2001, film, 57

287; *504*; tipi, 226–27; *379*
Whiz Bang Quick City West, design festival, near Pasadena, California, 287; inflatable, interior of, *502*
Whole Earth Catalog, The (Brand), 227, 228–29, 234, 236, 254, 274
Wilde, Oscar, 151
Wilford, Michael, and Associates, 321
Willard School, Troy, New York (Barnes), 151
Williamsburg, Virginia, 143
Williams-Ellis, Clough, 143
wind energy, *see* alternative energy, wind
Wines, James, 179
WOBO House, The Netherlands, 275; *476*
Wolfe, Tom, 223, 268
Wolfsburg Cultural Center (Aalto), 205
Wood and Thomason, 274; solar-heated house, *472*
Woods, Bill, 239; Church Dome, *400*; Spherical Dome, *401*
Woods, Brendan, 154
Woodstock Festival, 230, 249, 287
Woodstock Handmade Houses (Haney and Ballantine), 254; photograph from, *421*
World's Fairs, 21, 37, 237, 279; *58, 397, 486*
World Trade Centers, 91
Wright, Frank Lloyd, 77, 79, 200, 249, 256, 259, 284; Ennis House, 213; Falling Water, 213; Larkin Building, 21; Prairie House, 231

Xanadu, Calpe, Spain (Bofill), 166
Xanadune, St. Simon Island, Georgia (Moore Associates), 116; aerial view of model, *178*

Yamasaki, Minoru, 112
Yamashita, Kazumasa, 182, 183, 185, 325; Face House, 183, 185; *298*; Office Building, 183, 185; *299, 300*
Yin-Yang House, Hokkaido, Japan (Mozuna), 196; *319*; conceptual axonometric, *320*
You Only Live Twice, James Bond film, 55–56; slick-tech interior from, *84*

Zenghelis, Elia, 167–68; painting by, *268*
Zenghelis, Zoe, 167–68; paintings by, *268, 535*
Zen Temple, Tokyo (Mozuna), 197–98; axonometrics, *322*; interior, *323*
Zevi, Bruno, 16
Zimmerman House, Fairfax County, Virginia (MLTW/ Turnbull Associates), 204; exterior, *335*; ground-floor plan and cutaway isometric, *336*
Zimmermann, Dominikus, 89
Zimmermann, Johann, 89
zomes, 223, 228, 239, 272; *see also* domes, zonahedra
Zomeworks Humanufactory, Albuquerque, New Mexico, 228, 234, 272, 273, 274, 286
Zwolle Housing, Amsterdam (Eyck and Bosch), 31, 152; house units, *236*